THE

of

ASSASSINS

The Rise and Rise of Vladimir Putin

Yuri Felshtinsky
& Vladimir Pribylovsky

GIBSON SQUARE
London

By Yuri Felshtinsky:

Blowing up Russia (Gibson Square, 2007)
with Alexander Litvinenko

www.felshtinsky.com/index1.html

By Vladimir Pribylovsky

www.anticompromat.org

This edition first published in 2008 in the UK by

Gibson Square
47 Lonsdale Square
London N1 1EW

Tel: +44 (0)20 7096 1100
Fax: +44 (0)20 7993 2214

info@gibsonsquare.com
www.gibsonsquare.com

ISBN 978-1906142070 HB

Contents

Since Alexander Litvinenko, my co-author of *Blowing up Russia*, was killed in November 2006, it was painful to find out that in June 2007 the Moscow apartment of Vladimir Pribylovsky, a journalist and historian and friend, was searched by agents from the Russian secret service (the Federal Security Service or FSB—the KGB's successor organization). They were looking for our sources for this book on Vladimir Putin and the FSB.

Yuri Felshtinsky
February 13, 2008

'... until there is a public trial, until the former KGB officers feel the same shame as the former officers of the Fascist Gestapo or SS—until they're ashamed to admit where they served, until all this is done, terrorism won't stop.'

Alexander Litvinenko
former KGB officer, 2003

INTRODUCTION

Anna Politkovskaya

On October 7, 2006, Anna Politkovskaya was assassinated in her apartment building in Moscow. Those who killed Politkovskaya, whoever they are, had a choice. They could have murdered her on any day in October, or in any month for that matter. Instead they chose a day with a special significance for Vladimir Putin, the President of the Russian Federation. She was silenced forever on his birthday.

Politkovskaya was a well known Russian journalist who had published books in many languages. She was an uncompromising critic of the Russian government, of Russian policies in Chechnya, of the Russian army in Chechnya, and of President Putin as the head of a government that allowed crimes to be committed in Chechnya (like Alexander Litvinenko, who was poisoned in London 24 days after her death). It was natural to suspect that Politkovskaya's murder had been carried out on instructions from some pro-Kremlin Chechen leader, such as the president of Chechnya, Ramzan Kadyrov, who was only then negotiating with Putin about the possibility of becoming president in circumvention of the constitution of the Chechen Republic (Ramzan Kadyrov, born in 1976, was too young for this post). On March 2, 2007, Ramzan Kadyrov got what he wanted and became the president of the Chechen Republic, despite his age, and with the blessing of the Russian President.

It is the tale of this book. How, in eight short years, did the Kremlin move from Yeltsin's chaos to a situation where it no longer needs to issue orders for a problem to be cleaned up.

The twentieth century has entered history as an age of tyrants.

Stalin, Hitler, Mussolini, Mao Zedong... Great and small, extreme and moderate, communist and nationalist, they brought unspeakable evil to their victims and created rich materials for historians. Since we are used to thinking in terms of analogies, our inclination is to draw parallels between new phenomena that we are witnessing and familiar, old ones. We want to know: Is Putin a despot or not? Will he recreate something resembling the old Soviet Union? Will the world see a new cold—or perhaps even nuclear—war? Are we heading for a new cold war (books are already being published with that title).

Meanwhile, what we are really dealing with is another one of Russia's experiments. This experiment is being conducted not by the Communist Party, but by the Russian secret service. The goal of the experiment is to obtain absolute control over Russia and its resources. For the sake of unlimited power, which gives access to unlimited money, which in its turn creates the possibility of absolute power. Why? To paraphrase George Mallory's famous remark on Everest, the answer is: because it is there.

Under Soviet rule, everyone was poor, even the members of the ruling elite, the *nomenklatura*. Stalin and Brezhnev had power, but no money. Their apartments, cars, and dachas belonged to the state. They had no yachts and airplanes; they could not go carousing abroad. They did not put their children on the boards of directors of Russia's largest corporations. The members of the new ruling corporation—the Russian secret service—want both power and money, for themselves, for their children, and for their close relatives. Examples are not hard to find. The son of former Prime Minister Fradkov is the head of the board of directors of the state-run Bank for Development and Foreign Economic Affairs (Vnesheconombank). The son of secret service director Nikolai Patrushev is an advisor to the head of Rosneft. The youngest son of Deputy Prime Minister Sergei Ivanov is the deputy president of Gazprombank.

Putin himself also represents a completely new phenomenon, never before encountered in history. All of the dictators known to us have been self-motivated and self-appointed. All of them seized power by risking their lives and all of them held on to it by overcoming even greater difficulties. Usually, they died like Trotsky, Hitler, Mussolini, Ceausescu. Less often, they died like Franco,

Mao, Tito, and Pinochet. In some cases, we still do not know for certain whether a dictator died a natural death or was killed by his rivals (Lenin and Stalin).

Putin did not fight his way to the president's seat. He was selected by the secret service for the job. It was precisely this system—which secret service agents themselves often call the '*kontora*,' or the 'company'—that got President Yeltsin and the Russian oligarchs to appoint him as a successor. Putin does not thirst for power and does not enjoy it.

The oligarchs who helped Putin become president believed that these hands were theirs. It turned out, however, that the hands that steered Putin belonged to a completely different organization—the *kontora*. And these hands installed Putin as president precisely because they were not looking for a colourful, charismatic, independent person. Because an extraordinary person might come to like power and decide to become a dictator. And dictators always kill, as is well known, and they always begin by killing those who are close to them, those who brought them to power, their comrades, colleagues, and companions. The Stalin experience turned out to be very edifying in this respect. A new Stalin is not wanted either by the new businessmen or by the old state security agents. Putin suits everybody.

Under the old Soviet regime, the country was ruled by a single political party that was armed with a communist ideology. Under Putin, the numerous political parties that form the Russian parliament (the State Duma) are weak. This is no accident. He made them so, with the agreement of the Russian secret service. The secret service has no need of a strong political party, since a powerful political party will inevitably become a rival for power and thus pose a threat to the secret service. The same can be said about the Duma—weak, divided, and controlled by the president. And the same can be said about the lack of an ideology, which the secret service also has no interest in, since any ideology sooner or later leads to the creation of a political party, and a political party is called 'political' precisely because it strives for power (which, in the case of Russia, will have to be wrested away from the secret service). There is no room for a new cold war either, though this does not mean that the world can sleep safely.

One of the Russian secret service's distinctive characteristics, as a system, is its perpetual desire to monitor and control everything and everyone. Control on an individual level is difficult, not to say impossible. It is easier to control groups. The active part of the country's adult population is already organized into groups, one way or the other, and all of these groups (businesses, non-government organizations, political parties, etc.) have secret service personnel embedded in them. They inform their organization about everything that happens around them. Things are more difficult with young people. They are difficult to organize into groups, difficult to control, and extremely difficult to infiltrate, since the secret service's employees, agents, and informers are usually fully mature individuals. The old Soviet experience, of course, can be useful in this respect, and new creativity also helps. The secret service is able to monitor the grass-roots successes of different youth organizations. If they become successful—like the movement 'Nashi'—they are taken over and used to enforce the secret service's power, eliminating the possibility that they might become rival organizations.

In its modern incarnation, the secret service has adopted the mantra of capitalism—so hated by the Soviet ideology—and thinks like a corporation. It prefers to buy or to subjugate rather than to kill. Nonetheless, the secret service is an organization of killers. And if it believes that it has to protect itself from an imminent danger, a danger that can no longer be controlled, it kills. It is for this reason that Anna Politkovskaya and Alexander Litvinenko were murdered. Each of them represented a serious danger for the secret service corporation, and all other means of controlling, or buying, them had failed.

The secret service's system of corporate rule was not conceived and created by the secret service itself, but by the early Russian tycoons. In June 1996, Yeltsin, who seemed to have no chance of getting re-elected democratically, was leaning towards declaring a state of emergency in the country to prevent the victory of Communist Party candidate Gennady Zyuganov. This was the security services' first, awkward attempt to take over the government in Russia. But this attempt failed in the face of opposition from a rival secret-service faction outside the state departments and the Russian tycoons, who were connected to one another via shares in various joint-businesses. They threw their business resources behind Yeltsin and snatched 'victory' from the jaws of defeat.

In July 1996, Yeltsin was re-elected as president. But it came at a price. The young tycoons had become shareholders in the government as if it was another corporation. For the next four years, until the 2000 election, this corporation governed the country and its president was Yeltsin. Surrounded by the security services on all sides, clashing and contending with one another, inexperienced in politics (along with everyone else in democratic Russia), despising the people, and not believing in democracy in general and in Russian democracy in particular, the corporation of the Russian tycoons reached the conclusion that, in the election of 2000, a top official from the security services must be elected as president.

By 1999-2000, every tycoon had his own, high-ranking, tried-and-tested man in the security services. And every one of these state security men had his own tried-and-tested tycoon. Roman Abramovich, Boris Berezovsky, and Anatoly Chubais had Colonel Vladimir Putin, director of the secret service. The business tycoon, Vladimir Gusinsky had Army General Filipp Bobkov, deputy director of the KGB of the USSR. The tycoon Yuri Luzhkov had Yevgeny Primakov, deputy director of the KGB of the USSR, director of the Central Intelligence Service of the USSR, and director the Russia's Foreign Intelligence Service. Oil tycoon Mikhail Khodorkovsky had KGB General Alexei Kandaurov...

These tycoons and the state security men who were close to Yeltsin explained to the president that only a former head of the secret service would be able to become Russia's Pinochet and avoid plunging the country into chaos. It did not matter which former head it was (here Yeltsin was given a choice), but it had to be a former head of the secret service. In one year, Yeltsin tried out three different people for the role of successor. The first candidate for the position of Russia's future president was Yevgeny Primakov. He was appointed prime minister in August 1998, but dismissed in May 1999: he did not suit the Russian tycoons because he promised that, after he won, he would release 90,000 criminals from prison and fill their cells with 90,000 businessmen. The next candidate for president was Sergei Stepashin, director of the secret service in 1994-1995. He did not suit Yeltsin's 'family'—or more precisely, he did not suit some of its members: the oligarch Roman Abramovich, the president's advisor and future son-in-law Valentin Yumashev, and the president's chief of staff Alexander Voloshin. It seemed to them that Stepashin was shifting to the side of Yeltsin's rival for power in the country—the mayor of Moscow, Yuri Luzhkov. In August 1999, Stepashin was dismissed. In his place came Putin, up to that time the director of the secret service. Yeltsin liked Putin, and the oligarchs liked him. He had no ties to or yearnings for the old Soviet elite of the secret service. And on December 31, 1999, he was chosen to be Yeltsin's successor as the next president of Russia. For the first time since the short-lived reign of Yuri Andropov, the only other KGB head ever to lead Russia, the secret service had managed to plant their man at the head of the country.

The oligarchs (with the exception of Vladimir Gusinsky, who had bet on the wrong horse) believed that their corporation was still in power. It was they, after all, who had jointly supported Putin; it was they who, during the election campaign, had assisted him using all of the same mechanisms and managers that had secured victory for Yeltsin in 1996. But there was another corporation that, unbeknownst to the Russian tycoons, was supporting Putin and working to secure his victory using its own resources and its own methods: the *kontora* of the secret service. And Putin's first steps as president were marked by a conspicuous loyalty toward members of both corporations.

Little by little, however, the balance of power shifted in favour of the secret service. First, the empires of Gusinsky and Berezovsky—who had begun to oppose Putin—were destroyed, and Gusinsky and Berezovsky ended up in exile abroad. Then Mikhail Khodorkovsky's empire was dismantled, while Khodorkovsky himself was arrested and convicted. At the same time, a number of regional elected positions were replaced with positions appointed by the president. In the context of Russia's pervasive corruption—which blossomed particularly in local elections—the elimination of regional elections and the establishment of president-appointed positions in and of itself appeared in many respects to be something good and acceptable. But Putin began to appoint Russian secret service officers to all vacant positions—as well as to all government and political positions of any importance.

Not everyone understood what was going on, and not everyone understood all at once. And when they did understand, it was too late. Between 70% and 80% of all top positions in the government had been captured by the security services and the military. For the first time in history, the country's government had been captured by the Russian secret service—by people who had spent their whole adult lives working in the secret service system, who distrusted America and Western Europe, who had no positive program and no experience in building anything. They knew only how to destroy, to control, to subjugate, and to kill.

Today, the proportion between the two corporations' shares in the government—the secret service's and the Russian tycoons—is no longer what it was in 2000. Putin's Kremlin has created a new group of 200 to 300 shareholders who have replaced them and have inseparable ties to the secret service. They are the real oligarchs—in the classical sense of the word—and move effortlessly between government and the board rooms of Russian companies and back. For them elections are public relations shows in much the same way that corporations carefully plot and plan their shareholder meetings.

The new president of 2008 will scrupulously honour the shares the secret service corporation has in the government, since it will be this corporation that will get the next 'successor' elected as president. As in the handover of executive power in any large corporation like Shell, Exxon, GE, or American Express, it was the shareholders desire that Vladimir Putin would stay on as a guarantee of their rights. Nonetheless, they will not tolerate a new Stalin and former president Putin will have no way of avoiding the powerlessness that comes with leaving office, just as former president Yeltsin could not avoid it when he retired from the presidency. He will end up dying early if he acts above the rules.

Today, it is clear that 'Operation Successor'—which installed Putin as president of Russia—will have its sequel in March 2008. They will be looking for Putin's clone to be the secret service's new CEO of the corporation (like Dmitry Medvedev). The question for the rest of us is what will happen when the economy has a downturn and the Russian trough of plenty empties. Strife between the shareholders is likely to be fierce, manipulative and brutal. More likely than not, every part of the Russian state—from the army, to its ample resources—will be used by the secret service clans to destroy what gets in its way.

‘We are in power again, this time forever.’

Vladimir Putin

Prime Minister of the Russian Federation,
addressing an audience of FSB agents,
Moscow, 1999

CHAPTER ONE

War of the KGB Clans

KGB General Alexander Korzhakov

In August 1991, the putsch against Mikhail Gorbachev failed. Without doubt, much of the credit was due to Boris Yeltsin, who famously climbed on a tank to galvanize opposition against the plotters. Within weeks of the failed plot, the Soviet Union collapsed as well. As one of the leaders of the putsch was the head of the Soviet KGB (Committee of State Security), it was clear that the organization had to be formally dismantled and this enormous secretive structure was split up into various independent agencies in an attempt to decimate its power.

In many ways, nonetheless, this reorganization was business as usual. All power shifts in Russia since 1917 can be measured by the reorganization of the secret services—the Cheka, the mother of them all, was instituted by Lenin in that year. Until now, however, it has not been fully understood what unusual consequences flowed from the 1991 reorganization. The power vacuum that was left by the Soviet KGB was soon filled by former KGB agents who had never been part of the KGB elite, Putin included. Had anyone at the time suggested this was to happen, experts would have thought it not remotely likely that low-level officers would ever take the reigns. But the consequences of this unusual development are felt on the world to this day.

One of the first of the new agencies was the Presidential Security Service (the SBP—comparable in function to the US Secret Service that looks after the safety of the US President). It was regrouped from the KGB departments that had been responsible for the security of top government officials, members of the party nomenclature and their families, and the security of especially important government sites (The KGB's Ninth and Fifteenth Directorates). Despite the importance of providing security for top government officials, the agents of the new agency had previously been part of a lowly subdivision of the KGB. In terms of their level of skill and knowledge, the staff and directors were thought of as inferior to foreign intelligence and counterintelligence officers, as their main task was assuring the physical safety of the Soviet *nomenklatura* (elite).

General Alexander Korzhakov—a former bodyguard of KGB director and Soviet leader Andropov—who everyone believed was devoted to Yeltsin, headed the newly formed Presidential Security Service (SBP). He knew perfectly well that any new agency responsible for the security of the president, even such a wilful one as Yeltsin, would under ordinary circumstances remain as insignificant as it had always been. But in 1991 to 1992, the situation in Russia was not ordinary, and Korzhakov's influence over Yeltsin was great. He did everything he could to make the new presidential security service effectively his private mini-KGB.

The Ministry of Security (MB) of Russia was the new agency that took the place of the dismantled KGB in the Russian Federation and here Korzhakov used his influence to place his own man at the top, a colleague from the Kremlin regiment, former Kremlin commandant Mikhail Barsukov. Although he was the head of the MB—to which the SBP technically reported—he silently assented to General Korzhakov' superiority over him.

After successfully implementing the idea of creating an independent presidential security service and filling all key positions in other newly formed agencies with people personally loyal to himself, Korzhakov effectively became—without this being noticed by anyone, least of all by his boss, Yeltsin—the second man in Russia.

However, it's a bad soldier who doesn't dream of becoming a general. And in Russia, it's a bad security chief who doesn't dream of taking the place of the person he keeps secure. In Korzhakov's case, that place was occupied by Yeltsin. Ever since the historic days of August 1991—when Korzhakov, a man full of vigour and still unknown to the Russian nation, was seen on the news around the world standing behind Yeltsin's on the tank like a devoted dog, ready to tear any enemy to shreds or to protect Yeltsin from a bullet with his own body—Yeltsin's security chief wanted to replace Yeltsin at his post.

In order for this wish to be fulfilled, several parts had to fall into place first. Korzhakov built up his own security service (the SBP) with its own special forces, the Centre for Special Operations (TsSN), quickly and without much difficulty. What proved more difficult was shaping public opinion in the country in his favour. For this, Korzhakov needed his own television outlets and his own newspapers—especially so, since Korzhakov wasn't the only one who dreamed of occupying Yeltsin's seat. His main rival for Yeltsin's power was a man who had his own television and newspapers, his former senior KGB colleague Filipp Bobkov.

Filipp Bobkov

But who was Filipp Bobkov, this now almost forgotten man? In Soviet times, the KGB carried out a wide-scale fight against all expressions of dissent in Russia. It executed the political course laid down by the Central Committee of the Soviet Communist Party—specifically, by its Department of Agitation and Propaganda. A vital strategic aim was to consolidate the Party's ideological influence within the Soviet Union, the countries of the socialist bloc, and the world as a whole. The tactical aim was to install the agents of the security services at all positions in society at home and abroad, in order to counteract 'harmful ideological influences' on the population and to carry out counter-propaganda programs against enemy countries. To achieve total control over the political situation in the country and the mindset of its citizens, the security organs recruited agents among Soviet and foreign citizens alike, furthering important strategic and tactical aims in the process. Television, a particularly powerful instrument of propaganda and a means for shaping public opinion, had therefore always been under the constant control of the KGB.

The KGB had a special division whose main mission was fighting against 'ideological diversions by the enemy'. This was the Fifth Directorate of the KGB and its various local departments across the Soviet Union. The 'enemy' referred to countries with a different—bourgeois—ideology and morality, based on free enterprise and civil liberties. Thus, all of the capitalist countries and their allies were considered 'enemies'. The term 'ideological diversion' was quite broad. It included such concepts as 'harmful ideological orientation,' which could be applied to any aspects of human activity and creativity that did not fit within the frame work of the country's political structure, and did not correspond to the established ideological canon of the state.

For many years, practically since its inception in 1967, the KGB's Fifth Directorate had been headed by Filipp Bobkov. He retired from the KGB well before the putsch at the beginning of 1991, having attained the position of deputy director of the KGB and the rank of army general. Soon, he became quite well known as a 'consultant' to oligarch Vladimir Gusinsky, the owner of the Most Corporation, which included Most Bank, Media Most, and other enterprises. In reality, Bobkov was the head of this corporation's private KGB.

Gusinsky had been on Bobkov's radar for many years, as Gusinsky had become well-known to the Fifth Directorate during the preparations for the 1980 Olympics in Moscow. Bobkov's deputy in the Fifth Directorate was Ivan Abramov. When Bobkov became deputy director of the KGB in 1985—replacing Viktor Chebrikov, who moved on to become head of the KGB after Andropov became general secretary of the Communist Party—Abramov became the head of the Fifth Directorate and a lieutenant general. The officers who served under Abramov called him Vanya Palkin (from *palka*, 'stick') for his tendency to petty tyranny and his rigid, often unfair attitude toward his subordinates.

The KGB link to Gusinsky was first established by Abramov's deputy, Vitaly Ponomarev. A vet by training, and subsequently a party operative, Ponomarev was sent to work for the KGB in the beginning of the 1980s. He soon became the head of the KGB's regional office in the Chechen-Ingush Republic, and shortly after that he was transferred to Moscow and appointed deputy head of the KGB's Fifth Directorate. This occurred on the eve of the 1985 Moscow international youth and student festival, and it was precisely this politically significant event that Ponomarev was ordered to supervise. During this time, Ponomarev became acquainted with the main director of the festival's opening celebration, Vladimir Gusinsky, the very same person who, several years later, would become one of the richest and most influential people in Russia—and Bobkov's Most Corporation boss.

Another head of the Fifth Directorate after Bobkov's tenure was Yevgeny Ivanov. During the perestroika years, when the idea of ideological enemies vanished, Ivanov helped transform the KGB's Fifth Directorate into the 'Directorate for the Defence of the Constitutional Order' (the K-Directorate), to reflect the latest political changes in name at least. After the dismantling of the old Soviet KGB in 1991 in several new agencies, Ivanov became the head of the analytic department in Gusinsky's Most Corporation.

The Most Corporation's security service, headed by Bobkov, mainly consisted of Bobkov's former subordinates from the KGB's Fifth Directorate, and it soon became the largest and most powerful security service in the country. Its staff and its aims were substantially larger than that of the SBP, Korzhakov's mini-KGB. It collected information about a wide range of topics in contemporary Russian life. It assessed the landscape of competing political forces within the government and assembled files on prominent politicians, businessmen, bankers, and various state and commercial entities. In fact, Korzhakov's SBP analysts were no match for their former KGB colleagues, who now worked at the Most Corporation's security service not for the sake of an idea, but for high wages—and not in rubles, but dollars, receiving a salaries many times higher than General Korzhakov's own government income.

Thus, while Korzhakov was creating his mini-KGB through the Presidential Security Service of President Yeltsin, Bobkov was building his own mini-KGB through the empire of his former KGB client Vladimir Gusinsky. Bobkov's smart and experienced procurers of information and analysts could not but notice the steps that Korzhakov was taking towards increasing his influence and creating an influential group of supporters. In addition, Bobkov's employees maintained good professional relationships with their former colleagues who had stayed behind at the newly formed secret service agencies, particularly the FSK, later the secret service, headed by Korzhakov's protégé Barsukov.

Korzhakov vs. Bobkov

At the end of 1994, not long before the presidential election which was scheduled for 1996, Korzhakov and Bobkov went head to head. Gusinsky had declared that he could make president whomever he wanted. Korzhakov had retorted that 'it's not our place to choose the president' and, on December 2, 1994, entered into open war with Gusinsky and his security chief, Bobkov. As Viktor Portov, an officer of Korzhakov's Centre of Special Operations (TsSN), later recalled, 'our task was to provoke Gusinsky into action and to find out whose support he had secured in the government before making such declarations.'

On the morning of December 2, an armoured Mercedes and a jeep carrying Gusinsky's bodyguards were travelling from Gusinsky's dacha to Moscow on the Rublyovsko-Uspenskoye Highway. At a turn in the road, a Volvo with TsSN operatives wedged itself between the jeep and Gusinsky's Mercedes. Travelling neck-and-neck at 60-70 mph, the two cars reached Kutuzovsky Prospect in Moscow. They came to a stop between City Hall, where Gusinsky's office was located, and the White House, the seat of the Russian parliament.

During the chase, Gusinsky had called the head of the secret service directorate for Moscow, Yevgeny Savostyanov, and the Moscow Directorate of Internal Affairs and told them that he was being attacked by criminals (it was not yet clear to him who the people pursuing him were—they could have been simply hired killers). Savostyanov sent a unit from the anti-terrorism department; the head of the Internal Affairs dispatched a rapid response team.

A shootout ensued, during which, however, no one was hurt. At this point, it turned out to the hunted party that the attackers were agents from Korzhakov's SPB. Gusinsky's men had to give in. The TsSN agents dragged the passengers out of Gusinsky's jeep and laid them face down in the snow.

This marked the end of Korzhakov's operation. It entered history as 'Operation Face Down in the Snow.' The manoeuvre had done its job in revealing one of Gusinsky and Bobkov's key political ally: General Savostyanov, the head of the secret service directorate for Moscow. On the same day, at Korzhakov's request, General Savostyanov was relieved from his post by Yeltsin. He was replaced by one of Korzhakov's protégés, Anatoly Trofimov, whose job in Soviet times had been monitoring 'dissidents.'

Channel One

The victory of Operation Face Down in the Snow over his KGB

colleague proved, however, illusory for Korzhakov. From that day on, Korzhakov was doomed, although he realized it only in 1996, when it was already too late.

Under the Soviet KGB, the Ninth Directorate that formed the basis of Korzhakov's mini KGB protected sites and was traditionally separate from the others. Most of its divisions were situated around the Kremlin, since it was here that the people and sites that had to be protected were located. The employees and directors of the Ninth Directorate rarely came in contact with members of other divisions of the KGB's tentacles into Soviet public life. Consequently, the Ninth Directorate had no agents in the mass media, or among prominent politicians, or in academic circles.

Soon after Operation Face Down in the Snow, Korzhakov learned a key lesson. In post-Soviet Russia, control over one's own mini-KGB is not enough. One also needs a media empire—one's own private media outlets.

The most natural and tantalizing object to devour seemed to Korzhakov to be Russian TV's Channel One, which reached up to 180 million Russian viewers. However, here too Korzhakov's position turned out to be not particularly strong.

In an economic sense, the perestroika movement constituted primarily an unprecedented restructuring of hitherto national property. Among the first to catch the whiff of big money were the functionaries of Soviet television. Growing businesses needed advertising, and the possibilities of television in the realm of advertising were unlimited. Many television stations, competing with one another, rushed to offer their services to businesses seeking advertising on Russian central TV. The advertisements were paid for largely in U.S. dollars, and a substantial part of these payments ended up in the pockets of producers and their subordinates, who worked directly with clients.

By the early 1990s, fourteen newly formed advertising agencies were active on national TV. They purchased airtime from the producers of various television programs, divided it up as they saw fit, and sold it on to clients interested in placing commercials on television. The airtime was purchased at wholesale prices, and bought in chunks ranging from tens of minutes to several hours per day and for periods ranging from several days to several months per year before being re-sold in chunks of seconds and minutes, at considerably higher rates. The profit from such transactions was enormous, but the revenue obtained in this way was not credited to the accounts of state television. Instead, it was distributed among a group of people who had managed to divide the vast TV advertising market among themselves.

All of this activity—which took place at the Ostankino television centre, located in the Ostankino TV tower, the tallest building in Moscow—was monitored by at least 30 secret agents. They carefully reported everything about the black-market advertising business to their superiors, since all important correspondence with external agencies and organizations was conducted exclusively through the KGB department based at the television offices. All of these people had ties to Bobkov.

So how did they end up at the television centre and who were they, these people who knew, helped and promoted one another after the Soviet collapse?

Officers of the active reserve

The answer lies in a finely tuned infiltration system that had been set up by the KGB in Soviet times. In addition to the official KGB (after the collapse, secret service) agents who oversaw television, the various departments of the secret service employed many members who worked secretly in public life. These were agents recruited from the television staff, or retired KGB officers embedded among television employees. In secret service terminology, these operatives were called 'officers of the active reserve.'

The euphemistic concept of the 'active reserve' had first appeared during Yuri Andropov's tenure as head of the KGB from 1967 to 1982. The 'active reservists' existed in many ministries, departments, and government organizations (of course, prior to 1991, everything in the USSR belonged to the state). They would be established at specific places of work through a routine bureaucratic procedure. The KGB would submit a report to the Communist Party's Central Committee, justifying the need for such a position in one of the USSR's state structures. This would be followed by a resolution from the Central Committee's Secretariat, either in favour of or against the KGB's proposal. If the proposal was approved, the Politburo would ratify the new position and send appropriate instructions to the government.

Bobkov was the first deputy head of the KGB's active reservists, their second-in-command. On his initiative, an active reserve position was even created in the Central Committee of the Communist Party during the perestroika in an attempt to establish KGB control over so-called 'party money'. At the height of perestroika, such party funds were transferred abroad and never seen again—it seemed clear they were transferred by the active reserve officers that the KGB had planted in the Central Committee.

Gradually, active reserve officers were given positions in all organizations of any importance—enterprises, agencies, institutes, and businesses, including television. Those who were part of the active reserve remained on the staffs of their KGB departments, but worked at civilian or military agencies. There, while they did their new jobs, their main task was to promote state security interests. Even officers who had formally retired from the KGB/secret service would stay on at their new jobs as secret agents of the security services.

This was a truly revolutionary innovation on the part of the KGB, which was taking its precautions, in the event of unforeseen developments in the country. It was at this time that people started to say in Russia that there is no such thing as a former state security agent. Because they did not, in fact, ever retire—they became officers of the active reserve.

At the end of the 1980s, for example, Bobkov's successor Abramov, who had dreamed of becoming deputy director of the KGB and had a real chance of seeing this dream come true, was transferred—unexpectedly for everyone, most of all himself—to the General Prosecutor's Office and appointed deputy general prosecutor.

The next head of the Fifth Directorate, Yevgeny Ivanov, also became an active reserve officer at the Central Committee of the Communist Party. He was sent to work in the Soviet administrative department, which oversaw the Soviet Union's entire law enforcement system: the General Prosecutor's Office, the Supreme Court, the KGB, and the Ministry of Internal Affairs. After working there for about two years, he returned—now with the rank of lieutenant general—to the position of deputy director of the KGB. The deputy director had a great deal of power. In the absence of the director of the KGB, he oversaw foreign intelligence and the activities of the 'A' groups—elite commando units subordinated directly to the head of the KGB.

The active reserve officer position vacated by Ivanov after he left the Communist Party's Central Committee had been filled by another member of Bobkov's Fifth Directorate, Alexander Karbainov. Karbainov soon became the head of the Soviet KGB's press office, which was transformed under his supervision into the new propaganda outlet of Russia's restructured state security apparatus, KGB's Centre for Public Relations (TsOS) after the collapse of the Soviet Union.

Karbainov's next appointment could have been predicted. He was sent to work as an active reserve officer for the Russian oligarch Mikhail Khodorkovsky, owner of the Yukos oil company (prior to perestroika Khodorkovsky had been a leader of the Communist youth movement). Later, Karbainov's deputy at the TsOS, KGB General Alexei Kondaurov, also went over to Khodorkovsky as an officer of the active reserve—Kondaurov became the head of Yukos' analytic department, the company's own security service.

Alexander Komelkov

Korzhakov's reach into the lucrative business world was far less organised. His main ally was a former deputy director of the Fifth Directorate department who used to oversee Russian television, Major Alexander Komelkov. A graduate of the Moscow Institute of Culture, Komelkov was nicknamed 'Aubergine' for the beet-red and bluish colour of his face. He had come to the KGB's television department from another subdivision—the directorate that oversaw Moscow State and the Lumumba Peoples' Friendship universities.

Komelkov—who had served for 15 years in the KGB—had always wanted to work in Korzhakov's Ninth Directorate, particularly as an 'attached' officer, responsible for the personal security of a top official in the government or the Communist Party. However, he failed to meet the criteria that were used to select candidates. You had to be at least 5'9' tall and in excellent physical shape. Most of the 'attached' officers in the Ninth Directorate were in fact former Soviet athletes, who had achieved high degrees of success in various kinds of sports. Komelkov, on the other hand, was only 5'6' and had put on weight at an early age.

As head of the KGB's television department Komelkov had brought over his old friend, Valentin Malygin, whom he placed at the head of local KGB office at the Ostankino television centre. During the perestroika years, Komelkov and Malygin made skilful use of their positions through Vladimir Tsibizov, the active reservist who worked at the centre. He was responsible directly to Malygin. Like Komelkov, Tsibizov had come to the KGB through a relative after graduating from the State Institute of Theatre Arts. He oversaw the Goskontsert agency, which supervised the tours of Russian artists abroad and organized tours for foreign artists on the territory of the USSR.

The Ostankino television centre was a 'regime site'. Special passes were required to enter the building. As head of the 'regime department', Tsibizov was well acquainted with the list of people who visited Ostankino. If necessary, any visitor could be denied a pass on Tsibizov's orders, and any employee could have his belongings searched when entering or leaving the building. Komelkov and Malygin effectively leveraged this control over the Ostankino centre by selling airtime on television and radio stations and renting out facilities to commercial television enterprises. But for Komelkov, this had not ended well. He had been dishonourably discharged from the KGB in the late 1980s.

As Korzhakov needed people who were not loyal to Bobkov, this made Komelkov an eminently suitable candidate for him. Komelkov had been found guilty of corruption, fired from the KGB, and was upset at his former colleagues—especially his old boss, Bobkov. Korzhakov had good reasons to expect that Komelkov wanted to work against his former Fifth Directorate colleagues, who were all working for Bobkov's Most Bank staff at large salaries. He had been recommended to Korzhakov—despite the fact that he had been fired from the KGB—by Gennady Zotov, an old school friend from the Institute of Culture and a colleague at the Fifth Directorate who oversaw religion in the USSR and monitored religious activists (later, he became a head of department in the secret service). As someone who still retained a great deal of valuable information about TV workers, and who could renew his old contacts with them, Komelkov became Korzhakov's ideal man for working among television employees.

There was another reason why Komelkov was useful. After being dismissed, Komelkov had opened a restaurant on Kutuzovsky Prospect in Moscow, across from the Triumphal Arch. The heads of

Moscow's organized crime groups—particularly the Solntsevo gang—had been frequent visitors at Komelkov's restaurant. Kutuzovsky Prospect was also one of the government routes monitored by Korzhakov's agency. Consequently, Korzhakov knew everything about Komelkov's restaurant, just as he did about the details of another business venture of his new protégé's. During the summer 1992 Olympics in Barcelona, Komelkov had set up a successful business renting out Russian ships near the Spanish coast as hotels for tourists. The money had not been declared and was deposited in off-shore accounts. In other words, Korzhakov knew more than enough about Komelkov both to make him a loyal subordinate and to destroy him if necessary.

Korzhakov spoke with Komelkov in person about a new position at the Ostankino centre. He asked him to gather information about everything that took place there. Above all, he was interested in people and groups that had negative attitudes towards Boris Yeltsin and the SPB. Komelkov was also expected to influence editorial policies in a manner that was favourable to Korzhakov. Finally, Korzhakov warned Komelkov that there must be no leaks of information from him to his former colleagues who were now working under Bobkov for Gusinsky.

New Directions in Russian Television

Furthermore, Komelkov had also been instructed to use his old connections as much as possible in order to gather information about everything that went on at the Most Corporation. For many years, he had been acquainted with Yuri Balev, who had retired from the KGB.

The KGB department that Balev had headed dealt with ethnic problems in the USSR, one of the directorate's most important subdivisions in terms of the problems that it had to address, particularly during the perestroika years. Everywhere in the country, decentralising tendencies were on the rise. Many republics, from the Baltics to the Caucasus to Central Asia, had started thinking about their independence and the possibility of leaving the USSR, threatening the very fabric of the Soviet Union. It was these numerous nationalist movements that Balev's department had been instructed to fight. After the collapse of the Soviet Union, Bobkov, of course, invited his former subordinate Balev to join him at the new organization where he became one of Gusinsky's leading analysts at Most Bank's security service.

Nonetheless, Balev was on friendly terms with Komelkov, possibly with a view to obtaining information about Korzhakov's agency from him. Komelkov, in turn, had been instructed to obtain information about Bobkov's agency, and at one point he openly made Balev an offer to spy for Korzhakov. Balev, in response, not only rejected Komelkov's offer, he also declared that he was cutting all ties with him. Several days later, Balev was beaten near his home by unknown assailants.

Komelkov had a much easier time obtaining information about the goings on at the television centre. His old contacts and connections had remained at the centre. With Korzhakov's powerful backing, he quickly managed to become an influential person at the Ostankino tower. Komelkov's opinions mattered—few were willing to go against him, and most staff appointments were now coordinated with his approval.

During this whole period, the commercialization of state television went on unabated, and those who had been able to privatize TV channels made enormous private profits. Komelkov carefully monitored these deals and possessed reliable information about who had received how much and from whom.

Oleg Soskovets

With the enlisting of Komelkov, SBP General Korzhakov was playing a complicated and long-term political game. Having come to power at a relatively young age, he felt he was destined to remain in power for the foreseeable future. The possibility that he might fall from power, rather than rise to ever greater power, did not even occur to him. He was ready to fight for his ambitions using any means necessary—including deliberately encouraging President Yeltsin's drinking habit in order to incapacitate him.

For the role of Yeltsin's successor as President of the Russian Federation, Korzhakov had settled his choice on the deputy prime minister of the Russian government, Oleg Soskovets. True to his principle of promoting and employing only people with incriminating records, Korzhakov chose Soskovets because he knew that criminal proceedings had been initiated against him for large-scale theft at the Karaganda Metallurgical Combine, where Soskovets had been director. At the SBP, Korzhakov had access to all the incriminating evidence he needed to control him.

Korzhakov's plan was relatively simple. All Yeltsin's government power would effectively be concentrated in his hands, as the head of the SBP, those of Barsukov, as the director of state security, and those of Soskovets, as the deputy prime minister (somewhat analogous to vice president). They would retain control over all law enforcement agencies in the country, the military-industrial complex, and the arms trade within Russia and beyond its borders. The Russian Duma had to be transformed into a manageable instrument at any cost. Yeltsin either had to be kept drunk and perpetually incapacitated, or else to die of alcohol poisoning in the final stage of the plan. By that point, a state of emergency would be declared under some pretext as this would eliminate the need to hold a scheduled or early presidential election. Such a state of emergency would make it possible to appoint Soskovets as Yeltsin's successor, or as acting president. At some point, control would then be acquired over Channel One, Russia's main television channel. This would make it possible to conduct the right kind of election campaign, to hold a 'democratic' election at a moment advantageous to Soskovets, and to have Soskovets formally elected as president.

The deadline for Korzhakov's planned operation, which could be more accurately described as a government coup, was already known. It had to take place no later than the constitutionally-scheduled presidential election on June 16, 1996. Among his friends, Korzhakov would sometimes accidentally slip up and say something along the lines of: 'What do you think? Wouldn't I be able to govern a country like Russia?' For Korzhakov, Soskovets was merely a puppet appointee to be used to achieve his final goal: absolute power.

But to achieve his goal, Korzhakov needed money, a lot of it, so that he could buy up leading politicians, the Duma, and the voters. The question was where to get this money.

Before he appointed Komelkov to 'look after' Ostankino, Korzhakov had no idea what kinds of sums of money circulated at the television centre. Later, when he at last appreciated the level of profits that were coming in from advertising, he set himself the task of bringing these streams of revenue—which escaped the notice of the tax agencies and the state treasury—under his own control. This money would have undoubtedly been enough for any government coup. The SBP already extorted money from businesses, businessmen, and government officials, and Korzhakov disposed of considerable financial resources, including hard foreign currency.

These resources were spent with the aim of preparing a creeping government takeover. The SBP spent over $50 million to acquire sophisticated eavesdropping equipment from abroad, a large part of which was installed inside the Kremlin. The monitoring was all-pervasive. The Kremlin's offices were crammed with complex German bugging devices and, although the high-ranking officials who occupied these offices generally suspected that their premises had been bugged, nothing could be done to oppose Korzhakov's and Barsukov's system of total surveillance. Sergei Filatov, President Yeltsin's chief of staff at the time, constantly complained to reporters that he was forced to communicate with visitors in his own office by writing notes, and that the most important negotiations had to be conducted in the hallway outside.

According to the estimates of various rival organizations, by 1995 Korzhakov's SBP numbered over 40,000 people. Under Andropov, the KGB and the Foreign Intelligence Directorate together numbered about 37,000 employees.

Vladislav Listyev

What Korzhakov needed at the Ostankino was a man who was completely unaware of the ultimate aims of his superiors, who had no experience in the world of politics, who had no contacts in the Kremlin, and who at the same time was widely respected in the world of television. This man had to be convinced that everything he was doing was done for the good of the country, since everything had to appear as if financial order was being imposed on television in the interests of the state. Korzhakov relied on Komelkov, his man at the centre, to come up with the right person. Korzhakov's protégé knew just the man.

The recruitment of visiting foreign undergraduate and graduate students into the KGB's agent network required the active involvement of Soviet citizens. This was how, at the beginning of the 1980s, the path of future TV reporter Vladislav Listyev crossed that of KGB Senior Lieutenant Komelkov.

Listyev had grown up in a simple family, lost his father early on, and attended the best educational institution in the country, Moscow State University. There were many foreign students at Moscow State, coming to study in the USSR from all over the world. All of them were closely monitored by the KGB.

In order to achieve a more comprehensive surveillance over foreign students and a more thorough understanding of their political views and orientations, their personalities, and their psychological characteristics, university faculty and students—both Soviet citizens and foreigners—were recruited en masse by the KGB. Agents recruited among foreign students received considerable attention, since they were destined to become what the KGB referred to as 'subsidence agents'—known in the West as 'sleeper agents'.

Their principal mission was to establish a presence in any country that was of interest to the KGB, and to occupy a place in society that gave them access to information which was of interest to the Soviet Union's security organs. Many of these foreign graduates achieved advanced professional positions and high social status after returning to their own countries. They included members of ministers' cabinets, prominent political and social activists, diplomats, and famous journalists. In addition to their high levels of education, what facilitated their successes in life was the fact that most of them had influential relatives in their own countries.

Moscow's prestigious colleges were attended by the children of the Soviet and Communist Party elite and the children of the artistic community. Their status was similar to those of the foreign visitors. The children of the elite received the most interesting and promising internship assignments, both during the course of their schooling and after graduation. Consequently, their further careers unfolded with ease and success. They hardly needed a helping hand from the KGB.

To the small number of students who came from simple Soviet families it was obvious that their opportunities after graduation would be severely limited by comparison. On the other hand, those who lacked this kind of support had to rely on their own strengths and abilities, or else to try to obtain such support by marrying someone from the elite. The third means of support came from joining the ranks of the numerous agents and members of the KGB.

The process by which candidates were picked for subsequent recruitment constituted a kind of social selection. According to the

KGB's instructions, members of the top levels of the Communist Party nomenclature and members of their families could not be recruited into the KGB's agent network. The same constraints applied to the relatives of currently employed KGB officers.

As a result, the agents who were recruited among college students came for the most part from the middle and lower classes of Soviet society. A considerable number of them were children of simple working families, who thought that by helping the KGB they were demonstrating their loyalty to the Soviet regime and could count on assistance in their subsequent lives and careers. And, indeed, the KGB actively promoted its people, thus creating 'agents of influence' who occupied prominent places in the political and social life of the country while furthering the interests of state security.

Vladislav Listyev, a sociable and athletic student at Moscow State University's journalism faculty, could not but attract the attention of the KGB. With the help of the faculty's KGB supervisor, Listyev was able to join a group of students who were engaged in the intensive study of foreign languages. A couple of years later, he was able to transfer to the newly created faculty of international journalism—a faculty that a great many students wished to attend, including those with highly influential relatives. It was obvious to everyone that the new faculty's future graduates would have excellent prospects of working abroad—the greatest dream of many Soviet people. But in the selection of students for this faculty, the KGB had the last word. The phone calls made on Listyev's behalf went as high as the rector of the university and the dean of the faculty.

Shortly after being admitted to the international journalism faculty, Listyev was included in a group of students selected for pre-graduation internships abroad. Candidates for trips abroad were subjected to thorough investigations by the various subdivisions of the KGB, including a so-called 'home assessment', which involved the collection of information about the candidate's way of life and his relatives. Such 'assessment' projects were implemented by a KGB department specialising in surveillance over 'objects of operational interest', and of 'home assessments' for all operational and staff departments. 'Assessments' were also conducted at the request of departments that were responsible for doing background checks on Soviet citizens filing documents for travel abroad. Listyev's file (all Soviet citizens who filed documents for travelling outside the country had such files) contained the following note: 'Known to the Third Department of the Fifth Directorate of the KGB'. It meant that the 'subject' was either part of the KGB's agent network or that he was being examined as a potential candidate for recruitment.

Despite this endorsement, Listyev's 'home assessment' resulted in a negative characterization of him and his close relatives, and he was both denied the right to leave the country and excluded from the group of students selected for internships abroad. The KGB did not, however, forget about Listyev. When candidates were selected for work in the Soviet media—especially radio and television—their candidacies were also invariably coordinated with the KGB. Promotions to higher positions, as well as transfers to other forms of media, were likewise controlled by state security. With the help of his KGB supervisors, despite serious personal problems, he was hired in the 1980s to work at Soviet national radio, in the foreign broadcasting department.

Shortly afterwards, Listyev's path again crossed Alexander Komelkov, his former KGB overseer at university. With the support of Komelkov and the KGB, Listyev, despite his far from impeccable biography, was able in 1987 to join an elite group of young reporters who had been invited to work at the Ostankino centre for the new youth program '*Vzglyad*'. And although Listyev repeatedly came to work drunk, failed to come to work at all, and even missed his own broadcasts, a generous policy of 'forgive all' remained in effect toward him. No one touched Listyev.

Over the years, '*Vzglyad*' became one of the most popular shows on television, and its hosts became national favourites—Listyev included. With every year, he became more and more popular. His professional skills developed, as did his authority among his colleagues. In 1990, he became the artistic director of the extremely popular show 'Pole Chudes' ('Wheel of Fortune') as well as the programs 'Tema' ('Theme') and 'Chas Pik' ('Rush Hour'). After the failure of the August coup, he was appointed the general producer of the centre.

Korzhakov's plan comes together, almost

On Komelkov's recommendation, Listyev was chosen for the job of 'cleaning up' the television sector—and so Korzhakov started to sell Yeltsin on the idea that Listyev was the man who represented the future of Russian television. In September 1994, Korzhakov got Listyev appointed vice president of the Academy of Russian Television. And in January 1995, Listyev became the general manager of ORT, the television channel that had been created on November 30, 1994, following the privatization of the state-run Channel One. Yeltsin issued the decree on Korzhakov's initiative.

For Korzhakov, Listyev was an ideally naive figure. All Listyev wanted was to be the producer of entertaining TV shows on ORT and did not see himself in any larger capacity. What Korzhakov and Komelkov demanded of Listyev, in return, was to facilitate the takeover of ORT's entire advertising market, and to redirect all proceeds from the sales of airtime to accounts controlled by Korzhakov's SBP.

And so, a few days after his appointment, Listyev made a public announcement that henceforth all advertising on ORT would be restricted to a limited number of companies under his personal control. Television workers panicked, and the newspaper *Vecherny Klub* commented: 'This is understandable. Advertising means money. It is the income of television companies and of private individuals, both legal and illegal. Television workers even have a special word—*dzhinsa*—for shows, clips, and information programs that are produced off the books. Payment for such programming goes directly to its producers, bypassing official accounts. Now, Ostankino will no longer have this kind of trough at which to feed (according to estimates, the monthly fall in revenue will be 30 million rubles). Such a change is bound to have major consequences.'

The move reduced the channel's profits by millions of dollars. Listyev's SBP supervisor Komelkov was sufficiently familiar with the business plans of the principal advertisers. Thanks to his secret service colleagues who were still at the Ostankino centre—Tsibizov, and Malygin—Komelkov possessed information about all of the advertisers' connections and the organizations that provided for their financial support and security. In addition, the names of individuals who frequented the various television offices were known to him through the department that issued passes to the Ostankino tower. And secret service and Ministry of Internal Affairs records could be used to identify those among them who had links to various organized crime groups in Moscow.

One of the people who had come up with the idea of reforming and privatizing Channel One was Boris Berezovsky. Berezovsky proposed creating a joint-stock company: the government would retain control over 51% of the shares, and 49% would go to private investors loyal to President Yeltsin. This would give the president effective control over the newly-privatized TV station and, most importantly, it would allow him to use it as a resource in the 1996 presidential campaign.

This plan pleased Yeltsin, and it pleased Korzhakov, whom Berezovsky at that time considered an ally. Thanks to this, Berezovsky's political influence in the Kremlin undoubtedly increased, and his company LogoVAZ obtained access to Channel One's lucrative advertising market and signed an agreement with advertising magnate Sergei Lisovsky. In addition, 49% of ORT's shares were held by a group of private business people known to Berezovsky, and by Berezovsky himself.

The advertising magnate Lisovsky (a former leader of the Communist Party youth movement) had appeared at the television centre at the end of the 1980s. Prior to his arrival, he had become rather well known in Moscow for organising huge discos at the Olimpiysky sports complex. In 1991, he organized two television advertising agencies: LIS'S and Premier SV (in 1998, Premier SV controlled 65% of the TV advertising market). It was through him that Korzhakov now decided to get his share of the TV advertising business. Listyev as head of ORT was charged with opening negotiations with Lisovsky, who said he was prepared to offer ORT compensation in return for the right to supervise the channel's advertising and thus to retain his control. At the same time, Listyev began negotiations with another entrepreneur in the advertising business, Gleb Boky, who represented the BSG Industrial Trade Group.

The negotiations dragged on, however, and on February20, 1995, Listyev, who had in the meantime started his own advertising agency Intervid, announced a temporary moratorium on all forms of advertising until ORT worked out new ethical standards. It was clear that this was Korzhakov's attempt to deal a blow to Lisovsky and Boky, perhaps even to drive them out of the advertising business altogether, by switching all clients over to Intervid.

On 30 March 30, 1994, a meeting took place between Listyev, Lisovsky, and Boky in a small restaurant on Kropotkinskaya Street in Moscow. Over dinner Lisovsky and Boky demanded that Listyev share advertising airtime with them. The inexperienced Listyev gave in, thereby making a crucial mistake. On the following day, Listyev's mistake was quickly corrected. On Spartanskaya Street, Boky's Cadillac was riddled with six bullets from a TT-model pistol. Just to make sure, a grenade was tossed inside the vehicle as well. Boky died instantaneously.

Korzhakov now hurried Listyev. He needed the money to prime public opinion about the replacement of Yeltsin—whose drinking he continued to encourage—with the young and energetic deputy prime minister Soskovets. Time was running out as the Russian presidential election was approaching, and Korzhakov and his team had little confidence that Yeltsin, whose popularity rating was running extremely low, could win. Korzhakov determined that the necessary expenditure would amount to approximately $50-$60 million.

Listyev failed, however, to procure this kind of money for Korzhakov. It was becoming clear to all that Listyev had to be got rid of at once, and control over ORT passed on to someone else.

It is difficult to determine the exact moment at which the plan to murder Listyev took shape. But it is evident that this operation would fulfil many different goals. First, Listyev would be eliminated. Second, the blame for the organization of Listyev's murder would be cast on Listyev's main competitor in the advertising market, Lisovsky, and also on Boris Berezovsky—who was now an influential presence at ORT (and who at that time had Yeltsin's ear). Third, Berezovsky would be arrested, and Yeltsin—disappointed in Berezovsky, Lisovsky, and Anatoly Chubais, the influential reform-oriented politician with ties to both of them—would hand control over ORT to a new person named by Korzhakov, while Korzhakov and his people would get the 49% of ORT's non-government shares. Lisovsky, now a suspect, would also be unable continue his business dealings with ORT.

Someone began methodically to eliminate Listyev's rivals. Following Boky's assassination on 30 March 30, on 9 April 9, 1994, the head of Vargus-Video, G. Topadze, who owned 6.5% of ORT's advertising business, was shot. An assassination attempt against Berezovsky followed in June. Berezovsky's driver was killed and Berezovsky himself was injured. In order to prevent another assassination attempt, Gusinsky flew Berezovsky out of Russia on his private plane. Such open intervention by the Gusinsky-Bobkov axis on Berezovsky's behalf demonstrated to observers that the recent murders and assassination attempts had been carried out by rivals of the Most Corporation. Lisovsky's turn came next. It was believed that he was under the protection of the leader of the Orekhovo crime gang, Sergei Timofeyev ('Silvestr'). In September 1994, 'Silvestr' was blown up in his Mercedes along with his driver.

At around the same time, Listyev was anticipating a visit from the Solntsevo crime group. He had blocked a project that they were interested in, and he was expecting them to come to him and demand compensation in the million dollars. Listyev had asked Komelkov to intervene and to shield him from the gang's demands. The simplest form of protection, Listyev supposed, would be to deny them admission passes to the Ostankino building. But the members of the Solntsevo gang were allowed to enter the building and this indicated to Listyev that Komelkov and his SBP supervisors had abandoned him. It is even possible that the Solntsevo gangsters received the order to eliminate Listyev.

In any case, on March 1, 1995, Listyev was killed inside his apartment building. Shortly afterwards, the SPB attempted to arrest Berezovsky at the LogoVAZ office on Novokuznetskaya Street in Moscow after his return to Russia. They failed, however, to do so. He had time to get in touch with then prime minister Viktor Chernomyrdin, who prevented the arrest.

It spelled the end for the SBP's designs on Ostankino. Through the Gusinsky-controlled media, information was leaked that incriminated Korzhakov and Barsukov. Chubais, the privatization Czar, who was respected by Yeltsin, spoke out in support of Berezovsky and Gusinsky. ORT remained in Berezovsky's hands, and Korzhakov ended up not getting the advertising money and the \$50-\$60 million that he needed to reshape public opinion.

An alternative route

In Soviet times, arms exports were controlled by the Main Engineering Directorate (GIU) of the Ministry of Foreign Economic Relations. Most of the GIU's employees were staff officers of the intelligence agency of the military (the Main Intelligence Directorate, or GRU). After the revolution of August 1991, Korzhakov, had taken control of the stream of revenue that came from the arms trade. On November 18,

1993, in order to regulate and systematize the complicated business of selling armaments, Yeltsin signed a secret decree (No. 1932-s) that established a state-owned company, Rosvooruzhenie, to represent the interests of Russia's military-industrial complex in dealings with foreign companies involved in the arms trade. The same decree conferred control over Rosvooruzhenie's activities to Korzhakov's SBP.

To this end, a department 'V' (from *vooruzhenie*, 'armaments') was established in the SBP, whose main function was to control the activities of Rosvooruzhenie. At the head of department 'V,' Korzhakov placed a loyal subordinate Alexander Kotelkin. Born in 1954, Kotelkin graduated from Kiev's Higher Military Engineering School and for a number of years served in the air force. He was then hired by the GRU and sent to study at the Diplomatic Academy of the Soviet Union's Foreign Office where he served as a military intelligence officer under diplomatic cover at the permanent mission to the UN in New York.

While living in the United States, Kotelkin was noted for his many romantic liaisons with female of Soviet diplomats working at the UN. Kotelkin also maintained close relations with Sergei Glazyev, a deputy minister in the 1992 government of Yegor Gaidar, and later minister of foreign economic relations. With Glazyev's assistance, Kotelkin was appointed head of the successor organization to the GIU at the Ministry of Foreign Economic Relations where he received bonuses of tens of thousands of dollars from the enterprises under his control.

With such a chequered and well-documented background, he was the perfect candidate for Korzhakov. In November 1994, Kotelkin also became head of Rosvooruzhenie. And, from November 1994 onwards, Korzhakov and his people among Rosvooruzhenie's employees were able to arrange for the money the SBP needed for Korzhakov's ambitious designs to claim the presidency, and prepare the ground for the next stage.

The first Chechen War

Undeterred by the setback with ORT, Korzhakov then decided to opt for a cheaper strategy to trounce his KGB colleagues at the Most Corporation. It was a strategy that did not require a television-led public relations campaign—war. At this point in time, Chechnya had become the weakest link in the Russian Federation's multinational mosaic. The Soviet KGB had raised no objections when Dzhokhar Dudayev came to power in Chechnya in 1990, because they regarded him as one of their own.

General Dudayev, a member of the Communist Party since 1968, was transferred from Estonia to his home town of Grozny in order to oppose the local communists, to be elected president of the Chechen Republic, and then to proclaim Chechen independence in November 1991. But, rather than toe the line, it was as if he intended to show the Russian political elite what kind of disintegration was in store for Russia under Yeltsin's liberal regime. It was probably no accident that another Chechen who was close to Yeltsin, Ruslan Khasbulatov, would also be responsible for inflicting fatal damage on Yeltsin's regime. Khasbulatov, a Communist Party member since 1966, became speaker of the Russian parliament in September 1991, but it was precisely this Khasbulatov-led parliament that Yeltsin would forcibly dissolve—using tanks—in October 1993.

War in Chechnya offered a very easy way to finish off Yeltsin politically, a fact understood only too well by those who intended to provoke war with Chechnya. But there was also a simple financial aspect to relations between the Russian leadership and the president of the Chechen Republic. The Russians were continuously extorting money from Dudayev.

Some years later the Russian people would wonder why all the weapons that the Chechens were using to kill Russian soldiers had ever been left behind in Chechnya after the Soviet collapse. The answer was nothing if not mundane. They had been paid for by Dudayev in multi-million dollar bribes to the triumvirate of Korzhakov, Barsukov, and Soskovets. It began in 1992, when bribes were accepted from the Chechens in payment for leaving Soviet arms behind in Chechnya that year. Naturally, the Ministry of Defence was in on the deal. After 1992, Moscow bureaucrats continued their successful bribe-based collaboration with Dudayev, and the Chechen leadership continued sending money to Moscow on a regular basis. It was the only way in which Dudayev could get anything done in the Russian capital.

However, in 1994 the system began to falter, as Moscow extorted larger and larger sums of money in exchange for political favours relating to Chechen independence. Dudayev started refusing to pay.

The financial conflict gradually developed into a political standoff and finally a contest of strength between the Russian and Chechen leadership.

The threat of war hung heavily in the air. Dudayev requested a personal meeting with Yeltsin, perhaps even with the intention of telling him what had been going on. But the triumvirate of Korzhakov, Barsukov and Soskovets—which controlled access to Yeltsin—demanded a payment of several million dollars for organizing such a meeting between the two presidents. Dudayev refused and demanded that the meeting with Yeltsin take place without any money changing hands in advance. Furthermore, for the first time, he threatened the people who had been helping in exchange for bribes with the disclosure of documents in his possession, which contained compromising information about the self-serving dealings with the Chechens of certain functionaries.

Dudayev believed naively that possession of documents proving the bribes for arms was his insurance policy against arrest. Dudayev was correct in one way, he could not be arrested. But he was wrong in another, he now had to be killed, since he threatened to expose members of Yeltsin's entourage. His attempt at blackmail failed, and the meeting he wanted never took place. From a reliable source of revenue, the president of Chechnya had turned into a liability, a dangerous witness who had to be removed.

By 1994, the political leadership of Russia had reached the conclusion that it could not afford to grant Chechnya independence from the Russian Federation. To grant Chechnya sovereign status would make the disintegration of the rump that had left after the collapse of the Soviet Union a real possibility. But could it afford to start a civil war in the North Caucasus in order to liquidate the Chechen president? That was the question.

The 'party of war', which relied on the military and law enforcement ministries, believed that the answer was yes, as long as the public was prepared. It would be easy enough to influence public opinion if the Chechens were seen to resort to terrorist tactics in their struggle for independence. All that was needed was to arrange terrorist attacks in Moscow and to leave a trail leading back to Chechnya.

On 18 November, 1994, the secret service made its first recorded attempt to stir up anti-Chechen feeling by committing an act of terrorism and laying the blame on Chechen separatists. An explosion took place on a railroad track crossing the Yauza River in Moscow. According to experts, it was caused by two powerful charges of approximately 1.5 kilograms of TNT. About twenty meters of the railroad bed were ripped up, and the bridge almost collapsed.

Things did not, however, work out as the secret service had planned. The explosion occurred before a train was due to cross the bridge—the shattered fragments of the bomber's body were discovered about one hundred meters from the site of the explosion. The bomber's name was Captain Andrei Schelenkov, and he was an employee of the oil company Lanako. His own bomb had blown him up as he was planting it on the bridge.

It was only thanks to this blunder by the operative carrying out the bombing that the immediate organizers of the terrorist attack became known. Lanako's boss was 35-year-old Maxim Lazovsky, a highly valued agent of the secret service's bureau in Moscow, also known simply as 'Max.' It would later become apparent that every single one of Lanako's employees was a full-time or active reserve agent of the Russian security services. Several further 'terrorist' attacks occurred in Moscow during 1994-1995 which had also been organized by Lazovsky's group. In 1996, the terrorists from the secret service were arrested and convicted by a Moscow court.

But by that time, the first Chechen war had become a *fait accompli.* Max had done his job well enough. On 23 November, 1994, nine Russian army helicopters launched a rocket attack on the town of Shali, located approximately forty kilometres from the Chechen capital Grozny, in an attempt to destroy the armoured vehicles of a tank regiment located there. They were met with anti-aircraft artillery fire. There were wounded on the Chechen side, which announced that it had a video recording of helicopters with Russian identification markings.

The headquarters of Chechnya's armed forces also confirmed that Russian military units were being concentrated on the border, in the Stavropol region: there were heavy tanks, artillery, and as many as six battalions of infantry. It later became known that the backbone of the forces, drawn up for the storming of Grozny, consisted of a column of Russian armoured vehicles assembled on the initiative of the secret service. It had paid for it and also hired contract soldiers and officers, including members of the elite armed forces from the Taman and Kantemirov divisions.

On 25 November, seven Russian helicopters from a base in the Stavropol region fired several rocket salvoes at the airport in Grozny and at nearby apartment buildings, damaging the landing strip and the civilian aircraft standing on it. Six people were killed and about twenty-five were injured. In response to this raid, Chechnya's Ministry of Foreign Affairs forwarded a statement to the authorities of the Stavropol region stating that the region's leaders 'bear responsibility for such acts, and in the case of adequate responses being taken by the Chechen side', all complaints 'should be directed to Moscow'.

On November 26, the forces of Chechnya's Provisional Council (the Chechen anti-Dudayev opposition, and a puppet organization of Moscow), supported by helicopters and armoured vehicles of the Russian army, attacked Grozny from all four sides. More than 1,200 men, fifty tanks, eighty armoured personnel carriers, and six SU-27 planes took part in the operation. The Provisional Council's centre in Moscow soon announced, 'the demoralized forces of Dudayev's supporters are offering virtually no resistance, and everything will probably be over by morning.'

In fact, the operation was a total failure. The attackers lost about 500 men and more than twenty tanks, and another twenty tanks were captured by Dudayev's forces. About 200 members of the armed forces were taken prisoner. On 28 November, a column of prisoners was marched through the streets of Grozny 'to mark the victory over the forces of the opposition'. At the same time, the Chechen leadership disclosed a list of fourteen captured soldiers and officers who were members of the Russian armed forces.

Russia's minister of defence Pavel Grachev hinted that he had not been involved in the irresponsible attempt to take Grozny. From a military point of view, as Grachev declared at a press conference on 28 November 1996, it would be entirely possible to take Grozny 'in two hours with a single regiment of paratroopers... Introducing tanks into the city without infantry cover was really quite pointless.' Dudayev's forces were at full strength—those of the opposition were inadequate for the operation. The column could not possibly have been anything more than a moving target.

The general who later lead the second war in Chechnya, Gennady Troshev, confirmed the minister of defence's doubts concerning the Chechen campaign: '[Grachev] tried to do something about it. He tried to extract a clear assessment of the situation from [the secret services], he tried to delay the initial introduction of troops until the spring, and he even tried to reach a personal agreement with Dudayev. We know now that such a meeting did take place. They didn't come to any agreement.' The general could not understand how Grachev had failed to reach an understanding with Dudayev. The reason being that Dudayev insisted on a personal meeting with Yeltsin, and Korzhakov refused to set up the meeting unless he was paid.

Those who reported on the crude miscalculations of the Russian military leaders, who had sent the armoured column into the city to face-annihilation—failed to understand the subtle political calculations of the provocateurs who organized the war in Chechnya. The people who planned the introduction of troops into Grozny wanted the column to be wiped out in spectacular fashion by the Chechens.

The plan was to provoke Yeltsin into launching a full-scale war against Dudayev—which was indeed launched in December 1994.

State of Emergency

Just before the 1996 election, the triumvirate of Korzhakov, Barsukov, and Soskovets had finally managed to move the necessary pieces in place, or so they thought. They persuaded President Yeltsin that he had no chance of beating his main rival, Communist Party candidate Gennady Zyuganov, and that the only way to hold on to power in the country was to declare a state of emergency. The ongoing war in Chechnya since 1994 would be the pretext.

Their suggestion had a compelling logic to it. If the Communist Zyuganov came to power, he would undoubtedly put Yeltsin in jail for dissolving the parliament, The White House, in 1993 by force and shelling it. It was easy to portray the dissolution of Russia's legislative body as an unconstitutional act, or indeed a number of his other confrontations with parliament, with all the attendant consequences for Yeltsin. Furthermore, if anyone other than Yeltsin came to power, they could also prosecute him for starting the first Chechen war, for war crimes committed by the Russian army in Chechnya, and for the massive civilian casualties among the Chechen people. And any new president could question the legality of Yeltsin's privatization of the Russian economy. The list was long.

And so, Yeltsin signed a decree cancelling the presidential election and declaring a state of emergency. However, before this decree was made public, its contents became known to all those who opposed Korzhakov's coup: Gusinsky, Berezovsky, Chubais, Lisovsky, and all those who would later become known as the Russian oligarchs. In a single concerted effort—the likes of which has not been seen since in Russian history—they gained admittance to Yeltsin's office with help from his daughter Tatyana Dyachenko. They offered him the use of money, newspapers, and television instead of tanks and decrees declaring a state of emergency.

With such an offer to secure his position, Yeltsin recalled the decree which he had already signed. He summarily dismissed Korzhakov, Barsukov, and Soskovets, and appointed Chubais as his chief of staff. Berezovsky vouched for Yeltsin's support on ORT; Gusinsky on NTV; Lisovsky was in charge of advertising; Roman Abramovich, then almost unknown, handled the extra-budgetary financing.

Starting out with a popularity rating of just 3%, Yeltsin managed to get the highest percentage of votes in the first round of the presidential elections in June. In July's second round he beat his opponent, Zyuganov, by nearly 14% and over 10 million votes.

Shortly afterward, on August 31, 1996, Yeltsin signed a peace agreement with the Chechen Republic. The first Chechen war came to an end and Russia returned to the path of democracy. The SBP faction had lost, but behind the scenes new plans were brewing in Russia's sprawling network of secret service agents and active reservists.

CHAPTER TWO

St Petersburg Mafia and Chekists

The Collapse of the Iron Curtain

In 1996 Yeltsin supported elections, rather than the state of emergency advocated by the senior members of his cabinet (the so called *silivoki*[1]). This was a decision that, without doubt, offered some hope of democracy at the apex of the political pyramid. Sadly it barely reflected what was happening in the rest of the country. If there was severe tension at the top of the Russian Federation, there was a dense confusion at the bottom.

Normally, criminal offences are actions that violate existing laws. In this respect, the situation in Russia during the 1990s was unique. After the collapse of the Soviet Union in August 1991, the old Soviet laws were not formally repealed, but it became virtually impossible to apply them—apart from laws involving physical harm or property (murder, infliction of bodily injury, theft, and robbery).

Soviet laws were aimed at ensuring the absence of private property and banned private enterprise. They included prohibitions against the use and possession of foreign currency, and operations involving foreign currency were classified among the most serious crimes and in certain cases were punishable by death. The system of residence permits, which had not been formally repealed, essentially prohibited people from moving from one place of residence to another and from changing jobs. But with the collapse of communism, these laws no longer had any validity—though they remained on the statute books as legal ghosts. Thus, after August 1991, Russia was left in a state of utter lawlessness that would have made any lawyer or prosecutor despair. Every citizen of the Russian Federation was guilty of one crime or another, probably many.

Nonetheless, it is worth pointing out that, considering the atmosphere of anarchy in which this enormous country became submerged during these years—and contrary to what might seem to be the case at first glance—the level of self-regulation attained in Russia was extremely high rather than extremely low. The population relatively quickly developed its own rules of conduct, replacing the defunct Soviet laws with 'understandings.' And this was what the due process of law in Russia was based on, at all levels, on understandings.

Naturally, the number of holes in this alternative to law and order was endless. Many officials in Moscow and the other regions of the Federation invented and altered laws, decisions, resolutions, and regulations in accordance with their own political and economic interests, and those of their economic dependents and collaborators. Sometimes, a law could be tailored to a specific operation (such as the 'deposit auctions' for the privatization of government property in exchange for token money), and then radically altered to suit another analogous operation. Under such conditions, with legislation and enforcement being what they were, even the most innocent administrative-economic action by an official or businessman was bound to violate one rule or another.

At the same time, the most flagrant and unscrupulous economic and financial schemes often did not qualify as direct violations of the law and were not subject to prosecution. All financial transactions were handled in cash—so-called 'black money,' money that did not show up anywhere in the accounts—in rubles and foreign currency. Given the government's total lack of ability to monitor financial transactions, all attempts to collect taxes by relying on old Soviet tax regulations were meaningless. And no new federal tax code had been created to replace the old one. It was simply impossible to create any new tax code for the country that Russia had become, with its wild, embryonic, and rapidly developing dynamic capitalism.

As a consequence, Russia's entire population did not pay taxes on its grey income—which it received in cash. Russia's entire population was busily evading taxation, had there been any tax laws to speak of.

Active reservists of the KGB and Vladimir Putin

As before the collapse, ordinary Russians living in this enormous country did not often come into contact with the KGB. And if they did, they often did not know that their colleagues, friends, or even relatives were working for state security. Those who worked for state security knew each other, and knew about each other, exceedingly well. Through the mighty organization—the second in command in soviet times, and the structure that was mangled least in the Soviet collapse—that employed them, they helped one another, promoted one another, appointed one another to higher and higher positions, and were sooner or later soaked up in any organization of significance. As in Soviet times, the uninitiated population could never understand what it was that explained the career successes of this or that person, who often had no distinguishing professional abilities or sometimes was distinguished precisely by his lack of professionalism. Mediocre colleagues continued to become managers alongside the promotion of bright colleagues who would not have had a chance under Communism. It would have seemed odd if anyone had considered it in detail. But so much change, favouritism and nepotism, was going on that it remained under the radar. Meanwhile the system of the Russian secret service pursued its simple goal on autopilot: to use any means necessary to appoint its own active reserve officers or recruited agents to positions of influence: usually those 'assisting' decision makers. Slowly the corporation grew.

What mattered in the anarchic times that followed 1991 was the ability to strike an effective individual course through these nebulous circumstances in which laws were either treacherous, non-enforced or malleable to one's will. One active KGB reservist, in particular, was exemplary in his achievements—though he would perhaps not necessarily have been equally successful in Soviet times. His rise was typical of many others from 1991 throughout Russia and at all levels. The name of this particular agent was Vladimir Putin.

During the years of the Soviet Union, Vladimir Putin's career is perhaps best described as somewhat colourless. After graduating from the international law department of Leningrad State University in 1975, at the height of the Cold War when Brezhnev was still in power, Putin received an assignment to work at the KGB. His school record up till then was fine but not exceptionally different from his peers. From 1960 to 1968, he attended school No. 193 on the Griboyedov Canal in Leningrad and was the head of his Young Pioneer troop in the youth division of the Communist Party. After finishing eighth grade, he entered high school No. 281 in Sovietsky Pereulok (a magnet school affiliated with a technological institute and specializing in chemistry). After graduating in 1970, he entered the international law department of Leningrad State University's law faculty and became a member of the Communist Party. (He remained a member until it was banned in August, 1991.)

For about five months, the young Putin worked at the secretariat of the KGB's Leningrad office, 'pushing papers around.'[2] From February to June 1976, he attended retraining courses for operational personnel. Then, for half a year until 1977, he served at the Leningrad KGB directorate—according to him, in a 'counterintelligence unit... dealing with foreign elements,'[3] and according to the testimony of his co-workers, in the Leningrad KGB department, which oversaw the 'struggle against ideological diversions by the enemy' and the surveillance of dissidents (Fifth Department). While working at the 'counterintelligence unit,' Putin attracted the attention of foreign intelligence officers, after which he received an offer to transfer to foreign intelligence (the First Main Directorate) and was sent to attend a year-long retraining program in Moscow. After returning to Leningrad, he served from 1979 to 1983 in the Leningrad KGB.

In 1984, after being promoted to the rank of major, Putin was sent to the Higher Education School of the KGB in Moscow (the Andropov Red Banner Institute), which he attended under the assumed name 'Platov.' At the institute, Putin specialized in German-speaking countries (Austria, Switzerland, West Germany, East Germany). After completing his courses in 1985, he was sent to the KGB office in East Germany, where he served as director of the House of Soviet-German Friendship in Dresden. He lived on Radebergerstraße in Dresden.[4] As a KGB representative, he oversaw the conduct of Soviet students in East Germany. At one time, Putin's duties included surveillance over Hans Modrow, who would become East Germany's last communist premier and was at that time the secretary of the Dresden office of the Socialist Unity Party of Germany (SED). He also investigated anti-communist acts of protest in East Germany.[5]

It seems that KGB agent Putin's duties were somewhat undistinguished. In 1986, the then head of the KGB, Vladimir Kryuchkov, travelled to East Germany to meet Hans Modrow, yet he could not recall any Putin present at meetings attended by all KGB officers. In his view, Putin had most likely not been an active officer for the elite foreign intelligence unit of the KGB', but merely a staff member who had received a work assignment in East Germany for a standard period of five years.[6] Further light is cast by a retired KGB colleague of Putin's in East Germany, Vladimir Usoltsev (a pseudonym for KGB Lieutenant-Colonel Vladimir Gortanov), who published his memoirs in 2004.

Usoltsev had worked with Putin in Dresden and he writes about this period in Putin's life. He jokes that the Soviet Union's 'Berlin' agents spent most of their time collecting free fashion catalogues in department stores in West Berlin and then selling them to seamstresses and fashion designers back home. He and Putin had no such opportunities in Dresden, and they were forced to talk their Berlin colleagues into giving them some of their catalogues. Putin, 'Usoltsev' writes, was much more successful at this because many of the agents stationed in Berlin came from Putin's home town of Leningrad.

The head of the Dresden foreign intelligence group, the elderly Colonel Lazar Lazarevich Matveyev, was especially fond of Putin. Explaining how Putin managed to receive two promotions within the KGB and two promotions during his stay in Dresden, Usoltsev observes: 'Volodya knew how to be polite, friendly, obliging, and unobtrusive. He was capable of making anyone like him, but he was particularly successful with people who were old enough to be his father.' His simple motto was: 'why make things difficult for yourself by spitting against the wind?'[7]

Back in the Soviet Union

In the first half of 1990, Vladimir Putin, KGB officer, former secretary of the Communist Party at the KGB Dresden office, senior assistant to his department head, and a member of the Communist Party KGB's East German office—made plans to return to his home town of Leningrad. According to the long interview given by Putin to three *Kommersant* reporters at the beginning of 2000 (which formed the basis of his pre-election book *First Person*) he stayed in Dresden until January 1990: 'When In January 1990 we came back from Germany, I was still working for the state security organs, but was quietly starting to think about a back-up landing strip for myself.'[8] As well he might, because on 3 October 1990 the German Reunification of East and West would terminate Russian influence in Dresden and his pleasant existence.

Vladimir Putin's wife, Lyudmila, remembers almost the same date as her husband: 'We came back to the Soviet Union at the beginning of 1990, on February 3, I think.'[9] Lyudmila recalls this period of their life with some bitterness: 'As soon as we came back to Leningrad, my husband immediately threw himself into work. I think that he had become so tired of having a stable and regular routine in Dresden for four-and-a-half years that in St Petersburg he simply was never at home. It looked as if my husband has disappeared, as if he had run away from home.' Not only did Putin himself not show up at home; he also did not receive his salary in these turbulent times. But as a KGB officer he had the useful contacts that not many of his fellow returning Russians had, and it would seem that strings were soon pulled on his behalf. Lyudmila recalls: 'For three months, he was not paid his salary. I remember that by the end of the third month I started getting seriously alarmed because we simply had no money. But then, everything was paid to him all at once.'[10]

It seems, Putin finished up his business in East Germany from February to July 1990 lived (and worked) in two places at once, making periodic trips from Leningrad to East Germany and to Dresden in particular. One of the former KGB agents stationed in Berlin remembers arranging hotel accommodations for Putin in the spring of 1990 when he visited Berlin on a short work assignment. This co-worker of Putin's (who was an old friend and classmate from the Andropov Red Banner Institute, where Putin had spent a year) recalls that Putin 'wanted to write a doctoral dissertation.'[11]

It was an inspired ambition, because no later than the beginning of the spring of 1990, Putin's official place of work became Leningrad State University (LSU). It was perhaps not the most glamorous posting and former KGB Head Kryuchkov thought his return to the Leningrad KGB related to his rank in Dresden.[12] According to the president's official biographer Oleg Blotsky, at the LSU Putin became 'assistant to the rector on international issues—a position that was traditionally held by foreign intelligence officers.'[13] Former KGB General Oleg Kalugin, characterized Putin's official duties as not merely a 'foreign intelligence agent,' but the KGB's resident officer at the LSU.

But at the LSU, Putin displayed his managerial abilities for the first time. At this time, universities by law still had no right simply to rent out their facilities to foreigners. This prohibition could be circumvented, however. A lessor and lessee could set up a joint venture and legally use the lessor's property 'jointly.' The Soviet (government) side's share of such a joint venture's capital could be minimal. Putin established a joint venture of this kind between the LSU and Procter & Gamble (P&G). The LSU owned only 1% of it. Procter & Gamble acquired the right to occupy one of the mansions on Universitetskaya Embankment and for a whole year provided professors with hard-to-find American soap and laundry detergent.[14] It is not clear, whether some of the organizers of this creative arrangement were entitled to receive more than just soap and laundry detergent.

Second in command in St Petersburg

Simultaneously in the spring of 1990, active KGB reservist Putin was put to good use in another place of work, which he held simultaneously with the appointment at the LSU. Putin was sent to work with Anatoly Sobchak, a rising politician in the national parliament. Foreseeing Sobchak's prospects, the KGB wanted to attach someone to him early on.

Putin tells the story well in his autobiography:

> Stanislav Merkuriev was LSU's rector at the time.... It should be said that, by this time, Sobchak was already a well-known and popular figure. I myself followed what he said and what he did with great interest. I didn't like everything he did, that's true, but I respected him. It was also nice to know that he was a teacher from our university, a teacher with whom I had studied—although when I was a student, I had no personal contact with him. Later people often wrote that I'd been almost his favourite student. That wasn't true. He was simply one of the professors whose lectures I attended for one or two semesters. I met Anatoly at the Lensovet, in his office. I remember our meeting well. I came in, introduced myself, and told him everything. He was an impulsive person and immediately said to me:

'I'll talk to Merkuriev. Come to work for me. You can start on Monday. That's all. We'll work it out right now. You'll be transferred.'

I had to tell him:

'Anatoly, it would be a pleasure for me to do so. This work interests me. I even want to transfer. But there's one thing that will probably make this transfer difficult.'

He asked me: 'What is that?'

I said:

'I must tell you that I'm not simply an assistant to the rector. I'm a staff officer of the KGB.'

He started thinking. This really was a surprise for him. He thought about it for a while. Finally, he said:

'So, who gives a f**k?'[15]

Sobchak knew that the KGB was a very powerful force in Leningrad and that it was trying to plant its people in his entourage. The KGB defector Oleg Kalugin writes that Sobchak had told him: 'Dear Oleg, I feel isolated. I need a person who can maintain contacts with the KGB, which controls the city.' Sobchak asked Kalugin if he could recommend anyone. Kalugin, laughing, replied that no such person existed—Putin turned up not much later, by happy coincidence.

At the KGB, Putin's announcement that Sobchak had offered him a job was greeted with wild enthusiasm. No one expected that a KGB agent could be attached to the second-highest ranking democrat in Russia after Yeltsin with such ease. Putin recall telling his superiors at the KGB:

'Anatoly Alexandrovich has made me an offer to leave the university and to go work for him. If this is impossible, I am ready to resign.' To 'resign' from the university, naturally, not from the KGB.

They told me:

'No, why resign? Go and work for him, no problem.'[16]

Sobchak was indeed elected to the Leningrad city parliament (the Lensovet) on May 13, 1990—to a seat that had been left vacant after the March elections—so that he could be made the head of the Lensovet. The leaders of the Lensovet's democratic majority had been unable to decide which of them should occupy the top office, so they decided to invite one of the democratic members of the national parliament to become the head of the Lensovet and Sobchak had accepted. In a similar move member s of the national parliament had already become the heads of the Moscow city council (Mossovet). On May 23, ten days after being elected as a deputy to the Lensovet, Sobchak was chosen as the speaker of Leningrad's city council.[17]

It was exactly at this time, between May 13 and May 23, 1990, that Putin became Sobchak's assistant. Sobchak had already been elected to the Lensovet, but had not yet become its chairman. In democratic circles in Leningrad, few agreed that the eerie timing was a coincidence. At the university it was rumoured that Putin had got hold of compromising materials against Sobchak that permitted Putin to manipulate the mayor.[18] This was, for example, the opinion of the well-known Leningrad democrat Boris Vishnevsky: 'My explanation (you can quote me) is simple: as assistant to the pro-rector on international issues, Putin had to read all the denunciations that LSU professors wrote against one another. I do not rule out the possibility that Putin came across some document signed by Sobchak. And what would have become of Sobchak's unblemished image as the father of Russian democracy if this document had been published?'

The active reserve

The story of Putin's 'attachment' to Sobchak was no different from numerous other such stories involving the embedding of KGB agents in other political and business organizations. It was a pattern repeated throughout Russia, beginning with KGB general Korzhakov's 'attachment' to Yeltsin and KGB general Bobkov's 'attachment' to the business empire of Gusinsky. Moreover, this pattern was characteristic not only of Russia, but also of the other republics of what was then still the USSR. Thus, the already quoted 'Vladimir Usoltsev' (Gortanov), who had returned to the USSR before Putin, was dispatched by his KGB supervisors to Belorussia to serve as the deputy chief engineer at Minsk's Research and Manufacturing Electronic Technology Combine. There, Gortanov joined the team of Alexander Dobrovolsky, the leading Belorussian democrat at the time, and became the manager of his election campaign for the Congress of People's Deputies of the USSR.[19]

In Moscow, attempts were made to embed KGB Colonel Yevgeny Saushkin in the inner circle of mayor G. Popov, with Popov's own consent. Saushkin was an investigator who had once handled the case of the famous Soviet dissident Alexander Ginzburg. With Popov's support, Saushkin became a Mossovet deputy from the Democratic Russia movement. This was the end of his career as a democrat, however. After the Soviet Union collapsed in August 1991, he abandoned politics and went into business. But Popov acquired a new assistant and advisor in non-staff KGB agent Konstantin Zatulin, who made two unsuccessful attempts to get elected to the Mossovet as a deputy from the Democratic Russia movement (later, Zatulin became an advisor to Moscow mayor Yuri Luzhkov and, switching parties, a United Russia deputy in the State Duma). In Moldavia, Mircea Druk, who was presumably an agent of the KGB, became the head of the People's Front government. In Abkhazia, Tamaz Nadareishvili, also presumably a KGB agent, was elected as a deputy to Abkhazia's Supreme Council.

Thus, neither Putin, nor Gortanov, nor Saushkin were exceptions to the rule. Rather, all of them were examples of the KGB's general policy of embedding agents in democratic political organizations and private businesses. In this way, the KGB's active reserve officers became scouts in the enemy camp of the democrats (just as they had earlier served as scouts abroad).

Leningrad Politics

Sobchak was a politician who tended to get into conflicts and was not an easy person to deal with: he was conceited, arrogant, hot-tempered, and irritable. In the old Soviet Union, there was not much room for such characters. But, like Yeltsin, headstrong opinionated men like him were able to capture the moment and appeal to the hopes of the Russian people that the end of communism would spell the beginning of a bright future. Sobchak was a brilliant orator, but had absolutely no talent for or interest in forming agreements, reaching compromises, and coordinating his interests even with his allies and like-minded thinkers, not to mention his opponents or personal adversaries, who always surrounded him in large numbers. The politicians of Leningrad (which soon became St Petersburg) acknowledged Sobchak's popularity and were initially prepared to treat the speaker of the Lensovet as a first among equals. Sobchak, for his part, viewed them as nonentities and worthless demagogues. He recognized only Leningrad's famous writers and academicians as being more or less on his own level. He never regarded the city's democratic leaders, let alone ordinary Lensovet deputies, as his equals.

During his first months as Lensovet speaker, Sobchak lost the respect and support of St Petersburg's deputies and of his own executive committee (the Lensovet's governing body) in no time at all. At the same time, however, he retained the sympathy of the city's voters, which allowed him, after he resigned from the Lensovet, to become triumphantly elected as mayor in June 1991. Sobchak felt at ease in front of the awe-struck 'people,' when he was elevated above them on a speaker's podium; and when he was surrounded by respectful students; and when he was giving orders to obedient functionaries. But he had absolutely no interest in routine organizational-administrative work, and he constantly needed people who could free him of his daily administrative duties.

Therefore, Sobchak surrounded himself primarily by individuals who came out of the Communist Party or from managerial-administrative positions, and who knew how to read their boss's moods and how to please him—faceless executive managers without a sense of personal dignity, but with certain administrative talents.

This attitude suited Putin. As one of Putin's classmates from the Andropov Red Banner Institute recalled, at the institute they were taught 'the correct way to establish relations with people.... to form interpersonal relations, to influence people.'[20] And Putin himself liked to say, 'I am a specialist in dealing with people.'[21] He knew exactly what to say, without betraying his own views. His former Dresden KGB colleague recalled that in n conversations with outsiders, Putin knew how to be ironically hypocritical: 'In the presence of others, [Putin] without embarrassment engaged in conversations about 'Zionist influences' on [Soviet dissident] Sakharov. However, his tone of voice had a dose of irony that was always clear to me.'

Initially, Putin worked for Sobchak on a voluntary basis, continuing to toil away at the university at the same time. It was only after two months that he transferred to a permanent position under Sobchak as an officer of the active reserve.[22] From July 1990 to June

1991, Putin served as official advisor to Sobchak as head of the Lensovet.

A year later, on June 12, 1990, Sobchak was elected mayor of Leningrad. In accordance with a referendum held at the same time, the city was renamed St Petersburg in September 1991. 'I played a certain role in helping Sobchak to become the city's first popularly elected mayor,' Putin later recalled. It had little to do with increasing the role of elections, but more with controlling the uncertainty of democracy. 'I persuaded many council members to establish the position of mayor in St Petersburg, following Moscow's example. As head of the Lensovet, Sobchak could have been removed by the other council members at any moment.... In the end, I managed to convince some of them that a mayoral position would be beneficial for the city. In addition, we managed to mobilize the district heads who felt the same way. They could not vote, but they could influence their council members. As a result, the decision to establish a mayor's office in St Petersburg was passed by the Lensovet by a margin of one vote.'[23]

Others remember events differently. In 1991, Putin was unknown to most of the council members, however. The aim of establishing a mayor's office came was to force Sobchak to take responsibility for at least something in the city, and not to shift all accountability onto the Lensovet's executive committee. In any case, one of the first things that Sobchak did after becoming mayor was to establish the St Petersburg International Relations Committee (IRC) and to appoint Putin as its head. This happened on June 28, 1991. From then on, Putin's status indeed began to grow. It turned out to be a very lucrative agency.

In August 1991, Putin played a key role in the complicated negotiations that Sobchak was conducting with the Leningrad KGB in order to ensure that it would remain neutral in the conflict between the city's democratic government and the national State Emergency Committee that had mounted the putsch against Gorbachev. During the course of these negotiations, provisions were made to secure guarantees for KGB agents in the event of a victory by the democrats. After August 21, Leningrad's top KGB anti-Gorbachev plotter, Anatoly Kurkov—'a very decent man, by the way,' according to Putin[24]—not only escaped punishment, but he remained at his post as head of the KGB's Leningrad regional office until the end of

November 1991—when he transferred to the KGB's active reserve and went into the banking business. In his place, Sobchak—despite the protests of former dissidents—appointed Putin's friend Viktor Cherkesov, about whom Sobchak himself had said: 'Cherkesov works for those who are in control. These are people for whom the terms 'rule of law' and 'democracy' simply have no meaning. They only understand orders. For them, laws and rights are nothing but obstacles.' But since Sobchak believed that the KGB controlled the city, he concluded that it would be impossible to govern without them.

From June 1991 on, whenever the St Petersburg city government was reorganized, Putin's role and influence increased. After the termination of the State Emergency Committee that decided against Gorbachev, Putin resigned from the KGB, left the Communist Party and was transferred to the KGB's active reserve with the rank of lieutenant colonel. At the end of 1991, he was appointed deputy mayor of St Petersburg, while remaining the head of the IRC.

From 1992 on, it was Putin that Sobchak started leaving in charge during Sobchak's private trips abroad (although Putin, too, spent a great deal of time in other countries). It was Putin who kept the seal with Sobchak's signature. In the mayor's absence he always made independent decisions.[25] Putin has even described how, before leaving, Sobchak would give him blank sheets of paper that had been signed by him.[26] At the same time, Putin tried to remain in the shadows as much as possible, leaving all public functions to Sobchak; he avoided advertising himself and rarely made appearances on television or in the press. Possibly, his image as an éminence grise might have been due to the fact that speaking in public was always difficult for him. On the rare occasions when Putin had to appear before the Lensovet, his speeches sounded short and stiff. Putin was simply afraid of speaking at length, and he used stiffness to cover up his lack of oratorical skill. Sobchak once said: 'Putin came back from the meeting. I'd never seen him in such a state. He was all blue for some reason, and it looked like he had lost a few kilograms!'

Gradually, Putin acquired control not only over foreign economic relations, but also over many other important areas of the city's political and economic life. Specifically, he coordinated the work of all of St Petersburg's law enforcement agencies, including Internal Affairs, the Administrative Directorate, the Hotel Directorate, the

Justice Department, the Registration Chamber, and the Public Relations Directorate. As a result, an unwritten rule developed at the mayor's office: all key decisions had to pass through Putin. Sobchak, too, considered it important that the drafts of his decisions and resolutions be stamped with his deputy's approval. Putin was also put in charge of the mayor's office Committee on Operational Issues. Deputies who attended city government sessions that were chaired by Putin noted that, by contrast with Sobchak, Putin always conducted the sessions 'in a business-like and effective manner.'

In effect, while Sobchak's reshuffled city offices many times, St Petersburg was governed by two deputy mayors, Putin and a man called Vladimir Yakovlev. One might say that they divided the city's economy between themselves like chalk and cheese: Yakovlev inherited the old Soviet city economy, construction, the housing and residential complex, and transportation, while Putin was given control over the new capitalist economy, privatization, foreign investments, and joint ventures. Putin did not aspire to visible power. By contrast, Yakovlev cautiously (given Sobchak's jealous personality) but methodically promoted his image in the city, coming across as a business-like executive manager, a *khozyastvennik*, 'the Yuri Luzhkov of St Petersburg' (after the forceful mayor of Moscow).

Putin's IRC

As head of one of the mayor's office's most important committees, Putin took an active part in the region's economic activities. Putin's IRC co-founded several dozen and registered several thousand commercial enterprises in St Petersburg. No uniform system for registering businesses existed at that time, and such registrations were handled by several different departments of the city government, including the IRC, which mainly registered joint ventures and other companies with foreign involvement or export-import interests.[27]

According to Putin, his position at the mayor's office 'allowed him to solve a large number of problems that were of interest to various business organizations.'[28] For example, he was the co-founder of all of the city's elite clubs, which allowed him to become personally acquainted with or gave him access to all of the country's prominent businessmen, since all of them frequented these clubs. In 1992, as head of the IRC, Putin personally helped to facilitate a contract between the mayor's office and KPMG, a major international accounting firm, and oversaw an investment project to organize Coca-Cola production facilities in St Petersburg.

He also helped a number of German companies to get established in the city. His was instrumental in helping BNP-Dresdner Bank to open a branch in St Petersburg, making it one of the first foreign banks on Russian territory. Until December 2006, this bank's Russian subsidiary was headed by Putin's old German acquaintance Matthias Warnig. Warnig, a former Stasi officer, had been forced to flee to Russia after the unification of Germany in order to avoid possible persecution from the German government. (Later Putin would put his German banking contacts again to good use in Moscow and with the liquidation of Mikhail Khodorkovsky's oil giant Yukos, in which Dresdner bank was instrumental).

Putin also secretly controlled the Border Department at the mayor's office. This department had monopoly rights to trade in goods confiscated by customs. Since it set its own prices on resale of these goods, it could give trusted wholesale dealers privileged access to tons of confiscated metals, shipments of alcohol.

Vladimir Putin at the heart of Russia's crime capital

At the end of 1991, as head of the St Petersburg IRC, Putin initiated a program to provide food for St Petersburg from abroad in exchange for Russian raw materials exports. Putin himself described the situation as follows:

In 1992, when the country was basically going through a food crisis, St Petersburg was experiencing major problems. Our businessmen then proposed the following plan: they would be allowed to sell products abroad, mainly raw materials, and in return they would commit themselves to delivering food products [to St Petersburg]. We had no other options. Therefore, the International Relations Committee, of which I was the head, agreed to this proposal. We obtained permission from the head of the government and handed out the necessary authorizations. The plan started working. The firms exported raw materials.... Unfortunately, some of the firms failed to fulfil the main part of the agreement: they did not deliver food products from abroad or they did not deliver as much as they were supposed to. They did not fulfil their obligations to the city.[29]

The first known document signed by Putin is dated December 4, 1991. On that day, Putin sent a letter to the Committee for External

Economic Relations (CEER) of Russia's Ministry of Economy. This committee was headed by Pyotr Aven, a loyal friend of Vladimir Putin's who has since become one of Russia's oligarchs, a billionaire, and friend of Putin's. The letter gives a good indication of the amounts of money involved (the time of trading in West-German fashion magazines had long passed for Putin):From January to February 1992, the region will be able to obtain food products only by importing them in exchange for exports.... For the period of January-February 1992, the region needs: 83,000 tons of frozen meat, 11,000 tons of butter, 3 tons of evaporated milk, 0.4 tons of baby food, 4.5 tons of vegetable oil, 56 tons of sugar, 2 tons of garlic, 3.5 tons of citrus products, 8 tons of cocoa. The total cost is $122 million. In view of the urgency of the situation and the need to begin exchange transactions, I am requesting that quotas be set for the export of the following types of raw materials: 750,000 cubic meters of wood, 150,000 tons of petroleum products, 30,000 tons of non-ferrous scrap metal, 14 tons of rare earth metals (tantalum, niobium, gadolinium, cerium, zirconium, yttrium, scandium, ytterbium), 1,000 tons of aluminium, 1 ton of copper, 20 tons of cement, and 1 ton of ammonium, at a total cost of $124 million.

The crucial line followed at the end of the letter: 'In order to ensure the safety of the exchange transactions, I am also requesting permission to import 120,000 tons of cotton. Finally, I am requesting that the Committee headed by myself be given the right to assign quotas and to issue licenses.'[30]

The firms that received licenses were handpicked by Putin himself.[31] They were not raw materials exporters, they did not specialize in raw materials, and they did not present contracts with foreign firms for the import of food products. Some of the firms were foreign (and not subject to monitoring and review by the Russian government).

It did not take the Leningrad City Council a long time to investigate whether the deputy of the loathed Sobchak had issued these licenses before being authorised to do so. It started its investigation on 10 January 1992, well before the date of the order on March 25 1992. But this was because Putin's IRC had already issued 12 licenses, as he testified on 13 January to the City Council. (In his autobiography he flatly denied this, 'We had no right to issue licenses. That's the whole point. The licenses were issued by various offices at the

Ministry of Economy. This is a federal organization that had no relation to the city's administration.')[32] Putin himself signed two licenses. One of them was issued to the Nevsky Dom Company on December 20, 1991, granting it the right to export 150,000 tons of oil products (fuel oil, diesel oil, gasoline), costing over $32 million. The other was issued to a company called Fivekor, on December 26, authorizing it to export 50,000 cubic meters of wood, costing approximately $3,000,000 (in exchange for evaporated milk). In addition, Putin signed two contracts. The first, signed on December 25, was a contract to grant a license to Georgy Miroshnik, the president of the International Trade Centre Concern (Intercommerce-Formula 7), for the export of 150,000 tons of oil products in exchange for frozen meat, potatoes, and sugar (this license passed to Nevsky Dom a month later). The second, signed on January 3, 1992, was a contract with a local enterprise LOKK. This contract authorized LOKK to receive a license for the export of rare-earth metals and three tons of A5N-brand aluminium in exchange for 1,750 tons of meat.[33] Later that month, however, the license for the export of 150,000 tons of oil products passed from Miroshnik to Vladimir Smirnov's Nevsky Dom Company.

The choices of the companies were unusual. LOKK, which was ostensibly interested in exporting aluminium, was a publishing company of a local charity. The head of the firm was Sergei Platonov. He later became a business partner of Roman Tsepov, the head of the private security agency employed by Putin. Intercommerce-Formula 7—Miroshnik's Moscow-based company—was connected with ex-Stasi officer Mathias Warnig. At least Lyudmila Putin's German friend Irene Pietsch claims that, in 1996, she used to receive faxes from Lyudmila Putin on Intercommerce stationery when Lyudmila Putin was staying in Moscow with the Putins' friends: 'These were East Germans whom Putin had met in Dresden and who were now living in Moscow, where the husband occupied a managing position in one of the large German banks.'[34]

It seems that in many cases the true objective of the 'contracting parties' was not to deliver food to St Petersburg. The whole point of the operation was to do a deal with a person whom one trusted, to issue them with a license allowing safe passage of a shipment of raw materials abroad, and to sell the goods. As Putin admits, there were problems with 'fulfilment' of the final part of the contract—buying food for St Petersburg.

One reason for some IRC members not to supervise the final part of the licenses to closely were the colossal commission fees that were stipulated by the contracts, ranging from 25% to 50%. Meanwhile, the penalties for failing to deliver the food supplies were negligible. This, too, went against government regulations, which required all hard-currency proceeds from the barter operations to be used for the purchase of food for the city's population. Thus, the IRC's contract with LOKK, which Putin signed personally on January 3, 1992, stipulated a commission fee of $540,000 (25%). The contract between the IRC, 'represented by committee chairman V. V. Putin,' another contract of January 10, 1992, stipulated a commission fee of $5,983,900 (50%). Yet another IRC contract stipulated a commission fee of $12 million for the sale of 20,000 tons of cotton. The total commission fees for 12 contracts exceeded $34 million; on average, each commission fee constituted 37% of the sale.[35]

In addition to the unusually high commission fees, the contracts stipulated unusually low prices for the raw materials being exported. Thus, in the IRC's contract with the Dzhikop Corporation, to which the IRC had granted a license for the export of 13,997 kilograms of rare metals, the prices of most of them were as low as one seventh, one tenth, one twentieth, or even one two-thousandth of their market rates. For example, the contract stipulated a price of 72.6 DM for one kilogram of scandium, while the market price of the metal was higher than 150,000 DM. Through this contract alone, with its dumping-level prices, the city lost, and somebody made, over 14 million DM, or over $9,000,000.[36]

Sometimes, licenses were issued for transactions that were smaller than those agreed upon in the contracts that preceded them. Thus, the IRC's contract with the Interwood Corporation stipulated that the corporation would be issued a license to export 25,500 cubic meters of pine lumber, costing $2,805,000. The license the corporation actually received, referred only 500 cubic meters. The IRC made an identical contract with the Sansud Company. Customs did not accept the company's documents, however.[37] On January 15, 1992, the ship 'Kosmonavt Vladimir Komarov,' which was taking raw materials out of the country, was stopped. Only on February 23, when Putin intervened personally was the ship permitted to leave the country.[38]

Other price irregularities also turned up in the IRC's licensing agreements. For example, the same industrial wood cost $110 per ton in contract No. 4 and $140 per ton in contract No. 9. Ferrous scrap metal was assessed at $50 per ton in contract No. 6, while its real price in Czechoslovakia, where it was being exported, was at least $410 per ton. In contracts Nos. 3, 5, 7, and 8, sugar was assessed at $280 per ton, while its actual price at the time was less than $200.[39]

Putin acknowledges in his autobiography that 'the city, of course, did not do everything that it might have done. We should have worked more closely with law enforcement and we should have used coercive tactics to make these companies deliver what they had promised. But it was useless to take them to court: they dissolved immediately, ceased to operate, and exported their goods. In essence, we had nothing to charge them with. Think back on those years: all kinds of organizations and pyramid schemes appeared all over the place.... We simply were not expecting it.'[40]

Often one ceases to work with companies that do not 'deliver' what they are supposed to. But it is not clear that this is what happened. In 1992, Putin's IRC granted the right to export aluminium and nonferrous metals to the Strim Corporation (also known as the Kvark Corporation in 1992).[41] Strim was headed by KGB active reserve officer Vladimir Yakunin. Its board members included Andrei Fursenko, future minister of education and science, and three other KGB colleagues in the active reserve. The Strim Corporation sold its metal to obscure intermediaries at low prices; it then bought food products at prices that were high.

Through Yakunin, who was also a member of the board of directors of the Baltic Sea Steamship Company, Putin also controlled several other foreign trade organizations, which were given most-favourable treatment status: Lenimpex, Lenfintorg, Lenexpo, and Veliky Gorod (this last organization mainly handled the contraband export of nonferrous metals).

Approximately $100 million was lost through the IRC licenses. These are the losses that can be accounted for. But the government of Russia issued export quotas on raw materials to a value of about one billion dollars during those years. What happened to the remaining $900 million is not known. What is known is that 997 tons of highly refined A5-brand aluminium, costing over $717 million, disappeared—as did 20,000 tons of cement and 100,000 tons of cotton, costing $120 million.[42] Of the food imports received in exchange for what was exported and disappeared, only 128 tons of vegetable oil can be traced.[43]

Marina Salye, who headed the investigating commission of the St Petersburg City Council, still has all the documents. The committee's report concluded, 'the analysis of the situation surrounding the export-import operations to provide food for the population of St Petersburg was significantly hampered by the mayor's office officials responsible for the operations, V. V. Putin and A. G. Anikin [Putin's deputy],' who failed to submit information and documents detailing the licensing deals. 'The discrepancies in the documents analyzed [by the commission] cannot be accounted for merely by the unprecedented carelessness and irresponsibility with which A. A. Sobchak, V. V. Putin, and A. G. Anikin treated requests to provide answers to the deputies' questions.... These discrepancies stem from attempts to conceal the true state of affairs, to delay and confuse the investigation by making it necessary to verify an infinite number of facts.... From the legal point of view, most of the contracts signed by the IRC allow the intermediary firms to renege on their commitments.... The actions of IRC head V. V. Putin and his deputy A. G. Anikin reveal a special interest in forming contracts with and issuing licenses to specific individuals and firms.... The head of the IRC, V. V. Putin, and his deputy, A. G. Anikin, have displayed a degree of incompetence that borders on bad faith.'

As a result, the special commission recommended that Putin and Anikin be dismissed from their positions. The special commission's report was sent to the St Petersburg prosecutor's office and in Moscow to Putin's friend Minister Aven, the former head of CEER to whom Putin had sent his original request for the Leningrad barter licenses.

For a certain time, the deputies of the city council succeeded in prohibiting Putin to issue licenses. However, on March 25, 1992, Aven once again granted Putin's IRC committee the right to issue licenses (order No. 172). (In 1992, the St Petersburg affairs of Aven's ministry were supervised by the newly appointed deputy minister Mikhail Fradkov. In the spring of 2004, Mikhail Yefimovich Fradkov became the prime minister of Russia.)

On March 31, 1992, Yuri Boldyrev, the head of the Main Control Directorate of President Yeltsin's administration, made a resolution concerning the special commission's report: 'The Main Control Directorate has received documents from St Petersburg city council representatives attesting to the necessity of removing the head of the city's International Relations Committee Vladimir Vladimirovich Putin from his post. I request that the question of appointing him to any other post not be raised before the Main Control Directorate reaches its final decision regarding this issue.'[44]

On May 8, 1992, the findings of the special commission's investigation were heard by the city council. The city council made a decision to request that Mayor Sobchak dismiss Putin and Anikin from their posts. However, the St Petersburg prosecutor's office found nothing illegal in Putin's actions, although city prosecutor Yeremenko sent Sobchak a statement about 'the International Relations Committee's improperly written contracts and the incorrect procedure of certain licenses.'

Ultimately, the scandals surrounding the IRC forced Putin's deputy Anikin to resign (he became the general manager of another company), and some of the contracts made under Putin were dissolved. Anikin's position passed to his deputy Alexei Miller. (In May 2001, Miller became head of Gazprom's board of directors).

Of all the companies involved in the licenses for food, only the Moscow-based Intercommerce-Formula 7 company was dissolved. It was headed by a man called Georgy Miroshnik who had been adopted by a Moldavian NKVD (a previous incarnation of the KGB) officer. He was one of the two men with whom Putin had signed a licensing contract himself. In Soviet times, he had three convictions and served a total of four years in prison. During perestroika, he opened a cooperative and founded the Formula 7 concern. In 1991, he became an advisor to Russia's vice president Alexander Rutskoi and served as head of the Moscow Agroindustrial Market. He purchased goods from the Western Group of the Soviet Army (ZGV). He accused ZGV head Matvei Burlakov of theft when he himself was charged with appropriating $18 million. In July 1992, when Miroshnik was in Spain with Rutskoi as part of a government delegation to the Olympics, his dacha outside Moscow was raided and searched. Miroshnik did not come back to Russia and was put on the wanted list. In 1997, he was arrested in the United States and sentenced to a year in prison. After serving his sentence, he was deported to Greece where he served another prison sentence. On

December 9, 2001, Miroshnik was arrested in Moscow and given a further sentence.

The St Petersburg casinos

The IRC was not only involved in deals with other active reserve officers of the KGB (regrouped and renamed FSA, FSK and secret service, its current names, in a few years). At the end of 1991, St Petersburg's city agencies, headed by Putin's IRC, entered into partnerships with the city's organized crime groups. This period saw the first divisions of property between two groups of people who controlled St Petersburg: the chekists[45] and the criminals. The formal agreement between the 'city' (the KGB) and the 'businessmen' (the gangsters) concerning the joint organization of and control over the gambling business became a classic example of this kind of partnership.

In 2000, in his autobiography, Putin describes what happened to the proceeds from the gambling business:

I was studying their gambling houses in the line of duty, if you can believe it. At that time, we were trying to bring some order to St Petersburg's gambling business. I believed—I don't know whether I was right or not—that the gambling business is a form of enterprise that should be controlled by a state monopoly. But my position went against the anti-monopoly law, which had already been passed. Nonetheless, I tried to do things so that the government, represented by the city, might establish a firm control over the gambling industry. To this end, we created a municipal enterprise which did not own any casinos, but controlled 51% of the shares of the city's gambling establishments. This enterprise included representatives from the main regulatory organizations: the secret service, the tax police, the tax inspections office. The expectation was that the government, as a shareholder, would receive dividends from 51% of the shares.[46]

However, a contemporaneous order issued by Sobchak, the Mayor of St Petersburg, casts a very candid light on Putin's stake in the matter. On 24 December, 1991, Sobchak established a public licensing body, rather than a private company, and handed 'oversight' to 'the head of the International Relations Committee, V. V. Putin' alone (the full text is appendix 1). Sobchak's aim was to 'organize an open competition' for the casinos and for the city to collect taxes (not dividends) to 'be used to finance top-priority social programs'. One of the 6 members of this licensing body was Putin's close associate Medvedev, head of the St Petersburg Treasury (in December 2007 Vladimir Putin would designate him as his successor as president of the Federation).

In his autobiography, Putin complains that 'all the money left the gambling tables without leaving a trace. The casinos' owners showed us nothing but losses... they were laughing at us and showing us losses.' The excuse for the City of St Petersburg not receiving any money, Putin writes 'was a typical mistake made by people who are encountering a market for the first time.' Nonetheless, it is not easy to see how for a period of five years (1992-1996) a licensing body that included the St Petersburg secret service and Putin, St Petersburg most powerful *siloviki*, would allow itself to be laughed at by St Petersburg criminals.

The people who set up the 'municipal enterprise' referred to by Putin also seem to have been highly sophisticated. Originally, two subdivisions of the mayor's office—Putin's IRC and the city's property department had created a company simply called Casino. Putin's friend, secret service active reserve officer Valery Polomarchuk, was appointed head of the company.

The object was to become directly involved in the gambling business itself, so that its sizable proceeds would be channelled into the budgets of various departments of the mayor's office. Within a month, the joint-stock company Casino was dissolved, apparently for legal reasons, and in its place the mayor's office itself established a municipal enterprise called Neva Chance. But the address indicated on Neva Chance's official registration documents was the address of Putin's IRC—Antonenko Lane, 6. This new enterprise was headed by the same Polomarchuk. The city property department had effectively been squeezed out.

The municipal enterprise Neva Chance was not directly involved in gambling. It was registered as the co-owner of both newly created and already existing gambling establishments. Neva Chance's share of the authorized capital of these firms was usually 51%. It contributed this share not in money, which the mayor's office did not have, but by relinquishing the right to collect rent for the facilities that the casinos occupied. (This was a new way for share participation by St

Petersburg's *siloviki* in private enterprise, it soon caught on throughout the Federation) This arrangement had been invented by the IRC's legal expert Dmitry Medvedev. He was one of the first people in St Petersburg, and in Russia as a whole, who figured out how the government could 'join' a joint-stock company without breaking existing laws: not by contributing land or real estate, but by contributing rents on land and real estate.

In July 1992, a new company named Neva Chance was founded to supplement the Neva Chance municipal enterprise. The new company was registered at the same IRC address, Antonenko Lane, 6, and had the same Polomarchuk as its head. In February 1993, yet another organization was created, the Neva Chance, registered at Sadovaya Street, 53. This corporation had two different founders—replacing the mayor's office on this occasion—but was again headed by Polomarchuk. The new company's founders were the city's property department, the Telekazino company (founded earlier by the Neva Chance 'municipal enterprise'), and the Russkoye Video Company, headed by the former head of the 'T' ('terrorism') department of the Leningrad KGB.

This fine net of companies covering St Petersburg gambling aimed to confuse. This was precisely the purpose behind the constant creation of new organizations with the same name, registered at different or identical addresses, owned by different or identical co-founders, who often appeared as the co-owners of other organizations with the same names, but with other co-owners. With several different companies named Neva Chance to keep track of, neither the inquisitive city councillors nor the investigators in the prosecutor's office could ever determine who owned or co-owned what, who controlled what, and who received which profits to 'laugh at St Petersburg'.

At the beginning of 1994, secret service active reservist Polomarchuk was replaced by Igor Gorbenko, the founder and co-owner of the Conti casino, St Petersburg's very first gambling establishment. Gorbenko's partner and principal owner of Conti was the mafia boss Mirilashvili (who received an eight-year prison term for organizing a revenge killing of two small-time career criminals). At the same time, the firm acquired a third and altogether strange co-founder: St Petersburg's International Rescue Fund. Just how the fund contributed to the city's rescue by getting involved in the gambling business, no one knew.

All together, between 1992 and 1995, the Neva Chance company founded about 25 different commercial enterprises, predominantly in the gambling industry or serving the gambling industry (for example, the Polli Plyus Company, the St Petersburg Lotteries Company, several casinos—Telekazino, Fortuna Casino St Petersburg, Panda, Sirius, Venetsiya, Kleo, Arkada). At least one of them (Fortuna Casino St Petersburg) was again headed by Putin's friend Polomarchuk. The Arkada Casino Company was co-founded by Neva Chance, Mirilashvili and others. Neva Chance entered into partnerships with analogous organizations in Moscow, for example, with the Olbi Group owned by the Moscow-based financial magnate Oleg Boiko. The Planeta St Petersburg gambling establishment was co-founded by Neva Chance and Planeta Olbi, a Moscow-based company. One of the co-founders of the St Petersburg Lotteries Company was the Olbi Blok Company. In December 1993, Polomarchuk became the head the St Petersburg branch of the Olbi Group—Olbi St Petersburg (after resigning from his post as general manager of Neva Chance and being replaced by Gorbenko).

In May 1993, the St Petersburg municipal prosecutor's office (under city prosecutor Vladimir Yeremenko, who had already come up against Putin in the case of the illegal export licenses) conducted a review of the activities of one of the organizations connected with Putin's gambling business, the joint venture Melodiya. The investigators determined that the firm had illegally acquired a $16 million profit from the gambling business. This prompted a general investigation by the prosecutor's office, which revealed that there were 180 gambling houses and 1600 gambling machines operating in the city, and that in addition to the 26 registered casinos, the charters of over one hundred other commercial enterprises made provisions for gambling activities.

Meanwhile, a resolution passed on June 26, 1991, by Russia's Council of Ministers specified that businesses operating gambling establishments were required to obtain licenses from the Ministry of Finance. In St Petersburg, there was only one casino—the municipal casino Admiral—that had such a license, which had been given to it by the former deputy prime minister and minister of economics and finance, Yegor Gaidar. From the point of view of federal law, every other gambling establishment in the city was illegal. On February 12 and April 2, 1992, Mayor Anatoly Sobchak issued orders No. 134-R and No. 170-R instructing the administrative heads of the city's districts to shut down unlicensed gambling establishments.[47] However, these orders from the mayor were ignored by the gambling establishments, which had permissions from their local district governments and from officials at the mayor's office. In their defence, they argued that Russia had no formal federal law governing the gambling business.

On September 3, 1993, the St Petersburg prosecutor's office sent Sobchak an official report, notifying him that *all* gambling establishments in the city, with the exception of the Admiral casino, were operating without federal licenses and thus violating the law. The prosecutor's office also noted that the Lenatraksion company, which operated gambling machines, had been illegally given a special license—No. 274, dated May 27, 1992, signed by Putin—to run a gambling business.[48] The notice from the City's prosecutor's office produced no results.

Elections

In October 1993, the country was shaken by a general political crisis. In Moscow, tanks were used to lay siege to the White House, where the rebellious parliament was in session with the Chechen Ruslan Khasbulatov presiding.

Sobchak and Putin ended up on the winning side of this conflict. In 1993-1994, there were three election campaigns in a row: the elections for the new parliament at the end of 1993, the elections for the St Petersburg Legislative Assembly in the spring of 1994, and the special election for the Legislative Assembly. No one had any time to discuss the legality of the city's casinos, and thus the issue resurfaced only during the St Petersburg mayoral race in the spring of 1996.

In his autobiography, Putin waves the issues away as having been politically motivated:

Our political opponents tried to find some kind of incriminating evidence in our activities, to accuse us of corruption. They claimed that the mayor's office had been involved in the gambling business. These claims were ridiculous. Everything that we did was absolutely transparent.

Putin concedes that the arrangement he had allowed to remain in place for five years had 'turned out to be ineffective' and 'that it had not been properly thought through' from the point of view of the citizens of St Petersburg. If Sobchak had not lost the 1996 elections:

I would have finished off these casinos in any case. I would have forced them all to work for the needs of society and to share their profits with the city. This money would have gone to retired people, teachers, and doctors.

Putin did, however, not 'finish off' his associates in the gambling world—quite to the contrary. The former overseer of the entire network of St Petersburg's casinos, Polomarchuk, left the Olbi Group to become the representative in St Petersburg of Lukoil, Russia's largest oil company. (At least once after being elected president, Putin celebrated New Year's Eve at Polomarchuk's St Petersburg apartment, in 2002, and at Polomarchuk's instigation, Lukoil's president, Vagit Alekperov, was admitted into the tightly knit group of men and took part in the celebration.)

Polomarchuk's replacement, Igor Gorbenko, is today the president of the Conti Group and one of the leaders of the gambling industry in Moscow and in the country. He and another Putin associate of the St Petersburg gambling days, Boris Spektor (co-founder of the Arkada Casino Company and Planeta Olbi), created the Jackpot Unified Gambling System. Like many of Putin's friends from St Petersburg, Spektor followed Putin to Moscow, where he became the deputy general manager of the Jackpot Moscow Gambling System.

The one exception was a man called Rozhdestvensky. He co-founded the St Petersburg Arkada Casino Company, but, apart from gambling, he assisted Putin in other ways when he helped Putin set up a political party in 1995). Rozhdestvensky was arrested by the General Prosecutor's Office in September 1998, when Putin was director of the secret service. Tax claims were filed against the St Petersburg TV channel Russkoye Video (a co-founder of one of the Neva Chance companies), which had been privatized by Rozhdestvensky, and then the case snow-balled with further claims against the privatization of the channel itself. The claims started when Rozhdestvensky sold his channel to Vladimir Gusinsky. In the national political stakes, Gusinsky was betting not on other horses than Putin: Yuri Luzhkov (Mayor of Moscow), Yevgeny Primakov (then Prime Minister), and Grigory Yavlinsky (opposition politician). Rozhdestvensky was sent to the St Petersburg secret service's pre-trial detention facility but was released in August 2000, due to health problems, including a serious form of diabetes. In January 2002, he was sentenced to three years in prison, pardoned, and dead half-a-year later succumbing to a heart attack. Some argued Rozhdestvensky had been released from prison so that he might be poisoned without blame falling on the prison authorities.[49]

Dealings beyond Russia's borders

1991-1993 were heady and confused years and Vladimir Putin used his position at the St Petersburg international committee to set up international companies as well. In 1992, Putin led a delegation from St Petersburg on a visit to Frankfurt, where he and another member of the delegation, Vladimir Smirnov, persuaded a group of Frankfurt investors to create the SPAG Company. This was Putin's and Smirnov's second trip to Frankfurt. On August 4, 1992, the SPAG Company was established. Using Russian-German daughter companies as intermediaries, SPAG was supposed to become involved in investing in St Petersburg real estate, i.e. to use the money of foreign investors for purchasing, renovating, and building real estate in St Petersburg. The company's founders included lawyer Rudolf Ritter (the brother of Liechtenstein's National Economy Minister Michael Ritter), who was the deputy chairman of the company's advisory board and effectively the company's head. Other founders included the St Petersburg property department, the St Petersburg Bank; and a German-Russian joint venture Inform-Future.

In August 1992, the St Petersburg Bank was headed by future deputy minister of finance Yuri Lvov (Russia's deputy minister of finance in 2000-2001, and in 2001 the head of Gazprombank, part of the Gazprom conglomerate). The joint venture Inform-Future was headed by Vladimir Smirnov, who later became the head of the board of the St Petersburg Futures Exchange partnership in February 2002. From May 2000 to December 2001, he worked in Putin's Presidential staff on property. Throughout the various legal twists and turns, Smirnov remained the key man of the scheme.

Apart from Putin, various different individuals joined the constantly changing membership of SPAG's board of consultants. They included future minister of economic development and trade German Grefand Putin himself, who, according to the company's documentation from 1992, was the 'deputy head' of the company. According to other sources, he was merely a 'consultant.' Officially, Putin received no salary from SPAG. Another company headed by Smirnov was set up by the IRC, involving a similar byzantine group of interested parties.

The idea was that a hotel and a commercial centre would be built in return for use for a period of 50 years. (after various legal changes the city of St Petersburg had by now somehow evaporated). Another project concerned a whole block in the centre of the city for the creation of a 'business-centre.' The city was to be compensated 1.5 billion rubles for relocating the displaced residents of buildings that were demolished or rebuilt. (In 1996, St Petersburg's new mayor, Yaklovlev, demanded payment which suggested that the sum had never been paid.)

The subsequent dealings are as complex as any of the companies in which Vladimir Putin was involved. As in the case of the casinos, the St Petersburg underworld was involved in the project through a man called Kumarin (nicknamed 'Kum') Russia's law enforcement agencies considered him to be the founder, leader, and brains of the Tambov crime organization. In 1990-1993, Kumarin served a prison sentence for extortion. After being released in early 1993, he went into business in St Petersburg, including the restaurant and casino business. According to some accounts, his crime organization was the biggest in St Petersburg; according to other accounts, it was the second most important in terms of its power and size. In included 300-400 men who specialized in extortion, kidnapping, robbery, and criminal attacks. The organized crime group disposed of a surveillance service and a radio telephone monitoring service, had agents on the staff of St Petersburg's Internal Affairs Directorate and was considered the most disciplined of the city's criminal organizations. There was an assassination attempt against Kumarin in 1994. His driver and bodyguard were killed. Kumarin himself survived, but lost an arm. He spent a month in a coma, then left for Germany and Switzerland to receive medical treatment. He returned to St Petersburg in 1996, changing his name to Barsukov. It was at this point that Barsukov-Kumarin got involved: 'At that time, I was introduced to Rudi [Rudolf Ritter] and other people through mutual acquaintances, and they invited me to take part in the [SPAG] project—we had to relocate the residents of 300 communal apartments and build a business centre. I joined its board of directors as vice president of the St Petersburg Fuel Company in order to see if we should become involved in this project. We even relocated people from about seven communal apartments. But then we decided that we could make more money building gas stations, and I left the project.'[50]

In April 1999, in a report on Liechtenstein's role as a European centre for money laundering, the German intelligence agency (BND) and other intelligence agencies, including Liechtenstein's, first took note of SPAG because the Austrian prosecutor Spitze—who had been appointed by Hans-Adam II, Prince of Liechtenstein, to investigate money-laundering operations—had come to the conclusion that Ritter was helping to transfer substantial amounts of money from SPAG's St Petersburg headquarters to Vaduz, Liechtenstein's capital. On May 13, 1999, Rudolf Ritter was arrested in Vaduz in an operation carried out jointly by the Liechtenstein police and the Austrian finance team. Four other lawyers and businessmen were arrested along with him, including his partner, lawyer Eugen von Hoffen-Heeb. Ritter was charged with illegal transactions amounting to $6-$8 million, which he had carried out in 1995. The charges against them changed later and Von Hoffen-Heeb was given a sentence of nine years in total in 2003. Ritter was given a suspended sentence of 18 months for selling thirty SPAG shares to German investors not through the stock market and at inflated prices.

In 2000, the Ukrainian government, headed by Leonid Kuchma, suddenly became involved in the intrigues surrounding the SPAG affair. A group of Kuchma's security officers under orders from the former head of the Ukrainian KGB had started recording conversations in Kuchma's office. Known as 'The Kuchma Tapes'[51] they showed that German intelligence had a file on Putin's involvement in illegal operations, and that Russia's security services had spent a large amount of money in Germany to buy up documents that could compromise Putin (one set of files concerning Putin turned out to be in the possession of Ukrainian intelligence (having been given to the head of the Ukrainian Security Service, Leonid Derkach).

On May 13, 2003, 40 employees of Germany's federal police raided the offices of the SPAG in the little town of Mörfelden-

Walldorf, in the south of Hessen. At the same time, the apartments of the company's managers were searched. Gerhard Schröder was informed about the police operation. Russia's Ministry of Internal Affairs was also notified. The unusual openness of the police stemmed from apprehensions that actions affecting a firm that once had ties to Putin might lead to complications on the diplomatic front. On the same day, searches were conducted in a total of 28 business and residential locations in the Rhein-Main region, Hamburg, and Munich. One of the companies searched was the Bavarian bank Baader Wertpapierhandelsbank AG, which had acquired 30% of SPAG's shares and had put them up for sale on the stock exchange. In the Spring of 2003, SPAG's shares were still traded on the German stock exchange. They were traded in Berlin, Bremen, Stuttgart, München, and electronically. The shares cost 0.64 euros, having declined from the record high levels reached in the summer of 1999 (35.28 euros) by approximately 98%.

Rewards for hard working agents

In Soviet times, every Soviet citizen wanted to have a good apartment and a dacha. Few people had a good apartment, almost none had a dacha. Active reserve officer Putin had been a good Soviet citizen. He also wanted a good apartment and a dacha when he returned to Russia from East Germany. He wanted them as soon as circumstances allowed, but during his first three months home no salary was paid. Within a year, Vladimir Putin had acquired both a good apartment and a dacha, realising the dream of a Soviet citizen's lifetime.

One of the most fashionable neighbourhoods in St Petersburg is Vasilievsky Island. It was to this neighbourhood that Putin moved while working in St Petersburg city government. He acquired an apartment in building No. 17 on Vasilievsky Island's second metro line in a very strange way. Before he moved in this building underwent major renovation (at city expense). The renovated apartments were supposed to go to people who were on a waiting list. However, the apartments in the elite building went to completely different individuals, including Putin. Putin himself explains his move to building No. 17 by saying that he exchanged apartments with somebody else. Indeed, on February 23, 1991, Putin received an 'exchange authorization' (No. 205553/22). However, the column that was supposed to contain information about the person with whom Putin was exchanging apartments was left blank. At about the same time, at the end of 1992, Putin bought two adjacent plots of land—3302 and 3492 square meters in area—to build a dacha, in the town of Solovyevka of the Priozerny district of the Leningrad region.

How a government official could buy an apartment and a dacha on a meagre government salary was a mystery to most.

Democracy's musical chairs

At the end of April 1995, national elections loomed large. As described in the previous chapter, Yeltsin's popularity was at a low ebb. In defence of his position, Prime Minister Viktor Chernomyrdin instructed St Petersburg mayor Sobchak to establish a St Petersburg office for Our Home Is Russia (NDR), a pro-government party that was in the process of being created on Yeltsin's orders. It was evident that the party's political objective would be to support Yeltsin's candidacy in the 1996 presidential election.

Sobchak assigned the organization of the St Petersburg NDR office to his trusted right-hand man Putin, who became head of the party's organizational committee. The 21 members of the committee included a galaxy of useful people: deputy Vladimir Kolovay, president of the joint venture Lenvest; Anatoly Turchak, president of the Leninets concern; deputy Sergei Nikeshin, president of the finance and construction company Dvatsaty Trest; Boris Petrov, general manager of the St Petersburg office of the ITAR-TASS news agency; Lyudmila Verbitskaya, rector of St Petersburg State University; and Dmitry Rozhdestvensky, president of the television company Russkoye Video. Putin also successfully cannibalised the opposition. At the time, the St Petersburg branch of former prime minister Yegor Gaidar's party, the Democratic Rebirth of Russia (DVR), had two wings—a 'pragmatic wing' (mainly businessmen) and an unelectable 'human rights wing' (mainly old dissidents). Putin persuaded the DVR's pragmatic wing to help in the creation of NDR. On May 5, 1995, a ceremonial assembly was held to establish an NDR office in St Petersburg. At this assembly, Putin was elected head of the regional office's advisory board.

In the summer-fall of 1995, Putin supervised NDR's election campaign for the second convocation of the State Duma. The campaign was costly and elaborate, but Putin managed miraculously to raise 1.1 billion non-denominated rubles for the NDR (while NDR's central campaign headquarters raised no more than 15 million rubles). This money came mainly from St Petersburg banks. The residents of St Petersburg were overwhelmed by a multitude of colour posters with Chernomyrdin's picture on expensive advertising stands—up to five identical posters on a single stand and 10-15 posters on a single building wall (the same thing, however, could be observed in Moscow). Putin himself explained this excess by saying that NDR's national leadership had given him large numbers of posters and he saw no need for them to go to waste.

Nonetheless, despite its money, the NDR lost the election. The 'ruling party' managed to nominate a candidate (Alexei Alexandrov) only in the Northwestern District—one of eight city districts—and Putin's man lost the election to Yabloko candidate Anatoly Golov. In the party-list vote, the NDR's list received the third highest number of votes in the city (12.78% of the vote), coming in behind Yabloko (16.03%) and the Communist Party of the Russian Federation (13.21%), and slightly ahead of the DVR–United Democrats bloc (12.37%). The NDR won only two seats in St Petersburg, which went to Alexei Alexandrov and the mayor's wife, Lyudmila Narusova. Another member of St Petersburg's NDR—former Committee on City Property Management chairman Sergei Beliayev—also became a deputy; his votes came from the federal part of NDR's party list.

Undeterred by this failure, in March 1996, Putin joined the St Petersburg branch of a movement for the public support of the president, a coalition of organizations that were in favour of a second term for President Yeltsin. This move provoked a response from Igor Artemyev, the head of Yabloko's St Petersburg office and candidate Grigory Yavlinsky's representative in St Petersburg. Artemyev submitted a complaint to the city prosecutor's office, claiming that Putin's participation in the movement violated the law 'On the fundamental guarantees of citizens' voting rights,' and specifically the restriction against 'using specific official positions in order to create advantages for specific candidates.' The prosecutor's office did not pursue this complaint, choosing to accept Putin's official explanation that he had joined the movement not as first deputy mayor, but as the head of the regional office of NDR.

In the spring of 1996, while serving as head of the movement's and NDR's regional headquarters and working toward Yeltsin's re-election, Putin also flexed his muscles to get Sobchak re-elected as mayor of St Petersburg. It was precisely to Putin that Sobchak had assigned the task of persuading the deputies of the city's Assembly to change the date of the election from June 16 to May 19 in order to cut short the election campaigns of his opponents—the most dangerous of whom at that time appeared to be Yuri Boldyrev. As Vishnevsky tells it, on the early morning of March 13, Putin arrived at the Assembly with a presidential decree by Yeltsin that permitted the date of the election to be changed to May 19, and the draft of a resolution by Sobchak to reschedule the election. For a whole week, Putin literally 'twisted the arms' of the city parliament's deputies: he coaxed some, frankly promised top positions in the mayor's office to others, and asked yet others to come to terms with what was inevitable.[52] As a result of Putin's exertions, on March 20—the last day when the election could still be legally rescheduled—a majority of the deputies voted in favour of May 19. First deputy speaker Sergei Mironov, who presided over the hearing, proceeded as if a quorum had been reached, even though there was no quorum.

This bit of foul play, nonetheless, did not help Sobchak or the managers of his election campaign, Putin and Kudrin.

Sobchak lost the election to Yakovlev. The fact that he had little chance of getting re-elected became clear at the very beginning of the campaign. NDR's fund had allocated a modest amount of resources to print the posters that so appealed to Putin, but this was clearly not enough to secure victory for Sobchak. Putin understood this now also. More money was needed. At the beginning of April 1996, at the White Nights resort in Sestroretsk, Putin met with a group of heads of firms and joint-stock companies that had been co-founded by members of the city government. He proposed that they all chip in to Sobchak's campaign fund. Contrary to his expectations, the conversation turned out to be difficult and stiff. The entrepreneurs denied Putin's request, letting him know that he could count only on the dividends received by the mayor's office on the city's share of the capital. They did not wish to invest their own resources in Sobchak's campaign: they saw that Sobchak would not get re-elected while general Korzhakov, still Yeltsin's strongman at the time, was working against him.

As Sobchak's campaign manager, Putin also pinned great hopes on material support from the Congress of Small and Mid-Level Businesses. But Sobchak failed to appear at the congress's key session: he simply forgot. Naturally, the congress refused to help the mayor. Putin's old friends Miralishvili and Rozhdestvensky—the heads of the trusted Russkoye Video Company with whom so many lucrative private deals had been concocted—promised to provide advertising for Sobchak on St Petersburg's Channel Eleven and on federal television channels. In return, Sobchak promised to provide them with $300 million of subsidy credits. However, at general Korzhakov's instigation, the tax police began examining Russkoye Video's finances at this time, and Sobchak's public relations campaign on television never got off the ground.

Consequently, on the eve of the election, Sobchak and Putin were left without any resources. Putin was blamed for the defeat. He was accused of 'completely failing to grasp the specifics of electoral techniques' and of 'creating a political vacuum around Mayor Sobchak.' But what could Putin do with a lazy candidate without money?

Democracy's cruel hand

By the summer of 1996, when Sobchak lost the elections to his deputy mayor Yakovlev, Putin's two-story dacha of 152.9 square meters—'resembling a palace'—had been built. The house was worth about $500,000 and registered in the name of his wife, Lyudmila. 'The house was made of brick, but the interior had wood panelling,' Putin recalled, with a sauna on the first floor.

On August 12, 1996, Putin and his friends, including the husband of his secretary, celebrated a 'wake for his old job' in the sauna—the job that he had lost due to Sobchak's defeat in the election. After spending some time in the sauna, they went to take a dip in a lake and returned to a recreation room near the sauna without noticing that the sauna had caught fire in their absence. Putin's younger daughter, Katya, was in the kitchen on the first floor and ran outside immediately, while his older daughter, Masha, and secretary were getting ready for bed on the second floor. Wrapping himself in a sheet, Putin ran up to the second floor. He led his daughter and secretary out to the balcony, tied several sheets to the balcony railing, and lowered Masha and Marina Yentaltseva to the ground, while Yentaltseva's husband caught them below.

All of the Putins' cash went up in flames along with their dacha. Like all true Russians, the Putins did not keep their money (dollars, naturally) in a bank; they kept it all in a briefcase. After evacuating his daughter and secretary from the second floor, Putin tried to locate the briefcase with his savings, but he couldn't do it in the dark (the electricity went out as soon as the fire started):

The flames are roaring. I climb over the railing, grab the sheets, and begin to climb down. Suddenly, I realize: I'm naked. I only had time to wrap a sheet around myself. So picture the scene: the house is blazing, a naked man with a sheet wrapped around him is climbing down, the wind is spreading the sails, and people are standing around on the ground and watching in silence and with great interest....'[53]

The construction company could not refuse a request from a prominent official to 'reconstruct everything on the same scale as it was before,' free of charge.

The first option was for them to pay in money. But it wasn't clear what money.... Basically, it wasn't clear how to assess the damage. So I liked the second option better: to force them to reconstruct everything on the same scale as it was before. This is what they did. They built exactly the same frame and hired a Polish company that finished everything. The builders did all of this in a year-and-a-half. Everything became as it was before the fire and even a little better'[54]

In the meantime, Vladimir Putin seemed no longer welcome in Leningrad, where he had ruled with so much inventiveness over five years. One City official recalled 'Two days after Yakovlev became mayor, I was in Smolny on some kind of business. I ran into Yakovlev. We were standing and talking. Some bureaucrat came up to us and said: 'Vladimir, Putin is here. He's sitting and waiting to see how you will decide about him.' I will always remember Yakovlev's reply. He turned red and said: "I don't want to hear anything more about that asshole".'[55]

The vicissitudes of democracy had given active reservist Vladimir Putin a severe shock. With no money or a job, what was he going to do about it?

CHAPTER THREE

Moscow Fleshpots

One of the first to identify the post-Soviet regime as an oligarchy was Alexander Solzhenitsyn, one of Vladimir Putin's heroes. At the end of 1996, the year of Yeltsin's re-election, he wrote:

> Skilful members of the former upper and middle echelons of the old communist government, together with parvenus who have suddenly acquired wealth by devious means, have formed a stable and closed oligarchy of about 150-200 individuals, which decides the fate of the nation. This is the appropriate label for the current regime of the Russian government.... The members of this oligarchy are driven by a shared lust for power and money—they display no higher motives to serve the Fatherland and the people.[1]

In Plato's *Republic*, Book XIII, Socrates discusses oligarchy with Adeimantusas a form of government based on possession of wealth—only the wealthy have the right to govern. Because the rich are always many fewer in number than the poor, rule by the rich must necessarily be rule by 'the few.' Plato characterizes oligarchy as an unjust form of government, in which the rulers' goal is not the general welfare, but their personal interests.

Under the early Yeltsin, however, Russia had not yet fully formed an oligarchic regime. According to Aristotle, who developed Plato's ideas further, the three basic features of oligarchy are: rulers are recruited from among the rich or the rich select rulers from among their friends; rulers do not depend on citizens; rulers pursue their own interests rather than the general welfare. Drawing on the various political regimes that existed in Greece during his time, Aristotle distinguished oligarchies in terms of the ways in which the government is formed (whether government offices are bought, co-opted, inherited, or taken by force); the degree of economic disparity (from moderate to extreme); and the degree of lawlessness that exists in the state (from an unjust legislature that favours only the few to completely arbitrary rule).

Yeltsin's regime was nothing like this, and more like a benign form of tyranny (arbitrary rule by a single individual), oligarchy, as well as anarchy, as well as the frail beginnings of democracy. At the beginning of his rule, the many millions of Russians were separated from the few hundred thousand secret agents only by the fact that they did not have closely-forged bonds by years of secrecy—the differences in wealth were as they had always been in Soviet times. The state continued to follow the tracks laid by Stalin and the 'tyranny' of 'Czar Boris,' was quite good-natured on the whole, and manifested itself more in petty tyranny and wilfulness than in the systematic repression of citizens and due process. By far the most conspicuous under Yeltsin's rule were signs of anarchy, including the semi-feudal anarchy of the regional rulers, particularly during the periods when the president was 'working on documents' (incapacitated) or giving 'firm handshakes' to his spokesman Sergei Yastrzhembsky, when the latter was asked about the President's health.

But in post-Soviet Russia, as Yeltsin's rule progressed, the nascent oligarchic order was in 1996 ready to flex its muscles. In a five year span, personal fortunes had furiously been fought for at all levels of government. Due to the country's deeply rooted centralized bureaucratic system, and to the resulting super-presidential, quasi-monarchical nature of the Russian constitution, the oligarchy draped itself around the head of the government and developed a partly 'court-like' character. Typically, an oligarchy has a clan structure and is divided into competing groups and cliques. This was the case with the government of the Thirty Tyrants, the Roman Senate, the Venetian Council of Ten, the Latin American juntas of the nineteenth and twentieth centuries, and post-colonial Africa. Russia was and is no exception.

The most prominent oligarchic clan under Yeltsin was the oil-and-gas clan of Chernomyrdin-Vyakhirev. Its rival was the general

Korzhakov-Barsukov-Soskovets group (though deposed from political power after the elections in 1996, the group's hold over important parts of the economy did not diminish). A tight Moscow clan headed by Mayor Yuri Luzhkov also developed under Yeltsin. Finally, also under Yeltsin, the ideological group of 'Petersburg liberals' headed by Anatoly Chubais began its transformation into the independent oligarchic clan of the 'Petersburg economists.' By the end of Yeltsin's rule, the Yeltsin clan of 'the family', as they became known in Russia, had also taken shape, leaving the other groups with much less room to manoeuvre. It consisted of Roman Abramovich, Boris Berezovsky, Alexander Voloshin, Valentin Yumashev, Tatyana Dyachenko. Powerful regional clans became established in the provinces: the clan of Murtaza Rakhimov in Bashkiria, Mintimer Shaimiyev in Tatarstan, Kirsan Ilyumzhinov in Kalmykia, Eduard Rossel in the Urals, Vladimir Yakovlev in St Petersburg.

These oligarchic administrative-economic formations and clans became the principal players in the political process, while political parties, movements, blocs, and parliamentary factions became the clans' instruments. Official political entities were no longer independent (if they ever were); they came out of clans and cliques, their blocs and coalitions. Our Home Is Russia (NDR), the official 'ruling party' of the late Yeltsin period, was the political instrument of a coalition of several clans (Chernomyrdin's, Korzhakov's, Luzhkov's, certain regional clans, and an early grouping of 'the family'). (This coalition would three years later fall apart, in 1998-1999, and by the time of the 1999 election, several new parties had emerged from it: Fatherland, the instrument of Luzhkov's mayor's office, All Russia (a regional group), and Unity, 'the family's' political arm.

The secret service parachute

How did the clan system operate at the lower levels? After Sobchak was defeated in the St Petersburg election, clouds began to gather around active reservist Putin. Ousted from power by a hostile faction, he was at risk as a result of the investigation of the activities of the IRC, his former St Petersburg fiefdom. Hence, the question of transferring him to Moscow—with a promotion in rank for utmost loyalty to the Kremlin—became urgent. Anatoly Chubais, who in the summer of 1996 became Yeltsin's chief of staff, rendered the loyal Yeltsin supporter an invaluable service at this time: he obtained a transfer for Putin from St Petersburg to Moscow, and an appointment to the position of deputy head of the Presidential Property Management Department. For the St Petersburg investigators and councillors who were looking into corruption in the city, Putin was now well out of their reach.

Putin's new position promised work on a large scale for a capable pair of hands. As deputy head of the Presidential Property Management Department from June 1996, he oversaw the real estate valued at approximately $600 billion. After the collapse of the Soviet Union, by order of President Yeltsin, Russia's foreign possessions were also put under the management of this department. They consisted of 715 real estate properties in 78 different countries, comprising an area of over 550,000 square meters.

In turn, Putin co-opted his own supporters. Many of these friendships dated back to his Dresden time. In his book, his former colleague 'Usoltsev' lists them without giving their last names: Sergei, Boris, Nikolai, Viktor, Volodya-with-a-moustache, little Volodya and big Volodya. Putin everyone called 'little Volodya,' while Usoltsev himself was known as 'big Volodya.' The business-savvy Sergei, little Volodya's best friend when it came to drinking Radeberger beer, is undoubtedly Sergei Chemezov (currently the general manager of the Rosoboronexport Federal State Unitary Enterprise). Putin's fellow Leningrader Boris, is Boris Alexanderovich Mylnikov (until November 2006 the head of the Anti-Terrorist Centre of the CIS States Members). Sasha from the Penza region is Alexander Ivanovich Biriukov (the head of the tax collection service in the Penza region). Another, unnamed, Berlin agent is Andrei Yurievich Belyaninov, during Putin's Dresden tenure was the head of the Federal Service for Defence Contracts (since 2006 has been the director of the Federal Customs Service). The Dresden agent Nikolai is Nikolai Tokarev (since 2000 the general manager of the Zarubezhneft Company).

In her book *Heikle Freundschaften* (*Delicate Friendships*, 2001) on her friendship with Putin and his wife, the German memoirist Irene Pietsch also shed light on the East German Stasi colleagues at the time, carefully avoiding their names: 'These were East Germans whom Putin had met in Dresden and who were now living in

Moscow, where the husband occupied a managing position in one of the large German banks—the same one whose chairman had organized Lyudmila's trip...'; 'the husband was a Stasi colleague of Volodya's...'; 'in Hamburg... Lyudmila's hotel room had been reserved by the same German bank whose name was more and more often mentioned in connection with Lyudmila and Volodya.'

Thus, Putin was followed to Presidential Property Management Department by his old Dresden colleague, KGB officer Sergei Chemezov. Here is what Chemezov himself said about this transfer: 'I was recommended for the position of head of the Directorate of Foreign Economic Relations by Vladimir [Putin]. My work consisted of trying to bring some order into the use of Russia's foreign possessions, and of returning to the government what it had once owned but had lost due to poor management. Sometimes things came to light that made your hair stand up on end.'

A part of Russia's foreign property was located on the territory of former Soviet republics and the countries of the Eastern Bloc. When the group of Soviet forces stationed in East Germany and the Western Group of the Soviet Army stationed on the territory of Poland, Czechoslovakia, and Hungary—comprising three million and almost one-and-a-half million men, respectively, not counting their families—were sent back to Russia, they left empty a considerable amount of various kinds of property: kindergartens, schools, cultural centres, friendship society buildings, as well as buildings that housed various foreign trade agencies, press offices, and so on.

A certain part of the Russia's foreign property was handed over to Eastern European countries. By agreement, the real estate could be transferred for sums approved by both sides or even for nothing. For enterprising people, this opened up a realm of opportunities. Under these circumstances, real estate could be transferred for one price on paper and for a different price in reality. Naturally, the difference ended up in the pockets of the various interested parties who were responsible for carrying out these transactions, which amounted to many millions of dollars.

When interviewed, Filipp Turover, a former Soviet citizen residing in Switzerland and serving as a consultant to a major Swiss bank, has the following observations about corruption in the upper echelons of the Russian government: '[Vladimir] Putin—that is a special story and a long story. I had a chance to encounter him....

During his eight months in the Presidential Property Management Department in 1996-1997, Putin was responsible for Soviet property abroad. Let me explain. In addition to the former Soviet Union's debts, Russia inherited its foreign property, worth many billions of dollars, including property that belonged to the CPSU. In 1995-1996, various organizations made claims to this property: the Ministry of Internal Affairs, Minmorflot, and many others. But at the end of 1996, Yeltsin issued a decree that all of the USSR's and the CPSU's foreign property to was to be transferred not to the Ministry of State Property, but for some reason to the Presidential Property Management Department. And it was at this point that Mr. Putin got his hands on it. Naturally, on orders from above. When he undertook the so-called classification of the foreign property of the former USSR and the CPSU in 1997, all kinds of corporations, proxy firms, and joint-stock companies were immediately formed. A large part of the most expensive real estate and other foreign holdings was transferred to these organizations. Thus, its foreign possessions reached the government in a highly pilfered form. And it had been pilfered by [Vladimir Putin].'

The head of the Presidential Property Management Department, Putin's superior at the time, was Pavel Borodin. He was a typical Yeltsin appointee. Until 1993, he had been the head of the Yakutsk city council. At this post, he had had an opportunity to win over Boris Yeltsin, who visited Yakutia in 1990. Yeltsin remembered the warm reception he had been given in the middle of the frozen Yakutian winter: traditional Yakutian tents set up for the important guest right on the airfield, a magnificent traditional fur costume handed to him as he came out of his airplane, a big banquet held in his honour. On April 1, 1993, Borodin was appointed acting head of the Main Social-Manufacturing Directorate of the presidential administration. In November 1993, he became the head of a newly created agency, the Presidential Property Management Department. In 1996, he was given a new deputy—Vladimir Putin—who brought with him a tried and tested officer of the secret service's active reserve, Sergei Chemezov. It was a difficult appointment for both of them.

Borodin and Putin were unable to establish good relations with one another. It is possible that, as a representative of the old school of bureaucrats, Borodin perceived the young, energetic, and aggressive Putin as a threat to his own position (and rightly so). On other hand, it is obvious that Putin, as an officer of the secret service's active reserve in Borodin's agency, both from Borodin's point of view and in actual fact was a spy who had been sent to him and who acquired access to all of the secrets of the Presidential Property Management Department, which was comparable in size probably only to Gazprom.

Borodin, moreover, had good reason to feel threatened. On August 23, 1996, the Presidential Property Management Department signed a contract with Mercata, a Swiss company, for the renovation of the Grand Palace in the Kremlin. This lucrative contract was awarded to the company without a competitive bidding process. Shortly afterward, the same firm won a bid to renovate the building of the Accounts Chamber. The total cost of the contracts amounted to approximately $492 million. As Swiss investigators subsequently established, in exchange for obtaining these contracts, Mercata had paid $62 million in commission fees, 41% of which (equal to $25,607,978) were transferred to Swiss bank accounts controlled by Borodin and his relatives.

At the Presidential Property Management Department, Putin's first order of business was to find apartments in Moscow for himself and the colleagues that he had brought with him from St Petersburg (an apartment in Moscow is a very important step in a government official's career and financial wellbeing). Putin's job at the department was to oversee foreign economic relations and all of the department's contractual and legal affairs. He was also responsible for creating companies to manage the Kremlin's property in other countries.

People at the department suspected that Putin was loyal to other people and organizations, and that he had designs to take Borodin's place. Borodin did not intend to repeat Sobchak's mistake. Putin was not even admitted to the department's main office in Nikitsky Lane. Putin's office was located on Varvarka Street. True, Putin did end up occupying Borodin's seat for three days. On his daughter's advice, Yeltsin fired Borodin. But three days later, Yeltsin was persuaded to reinstate Borodin. No one except Borodin took any note of this temporary dismissal. But Borodin remembered it, and shortly after resuming his post he requested that Putin be taken away from him. (Putin paid Borodin back in time: as soon as he became acting president, he removed Borodin from his post and appointed him secretary of the Union of Russia and Belarus—the most meaningless of all government organizations.)

Continuing rewards for loyalty

As is the rule in Russia's bureaucratic machine, Putin was transferred and given a promotion at the same time. In March 1997, Chubais became first deputy prime minister (he was replaced as the president's chief of staff by Yeltsin's future son-in-law, Valentin Yumashev). Chubais and Yumashev, who supported Putin, soon managed to obtain a new appointment for him from the president. On March 25, 1997, Putin became deputy chief of staff and head of the Main Control Directorate (GKU). He replaced another member of 'Chubais's St Petersburg team' at this post—Sobchak's former deputy and Putin's old acquaintance Alexei Kudrin, who now became deputy minister of finance. In fact, it was precisely Kudrin who had recommended Putin as a replacement for himself, and since Putin was also backed by Chubais and Yumashev, the appointment to the high post went through.

Among the reasons cited for Yumashev's support of Putin's candidacy was the loyalty that Putin exhibited toward his former boss, Sobchak, and his lack of excessive interest in politics. Indeed, secret service active reserve officer Putin was not interested in politics at all, it seemed. From his cramped quarters on Varvarka St, Putin moved to a magnificent office in Staraya Square, which had once belonged to Arvid Pelshe, a member of the Soviet Politburo and the head of the Party Control Committee of the CPSU's Central Committee.

Outlining the policies for his new high-powered appointment, active reservist Putin stated that he planned to inspect various government organizations, natural monopolies, the armed forces, and the military-industrial complex. He intended to identify abuses within these organizations and thus to improve the state of the government budget. Putin emphasized that the GKU is an organization that acts in an advisory capacity: its findings about legal violations would be sent to the General Prosecutor's Office, while the inspections themselves would be carried out jointly by the GKU, the General Prosecutor's Office, and other law enforcement agencies. The main thrust of the GKU's work under Putin's leadership was aimed against the inappropriate use of budget resources in the various regions of the country and in Moscow itself. The first document that Putin signed as head of the GKU was an order to begin inspections precisely along these lines.

In his new post, Putin started actively gathering information about the 89 territories of the Russian Federation and, above all, about their governors. Under Putin, finally, sensible reports about the state of affairs in the regions began to arrive at the Kremlin from the depths of the GKU. Regional inspections, organized by the GKU and carried out by the federal government, became more frequent and strict. Some governors correctly assumed that this was Putin's way of gathering incriminating evidence against them, which was not difficult to do. During the Yeltsin years, a great deal of unfinished business concerning the corruption of local governments had piled up in the regional prosecutor's offices. Inappropriate use of budget resources was widespread. Perhaps it was precisely this incriminating evidence against the governors that became the golden key which opened up their hearts. During his one-year tenure at the GKU, Putin did not quarrel with a single governor and found a common ground with all of them—even the intractable governor of the Krasnoyarsk region, Lieutenant-General Alexander Lebed, the dry, straight-talking populist who ran as a candidate against Yeltsin in 1996.

Meteoric rise

In May 1998, major personnel changes occurred in the Yeltsin administration. On May 25, Putin was appointed deputy chief of staff with responsibility for regional policy. In contrast with his predecessor in the post (Yeltsin's old colleague Viktoria Mitina) Putin was given the title of first deputy chief of staff.

However, he did not occupy both positions for long. On June 1, he was replaced as head of the GKU by secret service Lieutenant General Nikolai Patrushev, also a product of St Petersburg. It was Putin who had brought Patrushev to Moscow and it was Putin who recommended him as his replacement. Mitina's resignation and Putin's appointment to her post was seen as a move by the administration to establish firm control over the regional governments in preparation for the 2000 election (among other things). Mitina, in the opinion of observers, had been unable to handle this task. It was expected that Putin—thanks to the appreciative contacts that he had established with the regional heads, and the leverage that he had acquired over them as director of the GKU—would be more effective.

On June 4, at the first press conference in his new capacity, Putin said that the country's leadership was going to devote greater attention to regional politics, and that the carrying out of presidential orders, decrees, and resolutions at the local level would be subjected to greater oversight and scrutiny. He added that there would be no 'tightening of the screws.' Quite how he would be able to achieve without the other no one asked.

Putin also talked about his achievements as head of the GKU: the abuses that had been discovered involving the inappropriate use of budgetary resources (tied to rival clans), and the criminal proceedings that had been initiated. Putin pointed, in particular, to violations that had come to light in the financial dealings of the Rosvooruzhenie company, the arms agency, and the ongoing inspection of this organization.

This inspection had been triggered off primarily by the fact that Rosvooruzhenie was headed by an appointee of the Korzhakov clan, Yevgeny Ananiev. Putin's plan was to install one of his own factotums—an officer of the secret service's active reserve—as head of this juicy piece of old-fashioned heavy industry of the Russian economy, the third in importance after oil and gas. Putin won this chess match brilliantly. He managed to get Ananiev dismissed, 'restructured' Rosvooruzhenie, and installed his old colleague from foreign intelligence Andrei Belyaninov at the head of the new organization. To secure matters further, Chemezov, his Dresden colleague became Belyaninov's first deputy.

On July 15, 1998, Putin also replaced Sergei Shakhrai as head of the presidential commission to prepare agreements on dividing authority between the federal government and the regions of the Russian Federation. Since that time, not one such agreement has been signed, leaving the regions in the dark as to what autonomy they had—if any.

Director of the secret service

On July 25, 1998, active-reservist Lieutenant-Colonel Putin returned to base. By order of President Yeltsin, Putin was appointed director of Russia's secret service (the Federal Security Service). His activities in his capacity as director of the secret service, responsible directly to the president, were coordinated in part by the then prime minister Sergei Kiriyenko. Kiriyenko's government was the youngest in all of Russia's history, and considered to be pro-Western and reform-oriented. He presented his new director to the staff of the secret service, characterising Putin as a man who had experience in working for the security services and fighting economic crime. Putin in his speech remarked that he was 'coming home' to the secret service and that he was set to embark on major constructive work.

In his book *First Person* (2000) Putin recalled, however, taking on his new appointment without much enthusiasm. Perhaps this was indeed the case at the time. His appointment was certainly greeted without much enthusiasm by many secret service staff employees. Things got worse. Shortly after his appointment, Kiriyenko's government was dismissed and Yevgeni Primakov replaced Kiriyenko. Primakov was the former deputy head of the KGB (1991), the director of the Foreign Intelligence Service (SVR), and an obvious opponent of both Yeltsin and the entire 'family'. For the high brass of the secret service, Primakov's appointment to the post prime minister meant, if not an already accomplished government coup, then at least the beginning of one. Putin, a Kiriyenko leftover, was not taken seriously any longer. On top of that, Putin was merely a lieutenant colonel. In a military organization, where people took such things seriously, Putin's military rank could not be mentioned without a smile or resentment.

The nature of Putin's former work at the KGB was also a cause for derision in the elitist corridors of its head office. Putin had worked in East Germany, where foreign intelligence employed its modest achievers. The top tier was, of course, sent to the mortal enemy—the capitalist countries, especially to the United States and Western Europe. Had the KGB taken Putin seriously as an expert of any kind, he would have worked in West Germany, not in East Germany.

But it was precisely because the central leadership of the secret service did not regard Putin as one of its own that the Chubais and Yumashev clan who had sponsored Kiriyenko, had positioned him at the head of the secret service. Putin's predecessor, secret service general Nikolai Kovalev, had been too much at home in the organization. And he had a long-nurtured political objective: to seize power in Russia, just as Korzhakov had once attempted to do. The only exception was that Kovalev's aim was to seize power not for himself, but for Yeltsin's ideological opponents.

Because obtaining power in Russia had become connected with possessing financial clout since Yeltsin, Kovalev had attempted to bring the country's main economic organizations under his control by using the secret service's two largest economic departments (the Department of Economic Counterintelligence and the Department of the Counterintelligence Provision of Strategic Objects). This blatant attempt to upset the oligarchic applecart led to Kovalev's dismissal and the beginning of the secret service reform that Putin was deputized to implement. People in Yeltsin's entourage reasoned that Putin, who had attained only the rank of lieutenant colonel in the provincial East German city of Dresden, must hold a grudge against the system and would remain loyal to the Kremlin, not to the Lubyanka (the street in which the secret service/KGB head office was located).

Putin's survival of Yeltsin's lurch to the old-soviets clan under Primakov was nothing short of remarkable. Seemingly one of Kovalev's young Turks, he was everything they despised. However, Putin's years in the mediocre KGB backwaters of Dresden—where there was no room for diva behaviour—paid off handsomely. A spy fishing for those with suspect beliefs, he was a master at ingratiating himself with his adversaries (who would one day include German Chancellor Gerhard Schröder; U.S. president George W. Bush and Italian prime minister Silvio Berlusconi)—while floating upwards.

Boris Berezovsky, then part of the Yeltsin 'family', recalled how Putin, as director of the secret service, came to his house with flowers to wish his wife, Yelena, a happy birthday—right at the time when Prime Minister Yevgeny Primakov's anti-Berezovsky campaign was at its height. 'You're crazy,' said the astonished Berezovsky. 'Primakov will find out...' 'He can go to hell,' Putin replied. 'I'm not afraid of him.'

Berezovsky was impressed and felt that here was a person he could trust, not knowing that Putin went to wish Yevgeny Primakov a happy birthday as well, with another bouquet of flowers.

Putin knew from long experience what the acceptable procedure for counter intelligence was. He was not afraid of repercussions, because all of his steps were discussed and logged with the *kontora* ('the company'), the leadership of the KGB. With the *kontora's* approval, he had been able support Sobchak in August 1991 as an active reservist, and wish Berezovsky's wife a happy birthday during the height of the harassment campaign against Berezovsky.

It had always allowed Putin to have it both ways. 'Usoltsev', Putin's Dresden KGB colleague, notes in his 2004 book that Putin's attitude toward the Soviet government in conversation with his friends was unusually critical for an agent:

Gradually, it became clear to me that Volodya had already absorbed all of this dissident wisdom back in Leningrad, while working at the Fifth Directorate, which was aimed at combating 'ideological subversion.' It appeared that, in the part of the battlefield that Volodya had been responsible for, the 'ideological subversives' had won. In our conversations, he mentioned many dissidents with esteem. He was especially respectful of Solzhenitsyn. I had never encountered anything even resembling such attitudes among the agents of the Fifth Directorate's Krasnoyarsk and Minsk offices.

The same section under Soviet times would attract praise as an excellent way of trapping fifth columnists.

Consolidation

One of Putin's objectives in his new job was to counteract the growing tendency for the mayor of Moscow, Yuri Luzhkov, and the governor of St Petersburg, his former colleague Vladimir Yakovlev who thought him an 'asshole', to exert a greater and greater influence on the regional heads of the secret service who were stationed in their towns. The secret service's Moscow and St Petersburg directorates were essentially under the command of the heads of the city governments first and only in a secondary way under that of the director of the secret service.

By coincidence, he was very well suited for this. The seemingly rather gray and solid Putin understood better—from personal experience—than anyone in the central government how the shoe twisted. It had been a long time since the good old Soviet times when secret service officers lived exclusively on his official government salary. In addition to their salaries, all of them now received bags of cash as the secret service's regional directorates were as free as any Russian citizen to enter into lucrative commercial agreements with city government officials, offering them various services: private security, businesses protection, and so on. The larger the city, the more influential the heads of its secret service directorate were. Prior to Putin's appointment as director of the secret service, the head of the secret service directorate for Moscow and the Moscow region were potentates who could compete with the director of the secret service in terms of his political influence in the government, and far outstripped the director of the secret service in terms of financial clout.

Putin handled the task of reforming the secret service brilliantly. First of all, he removed from the staff roster—i.e. fired—about two thousand secret service officers, including all of the employees of the two economic departments and the senior generals on the board of the secret service. He then appointed his own old KGB colleagues to vacant board positions. All of them were from St Petersburg and so, by default, Putin was the closest friend he had in their new town: General Viktor Cherkesov, General Sergei Ivanov, and General Alexander Grigoriev. In October 1998, Putin appointed Patrushev—another old colleague from St Petersburg—as his own deputy. Two other colleagues of Putin's from the Leningrad KGB were also transferred to Moscow: Vladimir Pronichev (who became the head of the Department for Combating Terrorism) and Viktor Ivanov (the head of the secret service's Departmental Security Service—internal counterintelligence). Captain Igor Sechin became Putin's assistant and representative in the secret service and in less than half a year, he rose to the rank of colonel (secret service director Putin was promoted to the rank of colonel as well).

In the classic move throughout the history of the Russian secret services, Putin made sure that he did not let any of the staff go—it would have created too many vengeful enemies and uncertainty throughout the secret service and the active reserve. All he wanted to do was to show each and every agent that he was the man who determined their fate. In place of the two economic departments he had closed down, he established six new departments, with freshly appointed directors. In these new departments he gathered the old employees from the secret service who had been removed from the staff roster. Their suspension had taken about a month. None of the employees who had been removed from the staff roster were left without a job, and Putin did not reduce the secret service's total number of employees, but there would be no further subordination.

Putin also made work at the secret service attractive from a financial point of view. He obtained regular financing for the secret service, and, going directly to Yeltsin, avoiding the bureaucratic ladder, he also obtained salary increases for secret service agents, bringing them up to the higher levels of SVR (Foreign Intelligence Service) and FAPSI (Federal Agency for Government Communication and Information) agents.

Assassinations

While Putin deftly handled the secret service threat to the Presidency, little in the way of crime fighting, the secret service's main area of responsibility, seemed to happen. The following political assassinations occurred during his tenure. Remarkably, secret service investigations of these cases led nowhere:

Murder of the president of the Association of Russian Diamond Manufacturers Alexander Shkadov at his dacha near Smolensk (August 1, 1998).

Assassination attempt against Makhachkala mayor Said Amirov (August 8, 1998).

Explosion outside the secret service's Lubyanka headquarters (August 13, 1998). Alexander Biriukov, from the left-wing group New Revolutionary Alternative was charged with organizing this explosion and arrested in 1999; he was subsequently diagnosed as a paranoid schizophrenic.

Murder of Anatoly Levin-Utkin, editor-in-chief of the magazine *Yuridichesky Peterburg Segodnya* ('Legal St Petersburg Today'; August 20, 1998).

Murder of the mufti of Dagestan Said-Muhammad Abubakarov and his brother in the courtyard of the Central Mosque of Makhachkhala (August 21, 1998).

Murder of the president of the Russian Public Fund of Disabled Army Veterans Alexei Vukolov outside Moscow (September 3, 1998).

Another assassination attempt against Said Amirov in Makhachkala (September 4, 1998).

Murder in St Petersburg of the deputy head of the City Committee on the Consumers' Market Yevgeny Agarev (September 28, 1998).

Kidnapping in Grozny (September 29, 1998) and murder (October 3, 1998) of the deputy representative of the government of the Russian Federation in Chechnya, Akmal Saidov.

Murder by radio-controlled mine of the president of the St Petersburg Fuel Company and former candidate for governor of St Petersburg Dmitry Filippov, a close associate of Gennady Seleznev (died on October 13,

1998 from wounds received on October 10).

Wounding in St Petersburg of Seleznev's advisor and sponsor Mikhail Osherov in an assassination attempt (October 16, 1998).

Murder in Moscow of the general manager of the Toms-Neft-Vostok company Alexander Berlyand (October 20, 1998).

Murder in the Moscow region of special prosecutor's office investigator Yuri Keres (October 20, 1998).

Assassination attempt in Grozny against the mufti of Chechnya Akhmed-Hadji Kadyrov (October 26, 1998).

Murder of the deputy general manager of the Chelyabenergo Company Nikolai Shapin (November 1, 1998).

Murder of Novorossiysk Transportation Police chief Yevgeny Fedoryakin (November 5, 1998).

Murder in Moscow of advisor to the governor of the Kemerovo region Alexander Gontov (November 18, 1998).

Murder in St Petersburg of Galina Starovoytova (November 28, 1998)

Assassination attempt against the first deputy prefect of Moscow's Central District Pyotr Biryukov (November 28, 1998).

Murder in Chechnya of three British citizens and one citizen of New Zealand (the foreign experts were kidnapped on October 3, 1998; their decapitated bodies were found on December 10).

Assassination attempt against lawyer Pyotr Kucheren (December 16, 1998).

Car explosion next to the U.S. embassy in Moscow (January 17, 1999).

Arson of Ministry of Internal Affairs building in Samara on February 10, 1999. Fifty seven employees died in the fire.

Murder in Moscow of A. Polyakov, editor of the magazine *Rossiysky Advokat* ('Russian Lawyer'; March 4, 1999).

Kidnapping in Grozny of the Russian Interior Ministry's special representative in Chechnya, Gennady Shpigun (March 5, 1999).

Pogrom in a synagogue in Novosibirsk (on the night of March 8, 1999).

Explosion in a market in Vladikavkaz, over 60 people killed, over 100 wounded (March 19, 1999).

Assassination attempt against the first deputy head of the Omsk region's administration Andrey Golushko. Golushko was seriously wounded (March 22, 1999).

Attempted grenade-launcher attack on the U.S. embassy in Moscow (March 28, 1999). One of the terrorists subsequently gave an interview describing his participation in the attack and was arrested and convicted.

Murder of the deputy general prosecutor of Dagestan Kurban Bulatov in Makhachkala (March 31, 1999).

Another explosion next to the wall of the secret service's Lubyanka headquarters (April 4, 1999). Subsequently, three young women from the underground group New Revolutionary Alternative were charged with organizing this explosion and convicted.

Murder in St Petersburg of the LDPR's head coordinator for St Petersburg and the Leningrad region, Gennady Tumanov (April 9, 1999).

Assassination attempt against the head of the Republican Court of the Karachay-Cherkess Republic Islam Burlakov (April 13, 1999).

Attempt to blow up Iosif Kobzon's office at the Intourist Hotel. Sixteen people wounded (April 26, 1999).

Mines planted in the Jewish theatre 'Sholom' in Moscow (May 10, 1999).

Assassination attempt against the deputy head of the Northwestern RUBOP office (Regional Agency for Combating Organized Crime) in St Petersburg, Colonel Nikolai Aulov, and his wife. Both are seriously wounded by shots from a sniper's rifle (May 26, 1999).

Second assassination attempt against the mufti of Chechnya Ahmed-Hadji Kadyrov (end of May, 1999).

Murder of the hetman of the Grand Army of the Don Cossacks Gennady Nedvigin (June 6, 1999).

Murder of the mayor of the city of Dedovsk, Moscow region, Valentin Kudinov (June 22, 1999).

Murder of the mayor of the city of Kyzyl, leader of the Tuva branch of the DVR party, Genrikh Epp (July 21, 1999).

Grenade-launcher attack on the LogoVAZ Reception House (August 8, 1999).

But there was one investigation that Putin carried out successfully: the operation to remove Russia's general prosecutor Yuri Skuratov from his post. In first-world countries this might have been an odd choice. The one thing, however, that Skuratov or any of the general prosecutors of Russia who came after him could *not* be accused of was a desire to fight corruption in the upper tiers of the Russian government blindly. From his position Skuratov was taking selective aim at the 'family'. Why Russia's general prosecutor decided to fight corruption in the Presidential Property Management Department and Yeltsin himself is hard to say. It may have been out of loyalty to General Korzhakov; or it may have been out of political sympathies with the Communists; or it may have been under pressure from Prime Minister Yevgeni Primakov, who had an extremely negative attitude toward Yeltsin and the 'family', including Presidential Property Management Department head Pavel Borodin and his former deputy Vladimir Putin.

On October 8, 1998, Skuratov initiated criminal proceedings on charges of corruption against the Presidential Property Management Department. In collaboration with their Swiss colleagues, Russian investigators had uncovered a series of abuses that had taken place in the making of contracts to renovate the Kremlin and to refurbish the president's airplane, including many millions of dollars deposited to the bank accounts of Pavel Borodin, his daughter, and his son-in-law.

Skuratov's findings shook Yeltsin's presidency hard. The word 'impeachment' began all of a sudden to be heard more and more often in the Duma, though not for long. Six months after the investigation began criminal proceedings were initiated against Skuratov himself. He was accused of conducting himself in a manner detrimental to his office. In March 1999, Putin's secret service obtained a video recording in which a naked person 'resembling' Skuratov was shown having sex with two equally naked prostitutes. On the night of April 1, 1999, Moscow's deputy prosecutor brought criminal charges against Skuratov.

The rush to initiate criminal proceedings was paramount. Swiss prosecutors were swiftly forging ahead in their investigation of the illegal dealings of the Swiss companies that had been engaged to renovate the Kremlin, and it was necessary to put an end to their investigation as quickly as possible to prevent toxic fall-out in Russia. Without criminal proceedings, this could only be done by replacing the general prosecutor. But replacement of a general prosecutor had to be approved by the upper house of the Russian parliament, the Federation Council, and the procedure was long and complicated.

Putin took the most important role in the operation to discredit and remove Skuratov. His agents had rented and paid for the apartment where Skuratov had his meeting with the prostitutes, and had videotaped the general prosecutor having sex. It was Putin who ended up in possession of the videotape that showed 'a person resembling the general prosecutor,' as Russian newspapers put it, since they had no right to assert that the man shown on the tape was Skuratov himself. And it was Putin who publicly voiced President Yeltsin's demand that Skuratov resign to avoid a scandal.

After Skuratov refused to resign, the video of the sexual escapades of 'a person resembling the general prosecutor' was shown on RTR, a state-run TV channel. The video had been delivered to RTR head Mikhail Shvydkov personally, as reporters joked, by 'a person resembling the director of the secret service.' (Somewhat later, the same video was also shown on Sergei Dorenko's program on Russia's main television channel, ORT.)

On April 7, 1999, secret service director Putin reported in a televised speech that the secret service's and Ministry of Internal Affairs' experts had made a preliminary assessment and had reached the conclusion that the video of the general prosecutor's sexual orgy was genuine. He then once again voiced the opinion that Skuratov should resign voluntarily. Putin also announced that the 'activities' recorded on the video had been paid for by 'individuals involved in criminal cases' under investigation by the General Prosecutor's Office, and demanded that the materials of the two criminal cases be 'merged' into one (the case against Skuratov, based on article 285 of the criminal code 'abuse of official position', and the case against the individuals who had illegally videotaped him, based on article 137 'interference into private life'). In the end, the scandalous individuals who had made the video remained officially unknown, and it was never legally established whether or not the 'person resembling the general prosecutor' was in fact Skuratov. Nonetheless, Skuratov was forced to resign.

In contrast to their Russian colleagues, the Swiss prosecutors saw their investigation through to the end. Their findings resulted in Pavel Borodin's highly publicized arrest in the United States—where he was attending the inauguration of President George W. Bush—followed by his extradition to Switzerland. Borodin's trial brought to light the corrupt arrangement that he and his Swiss accomplices had agreed upon. The Swiss court fined Borodin about $375,000, but Borodin refused to acknowledge his guilt and refused to pay the fine. The Russian Federation refused to pay Borodin's fine as well. The bail money to secure Borodin's release from the Swiss jail was put up by one of his Swiss partners. The Swiss case ultimately ended up being a farce.

The attacks on General Prosecutor Skuratov coincided with attacks on Filipp Turover, a witness for the Swiss prosecutor's office whose testimony was used by the Swiss and Russian investigators. After Skuratov resigned, the Moscow prosecutor's office also brought criminal charges against Turover, a Swiss citizen. He was accused of lying, incitement to crime, bribery, and theft. Due to the charges brought against him, Turover was put on the Russian wanted list and subsequently on the Interpol wanted list as well. In his book *A Version of the Dragon* (2000), Skuratov wrote: 'Turover helped us more than the secret service, the Ministry of Internal Affairs, and the SVR put together. All of his statements, alas, were confirmed. Not one instance of false testimony on his part was established. Our security services, in order to defend the Kremlin, started working on Turover and discrediting him.' After the headlines ceased, the case against Turover fizzled out.

Alexander Litvinenko

In November 1998, another scandal broke out. This one was linked to Putin himself and potentially very dangerous. On November 17, a group of secret service officers headed by secret service Lieutenant Colonel Alexander Litvinenko—although formally the senior member of this group was not Litvinenko, but Colonel Alexander Gusak—gave a press conference at Interfax, Russia's biggest news agency. At this time, the media was still free and the press conference was broadcast by all of Russia's television channels across the entire country. The group of officers stated that the leadership of the secret service had given them orders to kill Boris Berezovsky, the executive secretary of the Commonwealth of Independent States (CIS, a loose union between remaining Soviet States and the Russian Federation). It raised the suspicion that other political assassinations had also been secret service lead, authorised or condoned at least by Vladimir Putin.

Several days earlier, on November 13, the newspaper *Kommersant* had published an open letter from Berezovsky to Putin in which he wrote about the existence of a Communist nomenklatura conspiracy within the security services aimed at protecting criminals within the secret service. Although the criminal orders to assassinate Berezovsky had been issued under Putin's predecessor, Kovalev, the new director of the secret service did not take kindly to Berezovsky's statements. He countered frostily that his agency did not participate in political games but served to protect the constitutional order and the safety of the individual, society, and the government within the bounds of the law. He also condemned any interference by political forces (i.e. Berezovsky) into the work of the secret service, which, in his words, must receive guidance from the president alone. The director of the secret service considered any attempts at such interference to be destabilizing to the country as a whole.

The Litvinenko scandal put Putin's and his agency's reputation in acute danger. At a meeting with Putin, the president expressed deep concern about the situation and recommended that Putin look into the essence of the allegations advanced by Litvinenko's group against the leadership of the secret service. In response, Putin declared smoothly that 'in the event of a confirmation of any of the statements about the criminal activities of our employees, we will get rid of them mercilessly, regardless of their rank or position, and hand over their materials to the prosecutor's office.'

However, the country's public opinion and the press, which were inclined to ascribe control over top government officials to the Russian oligarch Berezovsky, began to suspect that everything that was happening represented a plot between Putin and Berezovsky whose ultimate objective was to hand control over the secret service to Berezovsky and his supporters, one of whom was believed to be Litvinenko. Such a public mindset represented a threat for Putin. People knew about the open warfare between Berezovsky and Prime Minister Primakov—in whose cabinet Putin was still a member, and that the General Prosecutor's Office was trying to bring charges against Berezovsky for committing economic crimes. Under these circumstances, an association between Putin and Berezovsky could clearly be only detrimental to Putin. This was especially so because Berezovsky had started losing his influence within Yeltsin's entourage, and Putin—who was part of this entourage and closely acquainted with everyone in it—was well aware of it.

Putin could have become the first victim of Berezovsky's war, while its last victim could have been Primakov himself. Former secret service director Kovalev, for example, claimed that Berezovsky tried to use the scandal that erupted after the Litvinenko press conference to undermine the influence of the secret service; and that this was connected to Berezovsky's long-standing plan—originally conceived when he became deputy secretary of Russia's Security Council in October 1996—to create a security service under the control of the Security Council and to place Litvinenko at its head.

It was a delicate matter. Putin took a neutral position with regard to the actions of Prime Minister Primakov and the General Prosecutor's Office against Berezovsky and his organizations (they were not part of his oligarchic clan). But he realized that the best way to defend himself against suspicions of having ties to Berezovsky, was to attack Berezovsky in public himself. He had the secret service fire Litvinenko and the other officers who had participated in the Interfax press conference on November 17, 1998, including Colonel Gusak, the senior officer in Litvinenko's group, who had not taken part in the press conference, but who had given testimony corroborating Litvinenko's charges. He then insisted that

Litvinenko and Gusak be arrested, and allowed Berezovsky to be essentially expelled from the country.

Security Council

In October 1998, just before the Litvinenko scandal broke, Putin became a permanent member of the Security Council of the Russian Federation. By a stroke of luck, from March to August, 1999, he served as its secretary as well. The real candidates for the position—which had earlier been occupied by Nikolai Bordyuzha (who had been previously fired from the post of Yeltsin's chief of staff)—included former prime ministers Sergei Kiriyenko and Viktor Chernomyrdin. However, after it proved impossible to reach an agreement with either of them that would also be acceptable to the Kremlin, the circle of possible candidates narrowed down to the heads of the law enforcement agencies. The selection among them was made based on which of them had the least loyalty toward Prime Minister Primakov. Thus, the candidacy of the director of the foreign intelligence service (SVR, Vyacheslav Trubnikov), was rejected due to his close ties to Primakov. Putin, on the other hand, although he did not quarrel with Primakov and maintained steady formal relations with him, oriented himself more towards allegiance to the Kremlin—Yeltsin and the family—rather than to Primakov, who was trying to control the work of the secret service. It is also possible that by nominating Putin for the Security Council, Yeltsin was trying to balance out his appointment of Alexander Voloshin as his chief of staff. Voloshin was seen as Berezovsky's man as he had worked in Berezovsky's organizations before being launched into politics. Voloshin's appointment as the president's chief of staff was generally interpreted as a sign of Berezovsky's growing influence on the Kremlin.

As both director of the secret service and secretary of the Security Council at the same time, Putin now had a degree of power comparable probably only with that of Prime Minister Primakov. It was during this period that an open standoff between Primakov and the Kremlin began. Exploiting the support of a parliamentary majority and General Prosecutor Skuratov's investigation into the Kremlin corruption racket, Primakov started something like a slow-motion coup.

In the State Duma, the Communists tried to turn against Yeltsin the wave of anti-American sentiment that arose as a result of the Yugoslavian crisis unleashed by Slobodan Milosovic and were hatching plans to impeach the president. Communist-leaning ministers received key positions in Primakov's cabinet. Gradually, all power in the government ended up in the hands of the former Soviet politicians. The only stronghold that President Yeltsin had left was the Kremlin, but it was powerless on its own. Primakov, meanwhile, skilfully created the impression that he was a bulwark against the Communist tide—the last barrier standing in the way of Yeltsin's overthrow.

At this moment—a moment critical for the country and for his rule—Yeltsin took an unusually decisive step which, it had seemed, he would never be able to bring himself to take. On May 19, he signed a decree to dismiss Primakov, who was then at the height of his power and popularity, from the position of prime minister. The Communist domination collapsed like a house of cards. The opposition in the Duma fell silent. All talk of impeachment ended. Skuratov resigned.

The silence, after the sharpening of knives, was deafening. What had sucked dry the resolve of the Communists? The answer to the mystery was soon revealed. Yeltsin had struck a Faustian bargain behind the scenes. After getting rid of a prime minister, who was the former head of the foreign intelligence service (SVR), Yeltsin picked a new prime minister, Sergei Stepashin, the former head of the FSK (the former KGB and the future secret service)and an active reservist. Yeltsin could now pick prime ministers only from among the officers of the secret service. This was the price he had to pay for remaining in power himself and for transferring power to a successor who could guarantee him and the family immunity from criminal prosecution by the Duma and the General Prosecutor's Office. The design on Yeltsin's presidency that secret service General Korzhakov had failed to realise before the presidential elections of 1996, was finally taking shape under the stewardship of secret service Colonel Putin.

During Putin's tenure as secretary of the Security Council, a number of topics were discussed at the council's meetings. First, there was the situation in the North Caucasus, particularly in Chechnya. In May 1999, after Stepashin was confirmed as prime minister, Putin obtained a presidential decree that increased the role of the secret service's subdivisions in the North Caucasus. Second, the Security Council deliberated over the development of Russia's nuclear potential in the face of what the Kremlin saw as the global hegemony of the United States, which had been demonstrated during the Yugoslavian crisis.

On May 12, 1999, the Security Council met to discuss the situation in the Balkans. Putin's remarks were brusque: 'Russia will not be satisfied with the role of a professional courier in the Yugoslavian crisis, the role of a country that merely carries proposals from one country to another.... We are seeing a one-sided attempt to destroy the world order that was created under the aegis of the United Nations after the Second World War. We must react to this challenge by changing our conception of our own national security.'

Putin repeatedly discussed the situation in the Balkans and various security-related aspects of Russian-American relations by telephone with Sandy Berger, national security advisor to the president of the United States. After one of the Security Council's meetings, Putin declared that Russia deserved a great deal of credit for the fact that a political settlement had been reached in the Balkan crisis, alluding to his own role in the process. Putin also worked on the issue of Russia's role in peace-keeping activities in Kosovo. And by June 1999, when the possibility of Stepashin's resignation was being mooted, Putin was already being considered as a possible successor.

Prime Minister

On August 9, 1999, by order of the president, one more deputy prime minister position (the third one) was created. By the same order, Putin was appointed to the new position. On the same day, Yeltsin issued another order dismissing Sergei Stepashin's cabinet and appointing Putin temporary acting prime minister (by law, only the deputy prime minister could be appointed to the position of acting prime minister).

Following the pact with the secret service who helped dispatch the old soviet guard run by Primakov earlier in the year, Yeltsin recommended on the same day Putin as his successor for the presidency of the Russian Federation in a televised address: 'I have now decided to name a person who, in my opinion, can bring society together. Relying on the broadest political powers, he will ensure the continuation of reforms in Russia. He will be able to surround himself with those who will have to bring renewal to great nation of Russia in the twenty-first century. This is the secretary of Russia's Security Council, the director of the secret service, Vladimir Vladimirovich Putin.... I have confidence in him. But I want everyone who will vote in July 2000 to have confidence in him as well. I think that he has enough time to show his worth.' In a televised interview on the same day Putin stated that he accepted Yeltsin's offer and would run for president in 2000.

On August 16, 1999, the State Duma confirmed Putin's nomination for the position of prime minister (223 votes in favour, 84 against, 17 abstentions). Thirty two CPRF deputies (including Duma speaker Gennady Seleznev) voted in favour of Putin; 52 CPRF deputies (including Anatoly Lukyanov and Albert Makashov) voted against him; the rest abstained or did not vote (Gennady Zyuganov did not vote). A number of deputies from the left-wing Narodovlastie party also voted against Putin. Eighteen deputies from the Yabloko party (including Grigory Yavlinsky) voted in favour. Eight Yabloko deputies voted against; the rest did not vote or abstained. The other parties voted in favour of the confirmation virtually unanimously.

Summing up Putin's first months in office as prime minister, the newspaper *Novaya Gazeta* wrote: 'Once upon a time, in a very democratic country, an elderly president appointed a young and energetic successor to the position of chancellor. Then the Reichstag went up in flames.... Historians still haven't established who it was that set it on fire, but history has shown who stood to benefit.' In Russia, however, 'the elderly chief handed the position of prime minister to a successor who had yet to be democratically elected. Then residential buildings started exploding and a new war in Chechnya began—a war that is now being praised to the skies by arch-liars.' These events which shook the nation were clearly connected to the advancement of yet another person: on August 16, 1999, Nikolai Patrushev was appointed director of the secret service. And then things really started to happen energetically...

CHAPTER FOUR

The Russian Pinochet

At the first session of Putin's cabinet as prime minister in August 1999, Putin announced that his predecessor Stepashin's resignation had been brought about 'not by a negative assessment of the actions of the prime minister and his cabinet, but by the president's desire to change the internal political configuration in the country in the run-up to the State Duma election, the presidential election, and in connection with the increasing hostilities in the Caucasus.' By 'increasing hostilities in the Caucasus,' Putin meant above all incursions into Dagestan by guerrilla troops from Chechnya under the command of Shamil Basayev, with whom Russian troops were engaged in prolonged battles in Dagestan.

Another change in the government was a risky move for Yeltsin, above all because no one in the country knew who Putin was. His career growth had been too rapid for people to become accustomed to seeing his face. He was unknown, unrecognizable and unloved. And perhaps it was for this reason that Yeltsin did not mind recommending Putin as his successor to the Russian people. Russian voters faced an all sorts list of candidates: the old-style KGB Yevgeny Primakov, who proclaimed that, if elected, he would arrest 90,000 businessmen, i.e. the entire Russian business elite; the communist Gennady Zyuganov, whose chances of winning were nil, despite him having come second in the 1996 election; and the young secret service man Vladimir Putin, who was thought to favour Yeltsin's policies (at least that is what the oligarchs thought who supported him).

The need to change the 'internal political configuration' stemmed from the ongoing opposition within the government between

Stepashin and First Deputy Prime Minister Nikolai Aksenenko—who was supported by Boris Berezovsky (still a political factor of consequence). Under Putin, the influence of Aksenenko was expected to decline, especially because Putin's nomination had been supported by the head of the Administration of the president, Voloshin, the oligarch Roman Abramovich, former deputy prime minister Chubais, former head of the Administration of the president and future Yeltsin's son-in-law Yumashev, and Yeltsin's daughter Tatyana Dyachenko, both of whom at that time occupied official positions as Yeltsin's advisors. But most importantly, of course, Putin had gained the confidence of Yeltsin.

On the day of his appointment, Putin announced his intention to stay the course set by the old government, both in terms of economic policy, and in terms of domestic political issues, especially those which concerned Chechnya and Dagestan. Nonetheless, when Putin came to power, reporters and members of the public expressed apprehensions of a severe clampdown in the federal government's policies in the North Caucasus and in domestic politics in general, including a possibility that the government might declare a state of emergency and call off the presidential election—especially if the Kremlin was uncertain of the victory of Yeltsin's chosen successor.

The new government was not only supposed to secure the outcome of the presidential election, but also to provide for a smooth parliamentary election, which was to take place in December 1999. Former Prime Minister Stepashin had refused to oppose the union of the Duma's two central parties—Fatherland, formed in January, and All Russia, formed by Mintimer Shaimiev in April. The union of these two parties represented a serious threat for the Kremlin. The Kremlin had reached the seemingly inescapable conclusion that Stepashin had reached a secret agreement with the parties' founders and former prime minister Primakov (who was in August of that year considered to be the favourite in the presidential race) to yield to Primakov's seemingly inescapable victory in the polls.

What the Kremlin really wanted was a 'firm hand'—much like that of Pinochet's for over twenty five years. Putin was seen as the man who could conquer the sympathies of Russia's voters. In fact, the same honour had been styled for Stepashin, previously. But Stepashin had proved flaccid rather than firm, in the eyes of the Kremlin. Among other things, as one of the initiators of the First

Chechen War in 1996—and having been burned badly—Stepashin was not at all enthusiastic about the idea of starting a second Chechen war. For less transparent reasons, Stepashin was also not willing to declare a state of emergency in the country.

Putin did not share Stepashin's reservations, and instead dedicated himself to the task at hand. He realised that he needed a henchman to his firm hand. On the same day, August 9, 1999, on Putin's advice, his successor as secret service director was named. It was his deputy (and fellow former St Petersburg KGB man) at the secret service, Nikolai Patrushev. The assassinations that occurred during Putin's tenure as director of the secret service would be small fry when compared with those committed under his successor. For Prime Minister Putin that kind of killer instinct was precisely what was needed from his secret service Director.

Also, Putin was intimately acquainted with the Chechen situation, and he and secret service Director Patrushev set to work on the plans that had been drafted some time ago. In January 2000, the former director of the secret service Sergei Stepashin, who had been Prime Minister until his replacement by Putin in August 1999, shed a certain amount of light on the issue of precisely when the decision to begin military operations in Chechnya had been made. 'The decision to invade Chechnya,' he remarked in an interview in the Nezavisimaya Gazeta of 14 January, 2000, 'was already made in March 1999'; 'I was preparing for an active intervention. We were planning to be on the north side of the Terek River by August-September' of 1999. Putin, 'who was the head of the secret service at the time, possessed this information.' Without delay, Putin and Patrushev pressed on.

The terrorist attacks

On September 4, 1999, in the city of Buynaksk in Dagestan in the Caucasus, a car packed with explosives was blown up next to a residential building in a military complex. Sixty-four residents—servicemen and members of their families—lost their lives. On the same day, an explosive-packed car was discovered in Buynaksk. The automobile contained 2,706 kilograms of explosive substances and was parked in a parking lot surrounded by residential buildings and an army hospital. The explosion was prevented due only to the vigilance of the local citizens, not by the security services.

In fact, the attack was organized by the Russian secret services. The September 4 terrorist attack in Buynaksk was prepared by the intelligence unit of the armed forces (GRU), headed by Colonel-General Valentin Korabelnikov. The operation was supervised by a senior GRU member (Lieutenant General Kostechko) and was carried out by a team of twelve officers, who had been sent to Dagestan specifically for this purpose.

We know this as from the testimony of one of them, Senior-Lieutenant Alexei Galkin, who was captured as prisoner of war by the Chechens in November 1999. It is clear that Galkin's testimony was given under torture. However, after escaping from captivity, he gave a second interview to *Novaya Gazeta*. This one was voluntary and Galkin did not retract this part of his statement.

The apartment-house bombings in Moscow, Volgodonsk, and Ryazan—which were also mentioned by Galkin when interrogated by the Chechen security service—took place a few days after the bombing in Buynaksk. On the early morning of September 9, a residential building on Guryanov Street in Moscow was blown up. On the early morning of September 13, another apartment building in the capital was bombed—this one on Kashirskoye Highway. On September 16, a residential building in Volgodonsk in Rostov Region exploded. On the evening of September 22, local residents and police averted the explosion of an apartment house in Ryazan, 200km south east of Moscow. These were all organised by the secret service, rather than the armed forces intelligence service (GRU). They would also have executed the one in the armed-forces complex in Buynaksk, except they wanted to avoid an interagency conflict between the secret service and the Ministry of Defence. The chain of command was as follows: Putin (former director of the secret service, future president)—Patrushev (Putin's successor as director of the secret service)—secret service General German Ugryumov (director of the counter-terrorism department). Maxim Lazovsky (the owner of Lanako, the company that employed the secret service agents behind the 1994-5 terrorist attacks) and Lieutenant-Colonel Abubakar were the two secret service operatives directly responsible for the practical organization of the bombings.

The individuals recruited by the 'Chechen separatists' (secret service agents) to deliver explosives disguised as bags of sugar to the basements of buildings destined for bombing in Volgodonsk and in Moscow were Adam Dekkushev, Yusup Krymshamkhalov, and Timur Batchayev. (They themselves were under the impression that the locations to which they were delivering the explosives were merely temporary storage spaces, and that the explosives would ultimately be used to blow up 'federal targets'.) Tatyana Korolyova, Achemez Gochiyaev, Alexander Karmishin were the founders of the company whose warehouses received shipments of the explosive, hexogen, disguised as bags of sugar. Finally there were secret service operatives Vladimir Romanovich and Ramazan Dyshekov, who carried out the apartment-house bombings in Moscow, and also the secret service agents who were apprehended and videotaped—but whose last names were not disclosed—after attempting to blow up a residential building in Ryazan on the night of September 22-23, 1999.

Apart from Galkin's statements, today we know a great deal more about the apartment-house bombings. The sources that have pointed to the involvement of the aforementioned individuals in the September 1999 terrorist campaign are many and varied. All kinds of people have contributed to the gathering and analysis of this information—reporters, human rights activists, and former secret service agents who cut their ties with the system. First and foremost among these are former secret service Lieutenant-Colonel Alexander Litvinenko—co-author of *Blowing Up Russia* (with Yuri Felshtinsky)—and former secret service Colonel Mikhail Trepashkin who, in an interview with the newspaper *Moskovskiye Novosti*, stated that he had recognized secret service agent Vladimir Romanovich in the photo fit issued of the terrorist 'Laypanov', suspected of blowing up the residential building on Guryanov Street.

On the day after his interview appeared in *Moskovskie Novosti*, Trepashkin was arrested on charges of illegally possessing a gun, divulging a state secret (Trepashkin was released from prison in 2007). Apparently, this state secret consisted precisely of the fact that 'Laypanov'—the criminal wanted by Russian law enforcement—and secret-service agent Romanovich were one and the same person. For his part, Romanovich emigrated to Cyprus some time after September 1999, where he later died—apparently in a car crash. Alexander Litvinenko, having claimed political asylum in the United Kingdom, was poisoned with the rare radioactive element Polonium-210 and died in London in November 2006.

These terrorist attacks were the largest in Russia's history and claimed the lives of approximately 300 people, and soon became the cause for a full-scale war of the Russian Federation with the Chechen Republic, according to plan.

The scheme comes together

On September 1999 14, shortly after the second apartment bombing in Moscow, Putin addressed the Duma on the issue of fighting terrorism from Chechnya and to be seen to make a fist he stated that Chechnya was clearly a terrorist camp. This was not a particular difficult argument to make. Islamic Chechnya—located on its extremities bordering only Georgia on the outside—has for centuries been a source of trouble for Russia and its inhabitants are viewed with suspicion. To combat Islamic terrorism, he stated the borders would be temporarily closed. There would be no question of Chechnya leaving the Russian Federation, and all bandits would persecuted without mercy.[1]

The day that the real war began, however, hastily followed the events of September 22-23 in Ryazan. The local Ryazan constabulary announced publicly, and proudly, that it had intercepted and disarmed terrorist bombing devices in an apartment block. Eyewitnesses described three 50 kg sacks of yellow granulated substance (later analysed as hexogen), and a device set to go off at 5:30 am. They soon apprehended the perpetrators who, to their surprise, however, produced secret service cards. In a reversal of fortunes that would suit a fairy tale, a public announcement followed thereafter that the devices in fact were bags of sugar. The Director of the secret service, Patrushev, explained in a separate statement that his department had started top-secret 'training exercises' to keep local counter-terrorist fighters on their toes, though he offered no praise to Ryazan for their vigil. The local secret service office Ryazan followed with its own public statement: 'This announcement came as a surprise to us... We will continue in the future to do everything possible to ensure the safety of the people of Ryazan.'

After the Ryazan fiasco, the secret service refused to undertake any further attempts to blow up residential buildings in Russia. Military operations had to be initiated on the day, in order to deflect Russian public opinion—then still based on independent media sources. It was only a matter of days before the facts would be put together, and the media would reach the conclusion that Ryazan was not an exception but that the terrorist atrocities in Russia were being organized by the security services in order to start a second Chechen war.

On September 23, the head of the Moscow secret service, Alexander Tsarenko, announced that the Moscow explosions had been organized by Chechens, and that the perpetrators had already been apprehended (later, after the favourable headlines had run, both of the Moscow-based 'Chechens' whom Tsarenko had in mind were released in view of the fact that neither had any relation to the explosions –for one, they were from Ingushetia, not Chechnya). On the same day, the Russian air force bombed Grozny airport, an oil refinery, and residential neighbourhoods on the northern outskirts of the Chechen capital. By 1st October, the war had started in earnest. In that month, over a relatively short period of time, the Russian army occupied about 80% of Chechnya's territory.

Brilliantly playing to Russian prejudices further, Putin presented the residents of Grozny with 'Putin's ultimatum' on 6 December. 'Persons remaining in the city,' the ultimatum stated, 'will be considered terrorists and bandits. They will be eliminated by the artillery and the air force.... All those who have not left the city will be eliminated.'[2] The firm hand was slapping the Chechnyans down hard. (Subsequently, the ultimatum was partly retracted when it was specified that its addressees were not all residents of Grozny, but only combatants.)

Apart from the small Ryazan mishap that was soon buried in the daily dispatches from the Second Chechen War, Putin had good reason to be pleased. On December 20 1999, 'the Day of the Chekist' (Lenin had founded the first Russian secret service, the Cheka on that date), Putin reinstated a memorial plaque in honour of Yuri Andropov, the former head of the KGB and the only one—so far—from the organization to lead the Russian nation, on the wall of the secret service building in Moscow. That evening, speaking at a banquet for secret service employees, he remarked: 'I wish to report that a group of secret service employees assigned to work undercover in the government has successfully completed the first phase of its mission.'[3] A widely-read Moscow newspaper also quoted Putin as saying the following: 'The criminal organization has been successfully infiltrated. Just a joke.'[4]

He was aggressively pushing through reforms in the same way he had reorganised the country. On 31st December, Putin signed a government decree reinstating military preparation in the schools. Ostensibly this was to fend off terrorist attacks that had claimed 300 casualties, from a region that may have loomed large in the Russian imagination but in comparison occupied the size of a postage stamp. On 21st January, at a meeting of the leadership of the Ministry of Internal Affairs, Putin warned about the growing danger of a new wave of terrorist atrocities by Chechen separatists in Russian cities. In February 2000, he signed an order to call up reserves for active duty, and then another order reinstating 'special departments' (military counterintelligence) in the army. The special departments (a kind of military KGB) had been dissolved after the collapse of the Soviet Union as an anachronistic relic of Soviet rule. But now these political agencies—whose aim was to monitor the ideological reliability of military personnel, including not just the officers, but the soldiers as well—were back with a new purpose, ostensibly.

Finally, on February 6, after completing the assault on Grozny, which had lasted many days, Putin announced that 'the terrorists' last remaining haven—Grozny's Zavodskoy district—has been taken and a Russian flag has been raised above one of the administrative buildings. So we can say that the operation to liberate Grozny has ended. Like President George W. Bush's famous statement about the war ending in Iraq, this was some exaggeration. The figures on both wars are similar. In October 2001, Putin's aide Sergei Yastrzhembsky reported the number of Russian casualties in Chechnya over the two years of the second Chechen war: 3,438 killed and 11,661 wounded. According to the Committee of Soldiers' Mothers, the number of casualties as of January 2002 was about two or two-and-a-half times greater than the official figure; in particular, about 6,000 soldiers and officers had been killed. In February 2003, new official figures were released for the total number of casualties sustained by Russia's armed forces as a whole between October 1, 1999 and December 23, 2002: 4,572 killed and 15,549 wounded.

On the whole, Russian public opinion, frightened by the September terrorist attacks in Russia, supported Putin's policies in Chechnya and even relished his crude remarks about 'whacking the terrorists in the outhouses'. After the beginning of the military campaign in Chechnya, Putin's popularity rating—thanks to the unswerving support of the Berezovsky-controlled Channel One of Russian television (ORT)—started steadily growing. By the beginning of the election campaign, he was no longer an unknown, but a candidate with a popularity rating as high as 50%.

Election fever

On December 19, 1999, in the national election for the third convocation of the State Duma, the Interregional Unity Movement ('Medved') won 23.32% of the vote, coming in second after the Communists (24.29%). Yevgeny Primakov's Fatherland–All Russia (Moscow mayor Yuri Luzhkov) bloc (OVR) won 13.33%; the Union of Right Forces (SPS) won 8.52%; The populist Zhirinovsky's bloc won 5.98%; and the pro-Western Yabloko won 5.93%.

The parliamentary election had been a resounding success for Putin. 'Medved'—formed shortly before the election by Boris Berezovsky, who had developed both the ideology and the symbolism of the new party—unexpectedly for everyone fell less than one percent short of the Communists in the party list vote. When the parliament's single-constituency votes were added to its total, Medved, nonetheless, became the largest party faction in the Duma.

Even more important was the fact that Medved's votes had been taken away from Primakov, Putin's main rival in the presidential election, and from Mayor Luzhkov. Their Fatherland–All Russia bloc had won only slightly more than 13% of the vote, instead of the 30%-40% that they had expected. The voters had also given considerable support to the Union of Right Forces, which was headed by Sergei Kiriyenko, the former Prime Minister who had appointed Putin as secret service Director. The Union of Right Forces supported Putin as a presidential candidate with the slogan: 'Putin for President! Kiriyenko for the State Duma! We need young people!' By contrast, the Communist opposition had lost its absolute majority in the Duma. Berezovsky, who controlled Channel One of the Russian television, had supported Unity and Putin with no attempt to achieve objectivity.

On the same day, Putin's principal opponent in the upcoming presidential election, Yevgeny Primakov, announced that he would not run for president. Those who had been planning Putin's campaign now shifted it in a higher gear. On December 31, 1999, in his New Year's address, President Yeltsin presented the citizens of Russia with a New Year's Czar-like gift and announced that he was abdicating from the presidency and appointing Putin as acting president until the presidential elections. He also announced that they would take place on March 26, earlier than previously scheduled. In return for this, in a secret agreement brokered between Yeltsin and Putin, Putin issued a decree in January 2000 granting the first president of Russia and his family immunity from all legal or administrative prosecution.

In January, two factions backing the acting president were formed in the new Duma—Unity (headed by Boris Gryzlov, Frants Klintsevich) and People's Deputy (Gennady Raykov). Two other centrist, establishment-oligarchic factions—Regions of Russia (Oleg Morozov) and Fatherland–All Russia (Yevgeny Primakov, Vyacheslav Volodin)—also declared their loyalty to Putin. These four centrist, pro-Putin factions had over half of the Duma's deputies. During the Duma's third session, 230-235 deputies formed a slim but significant majority. These deputies almost always voted in accordance with the orders of the president's deputy chief of staff, Vladislav Surkov. In addition to the Duma's centrist parties, populist Vladimir Zhirinovsky's LDPR became almost as loyal, as did a large part of the SPS (headed by Sergei Kiriyenko, as well as Boris Nemtsov and Irina Khakamada).

With this backing, the acting president was able to push whatever legislation it wanted through the Duma without encountering any obstacles, relying on an absolute majority of 226 votes. When it was necessary to enact constitutional reforms requiring a qualified-majority (300 votes), the administration relied either on the liberal-centrist, 'right-wing, pro-Putin' constitutional majority (the centrists, LDPR, SPS, Yabloko) or on the nationalist, 'left-wing, pro-Putin' majority (the centrists, and Nikolai Kharitonov's pro-Communist Agrarian group).

Independence from the Kremlin, and a measure of opposition was lead by the Communists. Occasionally, opposition from the liberal right would come from Yabloko, as well as certain independents (Vladimir Ryzhkov), and several SPS deputies (Sergei Kovalev, Yuli Rybakov, Sergei Yushenkov, Viktor Pokhmelkin, Vladimir

Golovlev). Boris Nemtsov sometimes wavered between loyalty and opposition—although this was reflected more in his rhetoric than in his votes. During the second session of the Federation Council of the Russian Federation, Putin was opposed to some extent only by president of the Chuvash Republic, Nikolai Fyodorov. However, Fyodorov soon thought better of it and his opposition also dwindled. The plan ran like clock-work.

The campaign

On January 13, 2000, during a trip to St Petersburg, Putin officially confirmed his intention to run for president of Russia (he had unofficially accepted Yeltsin's suggestion in August the previous year), and announced his support for Vladimir Yakovlev—Sobchak's assistant and subsequent rival—in the St Petersburg gubernatorial race. Since the time he had all but thrown Putin out of St Petersburg, Yakovlev had clearly had a change of mind and made up with his former colleague.

On February 15, 2000, Putin registered with the Central Election Commission (CEC) as a candidate for the presidency. On February 18, while campaigning in Irkutsk, he came out in support of the idea for a referendum on four issues, proposed by Kiriyenko's pro-West party: the necessity of increasing guarantees for the protection of private property; limiting deputies' immunity; sending only contractual military personnel to areas of armed conflict; and limiting the president's right to dismiss his cabinet without demonstrable cause. On the same day, Putin approved of the idea of 'prohibiting sex, violence, and terrorism' on television.

Putin had never before stood for elected office. Observers recalled an interview given by him two years earlier, in which Putin had talked about his unwillingness to participate in an election, citing the fact that during an election campaign the candidate must make promises that he cannot keep, and consequently, either must not be aware of the meaning of his own words or must deliberately lie. Putin's career also received some attention. His supporters pointed to his work in the Sobchak administration as proof of his commitment to reform. His opponents in the Presidential elections, particularly the no-hope candidate Grigory Yavlinsky, a liberal, stressed Putin's work for the KGB and the secret service, portraying him as a devotee of the old political order and the practices of the KGB.

On February 25, 'An Open Letter from Vladimir Putin to Russian Voters' was published in the press. Three days later, at a Moscow meeting with his supporters, Putin declared that 'it is vitally important to create equal conditions for all participants in the political and economic life of Russia. We must make it impossible for individuals to latch on to power and to use it for their own purposes. No clan, no oligarch must be involved in regional or federal government. All of them must be equally distanced from political power and all of them must rely on equal means.' The Acting President was of course thinking of his opponents, not of the clan he was heading.

First Person: Conversations with Vladimir Putin—a book compiled of three interviews with *Kommersant* reporters—was published during Putin's election campaign in 2000. This little volume, hastily assembled on Boris Berezovsky's initiative, was the only serious publication devoted to Putin that existed at that time. Today, many of the pronouncements published in this book can at best draw a smile. Thus, as a possible way of solving the problems facing Russia, Putin mentioned the monetarization of subsidies, i.e. the idea of replacing the numerous government benefits received by various groups of people—a system inherited from Soviet times—with loans. When the attempt to implement this undoubtedly progressive idea was eventually made, it turned out to be the most unpopular of Putin's economic policies and was never brought to fruition.

On the whole, however, Putin, as a staff employee of state security, who had spent his whole adult life working for the KGB under the ideological control of the Communist Party, had no ideology or political program of his own. He confined himself to general populist phrases. Back in 1999, at the beginning of his tenure as prime minister, Putin had given a very candid response to a question about his potential platform in the presidential race with a little whiff of the personality cult that was favoured by the fascists: 'My main objective is to improve people's lives. We will work out a political platform later.' Later, in 2001, in response to a question about how he envisioned the Russia of 2010, Putin said 'We will be happy,' adding utopia to the programme.

The Kremlin tried to foist upon voters the idea that there was no alternative to Putin, pointing out that Putin's main rival was the

Communist Party candidate, Zyuganov—who was undoubtedly a worse choice for Russia than Putin. Indeed, according to surveys, it was not only the adherents of Unity and the SPS that were intending to vote for Putin, but even supporters of Zyuganov's Communist Party and Yavlinsky's liberal Yabloko—even though the leaders of these parties were also taking part in the election.

Putin's candidacy was officially supported by Boris Gryzlov's and Sergei Shoygu's Unity bloc, Viktor Chernomyrdin's NDR, Yuri Luzhkov's Fatherland, Vladimir Yakovlev's and Mintimer Shaymiev's All Russia bloc, Gennady Raykov's People's Deputy bloc, the SPS, Mikhail Lapshin's Agrarian Party of Russia (APR), and a number of other organizations. Invaluable support for Putin continued to come from Boris Berezovsky's ORT television channel.

Somewhat disoriented by the demands of campaigning and with the finish line so close, Putin promised everything to everyone. On March 2, at a meeting with voters in Zvezdny Gorodok, he promised to support the 'Mir' space station, assuring his audience that 'the issue is merely one of financing and it will be resolved' (a year later, Putin as elected president approved the liquidation of the space station—it was sunk on March 6, 2001). On March 5, in a BBC interview, in a classic Putin move, he told viewers in the West that he did not rule out the possibility of Russia entering NATO. It was a statement that greatly perplexed many Russian politicians and government officials, but without it gave the international media a treat to suck on appreciatively. (Russia did not join NATO and, on the contrary, intensified its anti-NATO rhetoric, backing it up with declarations about withdrawing from various agreements, opposing ballistic missile defence, and resuming the practice of sending its strategic bombers on regular flights, which had been discontinued in 1992.) On March 20, during a 'working trip to the Chechen Republic,' Putin made a widely publicized flight on a Su-27 fighter aircraft as a second pilot-navigator. It is obvious that this circus performance was calculated to increase Putin's popularity among simple voters. But because the people who were making a president out of Putin had not explained to him why they had put him inside a military plane, Putin, in response to questions from American TV interviewer Ted Koppel, became confused and muttered that he had flown on the Su-27 in order to reduce costs.

Voting Russian style

Despite the overwhelming political and media support, the Kremlin were nonetheless not taking any chances. With so many candidates, it was possible that there would have to be a run-off. This would dissolve the advantage of the unexpectedly early elections Yeltsin had called, and allow Putin's opponents to regroup and cause trouble. Like Nixon in 1972, Putin and his clan did not trust that, rather than make the 'right' decision, the Russian voters would make the 'mistake' that had happened during the 1996 mayoral campaign in St Petersburg. As happens in democracies, the sitting mayor Sobchak was ousted and Putin's colleague Yakovlev was voted in. Not much later criminal investigations into Putin and his St Petersburg colleagues had commenced.

On March 9, 2000, a Yak-40 jet crashed seconds after taking off from Sheremetyevo Airport in Moscow. Nine people were on board: Artyom Borovik, president of the publishing concern Soveshenno Sekretno, Ziya Bazhayev, head of the Alliance Group Holding Company and a Chechen by nationality; his two bodyguards; and five crew members. The Yak-40, which Bazhayev had leased about a year earlier from the Vologda Air Company through Aerotex, a Moscow airline company, was supposed to fly to Kiev. The report of the committee investigating air travel incidents indicated that the Vologda air technicians had failed to treat the airplane with a special anti-freeze fluid prior to take-off and that its wing flaps had been opened to only 10° instead of the 20° required for takeoff. Meanwhile, however, the temperature on the morning of March 9 at Sheremetyevo had been only -4°C, with no precipitation, and there was no need to treat the airplane with Arktika anti-freeze. In addition, the Yak-40 could have easily taken off with the wing flaps open to only 10°: this would have simply meant a longer acceleration and a 'lazy' takeoff. Judging by the fact that the airplane crashed close in the middle of the runway, which in Sheremetyevo is 3.6 km long, its takeoff distance had been adequate—approximately 800 meters.

The relevance of this to the presidential elections was that they were in three days about to publish an article on Putin with potentially embarrassing details. In the preceding days and weeks, Borovik (through Bazhayev) had been active collecting materials about Putin's childhood, and the materials were supposed to be published on March 12, 2000.

Borovik had gathered evidence that Putin's real (biological) mother was not Maria Ivanovna Putin (née Shelomova), born in 1911 in St Petersburg, but a completely different woman—Vera Nikolayevna Putin, born in 1926 in the town of Achora (the Perm region in the Urals), who had moved to the village of Metekhi in Georgia, about an hour's drive from Tbilisi. The publication claimed that Putin had lived in the village of Metekhi between the ages of three and nine.

According to his official biography, Vladimir Putin was born on October 7, 1952, in Leningrad. He was the third child in his family (his parents' first two sons died in infancy, the first before the war, the second of diphtheria during the siege of Leningrad). His father, Vladimir Spiridonovich Putin, was born in 1911 in St Petersburg. At the beginning of the First World War, his entire family left St Petersburg for the town of Pominovo in the Tver region. Putin's mother, Maria Ivanovna Putin (née Shelomova), was born in the neighbouring town of Zarechye, also in 1911. His father served in the Red Army as a submariner and his family on his father's side had fought in various battles and had central Russian roots deep into the 17th century. Both parents died of cancer, the mother at the beginning of 1999, the father on August 2, 1999.

According to his official biography, Putin was born when his mother, Maria Ivanovna Putin, was 41 years old. This was a rare occurrence. In the Soviet Union, women as a rule did not give birth at such an age. Volodya entered the first grade in Leningrad on September 1, 1960, when he was almost eight years old. His school friend Vyacheslav Yakovlev has provided one of the few pieces of evidence that Putin grew up in Leningrad. 'The president could not have had a Georgian period in his life,' Yakovlev has stated, 'because we went to school together from first grade through tenth. Volodya and I entered the first grade together, at school No. 193, in 1959. I remember that he came with his mother, carrying an enormous bouquet of roses. We lived in the same building at the time, walked to school together, and came back home together. By the way, before entering school, I also saw Volodya in the yard with his parents.'[5]

This is the only—not particularly convincing—statement that exists about the pre-school period of Putin's life. In addition,

Yakovlev was off by a year, evidently adding the standard seven years to 1952, the year of Putin's birth. Putin entered the first grade of school No. 193 not in 1959, but in 1960.

Another statement sounds more credible: 'Putin and I are four years apart. I was probably about twelve when I first noticed him in the yard,' recalled Putin's neighbour Vyacheslav Chentsov.[6] In other words, children in the yard did not remember Putin before the first grade, when he was already eight years old.

What the new information did was cast a shadow on the Russianness of the Presidential hopeful. It was not only the embarrassment. Instead of having been born and bred in ur-Russian Leningrad, it was claimed that former secret service director Putin had grown up outside the Russian Federation in Georgia—the country from which the loathed Stalin and his henchman NKVD Director Beria hailed. As in the United States presidential elections, an association with alien country—and one with such emotional baggage from the past—was not the narrative that Putin's campaign masters needed at that tense moment in time while the election was only two weeks away.

Vera Nikolayevna, who claimed that she was Putin's real mother, said the following in a video interview of 1 March:

> Originally, I'm from the Urals. I went to a technical college there, too. In college, I met a young man. He was Vova [Putin]'s father. Vova was born in 1950. I don't even want to remember his father. He lied to me. I was already pregnant when I found out that he had a family. I left him immediately. Vova was raised for a whole year by my parents. Then, when I was sent to do my post-graduate service in Tashkent, I met my [current] husband, Georgy Osepashvili. He was in the army then. When I married him, we moved to Metekhi and after a while my mother brought Vova here too. He was three years old at the time.
>
> But soon, when we started having our own children, my husband didn't want Vova to live with us any more. He didn't beat him—he just didn't want Vova to be here. Who wants someone else's child? Once, my husband's sister even gave Vova away to some childless army major, keeping it a secret from me. I barely managed to find him and took him back. I

> had to take Vova back to my parents. They wanted me to keep my new family intact. Basically, I exchanged Vova for my girls. After that, I never saw Vova again, although I constantly looked for him and asked my parents where he was. Nobody wanted to tell me anything. Later, I found out that Vova was already in the KGB and had forbidden everyone to tell me where he was....
>
> Of course, I'd heard that Vova was working for the KGB, and then in the Russian government. Sometimes my daughters talked about him. The people in my village talk about him constantly. But now his childhood is classified information and he doesn't want to recognize me as his mother.... People from the KGB came to my house, took all my family photographs, and told me not to tell anyone about Vova.[7]

The photographs were according to her taken away in January 2000, when either secret service agents (according to one account by local residents), or Georgia law enforcement (according to another account) came to Metekhi and asked all about Volodya Putin. The agents confiscated Vera Nikolayevna's photographs of her son and warned her not to tell anyone about him.

When Vera Putin brought her son to her parents, Anna Ilyinichna and Mikhail Illarionovich, 'my father became ill and the child was sent to a boarding school.'[8] They, in turn, almost immediately handed him over to a childless relative, Vladimir Spiridonovich Putin.

Beset by reporters, Georgian president Eduard Shevarnadze felt compelled to make a statement about Putin's relatives. He suggested that it be left to 'Putin himself to get to the bottom of this issue.'[9]

Vera Putin was visited by reporters once again on March 11, 2000, the day of Artyom Borovik's funeral. This time she said, 'I'm afraid that Volodya won't become president because of me.' There were about twenty reporters in all, including correspondents from Russia's NTV Channel. They inspected Vera Putin's passport and birth certificate, checked the last names of her parents, and verified the name of Putin's father—Platon Privalov. Everything that she said was recorded by several cameras, including NTV's (the NTV interview was never aired).

The reporters also paid a visit to Putin's sister (on his mother's side), Sofia (Sofio) Georgievna Osepashvili, born in 1954, currently a nurse at a TB hospital in Tbilisi. After looking at a photograph of the 14-year-old Putin, which had by then been published in the book *First Person: Conversations with Vladimir Putin* (this was the earliest known photograph of the future president), Sofia said:

> Look at him and look at me—if this is not my brother, then show me my brother.... I sent him telegrams to Achora, to his commissariat. At first they told me that they didn't have any such Putin there. Then they told me that I shouldn't look for him anymore. It turns out that he was already working for the KGB by that time.

Vova Putin

The recollections from other Metekhi residents were plentiful, too. Volodya Putin from Metekhi received his education at the local high school. Some of his old classmates have been interviewed. Gabriel Datashvili, head of the Kaspi district planning organization and Putin's former classmate, said that he had been friends with Volodya and that the two of them were the best students in their class:

In school, we both got the best grades and were close friends. He basically had no other friends besides me.... He was a very quiet, secretive child. After school, he often went fishing or came to my house and we played together: war games, sword-fighting, lakhti, and wrestling.

The descriptions included details. One resident of Metekhi, uncle Gogi, described how Putin had seriously injured his finger while fishing:

> Vova was standing next to his school and bawling. There was a fishing hook stuck in the tip of his left-hand index finger. It couldn't be removed without pulling out a piece of flesh. The blood was gushing. 'Don't be afraid, sonny, it will heal,' I told him ... He cried a lot. I hugged him, calmed him down, and tore out the hook. He must have a small scar left.

Other distinctive marks were apparently two conspicuous bumps at the corners of his forehead (hidden by hair). People said that school-children in Metekhi even teased Volodya and called him the devil because of these bumps.

Nora Gogolashvili, an elementary school teacher, recalled her student Putin as follows:

> A quiet, sad, introverted child. His favourite activity was wrestling. He was almost always unhappy about something. Didn't do any physical work, but was a very good student. Had a very difficult family life.... Vova came to school in patched-up clothes. They called him my stepson. Whenever anyone hurt him, I defended him. I pitied him so much.... I felt so sorry for him. He stuck to me like a cat.

Oleg Iyadze, a wrestler from Metekhi and about ten years younger than Putin, met with the future president at wrestling meets. He recalls '[Putin] was a very reserved person. He was working in the KGB at the time and was as silent as the tomb. I saw him only at wrestling meets....'

After the death of Artyom Borovik, the newspapers of the publishing concern Sovershenno Sekretno that was to have published the book—the monthly *Sovershenno Sekretno* and the weekly *Versiya*—almost immediately halted their attacks on Putin personally and substantially tempered their critical stance toward his entourage. (After the election, one-time Presidential candidate Yevgeny Primakov—the political ideal and one of the sponsors of Borovik's publishing concern—ceased to be an active political player and began in all kinds of ways to emphasize his loyalty to the new regime—although he declined to join the pro-Putin United Russia party. Another one of Sovershenno Sekretno's guiding lights, Moscow mayor Yuri Luzhkov did join United Russia, taking his own Fatherland party with him.)

March 26, 2000, election day

In more direct ways, a run off was prevented too. Voter fraud in Putin's favour was discovered in a number of regions, including Dagestan, Bashkiria, the Saratov region, Tatarstan, and others. Putin was given tens of thousands of votes that had been cast for other candidates. In the three months between the parliamentary and the presidential elections, the Central Election Commission's official lists of registered voters increased by 1,300,000 people (from 108,072,000 in the parliamentary election to 109,372,000 in the presidential election), despite the annual 800,000 decrease in Russia's population. The extra million came in handy.

According to the records of the Central Election Commission (CEC), Vladimir Putin received 52.94% of the vote, enough to avoid a run-off without the media crying foul. On the night from March 26 to March 27, the number of votes cast for Putin until 2 a.m. did not reach 50% (by the time voting ended at 8 p.m., Putin had received only 44.5% of the vote), although his percentage continued to increase as voting moved from east to west. (Interestingly, in the Duma election of December 19, 1999, the opposite phenomenon was observed: as voting moved west, the numbers of the Communist Party consistently improved, while those of the pro-Putin Unity party consistently declined.) Another welcome development for Putin was the sudden spike in official voter turnout during the final hours of voting. Along with a constantly rising percentage of votes cast for Putin, turnout increased dramatically during the final two to three hours of voting. At 7 p.m. Moscow time, voter turnout was still 54%, but two hours later it had risen to 67%. Instead of watching the country's two most popular TV shows vast crowds of people were flooding the voting districts to vote and do their duty for the motherland.

At 2 a.m. on March 27, CEC Head Alexander Veshnyakov triumphantly announced: 'Vladimir Vladimirovich Putin, fifty and one hundredth of a percent.' At 10 a.m. on March 27, Putin already had 52%; and by the time of the final vote count on April 7, he had 52.94% (39,740,434 votes).

Investigations into fraud

Independent investigations to uncover voter fraud in the presidential election of March 26, 2000, took place in only two regions—Dagestan (the region neighbouring Chechnya) and the Saratov region. The infractions in Dagestan were investigated (following a complaint by Zyuganov's campaign headquarters at the Communist Party) by a

Duma, committee headed by Alexander Saliy (of the Communist CPRF). According to official records, Putin had received 877,853 votes (over 75%) in Dagestan. Saliy's committee did not recount the actual ballots and did not compare them with the official results. Fearing, nonetheless, that the committee would attempt to recount the ballots in at least some of the districts, the Dagestan government had taken precautions. Abdulla Magomedov, a Makhachkala police officer stationed at the entrance of the republic's government headquarters building, saw officials (who showed him their passes) carrying large bags with papers out of the building and burning them right on the street. The policeman, citing his official duty as security guard, insisted on inspecting the contents of the bags and determined that they were filled with voting ballots that had been cast for Zyuganov. 'I know what they look like—I was an observer during the voting,' the policeman said.[10]

Saliy's committee focused, instead, on comparing copies of the district records that had been given to observers with the official figures for the same districts as recorded at a higher level—by territorial election commissions. Saliy's committee analysed 453 copies of district records (Dagestan has 1550 voting districts in all; observers from Zyuganov's headquarters were unable to obtain copies of records from the other districts). Fourteen district territorial committees and two municipal ones came under investigation. All together, 174 different district records were examined.

The findings of Saliy's committee were self-explanatory. For example, district No. 1036 of the Suleyman-Stal territorial election commission: the observers' copy of the district records indicated 801 votes for Zyuganov, while official records showed 150 (651 votes stolen); the copy indicated 452 votes for Putin, while the official records showed 2038 (1568 added). District No. 1044 showed 862 of 863 votes stolen from Zyuganov, 1572 votes added to Putin's 227. All together, in 34 of the 40 examined districts of this territorial election commission, 8462 votes had been stolen from Zyuganov and 13805 votes had been added to Putin's total. Other districts showed similar discrepancies.

Saliy's committee discovered that when the signature of the district's electoral chairman on the copy of the records was identical with the signature on the original, no changes had been made in the copy, and that all such districts had been carried by Zyuganov. In cases when the signatures were not identical, Putin had won by a landslide, and the signatures that appeared in the observers' copies were identical to the genuine signatures of the district chairs, while the signatures in the official records were not.

Saliy's committee tallied the 'corrections' in all of the 16 territorial election commission records that it examined. All together, according to the composite table of falsifications published by Saliy, over 187,000 extra votes had been added to Putin's total vote count in Dagestan.[11] Saliy estimated that the figure of irregular Putin votes in Dagestan had been 700,000—based, evidently, on the figure of 180,000 for 16 territorial election commissions.

Saliy's committee sent these findings along with copies of the district records to the General Prosecutor's Office in the summer of 2000. The General Prosecutor's Office did not bring charges against the officials suspected of forgery.

Extra ballots were also added in Dagestan. The newspaper *Sovietskaya Rossiya* received 15 such ballots for Putin from the city of Izberbash, all bearing the stamp of district No. 0832. Their photocopies were reproduced in the newspaper.[12] Remarkably, forty percent of the districts in Dagestan had no cancelled ballots either. In each of these voting districts, exactly the same number of people had voted as there were ballots.

The Communist Party's past dealings with issues surrounding elections is not exactly without its blemishes, of course. But *Moscow Times* reporter Yevgenia Borisova conducted her own independent investigation of voter fraud in a number of regions, including Dagestan. Borisova checked the figures of Saliy's committee and reached the conclusion that 57,162 votes for Putin were unreliable. (Regarding the additional 130,000 or so that Saliy's committee found, she disagreed with the committee's methodology.)

Borisova also compared the territorial election commission tables with the copies of records from 71 voting districts that Saliy's committee had left unexamined. The picture in these districts was the same. Thus, according to the copy of the records of district No. 0876, 1070 votes had been cast for Putin, while the official records gave him 3535 (a difference of 2465 votes); according to the records of district No. 0903, Putin had won 480 votes, while according to the official records, he had won 1830; and so on. Sixty-three of the 71 records inspected by Borisova and her assistants contained evidence of falsification. They added up to another 31,101 votes for Putin that were unreliable. Having investigated 16% of Dagestan records she concluded 88,263 votes were unreliable and estimated that approximately 550,000 votes were unreliable.[13] As 877,853 votes were cast for Putin, according to official electoral records, even a fraction of 'miscounted' votes would have skewered the election result dramatically.

A similar situation was discovered in the Saratov region (near Kazakhstan), the only other voting region that was investigated. According to the testimony of a member of Saratov's official electoral committee, retired officer A. Bidonko, when figures from the districts began to arrive at 3 a.m. on March 27, it became clear that neither Putin nor Governor Dmitry Ayatskov (there was a simultaneous gubernatorial election in the region) would receive 50% of the vote. All night long, the records were rewritten, and the unused ballots were cancelled only in the morning.[14] The Communists brought charges on account of these events, but the court refused to hear the case, sending the complaint back to the Saratov electoral committee. It found that no rules had been broken.

Observers from Zyuganov's campaign headquarters were able to obtain 700 notarized copies of district records from the Saratov region, i.e. 38.6% of all records (the region had 1815 voting districts in all). Separately, *Sovietskaya Rossiya* reporter Zhanna Kasyanenko compared the records of 28 districts and found that 3769 votes for Putin in these districts were unreliable (according to the copies, pro-Western Yavlinsky should have had 1540 more votes in the official tally, and the Communist Zyuganov another 827). Other districts in Saratov showed similar discrepancies. In district No. 1576., for example, showed a frequently occurring discrepancy of a different kind. According to the copy 30 votes had been cast for 'none of the above', but only 10 were recorded on the official tally. It wasn't always Putin who was the beneficiary either. Kasyanenko inspected district No. 107 and found that unreliable votes trailed the strength of the parties in the Duma. The Communist Zyuganov had been given an extra 6 votes; while in district No. 452 Zyuganov received an extra 10 (Putin received an extra 31 votes and Zhirinovsky a single one).

After the General Prosecutor's Office in Moscow received complaints about voter fraud in the presidential election at voting districts in the Saratov region, the regional prosecutor's office in

Saratov was forced to recount the records of 20 districts. The results of the recount corroborated the discrepancy between the figures in the records and the notarized copies. Nonetheless, no criminal proceedings were initiated due to the fact that the heads of the Saratov election committee had told the general prosecutor's office, when copies of records had been released, that 'the figures contained in them had not been verified against the figures in the original records by the members of the committee.'[15]

Incidental reports appeared also from other regions. In district No. 207 of the city of Yoshkar-Ola, consultative district committee member L. Korostelev was removed by the police from the building where the vote count was taking place, on orders from district committee chair N. Bolshakov. When Korostelev was permitted to return to the building, he discovered 'a great number of defaced ballots for Zyuganov. I am convinced that they had been defaced on purpose, and deliberately during my absence—covered with additional dashes and signs.' The chair of the district election commission, his deputy, and his secretary refused to sign the copy of the district records assembled by Korostelev.

In Tatarstan President Mintimer Shaimiev once said: 'We position the voter, and he votes accordingly. This is a pragmatic approach, and this is how we work with voters.'[16] In voting district No. 2729 of 286 ballots, all but two turned out to have been for Putin. At another district in Tatarstan, voters were given a helping hand. Observer Olga Tarasova of the pro-West Yabloko party noted that extra ballots for Putin were added, and ballots for other candidates were removed, while votes were being counted. Alkhat Zaripov, a 65-year-old resident of a large apartment building in Kazan (Yu. Fyuchik Street, 107), noticed that the voting district showed 209 apartments for his building, while he knew there were only 180. The neighbouring building showed a vigorous 108 additional apartments: up from 17. The *Moscow Times* published a photograph of Pyotr Filippov, a retired 71-year-old resident of the town of Tatrsky Satlyk in Tatarstan, who arrived at the voting district late in the day on March 26 in order to vote for Zhirinovsky, but discovered that someone had already signed for him as having received a ballot.

In the Kaliningrad region, the chair of the electoral committee explained that due to the lack of copy machines, the copies of the records were filled out by hand, and then signed by members of the district committees without being verified.

Even allowing for Russian troops, terminators Putin and Zyuganov proved unexpectedly popular in Chechnya—as it was being pummelled into shape by the military: 191,000 votes for Putin, about 86,000 for the Communist Zyuganov, 35,000 for Yavlinsky, 22,000 for Dzhabrailov. As far as the outcome for the neighbouring Russian Republic Ingushetia (which sided with Chechnya in 1996 and was being treated like Chechnya) was concerned, peace reigned supreme at the ballot box: a miraculous 85% (94,000) of the voters who fought their way to the polling booths were in favour of Putin.

The winner is...

The effect of all the fraud on what would have been the outcome without is not easy to assess. In Dagestan, it seems beyond doubt that the electorate voted for the reactionary Communist Zyuganov rather than Putin. The scale of voting irregularities in Dagestan does not prove, however, that Putin would not have won the first round without fraud. Dagestan is both a 'Communist red' Muslim region, and precisely for this reason, it always votes differently from the rest of the country. In Chechnya figures always seem massaged. In 1996, during the first Chechen War, Yeltsin had received 65.11% in the first round of voting and 73.38% in the second! The Saratov region is perhaps more indicative of Russia as a whole. Had the vote been run without irregularities, it is estimated by some observers, Putin would have tallied about 4% fewer votes in a region in which he won 58% (and these 4% would have gone to the other candidates). In other words, the final outcome would not have changed in the region.

However, the real issue is that 2.94% (2,200,000 votes) made Putin president without the hazard of a second round. Given the level of grass-roots electoral 'organization' achieved by the Kremlin in hostile Dagestan, it is not very hard to reach the conclusion that distortions on this scale took place and a second round should have taken place on 7 May, a month and half later which can be a long time in politics when the media is free to go where it wants.

Perhaps they were concerned about what the still free media might find next. The botched Ryazan affair had suddenly reared to life again. In March 2000, criminal proceedings were initiated against a soldier of 137th Ryazan regiment of the airborne forces 'for stealing... a handful of sugar from an army munitions warehouse.' The regiment was located on the territory of a special base for training intelligence and sabotage units (part of the armed forces secret service GRU), close to Ryazan. In the fall of 1999, private Alexei Pinyaev and a fellow soldier, while guarding 'a storehouse with weapons and ammunition,' went inside a warehouse and saw sacks with the word 'sugar' on them. The two paratroopers cut a hole in one of the sacks with a bayonet and poured some of the state's sugar into a plastic bag. The tea made with the stolen sugar had an odd taste, however, and wasn't sweet at all. The soldiers confessed to their platoon commander. He suspected that something wasn't right, since everyone was talking about the story of the explosions, and he decided to have the 'sugar' checked out by an explosives specialist. The substance proved to be hexogen.

Private Pinyaev had made the mistake of giving an interview in September about this to Pavel Voloshin, a *Novaya Gazeta* journalist. Members of the secret service from Moscow and Tula (where an airborne division was stationed, just like in Ryazan) quickly descended on Pinyaev's unit. Pinyaev and the soldiers who had discovered the hexogen were interrogated because they had 'divulged a state secret.' 'You guys can't even imagine what serious business you've got yourselves tangled up in,' one officer told them. The press, however, was informed that there was no soldier in the unit by the name of Pinyaev, and that information about sacks containing hexogen being found in the military depot had simply been invented by Voloshin, the journalist. Pinyaev's immediate commander and fellow soldiers were sent off to serve in Chechnya. Pinyaev himself was forced to retract what he had said.

Paradoxically, also in March 2000, just before the election and alongside criminal proceedings, the 137th regiment sued *Novaya Gazeta* for printing Pinyaev's interview. The petition invoked 'the protection of honour, dignity and professional reputation,' and was submitted to the Basmansky Intermunicipal Court by the leadership of the regiment. The commander himself, Oleg Churilov, declared that the article in question had insulted the honour not only of the regiment, but of the entire Russian army, since in September 1999, there had not been any such private in the regiment. 'And it is not factually incorrect that a soldier can gain entry to a warehouse where weapons and explosives are stored, because he has no right to enter it while he is on guard duty.'

Probably no one doubts today that Putin would have won the election in the second round no matter what. But at the beginning of 2000, that victory was not a given—at least not to the president's staff or to the 'ministry of elections.' In any case, what Putin had planned for was a presidential inauguration legitimised by an attractive popular vote, and not a long-drawn electoral battle.

The failed secret service-Korzakhov coup of 1996 had finally come to fruition. Under Putin, for the second time in its existence (since the eighteen months of Andropov), the Cheka was leading Russia. A new horizon beckoned.

CHAPTER FIVE

Putin's Kremlin

During the 1999-2000 presidential election campaign, it was difficult to describe and explain Putin as a candidate. He was unknown outside of St Petersburg, if he can be said to have been known at all, which is what made it so hard to say anything good or bad about him. His meteoric rise was largely due to those essential chekist qualities of field operatives: complete loyalty, while favouring the secret service only in cases of a conflict of interest. With so many clans distrusting each other, it was a valuable commodity. As bureaucrat this lack of a profile caused no second look, but as the leader of the Russian Federation it left an empty space where other leading politicians could be placed in seconds. As any new politician, it gave him the benefit of the doubt nationally and internationally. In six short months he became Russia's Pinochet, transforming Yeltsin's legacy.

By definition, chekists have always considered those who are non-aligned (the rest of the Russian population) with suspicion. It is not surprising, therefore, that after coming to power, the corporation's members in Moscow and in local governments, from President Putin on down, have dedicated themselves to intensifying control over the population ('the vertical of power'), confiscating property (doing away with inconvenient oligarchs), planting secret service agents in the enemy's ranks (the officers of the active reserve), hunting down countless spies employed by an imaginary enemy (most often for the crime for 'divulging government secrets'). While Yeltsin was in charge the 'family', for one, held large swathes of the economy and state. The chekist were one among other groups and did not have absolute control. Influential positions could still be handed out to those who had no ties to them.

In his inaugural speech on May 7, 2000, Putin set out what he wanted to do and focused on the importance of preserving Russia’s unity and consolidating the government. What he meant became a little clearer a week later. (No, one of course, was aware how masterfully Putin had in a month turned the unruly elite of the secret service when he was first appointed.) On May 13, Putin signed a decree creating seven federal districts, with a representative of the president in each of them. On May 17, he addressed the nation on television to announce the beginning of a reform in the structure of federal relations. On May 18, Putin announced his appointments. secret service General Viktor Cherkesov became his representative in the Moscow district. secret service General Georgy Poltavchenko became his representative in the Northwestern District, which included St Petersburg. Three of the five remaining appointees were secret service officers as well.

Putin’s aim was to ‘consolidate government power.’ During the Yeltsin years, the Russian constitution did indeed have a weakness in that they had been created under exceptional historical circumstances and they were meant to suit an unusual president—Boris Yeltsin. Yeltsin endeavoured to create the greatest possible decentralization in Russia. He understood that the Soviet Union had fallen apart in August 1991 because of its excessive centralization, which had turned the USSR into an unmanageable white elephant that could not compete in the modern world. Putin now started moving the clock back.

‘‘Putin’s second most important innovation was a new law on the Federation Council of the Russian Federation. This law replaced the Federation Council, the elected upper chamber of the Russian Parliament, with an appointed one appointed by the president. The mechanism was as follows. The regional heads (governors elected by the regional population) who previously formed the Federation Council were now only given the right to delegate a representative to the new council, after coordinating their nominees with the Kremlin. Some regional heads were not even given the right to put forward their own representative.

Putin’s two-pronged attack at a stroke deprived the elected governors of their power at home and their influence in the capital.

Under the still unrepealed Soviet legal system local projects required the Kremlin's constant approval. Governors could, however, no longer solve local problems they encountered since federal and local government officials now looked to Putin's seven appointees. The federal leadership itself now also found it harder to resolve local issues through the governors' representatives in the Federation Council, since these representatives had no authority at the local level. No one had elected them and consequently, no one supported them.

Obviously, Putin's reforms amounted to constitutional change and required two thirds of the votes in the State Duma. But the proposal to create seven federal districts and to change the status of the Federation Council was not put before the State Duma for review, since Putin did not have two thirds of the votes in the parliament at that time. The Duma should have acted to protect its power, but Putin must have calculated shrewdly that concerted action by squabbling parties was not likely (and he was right).

The rise of Alexander Voloshin

The decree that created seven federal districts was the brainchild of the president's chief of staff, Alexander Voloshin (a member of the original Yeltsin family). This decree put all government power in the country into his hands. Stalin never even dreamed of the powers that Voloshin allocated to himself. The seven 'vice-presidents' inserted between the elected president and the 89 elected regional governors reported directly to Voloshin. The deputies of the seven 'vice-presidents also reported to the presidential Chief of Staff, as did their regional office. Likewise representatives in the Federation Council were appointed and dismissed 'at the discretion of the president's chief of staff'.

The annihilation of the power of the Federal Council and the local governors couldn't have been more devastating. But Voloshin, in fact, held a grudge against the Federation Council. It was he who had been deputized by Yeltsin to persuade the Federation Council to remove General Prosecutor Skuratov from his post after he started corruption investigations against the Kremlin. His speech before the Council, which was broadcast over the whole country, turned into a catastrophic defeat for Yeltsin. Voloshin, a bureaucrat through and through, turned out to be a worthless public speaker and was unable to put two words together. His speech was so unconvincing that the Federation Council voted against Skuratov's dismissal, and he was only removed when Putin's secret service released for viewing by public a compromising videotape of him with two call girls.

The legislative packet of regional reforms that was submitted for parliamentary review to the Duma was the third and final piece of the chekist plan. This entailed creating the right for the federal government to dissolve local legislative assemblies in the event that Moscow found their decisions to be at variance with federal law. It was a popular bill proposed primarily in order to safeguard the federal government against situations such as Chechnya, in which the legislative assembly had decided to secede from Russia (flying in the face, ostensibly, of the groundswell of popular support for Putin shown later in the elections).

The immunity of elected officials was also changed. Putin claimed the right to dismiss elected officials, including governors, on the advised of the prosecutor's office, both on the local and on the federal level. In a country where the prosecutor's office was one of the most corrupt parts of the government, the new law meant that the President would always be able to get prosecutors to agree to remove an obstreperous elected official. Finally, but not least of all, the federal government could now regulate laws and control local governments 'in cities of federal significance, capitals and administrative centres..., cities with a population over 50,000, border territories, closed administrative-territorial formations, closed military settlements.' In other words, the federal government got back direct control over almost all of Russia.

Solzhenitsyn

Putin's proposed legislation was duly confirmed by the Duma. The painstaking restoration of central government met no significant opposition and became a subject of discussion during Putin's first visit to writer and Nobel Prize winner Alexander Solzhenitsyn—of whom Putin said he had always been a great admirer. It was a magnificent publicity coup to get the seal of approval from the man who had opposed absolute power most famously. Putin visited Solzhenitsyn at his home on September 20, 2000, and had a long conversation with him. Looking at the famous portrait of Pyotr Stolypin that hung on the wall in the writer's office, Putin asked: 'Is that your grandfather?' Solzhenitsyn gently corrected him and told him that the man in the portrait was Stolypin, a prime minister in pre-Revolutionary Russia.

As always, Putin made an excellent impression on the elderly dissident. Solzhenitsyn's praise was ecstatic and widely publicised throughout Russia. 'His arguments are weighed with extreme care,' 'his mind is quick and alert,' 'no personal thirst for power, intoxication with power or with being in power,' 'self-regulation is the foundation of our existence.... He really understands and knows this. On this point, we were in remarkable agreement.'

Afterwards, Solzhenitsyn understood that, precisely in the matter of self-regulation, he had been the victim of a cheap stunt. Sozhenitsyn's interview with *Moskovskiye Novosti* on June 19-25, 2001, in which he said as much, was not reported elsewhere. 'I did indeed give him a few pieces of advice,' Solzhenitsyn said. 'But I have not seen him follow any of them. Of course, he agreed about self-regulation. But who would disagree about self-regulation? No one. Everyone praises it. And no one wants to promote it. On the contrary, they restrain it and choke it. I emphatically asked Putin not to destroy the state ecological committee, the independence of the forest management office. I saw no need whatsoever to wreck the Federation Council. It is completely unclear to me what they created in its place—some kind of intermediary, amoeba-like formation. Yes, I really did tell him what I could. And after that, we had no further contact.' (Putin visited Solzhenitsyn again only in 2007. This time, Solzhenitsyn had swung back to his previous laudatory position. He no longer had critical remarks to make about Putin. His reaction to everything that Putin was doing was positive.)

The assault on the regions

In May-June 2000, Putin began to flex his new regional powers. He repealed various pieces of regional legislation for being at variance with the Russian constitution. On May 11, he repealed statutes in Ingushetia and the Amur region. On May 16, he asked the governor of the Smolensk region to repeal resolutions made by the local executive government because they went against Russian law. On

June 8, he stopped a series of decrees by the president of Adygea, Aslan Dzharimov. On June 30, the stopped certain resolutions made by the Voronezh regional government, under Governor Ivan Shabanov, from going into effect.

Putin made skilful use of stick-and-carrot policies toward regional rulers. Many regional heads were in Yeltsin's position, and could not, under the Constitution, stay in office for a third term. In November 2000, the president's representative in the Duma, General Alexander Kotenkov, helped the governors' lobby to push through a legislative amendment that allowed 16 governors and regional presidents (including, retroactively, the president of Tatarstan, Mintimer Shaimiev) to run for a third term. In January 2001, Kotenkov facilitated the passage of the so-called 'Boos amendment' in the lower house of parliament, which enabled 69 heads of regional executive governments (including Primakov supporter, Yuri Luzhkov) to run for a third term, and 17 of them (including Shaimiev) to run for a fourth term. In return for this favour from Putin, Yuri Luzhkov gave the president control over his party in the Duma, Fatherland. On April 12, 2001, Fatherland merged with Unity into a single pro-Putin party. (Putin made no less skilful use of the conflicts between Yeltsin's entourage and the oligarchs, on the one hand, and the 'chekists', the secret service-KGB officers who he was bringing into the government, on the other), to whittle down the importance of the family.

Not an imperialist by conviction, Putin saw no reason at all to hold on to the diaspora of Russians who had not returned after the Soviet collapse from the former Soviet republics. It was a large group that the secret service neither wanted nor had infiltrated. On September 1, he signed a decree establishing the State Council, a new advisory organ consisting of the heads of the executive governments of all of the regions of the Russian Federation. On December 5, he withdrew the Federation from the Bishkek agreement on visa-free travel by citizens of the twelve members of the Commonwealth of Independent States (CIS). Foreign passports and foreign visas once again became necessary. As a pat to the army's sentiments about this, Putin changed the national symbols in the same month. The three-colour flag chosen under Yeltsin remained the flag of the Russian Federation. The two-headed eagle of pre-Revolutionary Russia remained Russia's coat of arms. But the red banner of Soviet times became the official banner of the Russian army, and the old anthem of the Soviet Union became the new national anthem—with the words changed where they referred to the defunct USSR.

On May 31, 2001, Putin signed a new citizenship law (passed by the Duma on April 19 and approved by the Federation Council on May 15). This law put former citizens of the USSR, including Russian emigrants (over 20 million Russians), on the same footing as all other foreigners if they wished to obtain Russian citizenship. As a result, tens of thousands of Russian army personnel—who prior to entering the military had had permanent resident permits in former Soviet republics that had separated from Russia—lost their Russian citizenship. During a visit to Moscow by the president of Turkmenistan, Saparmurat Niyazov, on April 10, 2003, Putin agreed to dissolve the Russian-Turkmen agreement on dual citizenship. On April 22, Niyazov signed a decree that gave holders of two passports two months to decide which of the two countries they wanted to be citizens of. After the end of this period, Russian citizens who lived in Turkmenistan and had Turkmen citizenship automatically forfeited their Russian citizenship. About 100,000 people lost their Russian citizenship as a result of this law.

Lawlessness

A crucial area for Putin's plans were the laws governing Russian citizens. There was the system of 'understandings' that had emerged unofficially after the soviet collapse. However, as none of the soviet laws had ever officially been repealed, Putin and the government that he headed had, in effect, acquired the ability to destroy any opponent by investigating the victim's economic activities during the 1990s. Everyone in Russia was after all guilty of something during those years, and whatever it was could be levelled at them at any citizen whenever this was convenient. There was no need to create new laws—which the Duma, filled with particularly successful economic criminals, would have blocked. All that was required was selecting an appropriate charge from the many. Judicial and law enforcement officials, appointed by the president, now began to investigate and prosecute actively the economic activities of the Russian population during the period of 1991-2000.

The problem, of course, was that these officials (and indeed the

President himself) were as guilty as any Russian—probably more so given their valuable closeness to the state's prize possessions. They had committed and contributed to the most rapacious economic 'crimes' of the previous decade. In fact, given that all property under the Soviet union was state property, they were probably the greatest bandits among the Russian population.

But the solution Putin found for the conundrum was elegant and simple. In May-June 2000, the president-controlled State Duma passed a resolution to pardon all Russian citizens for past crimes who had been decorated with government awards. It was a brilliant move, as this meant amnesty for all government officials, including the members of the Duma. Every official who had spent any length of time in either central or local government had received at least one government award, either during Soviet times or during the Yeltsin years. Essentially, the government had declared a qualified amnesty for its own members and put on notice anyone outside that they now had a big problem.

Mikhail Khodorkovsky—the arrested and convicted head of the Yukos Oil Company, one of the largest oil companies in the world before its forced dissolution—was less fortunate. Although Khodorkovsky had become an 'oligarch' and a billionaire over the years, he had nonetheless remained a private entrepreneur, not a government official. The Russian court (which is not that free or independent) found Khodorkovsky guilty of numerous violations committed by him and his company during the tumultuous preceding decade, and convicted him. By contrast with Khodorkovsky, Vasiliy Shakhnovsky, a former top official in the Moscow mayor's office, was not arrested. After leaving government service he became the owner of 7% of Menatep, the Gibraltar-based offshore bank that owned Yukos. Moreover, it was none other than Shakhnovsky—as an employee of Moscow city government—who had overseen the transfer of Yukos's Moscow holdings to Menatep. In other words, it was pretty obvious why Shakhnovsky had received 7% of the shares.

Putin was also covered by the pardon. By the time when the Russian parliament passed the amnesty law in June 2000, he had been decorated with the Order of Honour. His earlier activities in St Petersburg and Moscow could no longer serve as grounds for criminal prosecution against him by foes or friends. This was no small measure, as the question marks surrounding these activities proved to have a long and sticky tail. In August 2000 the newspaper *Sovershenno Sekretno* published an article about the cocaine trail to Europe through Russia. The narcotics trade was conducting operations on a very large scale: the shipments which were apprehended in Europe were hundreds of kilograms in size. However, there had been no evidence for the existence of a Russian delivery channel until a container with Columbian 'canned meat' was seized near Vyborg in February 1993. The weight of the cocaine packed inside jars amounted to a colossal 1,092 kilograms. The participants at the bottom rung of the operation—Russian, Columbian, and Israeli citizens—were arrested. But the organizers of the sale escaped.

The cocaine, obviously, was not meant for poverty-stricken Russia. The 'canned meat' was supposed to be delivered to Germany. The shipment was being monitored by European security services who were conducting an operation with the aim of uncovering the entire narcotics network that stretched from Columbia to Germany. In Germany, the cocaine was supposed to have been apprehended and destroyed, and all of the participants in the crime were supposed to have been arrested. Everything turned out quite differently, though. The cocaine was apprehended by the Russian security services instead. The drugs were stored for over two years at a warehouse in St Petersburg, although they were supposed to be destroyed. In 1996, when Putin moved to Moscow, they were shipped to Moscow, too, 'for further work'. No one heard anything about the cocaine ever again.

After the ton of cocaine was impounded in 1993, the heads of the drug trade created a whole network of companies in St Petersburg and Moscow, including a joint venture involving Putin's IRC. Foremost among these was the Belgian company DTI, created by Oskar Donat. Donat was arrested in Israel as a suspect in the Vyborg cocaine case, but soon released for lack of evidence. Suspicion had arisen because it was his company, DTI, which was supposed to deliver the Columbian 'meat products' from St Petersburg to Holland. Yuval Shemesh was a partner of Donat's family in this business. Shemesh was one of the people arrested and subsequently convicted on charges of organizing the delivery of the cocaine to Europe. Donat's and Shemesh's joint company JT Communications Services created one of the largest paging enterprises in St Petersburg and Moscow, a legitimate business. It was in order to provide for clandestine activity that DTI opened one of the largest customs terminals in St Petersburg. DTI's principal partners in this connection were the Security Association of the Directorate of Internal Affairs for St Petersburg and the Leningrad region and the Special Department of the St Petersburg military-naval base.

Other fortunate recipients of the amnesty were the children of Prime Minister Viktor Chernomyrdin and the children of the long-time head of Gazprom's board directors Rem Vyakhirev who had become major shareholders in Gazprom by the end of Chernomyrdin's tenure as prime minister. The case of army general Alexander Starovoitov, the head of the FAPSI (the former KGB department that intercepts communications and is, since 2003, once again part of the secret service), dragged on for several years. He was suspected of receiving a 20% commission fee on all purchases that his agency made from the German company Siemens. Siemens paid the commission fee officially, in accordance with its contract with FAPSI. Starovoitov, on the other hand, did not deposit these payments into treasury coffers. Repeated attempts were made to put him on trial for bribe-taking, but all of them came to nothing. While preventing uproar among his supporters, it was open season on any businessman, however.

Many factions shared their hatred of those who had made vast fortunes since 1991, but they distrusted each other even more. The way the Kremlin carefully picked his way through the fog was patient and methodical. This was a result of the fact that the main clans and groups had coalesced around the person of Putin.

But this did not mean that all interests were harmonized and that the new president's collaborators were monolithic in character. It merely meant that the Kremlin understood their agendas better than they each others.

When Vladimir Putin came to power, he did not become a sovereign ruler who made all decisions independently without taking the opinions of his entourage into account. Like other Pinochets in history, he did not enjoy—and continues not to enjoy—the nitty gritty of politics: the day-to-day government of the country. It is enough to notice how the traffic jams that paralyze one third of Moscow appear and disappear when the president drives to work and when he drives back home. The morning traffic jam usually occurs not before 11 a.m. when the president is driving to the Kremlin. Often, another traffic jam occurs as early as 5-6 p.m.—the president is coming home. Much more than political power, he enjoys a healthy way of life and sports.

In the tested tradition of the KGB, Putin always surrounded himself by workaholic collaborators—such people as Alexander Voloshin, Dmitry Medvedev, Vladislav Surkov, or Dmitry Kozak. These trusted lieutenants were on Putin's inner circle. Together they got work done through four administrative-economic clans: the 'old family' clan (inherited from Yeltsin); the 'St Petersburg economists,' or the 'Chubais clan' who were the architects of the new economy); the ascendant 'new Petersburg' or the 'Petersburg chekists' (*Novaya Gazeta* proposed the term 'junta' for this group); and the mayor's office in Moscow (Luzhkov's clan in the capital). New in the president's entourage are yet another influential clan—the clan of the 'Petersburg lawyers' (headed by Dmitry Medvedev, the man President Putin proposed as his successor). Each of these clans has commercial interests that it controls, and each of them has its own political instruments in the form of parties, Duma factions, and deputy coalitions. They are distinguished by their practical policies, by their preferred strategies, and in part by their ideologies.

All groups were rallied to clamp down on the businessmen without government posts. On June 19, addressing the Chamber of Commerce and Industry, Putin called on entrepreneurs who had taken their capital out of the country to bring it back to Russia, promising that they would not be penalized: 'The government must not pester people and ask where they got their funds if it itself was unable to ensure normal conditions for investment.' But Putin threatened sanctions if the entrepreneurs refused to bring their money back: 'I'm not going to say that your assets will be frozen tomorrow, but if decisions of this sort start being made.... you will choke on all the dust you'll swallow running around from court to court to have your assets unblocked.'

The background of the speech was the recently begun attack on Vladimir Gusinsky's media empire. His was the best established Russian power house since 1991 when, with a branch of the secret-service active reserve, he had vied for Yeltsin's power with the then official secret-service head, General Khorzakov. But Gusinsky had supported rival factions Primakov and Mayor Luzhkov in the presidential elections and made himself a personal enemy of both Putin and Voloshin through the attacks aired on his NTV, Russia's favourite TV channel, that were as partisan as those on Berezovsky's ORT channel, finding no fault with Putin. Having bet on the right horse, none of the other clans, of course, minded that Gusinsky's empire had to be sunk and regrouped. There was only a minor hiccup. It turned after his arrest that Gusinsky had been decorated with an Order of Friendship by Yeltsin. Any criminal prosecution was doomed to fail due to the amnesty. Consequently, he was merely 'asked' to hand over his property and leave the country—which he did.

The fall of Alexander Voloshin

At the same time, Putin entered into conflict with the other leading Russian tycoon, Boris Berezovsky, who spent many month abroad since he had been warned in 1998 by Alexander Litvinenko about the secret service assassination plot. Berezovsky did not like what the candidate he had supported so unswervingly was doing, and he and his media empire had publicly rebuked Putin on the creation of the seven federal districts, the dismissal of the Federation Council and other political matters.

Perhaps most damagingly for the image the Kremlin was building for Putin, was Berezovsky's unhelpful stance during the president's tactless conduct following the Kursk submarine disaster in August 2000. On August 12, 2000, Putin went on vacation and left for the Russian Riviera at Sochi (at the Bocharov Ruchey presidential residence), and he did not interrupt his vacation after being informed that an explosion had occurred aboard the Kursk submarine in the Barents Sea, killing 118 people. He remained at his residence while the Russian navy pretended to carry out rescue operations (it turned out later that this was a complete sham). On August 22, Putin met with relatives of the members of the submarine's crew in Vidyayevo and promised to rescue the bodies of the dead sailors for burial within a few weeks. When asked what happened to the submarine in a television interview with Larry King on September 8, Putin replied with a smile: 'It sank.' His response threw King and all of America into confusion. The Russian media felt consternated. Berezovsky, who still retained control over ORT at the time, probably could have swayed the management of the television channel to tone down the reporters' response. Instead, he decided not to interfere, and his silence was correctly interpreted by ORT's reporters that no molly-coddling was required. Russia's main television channel criticized Putin with a vehemence unmatched before or since.

It did not take long for the counter blow to land. The Kremlin remembered how brilliantly Berezovsky had conducted Putin's public relations campaign through ORT in 1999-2000; and it remembered the difficulties that had arisen because Putin's political opponents, Primakov and Luzhkov, used Gusinsky's NTV channel against Putin. Watching the anti-Kremlin campaign unleashed by indignant TV reporters on ORT and NTV because of the Kremlin's ineffective response to the Kursk submarine disaster, the Kremlin immediately started taking steps to take Russia's main television channels away from their owners. The person in charge was the Kremlin Chief of Staff, Voloshin. Berezovsky was a former boss, partner and friend and Berezovsky's refusal to submit to Putin's orders was particularly painful as these were relayed most often by Voloshin himself. Relations between Berezovsky and Voloshin became openly hostile.

The third most powerful businessman was Mikhail Khodorkovsky. He thought that under Putin economic power still meant autonomy. The head of Yukos started to compete with the Kremlin politically by giving financial support to the biggest oppositional forces in the Duma, from the pro-West Yabloko to the Communist CPRF. Moreover, at a meeting between Russian entrepreneurs and the president, Khodorkovsky openly challenged Putin by raising the issue of government corruption in the oil and gas industry—the elephant in the room.

The counterblow caught two birds with one stone. Some time before the unexpected arrest an agreement had been reached regarding the sale of 20% of Sibneft's shares to Yukos for three billion dollars. These shares were owned by Roman Abramovich. Khodorkovsky had already transferred money to accounts controlled by Abramovich and was waiting for the transfer of the Sibneft shares. It was at this moment that the government intervened: on October 25, 2003, Khodorkovsky was arrested on charges of tax evasion and fraud. Shortly after, the government cancelled the sale of 20% of Sibneft's shares to Yukos. The shares remained in Abramovich's possession, but Yukos claims the money that he had been paid for them was not given back. Abramovich bought the Sibneft shares that were controlled by Berezovsky for a price and then sold all 100% of Sibneft's shares to Gazprom for about $13 billion. Khodorkovsky learned about all of these mind-boggling developments from newspapers that were delivered to him in his jail cell.

Unfortunately for Voloshin, he became a casualty of the Yukos campaign. Voloshin had agreed to underwrite the deal between Abramovich and Khodorkovsky (for a price) without knowing the unification of Sibneft and Yukos, as had officially been declared, was not going to happen and that instead Gazprom would get the prize. Once he realized that he had been used, Voloshin resigned on October 30. On May 31, 2005, the Khodorkovsky trial ended and the former tycoon was sentenced to nine years in prison. On September 22, 2005, his sentence was reduced by one year. However, it is not likely that Khodorkovsky will ever be released.

The destruction of Yukos and the arrest of Khodorkovsky received a muted response from the majority of Russia's business elite. Realising that without amnesty they could be arrested at any time, they were stunned into silence. In addition, their profit and loss accounts gave them no reason to argue too much. The high price of oil and gas (as opposed to the exceptionally low oil and gas prices during the Yeltsin years) was spelling good news. Under Putin, Russia's GDP grew at an average annual rate of 6.5%, there was a budget surplus and a trade surplus, and the country's gold reserves increased, while its foreign debt fell from 50% of GDP to 30%.

Having sorted out the past, Putin introduced a new tax code with significant reductions in 'circulation taxes' for businesses and a flat personal income tax of 13%. As long as they did their job, Putin would do his. Not much was left of the Yeltsin 'family' after this, and those who continued to see eye to eye with Putin—such as Abramovich—became part of the Putin 'family'. Berezovsky's Unity party, Fatherland and All Russia essentially reconstituted itself under a new name, United Russia, the Putin party.

The Moscow Mayor's office

The more intractable problem was the Luzhkov clan, surrounding the mayor of Moscow. The administrative wing of this clan is represented by the leadership of the Moscow mayor's office—Yuri Luzhkov—the political wing include the Boos-Volodin group within the United Russia party and its economic wing consists of Vladimir Yevtushenkov and Yevgeny Novitsky (Sistema Corporation), Yelena Luzhkova-Baturina (Inteko). In the past, the 'protection' of the mayor's office facilitated the rise of Vladimir Gusinsky (Most Group) and Mikhail Khodorkovsky (Menatep Group). But Gusinsky lost his mayor's office patronage as early as 1995, when Luzhkov became afraid of entering into conflict with General Korzhakov following Korzhakov's anti-Gusinsky raid on Most Bank headquarters in December 1994. Khodorkovsky, after buying Yukos, relinquished his mayor's office patronage on the eve of the Russian financial crisis in August 1998.

Luzhkov had such control over United Russia's Moscow deputies in the Duma that, when the mayor's office needed them, they occasionally rebelled against their overseers from the president's staff. (In fact, the mayor's office has groups of influence in all major political parties, from the pro-Western Yabloko to the Communist CPRF.) Thus, United Russia's Fatherland-All Russia group in the Duma—in which most of Luzhkov's supporters were concentrated in the Duma's third session—and the Moscow deputies from the Regions of Russia group attempted to block a sales-tax cut planned by the Kremlin at the end of 2002 and beginning of 2003 (such taxes are extremely profitable for the capital's treasury). Surkov's admonitions were ineffectual, and it took a personal chat between Putin and Luzhkov to get Boos and Volodin to order their deputies to surrender. Not much later, Alexander Zhukov—one of the most influential and capable lobbyists for the mayor's office in the Duma (elected from the United Russia party, a member of the Regions of Russia group in the former Duma, first deputy speaker in the newly elected Duma)—was appointed to the post of first (and only) deputy prime minister. Despite his generally liberal views, in cases of conflict between liberal theory and 'Moscow's' (i.e. the mayor's office's) practical interests, Zhukov usually sided with the mayor's office in the Duma.

The main propaganda outlet of the Luzhkov clan was the local TVTs television channel, which is expanding its broadcasting facilities to reach the entire country. Media outlets that are controlled by commercial entities with links to the mayor's office included the

Sistema Mass-Media Holding Company (the newspapers *Rossiya* and *Literaturnaya Gazeta*, the Rosbalt news agency, and radio stations Govorit Moskva and Obschestvennoye Rossiyskoye Radio). Luzhkov was also supported by the popular newspaper *Moskovsky Komsomolets* and the Sovershenno Sekretno Holding Company (the newspapers *Versiya* and *Sovershenno Sekretno*).

Nonetheless, the political views of Luzhkov and his circle are in many respects close to those of the siloviki: economically anti-liberal, anti-Western, demanding a more 'active' foreign policy toward the former countries of the USSR and the Balkans, and supporting a full reinstatement of the institution of residence permits (at least in the capital). With respect to his neighbours in the Kremlin, Luzhkov expresses himself even more clearly—to the point of openly raising objections to the 'surrender' of the old Soviet Navy base of Sevastopol to the Ukraine (Sevastopol, of course, is a Black Sea city belonging to the Republic of the Ukraine, although the majority of the population of this city are Russians). The economic views of the Luzhkov and chekist clans were also similar in some respects. Indeed, the chekist wing of the Kremlin was aiming to establish on the scale of the country as a whole the kind of regulated capitalism that already exists in Moscow. The hungry siloviki from St Petersburg envied the overfed bureaucrats from Moscow and were not opposed to giving them a good shake.

Spymania

Under the Kremlin's barrage of Pinochet-like efficiency, the wilfulness and anarchy under Yeltsin dried up, but all traces of good-naturedness vanished as well. As the satirist Viktor Shenderovich, who ran a Spitting Image-like show on Gusinsky's NTV from 1994-2000, remarked, 'the old boss was big, bibulous, and blissful; the new one is small, sober, and mean.'

As early as April 2000, Putin planted a first warning to officials (elected or not), scientists and writers that he was about to take aim at their (sometimes lucrative and extra-curricular activities):

If the minister of foreign affairs is observed maintaining contacts with the representatives of foreign governments beyond the bounds of his official duties, then he, just like all other members of the government, State Duma deputies, leaders of Duma factions, just like all other citizens of the Russian Federation, will be subjected to specific procedures as prescribed by criminal law. And I must say that the latest operations being conducted within the Federal Security Service tell us that this is entirely possible.

Few, except those at the secret service Lublyanka headquarters, would have understood the point of the address. There was no such prohibition in the Criminal Code of the Russian Federation against contact with foreigners. One newspaper joked about the sudden foreign double agents rash in Kremlin bulletins, 'spies don't walk around in herds, but chekists don't know this.'

On September 9, 2000, Putin laid down the 'Doctrine of Informational Security,' which revived elements of state censorship—'in order to make more effective the body of legal limits on access to confidential information.' Relying on this document, the secret service began actively hunting after 'spies', while government officials started zealously protecting government secrets. The secret service was apparently so convinced that most of Russia's citizens were spying on their own country that it published the following announcement on its official website, fsb.ru:

Citizens who collaborate with foreign intelligence services may get in touch the secret service of Russia through a telephone hotline to become double agents. In such cases, the monetary compensation received by such agents from foreign security services will remain unaffected, and they will work with top level secret service employees. Anonymity and confidentiality are guaranteed.

This announcement was accompanied by a section from article 275 (high treason) of the Russian Criminal Code: 'A person who commits the crime described in this article, as well as those in articles 276 (espionage) and 278 (forcible seizure of power or forcible retention of power), will be absolved of criminal responsibility if his actions, by being communicated to the security organs in a voluntary and timely fashion, help to prevent further harm to the interests of the Russian Federation and if his actions do not constitute other crimes.'

Secrets were not those of a Soviet kind. What the Kremlin was concerned about was commercial and defence-related intellectual property leaving the country outside regulated channels. The wave of criminal cases against scientists, military personnel, and government officials began in the 1990s with two chemists who were working on problems associated with developing and destroying chemical weapons, Vil Mirzayanov and Lev Fyodorov. Despite the fact that their guilt could not be proved, Mirzayanov and Fyodorov were held for several months in a pre-trial detention facility. Their crime? They had been arrested for publishing an article in which they described the production of modern forms of chemical weapons in Russia.

For those who would have researched Putin's, the clues were there. At the end of 1995, charges were brought against environmentalist Alexander Nikitin. In February 1996, he was arrested and charged with treason in the form of espionage. The charge was brought by Vladimir Putin's friend Viktor Cherkesov, who was the head of the St Petersburg secret service office at that time. Nikitin had contributed to a report by the environment charity Bellona about nuclear safety in the Northern Fleet. Nikitin spent ten months in the secret service's pre-trial detention facility in St Petersburg until Deputy General Prosecutor Mikhail Katyshev signed an order for his release in December 1996.

Nevertheless, the charges against him were not withdrawn and the environmentalist continued to being harassed by being dragged from court to court for several more years. Then secret service director Vladimir Putin became involved in the trial. 'Our department acts on state interests,' Putin remarked. 'Let me make a comment about Nikitin. What was it that *really happened* in his case? He penetrated the library and obtained information that was *classified*. By the way, in return for this "public service" he received monetary compensation. Of course, there is another question that one might ask: how relevant is this information today? And from the point of view of tact, including international-ecological tact, one can probably consider reducing his punishment. But this is something that the court must decide. Unfortunately, in addition to using diplomatic cover, foreign security services very actively employ various ecological and public organizations, commercial enterprises, and philanthropic foundations. That is why such organizations will always be closely watched by us, no matter how much we are pressured by the media and by public opinion.'[1] In 1999 when Putin was not yet president, Nikitin was finally acquitted of all charges. The information that the secret service and Putin considered 'really classified' had not been found to be such by the court.

An even better indication of the new wind blowing from the

Kremlin was the espionage arrest in April 2000 of Anatoly Babkin, a professor at the Bauman Moscow State Technical University and chair of MSTU's rocket engineering department. Initially, Babkin had been the principal witness in the trial of Edmond Pope, a retired officer of U.S. naval intelligence (Pope was sentenced to 20 years, then pardoned by Putin and repatriated). Babkin had provided the testimony that had proved the American citizen's guilt. However, he had subsequently revoked his statements, claiming that he had given them under pressure and while suffering from a heart ailment. Pope had received documents, and Babkin had provided them, as part of a collaboration agreement between MSTU and Penn State University signed in 1996.

In February 2003, Babkin was convicted of high treason and given a suspended sentence of eight years in prison (in light of the professor's advanced age and reputation). The court found him guilty of passing technical reports about the Shkval rocket-propelled torpedo to American spy Edmond Pope. Babkin was put on probation for five years, stripped of his 'Honoured Science Worker' status, forbidden to engage in professional and scientific activity for three years, and prohibited from being the chair of MSTU's rocket engineering department for another three years.

In 2001, the tsunami of spy arrests started in earnest. The police arrested Viktor Kalyadin, the general manager of Elers-Electron Ltd. Kalyadin was charged with treason in the form of espionage. He was accused of passing classified information to the CIA and sentenced to five years in prison. Also arrested in that year was Valentin Moiseyev, deputy head of the First Asian Department of Russia's Ministry of Foreign Affairs. Moiseyev was accused of passing classified information to South Korean foreign intelligence (he got four-and-a-half years). Yet another official was Alexander Zaporozhsky, former deputy head of the First Department of SVR's Foreign Counterintelligence Directorate. Zaporozhsky was charged passing classified information about the activities and personnel of Russian foreign intelligence to the American security services (he was sentenced to 18 years in prison). The police, furthermore, arrested Mikhail Trepashkin, a lawyer and secret service colonel who had taken part in Litvinenko's press conference in 1998 (he was sentenced and released in 2007).

The Kremlin also clamped down on cases in the courts. In 1997, the Putin-led secret service claimed that Grigory Pasko, a correspondent for *Boyevaya Vakhta*, the newspaper of the Pacific Fleet, had disclosed information about the ways in which the military harmed the environment. Specifically, he was accused of passing classified information to the Japanese about a Russian submarine accident. He was arrested on ten counts of treason in the form of espionage. All of his correspondence had been read, his phone tapped, his apartment bugged, and he himself had been under close surveillance. The materials collected against him, however, contained no evidence that he had intended to pass his writings on to the Japanese media, even though the materials were voluminous. On July 20, 1999, Pasko was convicted of a different criminal charge relating to article 285, par. 1, the abuse of office. Presumably in view of the weakness of the case, he was immediately pardoned and released from custody.

Neither Pasko nor the secret service were satisfied with this outcome: the pardoned Pasko sent an appeal to the Supreme Court's military board (and also brought a suit to protect his honour and dignity against the head of the Pacific Fleet's regional secret service directorate, Rear Admiral Nikolai Sotskov), while the Pacific Fleet's regional secret service directorate sent the military board a protest against an 'unjustifiably lenient' sentence. With Putin's new directive on 'secrets' in place, the climate had changed, however.

On December 25, 2001, Pasko was found guilty of espionage and sentenced to four years in a maximum security prison. On January 15, 2002, at a press conference in Paris, President Putin said on the matter that he did not consider it feasible to interfere with the actions of the judicial system, but that he would be willing to consider Pasko's appeal for clemency if the latter were to submit such an appeal to him. In his remarks, Putin emphasized—as he had done in the case of Nikitin—that Pasko had been charged with passing documents marked 'classified' to foreign citizens for monetary compensation.

The misleading impression given by Putin was that this had been established as a fact in court, and was no longer contested by anyone, not even Pasko's lawyers.[2] In fact, on February 13, 2000, the Russian Supreme Court had ruled that the Ministry of Defence had had no authority to classify the information Pasko was investigating. Pasko never did submit an appeal for clemency to Putin. He was nonetheless released early by the Ussuriysk Municipal Court on January 23,

2003 after two-and-a-half years in prison.

Another trophy case in the courts in 2001 was that of Igor Sutyagin, head of military-technological and military-economic policy studies at the Institute of the United States and Canada where he had taught as a volunteer since 1994. He had been arrested on October 27, 1999, at his home in Obninsk (the warrant for his arrest was issued two days later). Sutyagin was charged with spying for the United States. Specifically, he was accused of selling classified information to U.S. military intelligence officers Nadya Locke and Sean Kidd, who were working under cover at Alternative Futures, a British consulting firm.

The secret service accused Sutyagin of criminal activity on five different counts: he was charged with having had five meetings with members of foreign security services and with having passed on to them information about five different topics. This information concerned the RVV-AG air-to-air missile and the Mig-29 SMT airplane. In addition, according to the prosecution, Sutyagin had conveyed information about the plans for Russia's strategic nuclear forces until 2007, about the Defence Ministry's work to develop permanent readiness units, and about the structure and current state of Russia's early warning system. The prosecution also alleged that, while Sutyagin was employed as a teacher at the Russian navy's Obninsk Educational Centre, he had solicited information from servicemen who attended classes at the centre with a view.

In 2001, Sutyagin was transferred to the Lefortovo pre-trial detention facility in Moscow after the Kaluga Regional Court determined that the agency which had carried out the preliminary investigation had violated criminal and procedural laws in appointing experts and obtaining expert opinions about the facts of the case. The court had ordered the case back for further 'investigation'. On March 15, 2004, Igor Sutyagin's trial in the Moscow Municipal Court finally began. On April 7, the court sentenced Sutyagin to 15 years in a maximum security prison.

Throughout these years, Sutyagin had insisted that he had no access to government secrets and had used only public sources in his studies. His innocence was supported by the Public Committee for the Defence of Scholars, the organization which had been founded on October 2, 2002, a year into the Kremlin's witch hunt on academic 'spies', by a group of scholars and members of public organizations.

On April 23, 2004, it sent an open letter to the Council of Europe in defence of Igor Sutyagin:

Even trial by jury turns out to be merely a clever imitation of fairness and justice if the case in question has been initiated by the secret service. Such, at any rate, was the trial of Igor Sutyagin. There was not even a hint of putting the two sides on an equal footing: all of the prosecution's wishes were satisfied, while the legitimate demands of the defence were ignored. The jury's unanimous votes on questions that distorted the meaning of the charges cast doubt on its independence. Even in theory, a group of 12 people could not have unanimously voted in favour of the prosecution's dubious evidence....'

The letter was signed by Vitaly Ginzburg (Nobel laureate, member of the Russian Academy of Sciences), Lev Ponomarev (National Movement for Human Rights), Sergei Kovalev (human rights activist), Grigory Pasko, Yuri Ryzhkov (member of the Russian Academy of Sciences), Alexei Simonov (Glasnost Defence Foundation), Ernst Cherny (human rights activist), and Father Gleb Yakunin (human rights activist).

On February 16, 2001, the police arrested another academic 'spy', the physicist Valentin Danilov, director of the thermophysics centre at Krasynoyarsk State Technical University (KSTU). In 1999, Danilov, representing KSTU, had signed a contract with the Lanchzhou Physics Institute of the China Aero Space Corporation to manufacture a research stand relating to satellites that are impacted by plasma in space. The scientist was arrested and put in Krasnoyarsk's pre-trial detention facility.

According to the secret service, Danilov had given the Chinese Russia's classified technological plans. But Danilov said he had ample evidence they had been declassified eight years earlier. After one-and-a-half years in prison, Danilov was released from custody (though the charges were not dismissed). During this whole time, the secret service had been unable to present any conclusive evidence of the physicist's guilt.

Danilov subsequently ran for the State Duma as a deputy from Yenisey electoral district No. 48. He lost the election, however, with only 6.42% of the vote. Nonetheless, in December 2003, Danilov was acquitted by a jury of all charges. Eight of the twelve jury members had found the prosecutor's office's evidence unconvincing and cleared the physicist of all charges. This prompted Danilov to comment critically that a satellite that had been created jointly by China and the European Space Agency (ESA) could have been created by China and Russia, since the Russian plans were better than those of the ESA. In January 2004, the Krasnoyarsk prosecutor's office appealed Danilov's acquittal. The Russian Supreme Court sent Danilov's case back to the lower court and in November 2004, he was convicted of spying for China and sentenced to 14 years in a maximum security prison.

Having set the bar so low, the courts accepted that any type of information could be deemed a secret. On December 15, 2002, secret service director Patrushev announced that the government was refusing to extend the visas of 30 Peace Corps volunteers (the Peace Corps had been working in Russia without any obstacles since 1992) because they had been 'collecting information about the sociopolitical and economic situation in Russia's regions, about government employees and administrators, and about the course of the elections.' Patrushev portrayed this refusal as a victory for the secret service in its battle against foreign spies in Russia. In 2007, the Novosibirsk region's secret service office initiated criminal proceedings against Igor and Oleg Manin, two employees of Novosibirsk State Technical University. The secret service's investigators had found classified materials in a book which the scientists had published for the fiftieth anniversary of the Siberian branch of the Russian Academy of Sciences. They were able to retrieve all 50 copies of 'the book of secrets.' As President Putin has said, 'Comrade wolf knows whom to eat. He eats and doesn't pay attention to anyone.'

The St Petersburg chekists

One of the reasons why Putin's ideological programme is so difficult to fathom is because it is no more than a managerial programme: the centralization of secret service control over all organizations, associations, parties, and groups. There are no goals as such, apart from inserting an secret service hierarchy and taxing (in whatever form) revenue. The objectives of Russia's security services were circulated explicitly in a memo obtained by Moskovskiye Novosti (published on October 8, 2002). In this brief, unnamed top officials recommended that former employees of Russia's security services 'directly embed themselves... in economic, commercial, entrepreneurial, and banking organizations, regulatory agencies, and organs of the executive government.' 'Creating cover organizations and firms,' the document stated, 'will make it possible to increase contacts with entrepreneurs and businessmen through such organizations, to establish a broad agent network, and to obtain information of operational interest through direct access to relevant documents.'

Thus, after March 2000, a great number of secret service officers, active reserve officers, and other law enforcement personnel—from the prosecutor's office, the police, and the army—flooded into the government at the local and federal level. It is difficult to trace all of the new promotions and appointments because not all former or currently active state security agents advertise their departmental affiliation.

At the Kremlin, the clan of the 'Petersburg chekists' were in charge of the embedding. The policy was initiated by secret service General Viktor Ivanov. After the quick demise of non-secret service workhorse Voloshin in the Yukos cross fire, it was Ivanov who promoted secret service officers—naturally, with the president's knowledge—to all vacant positions. Due to this network of loyalties, he is probably the most powerful of the entire clan while Putin is in power. Others powerful St Petersburg chekists are the Aide to the President Igor Sechin (who represents the President in the secret service), Director of the secret service Nikolai Patrushev, former Minister of Internal Affairs and speaker of the newly elected Duma Boris Gryzlov, former Minister of Defence Sergei Ivanov, Deputy Director of the secret service Yuri Zaostrovtsev, Director of the Federal Protection Service (FSO) Yevgeny Murov. Many of this clan's members (such as Ivanov, Gryzlov, Patrushev) were closely linked by their overlapping positions as secret service co-founders of a raft of lucrative commercial entities (Blok, Borg, Teleplus, and other companies) under the aegis of the St Petersburg International Relations Committee led by Putin.

Intelligence led-interests, such as the state system of arms production and trade, are under the administrative control of the chekist clan as well. In particular, Viktor Ivanov heads the board of directors of the Almaz-Antey Air Defence Concern, formed after the Antey Concern merged with Almaz (producers of air defence technologies). The clan has close ties with the following major entrepreneurs:

bankers Sergei Pugachev and Sergei Veremeyenko (Mezhprombank), oil magnates Vagit Alekperov (Lukoil), Sergei Bogdanichikov (the state-owned company Rosneft), Vladimir Bogdanov (Surgutneftegaz), Gennady Timchenko (Kirishineftekhimexport).

As Putin does not interfere with the detail how the clans use their clout, they are free to compete with other clans in politics. The chekist clan had initially chosen the People's Party of the Russian Federation (NPRF) as its central political tool (the party had actually been created under top Putin aide Vladislav Surkov's patronage, but he had no use for it and abandoned it). However, the NPRF failed to pass the five-percent threshold, although it did manage to get two dozen of its single-member constituency candidates elected to the Duma. Because there was no possibility of creating even a separate deputy group out of the NPRF deputies, most of them were herded into the United Russia faction.

While cultivating the NPRF, the St Petersburg chekist did not neglect to work on United Russia as well. Initially, Vladimir Bespalov, an old colleague of Putin's from the St Petersburg NDR office, was delegated to take over the party. The task proved too much for him and he was transferred to Gazprom, while Viktor Ivanov's protégé Valery Bogomolov became the secretary of United Russia's general council. The party's former leader, Boris Grzylov, was brought back to party work, becoming the head of the party's Supreme Council, initially while still remaining head of the Ministry of Internal Affairs.

In the regions, the chekists prefer to bulldoze over all obstacles, without being particular about their means; they replace governors at will—as long as they have people available. It was the chekists—on orders from the vengeful Putin, who never forgave governor Rutskoy his harsh criticism of the handling the Kursk submarine disaster—who overthrew Rutskoy in the city of Kursk, forced the Ingushes to accept Zyazikov, schemed against Mikhail Nikolaiev in Yakutia, and attempted to unseat Kirsan Ilyumzhinov in Kalmykia and Murtaza Rakhimov in Bashkiria. They have enjoyed relatively peaceful successes as well: the gubernatorial victories of secret service agents Viktor Maslov in the Smolensk region and Vladimir Kulakov in the Voronezh region (the latter has by now won twice), as well as the election of General Vladimir Shamanov as governor of the Ulyanov region.

The chekists are, not without reason, considered to be the source of President Putin's 'new course' initiative—the policy of reorganizing the 'protection' arrangements of various economic entities on the pretext of restoring rule of law. First, the chekists destroyed Gusinsky's media business, instigated a rupture between Putin and Berezovsky (Putin himself, of course, welcomed such a rupture), and pushed Berezovsky out of Russia. Then they attacked Vladimir Potanin's Interros, a business that had expanded under Chubais's patronage, and evidently subordinated Potanin to their own agenda (in return for his understanding, they supported the candidacy of Potanin's partner Khloponin in the gubernatorial election in the Krasnoyarsk region). The partly state-owned Gazprom was swept clean of private commercial hangers-on associated with Chernomyrdin-Vyakhirev (Itera) and then connected with other commercial hangers-on (Eural TG).

One of the subdivisions of the chekist clan (Yu. Zaostrovtsev and his allies in the General Prosecutor's Office) played an excessively obvious and active role in the rivalry to offer 'protection' to the furniture import business, coming into conflict with the interests of the Yeltsin 'family's' Customs Committee (M. Vanin). The scandal surrounding two companies (Tri Kita and Grand) became an example of the open rivalry between government law enforcement agencies over the right to offer protection to businesses. The Customs Committee was ostensibly trying to convict lawbreaking businessmen, while the secret service and the General Prosecutor's Office were defending them and trying to convict the prosecutors who were trying to convict the businessmen.

The clan of St Petersburg lawyers

As the members of the chekist clan are not selected for their brilliance but for their ability to follow orders, the brains of the Kremlin is formed by Putin's work horses, the St Petersburg Lawyers. They are the people he most trusts and relies on—not being chekists themselves they have very little room for manoeuvre without the patronage of Putin. Most of them once attended the law faculty of Leningrad State University, or indeed studied with Sobchak who gave Putin his job when he returned from Dresden. This group included the co-owner of the Ilim Pulp Corporation, Dmitry Kozak;

the then-speaker of the St Petersburg city legislature, Yuri Kravtsov; the speaker of the Federation Council, Sergei Mironov; and the head of the Vozrozhdenie Peterburga Corporation, Yuri Molchanov (currently deputy governor of St Petersburg and former pro-rector of Leningrad State University, who recommended Vladimir Putin to Anatoly Sobchak in 1990). Viktor Zolotov, head of Putin's personal security service, is also close to this group. Dmitry Medvedev; the head of the legal committee of the St Petersburg mayor's office, however, is the most important of the group. After becoming president, Putin brought Medvedev and Kozak to Moscow. In January 2004, Valery Nazarov, the former head of the St Petersburg Committee on City Property Management, who is also considered to be close to Kozak and Medvedev, was transferred to Moscow as well.

As a graduate student, Medvedev studied with Sobchak and was the informal head of Sobchak's election campaign for the Soviet Union parliament in 1989. He also served as the legal expert for Putin's International Relations Committee. His legal creativity has been one of the greatest boons to Putin in steering a way through the trench warfare of the clans. Medvedev is considered to have invented a widely used method by which government organs could legally become co-founders and co-owners of joint stock companies: namely, by contributing their share of a company's statutory fund in rent payments that were due to them. He was one of the first people in St Petersburg, and in Russia as a whole, who figured out how the government could 'join' a joint-stock company without breaking existing laws: not by contributing land or real estate, but by contributing rents on land and real estate.

From this lucrative time, Medvedev has his own souvenirs. On April 30, 1992, the Ilim Pulp Enterprise (IPE), a Russian-Swiss joint enterprise, was registered with the International Relations Committee (registration number AOL-1546), with a fund of 1,000,000 rubles. The manager in charge of legal issues was Dmitry Medvedev. IPE became one of the co-founders of the previously registered Rus' insurance company, founded in 1990 by A. Krutikhin. Some time later, the joint enterprise limited liability partnership Ilim Pulp Enterprise was re-registered as a closed joint stock company, no longer with the International Relations Committee, but now with the participation of the closed joint stock company Fincell, 50% of whose shares were owned by Dmitry Medvedev.

When Voloshin's star fell due to the Berezovsky-Abramovich struggle over Yukos, Dmitry Medvedev was promoted to the powerful post Voloshin had created for himself. Medvedev began playing his own game in regional politics (as Putin would expect him to). His approach was entirely in keeping with the traditions of the workaholic but generally cautious Alexander Voloshin. When the chekists were ready to pounce on Bashkir president Rakhimov: they didn't allow him to deny his opponents the right to register, caught him printing additional voting ballots that were to be used to falsify election outcomes, and brought the Bashkiria elections to a seemingly impossible second round. It was only a short step to the 'liberation of the Bashkir nation from the criminal regime of Rakhimov' by the Kremlin, but at the last moment Medvedev helped convince Putin that the old and reliable Rakhimov was preferable to a new face whose loyalties were untested. Observing the Putin chain of command, the chekists called off their opposition candidate, leaving no one to catch Rakhimov's forgeries and falsifications, and the Bashkir president easily won the second round. (In return Rakhimov thanked the Kremlin with a record-high percentage of votes for Putin in the presidential election.)

Medvedev anointment as Putin's successor to the presidency in 2007 was a Kremlin move that resembled Yeltsin's choice of Putin. Like Putin, he was loyal and possessed the elusive Pinochet quality of making the right decisions. But mostly it was what he was not that appealed most. Those who had a lot to lose under a new President felt happy that Medvedev was not an active secret service reservist (as far as anyone knows). None of the various secret service clans with their vice-like grip on the country felt that the other was being favoured. At the same time, they knew that he lacked a loyal secret service power base of his own to challenge them. In addition, the Kremlin could tow the line to the world and the Russian electorate that there is no question that the secret service controlled the Russian state, economy, and resources.

CHAPTER SIX

The Magic Wand

'People who came to power by relying exclusively on TV are doomed to see TV the way Ivan the Fool saw the magic wand in the fairy tale. If the magic wand is theirs, then everything will be all right; if someone steals it, then everything is over.'
Yulia Latynina, *Novaya Gazeta*

After the successful re-election of Yeltsin in 1996, the Kremlin had grudgingly come to see a free media as a counter weight of sorts against the clan power that surrounded it. Not that it had a particular liking for the media, but on the whole it had proved to be a necessary (and sometimes useful) evil. But this changed in 2000. Putin's Kremlin no longer had any real use for it. It wasn't so much ideological concern about the media's influence on the Russian people. The past decade had thrown the electorate into a state of confusion about the new freedoms; it had discovered that real votes meant it was now part-responsible for the chaos at the top. The real issue for the Kremlin was that the secret service had its own, and much more smoothly-run, mechanisms in place to resolve the usual squabble of petty conflicts between the clans. The Russian media raked muck thinly, and mainly as part of the partisan struggle between the clans. But it managed to spread it amply enough to dislocate erratically other lines of command and delicate power balances that were only distantly connected to what was publicised.

A good example of the old media approach under Yeltsin was the 'Khinshtein affair' of January-February 2000. Khinshtein was a widely-read columnist for *Moskovsky Komsomolets* and he published exposés about various figures in the Ministry of Internal Affairs, including ministry head Vladimir Rushailo.

Under Yeltsin, Khinshtein's exposés had a natural place within the political bear pit—they were just another round of ammunition in the fight between the various groups in the Kremlin. In fact, already during the perestroika years, Alexander Khinshtein—a very young reporter at the time—had been talent-spotted by the agents of the central KGB who gathered information on the work of the regional KGB offices. At first, the KGB would itself leak information during the early 1990s. But later it simply enlisted reporters and published materials under their by-line. Khinshtein had thus been tapped by KGB analyst Oleg Mikarenko, and he had not been out of work since the KGB created a PR department to which Mikarenko had been transferred. During 1999 Khinshtein had, for example, taken an active part in the mud-slinging between the various rival parties, lending his support to the Fatherland–All Russia bloc headed by the reactionary Yevgeny Primakov and Moscow mayor Yuri Luzhkov. He repeatedly wrote extremely unflattering pieces not only about 'the family' and 'the family's' Unity bloc, but also about Vladimir Putin. Although Khinshtein had already ceased his attacks on Putin in 2000, Minister of Internal Affairs Vladimir Rushailo assumed that the gadfly editorialist who continued to come after him, could be dislodged quickly and easily. Khinstein had been charged with forging a driver's licence, and attempts had been made to commit him in a lunatic asylum. In the end, however, the minister had to draw in his horns. In the clan tug-of-war, the Kremlin power-seeker Rushailo turned out to have very influential enemies (at the Moscow mayor's office and in the secret service), and the journalist discovered powerful protectors in the secret service.

But now, assembling the media into a unified front was a top priority of President Putin. It was the leading policy for the entire duration of his first term in office. It was more important than 'establishing a constitutional order in Chechnya,' (a matter of great symbolic but not earth-shattering relevance given the diminutive size of the region), and more important than the makeover in federal-regional government relations, more important even than all judicial transformations, far more important than talk of military reform. In no other sphere was the Putin administration's approach as systematic and methodical as in this one. And in almost no other sphere (except perhaps in the fight against Chechen separatists) did Putin display such an active personal interest.

To the extent that this was possible, these operations were portrayed either as a non-political 'property rights conflict' or as a fight against economic abuses. Attempts were made to camouflage Putin's personal involvement, but it was practically impossible to conceal his interest in these matters.

The number of criminal charges filed against reporters and editors during Putin's first term from 2001-2003 was several times greater than in the 1990s. In the far more unsettled 1990s, the initiation of criminal proceedings against a reporter would create a big controversy and be a sufficiently rare occurrence. In 2000, the Centre for Journalism in Extreme Situations counted 19 cases of reporters being accused of crimes; in 2001, it counted 31; in 2002, 49.[1] These tallies merely measure the official proceedings. There were also the unofficial campaigns. These years saw a remarkable increase in criminal actions against representatives of the press and media, particularly in the provinces: murders of reporters (up to two-three per month in the fall of 2003), attacks on reporters, attacks on editorial offices. Hundreds of such episodes are well documented by the Centre. All of a sudden, criminals showed an unprecedented appetite for those with a reporter's card—even though crime rates for ordinary Russians were steadily going down. No investigation of this remarkable rise was undertaken by official crime fighters such as the secret service, the police, or ordered by the Interior Minister.

The Andrei Babitsky affair

The new Kremlin's policy took shape as Yeltsin had barely vacated the presidency. At the beginning of January 2000, Radio Liberty correspondent Andrei Babitsky, known for his reports from Chechnya—which were extremely disagreeable for the acting president and his election campaign—disappeared in Grozny. Radio Liberty's management supposed that Babitsky had most likely been arrested by Russian security services and interned at the Chenokozovo interrogation camp.

The government categorically denied that Babitsky had been arrested, until finally reports began appearing in the Moscow papers from witnesses who had seen federal officers apprehend Babitsky on his way out of Grozny. At this point, Acting General Prosecutor Vladimir Ustinov was forced to admit that, on January 27, 2000, Babitsky had indeed been arrested for criminal breach of 'the rules of conduct for journalists working in a zone of anti-terrorist operations.'

Attempting to blandish Western public opinion, the Putin's assistant Sergei Yastrzhembsky assured everyone who wanted to listen that the Babitsky incident was 'under the personal control' of Putin. Soon, it was officially announced that on February 2, Babitsky had been released on the condition that he not leave the location. In the headlines, Putin had saved the day with his personal intervention.

In the following days there seemed something odd about this new arrangement by the acting president. The 'released' Babitsky failed to get in touch with his family or his co-workers. On February 3, 2000, Babitsky, allegedly with his consent, had been handed over to Chechen 'field commander Sayid Usakhodzhayev' in exchange for a group of Russian prisoners of war who had been captured by Chechen combatants. Anticipating questions about the Putin's 'personal control' of the matter, Yastrzhembsky announced that, from the moment of the 'exchange,' 'the federal government [was] no longer responsible for what happens to Babitsky.'

Footage of the 'exchange,' made by the secret service, was shown on television. Babitsky looked nothing like a person acting on his own free will. On the contrary, it was clear from what could be seen and heard on the footage that the video had been made with Babitsky protesting, and that his transfer to unknown people in masks took place under the escort of federal troops with automatic weapons. The government-released document in which Babitsky gave his consent to be handed over to Chechen combatants was dated January 31, i.e. *before* the date when it was announced that he had been released after promising not to leave the location.

The case got more curious. Both the president of the Chechen separatists, Aslan Maskhadov, and their main propagandist informed Radio Liberty that they knew nothing about any exchange and that there was no field commander with the Uzbek last name 'Usakhodzhayev.' They were unaware of Babitsky's fate following his arrest. All Russian security services and law enforcement agencies denied their involvement in the exchange, including the Ministry of Defence, although defence minister Igor Sergeyev did offer the comment on ORT that he 'wouldn't be sorry to exchange ten Babitskys' for one of his soldiers.

In the independent media—for example, in the *Segodnya* newspaper—speculations began to appear that there had not been any exchange at all: 'someone was [simply] covering their tracks, and not doing a very good job at it.'[2] The Babitsky affair was analyzed most exhaustively on NTV, in the newspapers *Obschaya Gazeta* (a special edition was devoted to the incident), *Novaya Gazeta*, *Segodnya*, *Novye Izvestiya*, *Moskovskie Novosti*, and in the magazines *Itogi* and *Novoye Vremya*. Commentators expressed fears that Babitsky had already been killed by the security services. The likelihood that Babitsky was indeed no longer alive—or would soon cease to be so—was far from negligible. During the first Chechen war ahead of the 1996 secret service putsch led by General Korzhakov, reporter Nadezhda Chaykova had been kidnapped, tortured, and shot. Chaykova was hated by the federal authorities for reporting on war crimes in Chechnya and for not concealing her sympathy toward the idea of an independent Ichkeria. The fact that federal organs were denying their involvement in the 'exchange' gave reason to suspect the worst.

Izvestiya, however, the old Soviet faithful, came to Putin's defence against charges that Putin was responsible for Babitsky's fate:

> There are certain 'hot spot' fanatics who can no longer live without these spots and without the adrenalin that is to be had there.... Meanwhile, the government-guaranteed right to adrenalin has yet to appear in any constitution. At your own risk, please.[3]

Then, on February 7, 2000, Andrei Babitsky—who had officially been handed over to 'combatants', if not with his agreement at least with theirs—was 'called in for questioning' by the General Prosecutor's Office. The prosecutor's office announced for good measure that if the reporter failed to come of his own free will, he would be placed on a wanted list and arrested when found.[4]

All of February, more contradictory information circulated concerning Babitsky's location. From time to time, government officials fed names of Chechen villages in which Babitsky was supposed to be hiding, and of field commanders who were supposedly hosting him. From their end, the separatists stubbornly denied these reports and continued to insist that Babitsky had not been handed over to them.

Finally, on February 25, 2000, it was announced that the reporter had been arrested in Dagestan, while carrying a false passport with another person's name. Babitsky was delivered to the Makhachkala hospital in the trunk of a car by unknown individuals, who had been holding him in a Chechen village after the 'exchange.' In Makhachkala, Babitsky did not immediately turn himself in to the police, but rented a hotel room and made several phone calls, including calls to his wife in Prague and to Radio Liberty in Moscow. After this, he was arrested for carrying a false passport in an extremely short period of time.

In his opinion, the masked combatants to whom he had been handed over by the federal agents were indeed Chechens; however, they were not separatists and Maskhadov-supporters, but on the contrary, combatants with pro-federal leanings who supported some collaborationist field commander. They had tried to pass themselves off as Maskhadov-supporters, and Babitsky had in general pretended that he believed them. Subsequently, just as he had supposed, they turned out to be not separatists but fighters from the armed formation of the Adamallah party, headed by Adam Deniev. Deniev's younger brother, Gazi Deniev, was an active lieutenant colonel in the secret service, while the Adamallah party stood for Chechnya remaining a part of Russia. Deniev's fighters had taken away both of Babitsky's passports—domestic and foreign—and instead had given him a passport bearing his photograph but under an Azerbaijani name, Aliyev.

At the Makhachkala temporary detention facility, Babitsky went on a hunger strike. On February 28, Putin once again personally remarked that he saw no need to keep Babitsky under guard in Makhachkala. On February 29, Babitsky was put on the empty plane of internal affairs minister Vladimir Rushailo and flown to Moscow's Chkalovsky airport, where he was set free, with an injunction not to leave the city. In October of the same year, Babitsky was sentenced for using a false passport, but was pardoned by the court.

At approximately the same time, in October 2000, secret service Lieutenant Colonel Gazi Deniev was shot and killed in Moscow by a businessman from whom he was extorting one million dollars. While the head of the Adamallah party Adam Deniev was blown up by Chechen separatists in April 2001. Whether there was any connection between the Deniev brothers' involvement in the Babitsky affair and their deaths remains unknown.

Babitsky had signed his consent to the 'exchange' without yet knowing that news of his arrest had already got out. Putin's reputation in the West had been saved, and so had Babitsky's life.

The 'Dolls'

The 'NTV affair' effectively began on February 8, 2000, when the newspaper *Sankt-Peterburgskie Vedomosti* published a written declaration by St Petersburg University's Task Force to Nominate Acting President Vladimir Putin for President of Russia.

The authors of the declaration, headed by university rector Lyudmila Verbitskaya and the dean of the law faculty Nikolai Kropachev, expressed grievances against the two latest episodes of Viktor Shenderovich's TV show 'Dolls' (*Kukly*, akin to Spitting Image) on NTV (then still owned by the anti-Putin tycoon Gusinsky), which had left them with 'a feeling of profound indignation and revulsion and [constitute] eloquent examples of the abuse of freedom of speech with which Russian citizens are confronted more and more often in anticipation of the election, however deplorable this may be.'

In the opinion of the professors of Putin's alma mater, their illustrious alumnus had been 'the victim of egregiously vicious and furious defamation that displayed no regard for his dignity and honour.' The law professors spelled out that since this defamation occurred while he was serving in an official capacity (as acting president), the actions of the creators of the show were 'subject to prosecution in accordance with article 319 of the Russian Criminal Code.' And, as the authors of the declaration pointed out, criminal proceedings based on article 319 could be 'initiated regardless of the wishes of the person who has been wronged.'

In this way, the obliging law professors from the university shielded the acting president in advance from the necessity of any personal involvement on his part in the criminal prosecution of NTV and exonerated him of any criticism that such prosecution might draw. But, as the show's creator Viktor Shenderovich wrote, 'there are certain doubts concerning the authorship [of the declaration] (rumour has it that a fax with the text of the letter came from Moscow).'[5]

Verbitskaya and the others were particularly outraged by Shenderovich's fairy tale 'Little Zaches' (based on the story by E. T. A. Hoffmann), whose main character was 'Putin-Zinnober'—an acting president whose hair had been combed with a 'magic television comb.' 'After 'Little Zaches,' Anna Bossart wrote in *Novaya Gazeta*, 'it was as if the character's source of inspiration had declared: 'I'll put him in jail.' Not the author, of course—we have freedom of speech, after all. But the man who owns the store [Gusinsky].'[6] Similar reports reached Viktor Shenderovich: '*Up there* (upward glance), they are particularly offended by the fact that the show's hero turned out to be a creature of diminutive height.'[7]

By this time Putin and his entourage had a whole series of grievances against Gusinsky's media outlets, and first and foremost against the influential NTV channel: NTV coverage of Chechnya was not on message, nor their support for anyone but the non-'family' clan in elections. It didn't help that NTV doggedly tried to find out the truth about the apartment-house bombings in Moscow, and the awkward secret service-organized stockpiling of explosives (or sugar in official readings) in an apartment house in Ryazan—or 'educational tests'—in September 1999.

But the greatest infraction was the stirring in corruption scandals surrounding Kremlin Property Manager Pavel Borodin, Acting General Prosecutor Vladimir Ustinov, the President's Chief of Staff Alexander Voloshin, Prime Minister Mikhail Kasyanov, Deputy Director of the secret service Yuri Zaostrovtsev, and other people close to the president.

At the end of April and the beginning of May 2000, the editors of *Segodnya*—a newspaper belonging to Vladimir Gusinsky's Media Most holdings—wrote and mailed what turned out to be three toxic letters. The first (dated April 28) was sent to the Deputy General Prosecutor, the second (dated May 3) to the Deputy Director of the secret service, and the third (dated April 27) to Vladimir Putin himself, who had already been elected president, but had not yet been inaugurated.

Each of these government officials was presented by the newspaper with several waspish leading questions. For example, the deputy general prosecutor was asked:

Did Assistant General Prosecutor of the Russian Federation

Nikolai Yemelyanov write a report in 1994 about you using your official position in the interests of the Balkar Trading Corporation?

Do you or your close relatives have any relation to Mosstroyeconombank?

With what resources was your son Artur's apartment purchased in 1997, at such-and-such an address?

The Deputy Director of the secret service was asked:

Why did you resign from the secret service in 1993?

What caused your departure from Tveruniversalbank?

What happened to the security and sourcing companies that you founded during your years of commercial activity?

Do you help your father, the founder of the private security company Fort Professional, with his work?

And in a bold letter sent to Putin at the Kremlin, *Segodnya*'s editor-in-chief Mikhail Berger complained that after *Segodnya* became interested in General Zaostrovtsev's past history in business and published an article about it, secret service General Zaostrovtsev began intensively gathering incriminating evidence against the Media Most group. In doing so, Berger stated, 'whenever Zaostrovtsev has tried to exert pressure on the group's subdivisions, he has claimed that with respect to Media Most, he was acting on your'—i.e. Putin's—'personal instructions.'

The Deputy General Prosecutor (Sabir Kekhlerov) was not subtle in his counter blow. He started a criminal investigation against Media Most regarding violation of personal privacy, private correspondence; illegally obtaining and distributing commercial secrets. Two days after Putin's inauguration on May 7, 2000, Media Most's offices were raided and searched on orders of his office.

At first, the masked agents claimed that they were merely the 'tax police,' while the General Prosecutor's Office stated that the search had been carried out as part of a two-year-old criminal case involving an unnamed Ministry of Finance official. But one of the officers in charge of the search admitted in front of a TV camera that he was not from the tax police, but from the secret service. By that evening, the official reason for the searches had changed: it was no longer a criminal case involving a Ministry of Finance official, but 'illegal invasion into citizens' private lives using special technical means' (a charge formulated by Sergei Debitsky, the General Prosecutor's Office's investigator on cases of special importance). The 'illegal invasion into... private lives' seems to have referred to the journalistic investigation into secret service General Zaostrovtsev's business dealings.

The secretariat of the Russian Reporters' Union stated that it viewed this operation as an 'unconstitutional act and an expression of arbitrary rule intended to intimidate the independent media.' Putin, however, categorically denied that the operation had any political subtext. He assured the public that he was an adherent of the principle of free speech. However, he let it be known that he had no intention of interfering in the matter, since the law was the same for everybody, including tycoons such as Gusinsky. The following joke, however, quickly surfaced on the internet: 'Why did the people who raided Media Most wear masks? Because the new president likes to do everything himself.'

On Yevgeny Kiselev's Sunday TV show 'Itogi,' which followed the Thursday raid, all of Media Most's enemies were again given their due: Kekhlerov, and Zaostrovtsev, and the leadership of the secret service in general (for the 'educational' stockpiling of the explosive hexogen in a residential building in Ryazan), and Alexander Voloshin (for his involvement in a swindle), and Mikhail Kasyanov ('Mr. Two Percent'), and Putin himself (for the Babitsky affair). The programme also included an appropriately sombre monologue by Alexander Solzhenitsyn, which had been recorded by NTV on May 4 but was shown only now. And concluding this two-hour-long bout of artillery fire—which delayed all other programming on the network by about 40 minutes—was another acid episode of Viktor Shenderovich's 'Dolls'.

There was no unanimity inside the Kremlin how to deal with 'NTV. The chekists wanted to rely on the law and the prosecutor's office. The more flexible 'family' was willing to employ the carrot as well as the stick. What happened next was described by Viktor Shenderovich, 'in May 2000, Media Most was contacted by a top Kremlin official. During a personal meeting, he produced a list of conditions and said that if they were fulfilled, the attack against NTV would be called off. There were several conditions—changing news policies with regard to Chechnya, stopping attacks against the so-called 'family'—but the first thing on the list was that the president's puppet had to be removed from "Dolls".'[8]

In the next episode of 'Dolls'—with presenter Kiselev's agreement—Shenderovich teasingly observed his Kremlin critics to the letter: in place of the president, the story of the 'Ten Commandments' featured a cloud on a mountain and a burning bush, which were interpreted by Moses-Voloshin as 'simply *Gospod Bog* [the Lord God]. Abbreviated as *GB* [Russian slang for KGB].'

Two weeks later, on June 13, 2000, NTV's owner Gusinsky was arrested for the third time in one month, indicated that the security organs had not been sufficiently prepared: the order to attack had come too suddenly. The journalist V. Kara-Murza was involved in the freeing of Gusinsky. 'We got him released after three days. I called Gorbachev, he called Juan Carlos, and Juan Carlos told Putin that if he, Putin, didn't let Gusinsky go, he himself would regret it later. And Putin was forced to send Minister [Mikhael] Lesin to [Gusinsky's] jail. But he gave him instructions: 'Bargain with him, make sure he gives all those shares away. We'll have to let him go in any case.'[9]

With the scale of attacks on NTV rising, it made the channel's reporters feel like they had nothing left to lose. All of the critical arrows from presenter Kiselev's team were now aimed directly at Putin. On July 15, 2000, 'Dolls' featured another puppet play by V. Shenderovich. This episode was about Girolamo Savonarola (burnt at the stake by his countrymen), who was made to look like President Putin. In Shenderovich's funny and inflammatory satire, the citizens of Florence (who were made to look like Russians) are disappointed that their preacher's fight against the luxury and decadence of the rich has not had any effect on their own lives 'Do something at least!' the Florentines yell at Savonarola. Then one of them flips an hourglass and says: 'Time's up.'

On July 19, 2000, General Prosecutor's Office investigators, accompanied by a car with secret service security agents, paid a visit to the home of NTV's owner Vladimir Gusinsky in the town of Chigasovo outside Moscow. The search was officially called an 'inventory of the property,' and impounded Gusinsky's luxury possessions in connection with the criminal case of 'large-scale embezzlement by means of fraud and breach of trust.'

The sixth protocol

On the following day, Gusinsky signed an agreement to hand over to the Gazprom Media Holding Company all media outlets belonging to Media Most, as payment for (bona fide) debts amounting to $300 million. Minister of the Press Mikhail Lesin participated in the negotiations. At Gusinsky's insistence, he signed the agreement's 'Appendix 6,' It stipulated that, in lieu of Media Most's agreement to pay back these debts, the criminal case against Gusinsky would be dropped.

But the Kremlin was somewhat premature in celebrating its victory over Media Most. After leaving the country, Gusinsky immediately disavowed his agreement with Gazprom Media as he had signed under duress. As proof of this, Gusinsky presented the same Appendix 6—or the 'sixth protocol,' as it came to be known. Gusinsky did not deny his debts. But he refused to settle them by handing over his media assets.

Shielding Putin from charges of extortion, Media Minister Mikhael Lesin stated that he 'had not informed' the president about the agreement that he had signed with Gusinsky, although he had informed Prime Minister Kasyanov. On September 26, 2000, Putin issued a statement that he would not get involved and all disputes should be settled in accordance with Russian law.

In its caustic approach to the Kursk submarine disaster (it happened while the Gusinsky affair dragged on), NTV found an unexpected ally. Berezovsky's much more populist and popular ORT (Channel One)—which had previously lambasted all of Putin's enemies. News anchor Sergei Dorenko's criticism of the government differed from Shenderovich's in style, but was the same in substance. In contrast to NTV, ORT was watched by the entire country. If Shenderovich was loved by the Moscow intelligentsia, then Dorenko was popular among the people. For the first time, Putin's popularity rating shuddered.

According to Berezovsky, he first had 'serious doubts' about Putin 'in December 1999, after the Duma election. 'This was when Putin didn't stop in Chechnya,.... But these were not yet serious differences.... But the disagreements about the seven federal electoral districts, the Federation Council, and the right to remove elected governors—yes, these were already insurmountable differences.... The turning point, of course, was the Kursk submarine tragedy. Channel One, which I still owned, covered it in a very critical way. It showed the despair of the widows, and the cowardice and hypocrisy of the government officials.'[10]

In August 2000, Berezovsky was told by his former protégé, Putin's chief of staff Alexander Voloshin, that if he did let go of his shares in ORT, he would 'follow in Gusinsky's footsteps.'[11]

Berezovsky attempted, if not to save ORT from Putin, then at least to drag out the process. To this end, the attempt was made to transfer ORT's shares not to the government or its representatives, but to a newly-formed, privately-owned company named Teletrust, which consisted of members of the creative intelligentsia, including a number of NTV reporters. The Teletrust idea was probably unfeasible for many reasons—not least the fact that without sponsorship and financing, the creative intelligentsia would not be able to maintain the television channel.

However, Berezovsky did indeed succeed in somewhat delaying the transfer of ORT to the president's chekist entourage. In addition, by opening this 'second front,' he drew the Kremlin's attention away from finishing off NTV, which was delayed because of this.

But in December 2000, the Kremlin took a 'hostage' from Berezovsky: the media magnate's close friend and collaborator Nikolai Glushkov was arrested. Previously, Glushkov had been forbidden to leave the country in connection with his and Berezovsky's financial operations involving the Aeroflot joint-stock company. And so, in January 2001, Berezovsky was finally forced to sell his ORT shares to the person from the Yeltsin family Voloshin had instructed him to sell them to.

The attack on NTV continues

Although Gusinsky had disavowed his agreement to transfer his media assets to Gazprom, and the criminal case against him had effectively fallen apart, Media Most's debt to Gazprom remained outstanding. The task of subjugating NTV, which the secret service and the General Prosecutor's Office had been unable to manage, was assigned to the general manager of Gazprom Media, Alfred Kokh.

To help things along, on December 9, 2000, the Russian tax

agency initiated court proceedings against NTV. It filed a suit with the Moscow arbitration court to 'liquidate the NTV Television Company, as well as a number of other companies belonging to Media Most.' The suit was based on a provision that allowed liquidation if a company's assets fall below the minimum size of the authorized capital fixed by the law,. It was the first time the government used the provision.

Trying to turn the public against NTV, the General Prosecutor's Office began disclosing facts to the press about the cost of apartments that NTV reporters had received from Media Most. Also, since the 'hostage experiment' had produced results (Berezovsky sold ORT in return for a promise that his associate Glushkov would be released), the government 'took a hostage' from Gusinsky as well. On January 16, 2001, the former head of Media Most's financial department, was arrested. At the end of January 2001, 'TV presenter Kiselev's team' made an attempt to bring its conflict with Putin under control. On January 29 Putin received a large group of NTV reporters, with Kiselev at their head, in his office in the Kremlin. The meeting produced no results: the reporters expressed no signs of contrition, while the president assured them that he had no connection to the pressures being exerted on Media Most by Gazprom, the General Prosecutor's Office, and the secret service. In response to the request that Titov be released, Putin replied that, as a democrat, he did not wish to resort to 'law by telephone.' (Titov ended up remaining in custody until December 2002, when he was finally tried, sentenced to three years in prison, and then pardoned; during his trial, most of the charges against him were dropped.)

In the spring of 2001, a number of reporters fled from the sinking ship of NTV. As Viktor Shenderovich recalls, 'reporters who agreed to leave NTV had their debts cancelled and their salaries increased.'[12]

On April 3, Gazprom Media called a meeting of NTV shareholders at which a decision was made to remove Kiselev from the positions of general manager and editor-in-chief, and to appoint a new management for the television company under the leadership of the general manager of Gazprom Media and an American businessman.

Kiselev blamed the president personally for what had happened: 'Putin's signature style is to start a war and then to step aside' (NTV, April 4, 2001).

NTV's staff reporters became divided: some prominent journalists agreed to accept the new management, while others refused to do so.

On April 7, 2001, Yeltsin's privatization Czar Anatoly Chubais, responding to reporters' questions about his attitude toward the situation surrounding NTV and its possible occupation by Gazprom, stated that Gazprom 'was asserting its ownership rights—rights that are sacred and untouchable.' Moreover, Chubais emphasized that Gazprom was acting in accordance with the law and doing so 'very carefully,' even though, 'with a court decision in its hands, it could act in a much more forceful manner.' According to him, 'Alfred Kokh is proceeding with caution, trying not to hurt the dignity of NTV's people and unique staff.' On the night between April 13 to April 14, 2001, the occupation of NTV was completed: security workers from the Invest Security agency, brought over took over the TV company together with its 'unique staff.'

As a side effect of the Kremlin's victory over Media Most, the publication of the newspaper *Segodnya* was discontinued. In addition, the management of the magazine *Itogi* changed to one that was loyal to the Kremlin (by the end of the year, the staff of the old *Itogi*, headed by Sergei Parkhomenko, created the magazine *Yezhenedelny Zhurnal*).

In June-July 2001, Gazprom Media also acquired controlling shares in the radio station Ekho Moskvy as part of its debt settlement. However, Gazprom did not replace the station's management, headed by Alexei Venediktov, and Venediktov has seemingly been able to preserve an independent editorial policy at the station.

When a new manager was appointed at NTV, the head of Gazprom Media offered an intriguing insight to his successor to journalist Yevgenia Albats: '[He] is the ideal choice. He's the great-grandson of a White Army officer who ran away from the Bolsheviks shortly after the Revolution. He's Russian Orthodox, with an American passport in his pocket, and on top of everything not a Jew, an anti-Semite—only such a person could be accepted by the chekists as head of NTV.'[13] (In addition, two relatives of the new head had been officers in Hitler's Wehrmacht fighting against the Yugoslavian resistance under the command of SS Gruppenführer Neuhausen.[14]

The TV-6 affair

The core of 'Kiselev's team,' exiled from NTV, found a refuge in

June 2001 on the previously apolitical TV-6 channel ('the sixth button'), owned by the Moscow Independent Broadcasting Corporation (MNVK) It was then still owned by Boris Berezovsky, though not for long. Putin had already begun an operation to take TV-6 away from Berezovsky. In order to push Berezovsky out of the media business, he kept using his 'hostage'—Nikolai Glushkov. Berezovsky had to renounce all political activity and sell of all his media holdings (including the newspapers *Nezavisimaya Gazeta and Kommersant*). Further negotiations were handed to Lukoil head Vagit Alekperov, who wanted to please the Kremlin and pay nothing for the company. In April 2001, Lukoil initiated court proceedings through its daughter foundation Lukoil-Garant (a minority shareholder in TV-6) to liquidate TV-6, claiming that TV-6 had violated the rights of minority shareholders.

In June 2001, the court failed to satisfy Lukoil's claims, but in the fall of 2001 a court decision was finally made to liquidate TV-6. At the beginning of January 2002, TV-6's appeal contesting the court's decision was rejected by the Arbitration Court. It was an extraordinary legal decision because the law on which the decision to liquidate TV-6 was based had just then—on January 1, 2002—been repealed.

On January 15, 2002, President Putin announced with chutzpah that the government would not interfere in the situation surrounding TV-6: the TV channel was involved in 'a conflict between absolutely independent economic entities, to which the government has virtually no relation.' A few days later, on the night of January 21, TV-6's broadcasting was suspended by order of Minister Mikhael Lesin in accordance with the decision of the court. On January 29, 2002, the president ordered the government to come up with a plan for the creation of a national sports channel on Russian television. The liquidation of TV-6 was met with loud cheers by the reactionary press. Dmitry Dudko, a priest who enjoys popularity among nationalists, welcomed this move by the government:

> I am now putting very high hopes on Vladimir Putin... in many ways, he reminds me of Joseph Stalin.... Putin, I hope, will take the same path. He is difficult to understand. Many bad things are still done in the country. But Stalin also did not become resolute all at once. We are witnessing a fight over television, a fight with the oligarchs, a fight for the health of the nation, for our children. [15]

In the Kremlin, however, no final decision about either the fate of the 'sixth button' or the mega sports channel had yet been reached. Vladimir Putin had painted himself in a corner with the speech on the sports channel. If it happened, it was sitting proof for the international media that the Kremlin slapped the Russian press around in the same way as companies such as Yukos. The rump of the Yeltsin 'family' members within the Kremlin administration were still hoping to tame NTV's former staff. They won the day under the circumstances, and it was announced that the TV-6 would be auctioned off to the highest bidder. TV presenter Kiselev's banished team was able twice to take part in the scrupulously fair auction as part of the nonprofit partnership Mediasocium—headed by Yevgeny Primakov. On March 27, 2002, Mediasocium won the auction. The reporters who had lost now won, and clearly the decision had been made objectively.

The carrot had been handed to Kiselev, but now came the stick. While the former staff of NTV was preparing the renew broadcasting, on May 17, 2002, the Khimkinsky Municipal Court of the Moscow region ruled the owner MNVK's 'actions' to suspend TV-6's broadcasting to be 'illegal, infringing on the constitutional right of television viewers to obtain information freely' and ordered the MNVK (which continued to exist as a formal entity) to put TV-6 back on the air.

The situation around Channel Six thus became a legal cesspit for the new TV company. Two 'legal' licenses to one and the same frequency had been issued—Berezovsky's old MNVK license (now without Kiselev, and also without a company as MNKV had ceased to exist) and Primakov-Volsky's new Mediasocium license (with Kiselev). The new television channel (restyled 'TVS') began broadcasting in June 2002 and was mired in legal limbo as a result of this court decision. It was such a technical and seemingly mundane detail that it bypassed the radar of all of the international media. In fact, it meant that the government, could always put this court MNVK decision into effect and remove the station from the air.

The new TVS channel (and the non-profit Mediasocium) received sponsorship and investment from the Shestoy Kanal (Channel Six) joint-stock company, a consortium of business magnates to whom the Kremlin had effectively assigned the custodianship of TVS.

During the whole period of TVS's existence, two competing groups of co-owners in the TV consortium (headed by Anatoly

Chubais and the aluminium oligarch Oleg Deripaska, respectively) tried, first, to establish their clan's complete control over the channel, and second, to force the reporters to apply self-censorship. Their success in achieving the second of these goals did not come up to the Kremlin's exacting standards, while their success in achieving the first was nonexistent. Neither Chubais's nor Deripaska's group were able to derive any kind of commercial or semi-commercial benefit from channel's existence. Meanwhile, the Kremlin constantly expressed displeasure at the continuing opposition of TV presenter Kiselev.

TVS—which lasted exactly one year, from June 2002 to June 2003—was significantly different from the 'old' NTV and from TV-6 from which it had phoenix-like arisen. It featured programming that would have been inconceivable on the 'old' NTV and TV-6, such as the Islamophobic TV show 'Men's Work' (the heroic struggle of secret service agents against Chechen bandits, including a traitor-reporter who was easily recognizable as modelled on Radio Liberty's Chechnya correspondent Andrei Babitsky) or the white-washing 'examination' of the case of Colonel Yuri Budanov, who had strangled an 18-year-old Chechen girl to death during 'questioning.' TV-6 had already made an attempt to attract a new kind of viewer (and new advertising sponsors) through fundamentally apolitical 'reality shows' (such as the primitive and ethically suspect 'Behind Glass'). This attempt continued on TVS: the reality show 'Behind Glass: You're in the Army Now' was as low-brow as its predecessor, but in addition presented itself as promoting military-patriotic values.

Yevgeny Kiselev himself became so cautious on his show 'Itogi' that it sometimes seemed as if the calmly ironic Leonid Parfenov over on the 'new' NTV was allowing himself greater liberties. However, Viktor Shenderovich's brilliant 'Free Cheese' and Andrei Cherkizov's 'Out of Spite!' were fully in keeping with the traditions of the 'old' NTV from which the team hailed. Other great shows were Alexander Tatarsky and Vladimir Neklyudov's shows 'Kremlin Concert' and 'Shut the Lights!' But the second half of 2003 and the first half of 2004 were periods of two national election campaigns—for the parliament and for the presidency. It was completely inconceivable that 'Free Cheese,' 'Out of Spite!,' 'Kremlin Concert,' and 'Shut the Lights!' would be allowed to survive until the election.

At the end of April 2003, the co-owners of the consortium terminated TVS's financing. In the middle of May 2003, Pilot TV's shows 'Shut the Lights!' and 'Kremlin Concert' stopped appearing. Mostelecom—a joint-stock company owned by the Moscow government—stopped receiving payments for the TV signal and at the beginning of June 2003 and began shutting down TVS's broadcasting in Moscow, district by district.

Then the Ministry of the Press took advantage of the Khimkinsky Municipal Court's decision from the previous year and on June 22, 2003 announced the termination of TVS's broadcasting. Naturally, the 'sixth button' license was not returned to Berezovsky's paralyzed MNVK. The frequency was taken over by the new Sport Channel: President Putin's demand for a 'national sports channel' had come true at last.

Despite the love of Russians for televised sports events, the Sport Channel was still not making a profit as of the summer of 2004. Formally, the programmes are acquired by the state company VGTRK, but in practice they are used for the Sport Channel. According to the director of the National Research Centre for Television and Radio Alexei Samokhvalov, 'VGTRK's international partners do not even suspect that their programs are being illegally used by a different channel.' The transmission of the European soccer championship cost the government $10 million, the American hockey championship cost $4 million, the Winter Olympics cost approximately $7.5 million.[16]

New purges

Over at the 'new' NTV things were not much better for the Kremlin. Despite credentials that had apparently pleased the secret service, the promising new head of NTV did not lead NTV for long. His advance was routed by the 'Nord Ost' catastrophe of October 23 in 2002, when Chechen rebels took hostage the audience at the Dubrovka theatre during a performance of the musical 'Nord Ost'. He had started his rule by treating NTV as a business that must sooner or later begin to yield a profit and freed the reporters from petty surveillance. For a while, this drew no direct censure from the Kremlin. But during the 'Nord-Ost' crisis, NTV's reporters covered the news in a way that angered the president personally. Putin was 'infuriated by the fact that NTV had shown the storming of the theatre on the air.'[17]

No important reporters were fired at the time, but the new head was dismissed during the second half of January 2003—first from one general manager's position (Gazprom Media), then from another (NTV).

On January 22, 2003, a doctor by profession was appointed acting general manager of NTV. NTV's journalists protested against this baffling appointment. On February 6, the prominent journalist Leonid Parfenov stated in an interview with Ekho Moskvy radio that his popular programme 'Namedni' ('The Other Day') was going to end production and that he was going to take a three month vacation beginning on February 10, 2003. In addition to Parfenov, reporter heavy-weights Tatyana Mitkova and Savik Shuster also expressed dismay at the fact that NTV's new head had no connection to journalism. However, the new management showed greater powers of persuasion. On May 18, 2003, 'Namedni' came back on the air.

On November 15, 2002, NTV announced that Leonid Parfenov's show 'Namedni' would feature a segment of *The Tales of a Kremlin Digger*. It was a controversial book about the mores and morals of the Kremlin under Boris Yeltsin written by reporter Yelena Tregubova. One of 'Czar Boris's' courtiers in the book was secret service director Vladimir Putin. According to the reporter's account, Putin either wanted to have an affair with her or to recruit her as an agent—she herself could not figure out which. The three-and-a-half minute segment included an interview with Tregubova, as well as with Kremlin officials Mikhail Margelov and Alexei Volin, who also figured in the book. In addition, one of the scenes from the book was recreated in Parfenov's studio: a sushi dinner at the Japanese restaurant 'Izumi,' where secret service director Putin had invited Tregubova in December 1998.

The segment was never aired. According to Parfenov, NTV's new director called him on November 16, 2003, and proscribed the broadcast. In an interview with Ekho Moskvy radio, the new director explained himself:

> NTV is not a garbage dump that has room for insults and vulgarity... NTV cannot be accused of being insufficiently critical, and the program 'Namedni' especially cannot be accused of this... Freedom of speech is one thing, but insults and vulgarity are another. There is a big difference. I will not

allow such things to go on the air from now on.[18]

Under the new regime, NTV's political programming began to retreat into the background, yielding to talk and reality shows. The weekly program 'Faktor Strakha' ('Fear Factor') became typical of the 'new new' NTV ordered by the doctor. Disguised as a fight against phobias and squeamishness, 'Faktor Strakha' shows how participants kill, torture, and eat small animals alive and eat their faeces.

The case of the wilting newspapers

While the TV stations were being refurnished, the independent newspapers were the few remaining flies in the ointment. In April 2002, Mezhprombank was awarded 15 million rubles (about $500,000) for 'lost profits' in its suit against *Novaya Gazeta*, the newspaper Mikhail Gorbachev helped to set up with his Nobel Peace Prize. It was uncertain whether *Novaya Gazeta* (with a circulation of around 500,000) would be able to survive this body blow.

The suit was prompted by a November 2001 article in *Novaya Gazeta* that claimed that Mezhprombank's management and its head Sergei Pugachev (close to Putin and the chekists clan in his entourage) were involved in laundering money for the Russian mafia at the Bank of New York. Mezhprombank filed a suit for the protection of its business reputation. One of its clients—the joint-stock company Veststroyservis—the bank claimed, had become so concerned that it altered the terms of its account with the bank, which caused substantial financial losses. The unprecedented severity of the fine meant that those who had organized the lawsuit not merely to punish the reporters, but to terminate the existence of the newspaper altogether.

The only thing that ended up saving *Novaya Gazeta* was the fact that the evidence presented by Mezhprombank about its 'losses' had one flaw that had been 'overlooked' by the court. It was brilliantly demonstrated by *Novaya Gazeta* editor Yulia Latynina. The companies 'due to whose agreements and letters Mezhprombank incurred losses, are controlled either by Mezhprombank itself or by Mezhprombank's managers and founders.' Among the managers of the companies named in the article were one S. Pugachev himself, his wife Galina Pugacheva, and other managers employed by the same Mezhprombank that losses had been inflicted on it.[19]

At the end of May 2002, *Novaya Gazeta*'s editorial board filed a request with the Moscow prosecutor's office and law enforcement agencies to 'look into instances of swindling... against *Novaya Gazeta* committed by Mezhprombank's management and a number of companies affiliated with the bank.' Mezhprombank became frightened of a public scandal and in June 2002 decided not to claim the money that it had won in court.

As newspapers are relatively cheap for the Kremlin clans, the fate of another independent newspaper—*Obschaya Gazeta*, the last mouthpiece of the 60s generation'—was decided in a much more productive way.

Its founder and editor-in-chief (the glasnost journalist Yegor Yakovlev) was unable to find financing to continue its publication. He then sold the newspaper to the St Petersburg businessman Vyacheslav Leibman (better known as the former boyfriend of Ksenia Sobchak, a popular figure in the gossip columns and daughter of St Petersburg's first mayor under whom Putin served). Leibman immediately shut down *Obschaya Gazeta*, and in its place he began to publish *Konservator*—a newspaper with a completely different (pro-Putin) political slant. Up to the very end, Yakovlev seems to have been convinced that *Obschaya Gazeta* would survive after its sale—even if it would assume a different form—and that its staff would not be dismissed, at least not all at once. Some speculated that Leibman did not spend his own money to buy the newspaper with only one goal—to prevent someone like Berezovsky buying it. The *Konservator* closed within half a year. Despite the ostensible popular support for their President, it seems, Russians had little appetite for buying a print-out of the Kremlin's policies.

As good as done

Nonetheless, under editor-in-chief Rustam Arifdzhanov, *Versiya* and *Sovershenno Sekretno* continued to maintain a sufficiently independent stance. These newspapers could be accused of indulging in a certain amount of 'yellow journalism,' of taking part in feuds between the oligarchs (publishing compromising stories about members of 'the family,' apparently at the behest of the Moscow mayor's office), but they could not be accused of toadyism to the Kremlin.

In September 2000, the newspaper *Versiya* was raided, searched, and had its files confiscated by the secret service, when it was preparing to publish exclusive materials concerning the sinking of the Kursk submarine. The government's criticism focused mainly on TV reporters, whose mistakes in covering the event may have allegedly helped the terrorists.

Versiya was the first newspaper to be hit after its reporters undertook an independent investigation of the tragedy. On November 1, 2002, secret service operatives showed up at *Versiya*'s offices and confiscated the newspaper's computer and server, paralyzing its work for several days. Back in May 2002, *Versiya* had published an article entitle 'Camouflage,' describing illegal construction projects at classified government sites. A criminal suit against the newspaper had been filed on October 18, 2002, and this was offered as the reason given for the confiscation of its property.

However, the real reason, as the editor Arifdzhanov immediately surmised, was the secret service's desire to prevent *Versiya* from publishing a detailed report about the elimination of the terrorists along with the hostages at the Dubrovka theatre. It so happened that on October 26, 2002, *Versiya's* deputy editor-in-chief Andrei Soldatov had been a witness to the operation to 'rescue' the hostages, and his reports about the victims differed rather significantly from the official accounts. He observed first hand that many hostages were already dead when they were carried out of the theatre, and yet that, they were immediately taken to the hospital, apparently in order to save their lives.

When the truth about this appeared in *Versiya*, it seemed the secret service had overreacted to what it thought the paper would write. The criminal case against the 'Camouflage' article was closed, and *Versiya*'s computers and files about the hostage crisis were returned to its offices. Soldatov's exposés of the government's lies about the hostage crisis were ignored.

Immediately following the hostage crisis, the Kremlin and Duma passed new legislation aimed at the media. The new regulations included numerous restrictions on reporters' activities during a state of emergency, effectively making it illegal even to criticize 'anti-terrorist operations.'

On November 25, 2002, at a meeting with the heads of pro-government media outlets, Putin announced that he had vetoed the legislation—which had already passed both houses of parliament—after it drew criticism and calls for a presidential veto from the press. The reporters, however, were too quick with their celebrations: on November 27, the president sent a letter to the heads of both houses of parliament with the recommendation to continue developing the new media law, proposing the introduction of 'additional regulations for media activities during states of emergency, under martial law, and in the coverage of emergency situations of a natural or technological character.'

Putin's veto did not signify a refusal to 'develop and pass into law of a set of restrictions on reporters' activities, as it has been portrayed by enthusiastic staff reporters and well-paid optimists, but [was] merely the formal expression of the president's displeasure at the imperfection of the proposed measures.'[20]

On December 15, 2002, secret service Director Patrushev opened a meeting with the heads of a number of Russian media outlets (ITAR-TASS, Interfax, RIA Novosti, ORT, and the Rossiya Channel) by noting that he was satisfied with the cooperation between his agency and the Russian media: 'We are doing the same thing—working for the society, for the state.' If the secret service and the media in Russia are 'doing the same thing,' then the 'thing' can be considered as good as done.

Novye Izvestiya

Novye Izvestiya, along with *Novaya Gazeta,* was one of two newspapers which from the very beginning criticised President Putin. The financial sponsor of *Novye Izvestiya* was Boris Berezovsky, but the formal owner of more than the controlling percentage of the shares was businessman Oleg Mitvol. Seventy-four percent of the shares of the Novye Izvestiya News Publishing Group were in the name of a businessman in the canning industry and green pea production, Oleg Mitvol (they had been transferred to him by Berezovsky when he left Russia), and 24% were owned by the newspaper's staff.

Novye Izvestiya's formal owner did not interfere with its editorial policies, nor did he contribute anything to its financing—the newspaper continued to be financed by Berezovsky. Nonetheless, on February 20, 2003, Mitvol presented the newspaper's management with a complaint that 'his' financial contributions were being improperly handled and he fired the general manager and stopped the newspaper's publication. Mitvol also notified the public prosecutor's office.

'What Oleg Mitvol says about financial schemes is curious,' *Novye Izvestiya*'s deputy general manager Valery Yakov noted in an interview with *Kommersant*. 'It was precisely Mitvol who was in charge of our finances. We believe that the events at the newspaper are connected with the fact that it has recently published critical articles about Putin. For example, the last issue contained a long article entitled "... Plus Putinization of the Whole Country".'[21]

In an interview, Berezovsky expressed a similar view: 'Yesterday, for example, they published an article about the revival of a cult of personality around Putin [written by Vladimir Pribylovsky, co-author of this book], and the Kremlin evidently did not like it. I think that Mitvol got a signal from the Kremlin, because he himself is a cowardly person.'[22]

Two months later, a group of former *Novye Izvestiya* employees founded the newspaper *Russky Kurier*, while the remaining staff began once more to publish *Novye Izvestiya.* As a result of this one of the pro-Putin pundits sarcastically remarked in the English-language *Moscow Times* how scary Putin's autocratic regime truly was—as soon as one opposition newspaper closed, sponsors were found to replace it with two new ones.[23]

In truth, the 'new' *Novye Izvestiya* has a neutral editorial policy rather than an oppositional one, and the *Russky Kurier* lasted as an opposition newspaper (although a notably more cautious one than the 'old' *Novye Izvestiya*) for less than two years (until February 2005).

On June 18, 2004, the criminal investigation of the 'old' *Novye Izvestiya* was completed. On August 16, 2004, the prosecutor's office handed the case over to the court, after which, however, it was returned to the public prosecutor for further inquiry, and then forgotten (it seems).

Marginal comment

Only two books caught the eye of the Kremlin in this period. They both deal with the same matter, the Chechen terrorist attacks as fronts for secret service operations—one as fiction, and so less damaging, the other as non-fiction, far more damaging because the author was a former member of the secret service. One is Alexander Prokhanov's political thriller *Mr. Hexogen.*[24] *Mr. Hexogen* is devoted to the Moscow apartment-house bombings as a chekist electoral technique. Even the old Gusinsky/Primakov-protected NTV went only so far as to raise this question—without ever answering it so unequivocally. The book stung the Kremlin even harder, because it had won the National Bestseller Award.

The attack was made in a crab-like fashion via a different book by the same publishing house, Ad Marginem, and charging it with distributing pornography. (This book was called *Blue Lard*, and had sex scenes with Brezhnev and Stalin, but had otherwise been out for three years.)

Later, at the beginning of 2004 just before the presidential elections, the secret service tried to initiate criminal proceedings against a legendary dissident, the head of the Prima News Agency, and former editor-in-chief of *Express Khronika*, a newspaper devoted to defending human rights, Alexander Podrabinek. On January 28, 2004, Podrabinek was called in for questioning, as a witness, to the secret service's Investigations Directorate at Lefortovo Prison, where he was asked to answer a series of questions about the publication and shipment to Russia of Alexander Litvinenko and Yuri Felshtinsky's *FSB vzryvaet Rossiu (Blowing Up Russia).*

It turned out that the publication of this book had provoked a criminal investigation into 'divulging state secrets'. According to a new Russian law, only people who have official access to classified information may be charged with divulging state secrets if they publish them. This is in contrast to the findings of a newspaper investigation by a non-official, which does not amount to the disclosure of a state secret, even if from the point of view of the security organs they contain information that is highly classified. As Alexander Litvinenko was a former secret service officer, his involvement triggered the investigation. Neither his co-author, Felshtinsky, nor the book's publisher, nor its Russian distributor—Podrabinek's Prima News Agency—were subject to criminal charges for divulging this government secrets.

Podrabinek was called in for questioning by the secret service as he had placed the order for the book. On December 31, 2003, a shipment of 5000 copies of *secret service vzryvaet Rossiu* was to be delivered from Riga to Moscow. The shipment successfully crossed the Latvian-Russian border, but on the half way down the Volokolamskoye Highway, the truck with the books was stopped and confiscated. Thus the book became the first to be banned in free Russia since Solzenitsyn's *Gulag Archipelago*. As they could only charge Lieutenant-Colonel Alexander Litvinenko—and despite his interrogators' threats to turn him from a witness into a defendant—they let Podrabinek go in the end.

There is no better example of the two vice-like grips on the media's access and self-censorship that the Kremlin had developed ahead of the re-election campaign of Vladimir Putin.

CHAPTER SEVEN

Vertical Democracy

Only two years into his presidency, Putin had transformed the Russian state into something beyond Pinochet's achievements. The Kremlin had on the one hand successfully insulated the Russian media from the world press and on the other cut the transfusion of information from state officials to the media associated with their secret service clan. It was in a good position to apply itself to the upcoming Duma and Presidential elections in the winter of 2003/4, without the need (in principle) to provide the Russian electorate with a fresh dose of Chechen events to occupy themselves with.

Apart from the usual resources that an elected government has at its disposal, the Kremlin had an enviable arsenal of additional aids with which it could steer outcomes in the desired direction. The 'administrative resources' used to arrange a managed election include a variety of different methodologies. These range from extreme techniques (starting a war before an election, reaching a peace settlement before an election, campaigns against corrupt law enforcement agents, persecuting an 'oil oligarch,' physically eliminating a separatist leader, etc.) to routine methods (using convenient laws, relying on media monopolies).

The most sophisticated arsenal was the development of the 'Bashkirian election technology.' It included preventing the opposition candidate from registering his candidacy, or to have his registration disqualified. Second, it consists in the 'right' the replace the owner of an opposition media outlet by orchestrating a 'conflict relating to property.' Third, it consists in criminal proceedings against opposition candidates, including ones based entirely on trumped-up charges. Fourth, it consists in the possibility of 'correcting' election outcomes through dishonest vote counts, the addition of extra ballots, and the defacement of 'undesirable' ballots.

The method had been pioneered under Yeltsin's Kremlin, where it was tolerated on a local level in order to prevent to Federation from collapsing. In addition, the methodology was not deployed universally but only in a limited number of regions—first and foremost in oil rich Bashkiria—hence the expression 'Bashkirian election technology'—where the governor (arguably dictator) Murtaza Rakhimov has remained in power since Soviet times; Buddhist Kalmykia; and pacific-port region Primorye.

But from 2000, the 'Bashkirian election technology' was deployed by the Kremlin in the elections for governor of the Saratov region (March 2000, the sitting pro-Kremlin governor faced down his main rival, a Communist who even had the support of local businessmen, by refusing to register him; the Russian courts backed his decision), governor of the oil-producing Khanty-Mansi region (March 2000, the sitting pro-Putin governor disqualified his main opponent—his popular election platform for locals to receive a share in the oil proceeds 'violated' campaign spending rules).

These regional two elections happened simultaneously with the 2000 Presidential elections. One that followed after Putin's inauguration was the election of the governor of the Kursk region in October 2000. Here, the sitting governor was the tricky Alexander Rutskoy. He was a one-time rival Acting President appointed by the Duma during its 1993 stand-off with Yeltsin. In 1996 his candidacy for the Kursk governorship reached the Presidium of the Russian Supreme Court (where he must have had powerful friends) before his registration was allowed, after which the popular Rutskoy had a walk-over with almost 80% of the vote. During his 2000 re-election campaign, however, he was disqualified thirteen and a half hours before the first round was to have taken place. It would otherwise have been a foregone conclusion, and his re-election was in fact expected given his reasonable loyal membership of the pro-Putin Unity party. But the operation to 'show-whip' him for his non-Kremlin stance during the Kursk submarine affair that summer was guided from the local office of the seven newly created Presidential representatives. The Presidential representative in the area, General Georgy Poltavchenko (the Kremlin itself remained outwardly 'neutral'), favoured an secret service Major-General as candidate and had managed a last minute betrayal of Rutskoy by his own party—sealing access to the media on election day in case Rutskoy might attempt to address the electorate. The election without Rutskoy was not a success, however. In the first round the electorate ignored the secret service candidate, and in the second they voted in a Communist. It was the first and last election in Russia in which a sitting governor was disqualified from running.

The Bashkirian technology spread to those locations where the likely election outcome was not the one wished for at the Kremlin—but with mixed results. In the Komi-Permyak governor elections of December 2000, the leading candidate was a nominee of the reactionary pro-Soviet movement backed by a good deal of local money. On the eve of the election, he was disqualified for violating election rules. The incumbent governor was narrowly not re-elected, but a candidate from the same clan was. The mayoral elections of the Russian Riviera town Sochi, where the Moscow elite has its palaces and dachas, in April-May 2001 spelled another defeat for the Kremlin. The Kremlin-favoured candidate, a former reporter supported by the Press Minister Mikhael Lesin and others, lost against the candidate promoted by a clan led by Moscow mayor Luzhkov. The same happened during the governor elections in Primorye in June 2001. This pivotal region's elections had been 'technologically' managed since Yeltsin's time and the Kremlin had to admit defeat against the clan of the sitting governor, even though he was not a candidate because they had lured him to Moscow promising him a seat as minister, likewise, the governorship of the Nizhny Novgorod region in July 2001. The candidate favoured by the Presidential representative, Sergei Kiriyenko, the man who had appointed Putin as secret service director, lost against a Communist.

Successes for the Kremlin were the governor elections of the Rostov region in September 2001. The leading candidate in this Communist region was a Communist, whose registration was nonetheless disqualified due to irregularities the election committee discovered with 10% of the signatures required for his candidacy. The sitting governor remained on the ballot, while an unknown local politician was chosen to oppose him. He was duly elected after the Presidential representative had a chat with the disqualified Communist before the elections. Another success was the presidency election in Yakutia of December 2001-January 2002. The sitting president had overlooked to change the local constitution about sitting for a third term and was deemed (not unreasonably) not eligible by the election committee. Tempers flared and reporters dispatched by the Kremlin to report for national papers on the elections were briefly arrested. After a rumoured chat with Putin, the sitting president of Yakutia withdrew his candidacy and was appointed as vice-president by the person who won the elections.

The presidential elections of North Ossetia in January 2002 were a struggle but nonetheless a success. The leading opponent to the incumbent was an old-style Soviet who was a member of the Duma, Sergei Khetagurov. The Kremlin feared that the old hardliner he would fan the nearby Chechen conflict. A few months before the elections, criminal proceedings commenced with regards to corruption during the 1990s in which Khetagurov was called in as a witness. He was subsequently disqualified because he had provided unreliable evidence of his family's income and had provided the wrong place of residence (he had two, Moscow and a local city) and 'false passports' (he had two, an old Soviet one and a replacement for one that he had lost). The presidential elections of Ingushetia (next to Chechnya) in April 2002 were another victory for the Kremlin. The sitting president had to resign under pressure of the Presidential representative, with whom he had been in open conflict about Chechnya. In order to avoid disqualification, his clan had registered several candidates, but the President's representative backed secret service candidate Major-General Murat Zyazikov. In an ad in the national paper *Kommersant* the opposition complained, 'Ingushetia public television and radio reporters have been subjected to unprecedented and unembarrassed pressure from the representatives of the Southern Federal District, who have demanded greater and better coverage of the activities of one of the deputies of the president's representative in the Southern Federal District, an secret service general who is registered as a candidate for the presidency of Ingushetia.' It was in vain, the Russian Supreme Court confirmed the disqualification of the general's leading opponent due to not resigning from his post as Minister of Interior Affairs of Ingushetia. Against complaints that there were 25% more votes than ballots, the general beat the other leading candidate, a Duma deputy, narrowly.

Vladimir Putin himself got entangled in the mayoral elections of Nizhny Novgorod in September 2002. The leading candidate was a populist entrepreneur Andrei Klimentyev. He had won in March 1998, but been removed for currency 'theft' the day after his victory. Another win by this 'criminal' many times over would mean that Putin's Presidential representative Kiriyenko was not in charge of his federal district. But Kiriyenko could not back the sitting mayor Yuri Lebedev either. Unhappy with the incumbent mayor, Putin had predicted that Lebedev 'had no chance of getting re-elected' because 'he has a miserable approval rating.'[1] Klimentyev was disqualified twenty four hours before polls started when one of his sponsors came forward to say she had given money handed to her by a third party. In the first round the favoured mayoral candidate—a deputy in the Duma—received almost as many votes as the sitting mayor (though there were as many defaced and 'none of the above' ballots as there were votes for the incumbent). On 29 September, election night for the second round, the electoral committee had the ballot papers impounded. The papers were released when it was clear the right candidate had won. Putin's Presidential representative issued a statement that he had 'absolutely certain information that on the night after the mayoral election... those ballots which had been cast for the winner' would be defaced.[2]

Changes in electoral legislation

As the Bashkirian technology was being rolled out throughout the federation, it became clear that new legislation was required to make it work more efficiently. Thus, on June 12, 2002, President Putin signed a new law: 'On the Basic Guarantees of Electoral Rights and the Right of Citizens of the Russian Federation to Participate in a Referendum' (passed smoothly through the State Duma on May 22, 2002, and approved in record time by the Federation Council on May 29, 2002).

On the face of it, the new law—which was adopted in June 12, 2002, and went into effect in November 2002—boasted a number of very fair provisions. The registration of a candidate (or list of candidates) could no longer be revoked within five days or less before an election, and mainly through the courts. It prevented last-minute surprises as a result of unfavourable polls. Inaccuracies and omissions in a candidate's declaration of property ceased to be a basis for denying him registration or disqualifying him from an election

(election commissions retained the right to inform voters about the omissions or distortions in a candidate's declaration of property). It also became possible to nominate party candidates without collecting lists of signatures and making a monetary deposit. Yabloko party deputy Sergei Mitrokhin, furthermore, introduced an amendment that required elections to go to a second round when no candidate had won an absolute majority in the first round.

On the other hand, the new regulations greatly enhance the capacity of the Ministry of Elections and its local offices to 'manage democracy.' The new law recognizes thirteen (!) reasons for denying a candidate the right to register, another four reasons for annulling a candidate's registration, and another six reasons for revoking a candidate's registration through a court decision requested by the election commission. In addition, election outcomes can also be invalidated, either by higher-level election commissions ('if, in the course of an election or while the outcome of an election was being determined, this federal law was violated, or if another law governing the said election was violated...') or by a decision of the court. The new law recognizes four different reasons for invalidating election outcomes.

The following three grounds offer the Ministry for Elections the greatest latitude whether to allow or disallow registration:—A candidate or bloc must not exceed the campaign spending limits established by law by more than 5%. Where the spending is in excess of 10%, the election is invalid;—A candidate, coalition, or bloc must not 'abuse the right to campaign before an election'—which is open to a very broad interpretation;—A candidate must indicate his position and place of work correctly. During the State Duma election campaign in 2003, the government made especially broad use of this to cull candidates from registration. These new regulations made it possible to block candidates from participating for a wide range of facts: for example, due to an 'expired passport'. This is what happened in the summer of 2004 with the passport of the opposition candidate for the presidency of Chechnya, Malik Saidullaev. Or because a candidate had 'concealed' the fact that he was a professor (the case of ex-general prosecutor Yuri Skuratov in the 2003 Duma election).

New regulations strengthened the possibility of using the law in an instrumental and selective fashion. For the duration of an election campaign, the new law prohibited any 'actions intended to induce or inducing voters to vote for or against candidates (lists) or for "none of the above",' except by advertisements paid for with registered campaign funds. In other words, the new law substantially restricted how could voice their opinions to what it could pay for. In effect, it meant a ban on political analysis for the duration of an election campaign, since the law equated it with campaigning, which was legal only when it was paid for with official campaign funds. 'Violations' of this ban by supporters of opposition parties have invariably led to charges of 'abusing the right to conduct an election campaign,' which constitute legal grounds for disqualifying a candidate's or a political bloc's registration.

The new law gave the Ministry's electoral commission (CEC) broad discretion to resolve 'contradictions' in the new legislation. For example, financing an election campaign was forbidden, unless it happened through a campaign fund. But at the same time media regulations require the media to inform the population about all significant events. Therefore, a TV channel that promotes a president or a minister—the leader of United Russia—will be seen by the CEC as lawfully informing the population. But if an opposition candidate appears on a programme, then the question becomes whether he paid for the program out of his campaign fund. If this is not the case, then he can be disqualified.

The new law also prohibited government officials from campaigning, or making use of their official positions in elections. It is a sensible provision. In practice, however, the CEC's discretionary powers seemed to mean it can elect whether or not to exercise its rights. When the President campaigns for his party United Russia or for his own candidate in a governor race, this incurs no censure from the Ministry of Elections. But if the assistant of an opposition deputy takes part in the campaign for his boss, then the deputy is using his official position in an *illegal* manner. Then again, if a candidate for the Duma from a pro-presidential party uses his assistant in exactly the same way, the issue of its legality or illegality does not seem to surface.

Voters themselves had previously found a way around the 'Bashkirian election technology' by voting for the Nota ('none of the above') team and expressing their dissatisfaction. The new law blocked this route as well. Only registered candidates were allowed to 'campaign' or in any other way 'suggest' voters choose 'none of the above,' because other supporters of Nota by definition cannot have a campaign fund to fund such a vote. Private individuals who campaign for Nota can do so without having officially registered campaign funds, but media outlets that air this viewpoint can be penalised.

Putin's new law also weakened the right to a referendum substantially, From now on, it was prohibited to hold a referendum during the year preceding and the three months following a federal election for the Duma and for the presidency. Votes in favour of this amendment were cast not only by Chubais' pro-business Union of Right Forces (SPS) deputies (apart from human rights activist Sergei Kovalev, who voted against it), but by the pro-Western Yabloko's deputies as well.

The law furthermore moved supervision of Russia's GAS-Vybory electronic voting system to a new department. In March 2003, as part of a reform of the security services, the secret service was given administrative control over the system. Prior to March 11, 2003, GAS-Vybory had been controlled by the Federal Agency for Government Communication and Information (FAPSI), but this agency was dissolved and regrouped under existing parts of the Russian secret service (like Freddie Krueger, the KGB had now completely healed itself from the 1991 break-up under Yeltsin). The secret service had concluded that it was 'administratively' easier to have one central computer rather than multiple regional ones at different locations.

In June 2003, the Kremlin introduced (under generous discretionary powers of the President provided for in the new election law) a mechanism that had previously been lacking—punishment of the media for violating election regulations. At the height of the Duma election campaign in the fall of 2003—in response to a claim brought by a number of reporters and deputies—the Russian Constitutional Court took aim at the new law. The court ruled that the new law did not effectively prohibit, for the duration of the campaign, information and political analysis that was not paid for out of candidates' campaign funds. It was nonetheless, not clear whether this judgement was a victory for reporters or for the Kremlin. The ruling only provided reporters with a means to challenge the most blatant excesses, that is to say, file a complaint with the appropriate electoral committee citing the court's decision. The Ministry's election committees still retained the discretionary power to decide which information and political analysis should, as a matter of fact, be considered political advertising, and which should not. The court had merely rebutted the accusation that in Putin's Russia political analysis during elections was not allowed.

On May 19, 2004, the president introduced further amendments to legislation governing referendums. In a federation where regions so often want to secede, these are important electoral instruments. Putin's amendments were passed by the Duma on June 11 (the Federation Council approved them on June 23, and the president ratified them on June 28, 2004). The law made it considerably more difficult to initiate a referendum. In particular, instead of a single initiative group, the law now required the existence of a minimum of 45 initiative groups, in different constituent subjects of the federation, each with at least 100 members. The deadline for collecting two million signatures in support of the initiative was shortened from three months to two.

Results

The results quickly showed after the new law came in force. In 2003-2004—after the new electoral legislation went into effect—candidates were not allowed to register or had their registrations disqualified in the elections for: the Bashkortostan state assembly (March 2003), the mayor of Novorossiysk (March 2003), the Rostov region legislative assembly (March 2003), the mayor of Norilsk (April 2003), the Vladivostok municipal duma (June 2003), the administrative head of the Omsk region (August-September 2003), the president of Chechnya (September-October 2003), the State Duma of the Russian Federation (December 2003), the administrative head of the Kirov region (December 2003), the runoff election for mayor of Noyabrsk (January 2004), the Krasnodar region gubernatorial race (March 2004), the Vladivostok mayoral race (July 2004), and the Chechnya presidential election (August 2004). Only the Vladivostok Duma election in June 2003 ended with a victory for the opposition—despite the fact that a number of opposition candidates had their registrations disqualified. However, on the initiative of the municipal election commission, the court rejected the election outcomes for two districts carried by candidates unfavoured by the local authorities, thus depriving the opposition bloc Freedom and People's Government of the majority that it had won.

The time was there to impose order on the larger national power blocs, such as St Petersburg.

Rumours of St Petersburg governor Vladimir Yakovlev's impending replacement circulated for almost four years. Under Anatoly Sobchak, his two discreet deputy mayors, Vladimir Yakovlev and Vladimir Putin, effectively governed the city for the charismatic mayor, who travelled around the world and would be gone from the northern capital for months at a time. No conflicts between Putin, who was involved in the 'new economy,' and Yakovlev, who was in charge of the 'old economy,' were observed at the time. But in the spring of 1996, when Yakovlev suddenly ran against their common boss in the mayoral election, Putin publicly (although behind Yakovlev's back) called Yakovlev 'Judas.' After Yakovlev won, he called Putin (also behind his back) an 'asshole.'[3]

When he became president, Putin was widely expected to punish Yakovlev. Sobchak's widow, Lyudmila, was particularly passionate in encouraging him to do so. However, despite Yakovlev's obvious shortcomings as an administrator (he had the habits and style of a Soviet-era paymaster, the corruption of the governor's and his wife's inner circle) no one doubted that he would win again in the next mayoral election. Under Yakovlev, some kind of order had finally been established in St Petersburg—which had been absent under Sobchak. A straightforward system for 'resolving problems' developed in the city (including a reliable, 'single-channel' method for handling bribes), based on the same principles as the one that had been set up years earlier in Luzhkov's Moscow. This bureaucratic, corrupt, but functioning system was more or less acceptable to both large-scale and mid-level businesses and even to a considerable part of the ordinary population. (In fact, it is just this kind of order that Putin's bureaucracy would later try to establish on the scale of Russia as a whole—only with military-police overtones and centred on a somewhat different group of individuals.)

The office of the Presidential representative under which St Petersburg resorted did its best to bring one criminal charge after another against Yakovlev's corrupt deputies, but paradoxically this only increased the governor's electoral potential. In addition, the 'anti-corruption' campaign against Yakovlev's team was conducted in a highly erratic fashion. As the reporter Yulia Latynina rightly noted, 'by initiating criminal proceedings in connection with shortfalls in the city budget and then abandoning them halfway, like casual lovers, the government has shown St Petersburg residents that it does not consider theft to be a wrongdoing. By intending to replace the governor and then dragging it out for four years, the government has discredited its own intention to seek revenge.'[4] She suggested a simple explanation for this erratic approach: 'St. Petersburg is a small city. And too many of the president's friends are also friends of Yakovlev's.'[5] To this it may be added that too much of the corrupt business of Yakovlev's friends is also the business of certain friends of Putin's.

It seemed that only a direct declaration by the president that Yakovlev was an absolutely unacceptable head for the second capital could have overthrown the 'boss' of St Petersburg. Putin, however, found another method—the same that he had used to unseat Yevgeny Nazdratenko, the governor of Primorye, three years earlier. On June 16, 2003, Yakovlev was appointed deputy prime minister for social issues in the federal government. An early mayoral election was scheduled for September. It is not known for certain what arguments persuaded Yakovlev to accept a position that he could lose at any time at Putin's whim. Nonetheless, Yakovlev agreed, and the Kremlin inaugurated a meddlesome campaign to promote the bland Valentina Matviyenko (who had shortly before been appointed the President's representative for the area) as a loyal supporter of Putin and therefore the inevitable winner in the gubernatorial race.

All of the pro-Putin parties in St Petersburg approved of the president's choice. The Kremlin managed to persuade almost all candidates for the mayoral post from Yakovlev's old team to abandon their ambitions. The only exception was Anna Markova, who had earlier been one of Yakovlev's deputies.

On September 2, 2003, Putin met with Matviyenko as his plenipotentiary representative, despite the fact that she was on official leave precisely in connection with her participation in the mayoral race. After discussing plans for the 'revival of St Petersburg' with her, the president wished Matviyenko success in the election. All state-run television channels ran long stories about this meeting. It seemed like campaigning by a top government official on behalf one of the candidates in a way that was 'not paid for with campaign funds'. However, the Kremlin's political analysts had convinced the president that without him Matviyenko would lose, but that with his support she would definitely win, and maybe even in the first round.

Markova, naturally, accused Matviyenko of using illegal campaign methods. 'How much does it cost to make a political commercial with the president of the country and to have it shown on federal television? Did the deputy pay for this commercial out of her campaign fund?'[6] Markova dared to charge even Putin himself with violating a number of the new electoral law's provisions.[7] The national electoral committee (CEC) agreed that she had point, though it was the media who was to blame. If the media had not run stories about the president's meeting with one of the candidates, everything would have been ethical and legal.

The candidates who had no ties to Yakovlev—including Mikhail Amosov, the leader of the regional branch of Yabloko and in opposition to both Moscow and Matviyenko, and Sergei Beliayev, former minister of federal property management—had no chances of winning from the start.

Since Markova, contrary to expectations, was able to achieve a high approval rating relatively quickly, Matviyenko attempted to use the old Bashkirian methods to get her thrown out of the election. The St Petersburg Directorate of Internal Affairs (GUVD) was requested to check the lists of signatures gathered in support of Markova's nomination, and it 'identified' over 25% of the signatures as questionable (despite the fact that the initial check by the municipal election commission had determined only 701 signatures to be invalid, which constituted 9.4% of the signatures submitted for verification). Another candidate, the businessman Viktor Yefimov (effectively a default opponent for Matviyenko in case the other candidates should suddenly collectively withdraw from the election in order to undermine it), brought a claim before the municipal court, requesting that Markova's registration be revoked due to the forged signatures.

Markova was, however, able to prove the authenticity of most of the signatures that the police had declared invalid. A few days before the election: on September 18, 2003, the Supreme Court ruled that Markova could remain a candidate. This decision came after a team of political analysts who were working for Matviyenko had determined that if Markova was barred from the election, either the election would be called off due to a voter turnout of less than 25%

in the first round of voting, or 'none of the above' would come in first in the first or second round.

Over the course of the election campaign, the police regularly detained Markova's supporters, and also the distributors of the *Peterburgskaya Liniya* newspaper, which advocated voting for 'none of the above.' On September 4, 2003, in the Moskovsky district of St Petersburg, law enforcement officials confiscated campaign flyers 'with a negative content' aimed against Matviyenko. On September 17, 2003, the general manager of the typesetting company that had printed the flyers was charged with libel. Beliayev's campaign flyers were impounded when they were being transported to St Petersburg: the pretext was that the shipment might contain materials that discredited Beliayev himself.

The first round of voting took place on September 21, 2003. Matviyenko got 48.73% of the vote and was unable to win in the first round. Markova won 15.84% (10.97% had voted for 'none of the above,' 8.8% for Beliayev, 7.5% for Amosov). The official voter turnout of 29% was incredibly low for the normally politically active city of St Petersburg—and it is possible that this figure itself was a deliberate overestimate.

After Yabloko's defeat in the first round (third place might have constituted some kind of victory, but fourth place was definitely a defeat), the party's St Petersburg branch gave in to Grigory Yavlinsky (who was being pressured by the Kremlin, which had demanded that Yabloko withdraw Amosov from the running and endorse Matviyenko even before the first round) and called on its supporters to vote for Matviyenko in the second round. On October 5, 2003, Matviyenko was elected with 63.16% of the vote and an official voter turnout of 28.25%. (Markova won 24.18%, and 11.75% went to 'none of the above.')

The state Duma elections

The State Duma on December 7, 2003 was the real testing ground for the new legislation. Twenty three parties and blocs were allowed to register. Two relatively well-known and significant parties were barred from participating in the election: Eduard Limonov's National Bolshevik Party (NBP) and Boris Berezovsky's and Ivan Rybkin's Liberal Russia.

The NBP's attempts to participate in the election were nipped in the bud. Despite its efforts, the party was unable to obtain a registration from the Ministry of Justice. The NBP is popular among young people (and has even greater potential popularity among young people). Under the right conditions, the NBP could even hope to pass the five-percent threshold. It certainly was a more real prospect than half of the twenty three parties that did take part in the elections. As a result of being barred from the race, the NBP remained nothing more than a gang of tomato-, egg-, and mayonnaise-throwing hoodlums, and the votes of the teenagers who showed up at the polls, instead of going to the NBP, went to Vladimir Zhirinovsky's centrist LDPR, which with every election loses more and more of its support among older voters. And this was, apparently, just what was wanted inside the Kremlin, where Zhirinovsky's party has been prized and cherished since the time of Yeltsin, while Limonov's NBP is hated and feared.

Berezovsky's and Rybkin's Liberal Russia party emerged after the old Liberal Russia split into two identically-named parties. The Ministry of Justice allowed the non-Berezovsky Liberal Russia to proceed, and it was this party that took part in the election under the name 'The New Course–Automobile Russia' (it won 0.84% of the vote, coming in twelfth).

Participants who were not favoured by the government were barred from the race in a particularly shameless, frank, and disdainful manner in majoritarian, single-constituency districts. In the Duma election of 2003, dozens of candidates were denied registration or had their registrations revoked. Sometimes this was simply the result of a struggle between rival candidates themselves, who tried to remove each other from the election by using the courts and the election commissions: in such cases, the CEC and the Supreme Court in Moscow sometimes displayed impartiality and reinstated candidates' registrations. Sometimes this was done by local governments intent on eliminating their critics: in such cases, Moscow could either uphold or not uphold a candidate's disqualification, based on its political desirability.

Outcome of the Election of December 7, 2003

On December 7, 2003, with a voter turnout of 55.75%, the United

Russia party—whose slogan was 'Together with the president!'—won 37.57% of the vote, according to official records, and 228 out of the Duma's 450 seats (120 party list candidates, 100 candidates from majoritarian districts, and eight more non-party candidates backed by United Russia or candidates from affiliated parties). With the addition of single-constituency deputies from the People's Party (17 seats), the Union of Right Forces (three seats), the Agrarian Party of Russia (two seats), as well as the non-party candidates and candidates who had switched parties (two from Homeland, one from Yabloko, one from the CPRF), United Russia's faction in the Duma added up to 306 seats. In other words, through United Russia the Kremlin had won more than a constitutional majority in the Duma.

The oppositional Communist CPRF won only 12.61% of the vote and 51 seats (40+11). The centrist LDRP, which sells its votes to the highest bidder in the Duma, won 11.45% and 36 seats. The semi-oppositional, left-nationalist Homeland party won 9.02% and 37 seats (29+8); 38 deputies entered the Homeland faction; and in February 2004, a pro-Putin subgroup effectively emerged within the faction (at least 17 out of 38 deputies), under the leadership of Dmitry Rogozin.

Yabloko and the SPS failed to pass the five-percent threshold, winning four and three seats, respectively, in majoritarian districts (immediately following the election, all three SPS candidates and one Yabloko candidate joined the United Russia faction). In addition, about five small-party and non-party democrats were elected to the Duma. Three seats remained empty (districts in which the greatest number of votes had been cast 'none of the above').

Eligible voters

According to the State Committee on Statistics, 2,160,500 people died in Russia in 2003. Taking into account the birth rate and immigration, the population of the country fell by 767,600 during the same year.[8] By necessity, the vast majority of the over two million people who died were voters. Newborn babies and practically all immigrants (with the exception of a few thousand) are not voters. Nonetheless, astonishingly, according to official statistics, the number of voters in the country did not fall in 2003, but rose. In the first half of 2003 alone, according to the records of the CEC, the electorate grew by two million.[9]

When asked what explained these remarkable figures, Irina Zbarskaya, head of the directorate for the census of the population and demographic statistics, gave the following official response to *Nezavisimaya Gazeta*:

Despite the fact that Russia's population has been shrinking since 1992, the number of people of age 18 years and over has grown by 3.7 million over the past 10 years, which has resulted in a growing number of voters. This increase has been due to the aging of people born at the end of the 1970s and the beginning of the 1980s, and to immigration.... According to estimates, the increase in the number of people in this age group in 2003 may have amounted to approximately 300,000.[10]

This left the remaining rise unexplained, however. In the first half of 2003 alone, the CEC (or its sources of information) counted an increase in the number of voters that was almost seven times as great as the State Committee of Statistics' forecast. It turned out, however, that the Russian electorate had further surprises in store. 'At a CEC meeting on February 10, 2004, it was revealed that, in the span of only a few months, the number of voters had unaccountably risen by 400,000.'[11] Thus, in 2003 the number of voters grew by 2,400,000, 8 times the upper end of the census forecast. At the same time, the figure of those who died in 2003 (2,160,500) added to the estimated increase of 300,000 was almost identical to the electoral bull market. It seems that the 'dead souls' first spotted by the 19th-century Russian satirist's Gogol had staged a spectacular 21st century comeback.

The CEC receives its information about citizens who are eligible to vote from the regional governments. These regional governments are responsible to the central government for carrying out its voting plans, and it is precisely they that are most interested in 'dead souls'. In an interview with *Nezavisimaya Gazeta*, Boris Makarenko, deputy general manager of the Centre of Political Technologies, pointed out that 'dead souls' cannot vote. And since they won't show up at the polls, their ballots can be cast for them by someone named "the administrative resource".'[12]

With 2,100,000 votes at their disposal, local governments and election commissions possessed a silent but influential majority.

Observers from different parties, reporters, and ordinary citizens who came to vote on December 7, noted an enormous number of irregularities that might show the tracks of this army of deceased voters.

In electoral area No. 1714 (Orekhovo-Borisovo's district No. 197 in Moscow, returned secret-service agent Konstantin Zatulin for United Russia), the lights were suddenly turned off while ballots were being counted. The committee sent all of the observers out of the room while, for an unexplained reason, all of the windows were opened. In other areas in the same district, the lights were turned off as well, and all of the observers were told to come back later. In electoral area No. 2702 (Tushinsky district No. 200 in Moscow, returned former minister Vladimir Vasiliev), an elderly female voter, who had a portable ballot box carried out to her, noticed that the ballot box was not sealed. At the voter's request, attempts were made to reseal the ballot box, but as it turned out, the paper could not be glued onto the plastic of which the ballot box was made. Other portable ballot boxes possessed similar properties. In Babushkinsky district No. 192 in Moscow (returned Sergei Shirokov for United Russia), observers from the camp of Yabloko candidate Sergei Mitrokhin were denied copies of the voting records until OSCE representatives intervened at their request. After the polls closed, Yabloko's observers noted that unsealed ballots were being transported from precinct election commissions to the regional election commission.[13] (According to the official data, Mitrokhin lost to Shirokov by 1.5%.) In area No. 1064 of Balashov's electoral district No. 157 (election of Pyotr Kamshilov; Krasnoznamenny village, Samoilov district, Saratov region), the secretary of the precinct committee added a packet of ballots to the ballot box in front of the voters; the head of the committee refused to listen to observers' complaints.[14] In area No. 1546 in the Rostov region, the composite records of the GAS-Vybory electronic voting system showed that zero absentee ballots had been handed out, while the copies of the same committee's records received by the CPRF observer indicate that 406 absentee ballots had been handed out.[15]

In contrast to previous Duma elections, observers in Moscow who asked for copies of records had to sit out the procedure common in Bashkiria. Local electoral committees refused to sign the records without first having them approved by the regional committees. Observers were given copies of records only after they had been 'checked' and approved by the territorial committees.

In areas where election fraud was common, the methods were more blatant. In Ingushetia, one of the losing candidates, Musa Ozdoyev (by no means a marginal candidate, the head of the Ingush office of the People's Party), checked the records of several precinct committees by going around to voters' homes and interviewing them with the assistance of his friends and relatives. In area No. 67 (Ingush district No. 13, returned Bashir Kodzoyev for United Russia), 53 people failed to recognize their own signatures, their passport information, or both. Forty-six citizens could not be interviewed, because they did not reside at the addresses indicated in the voters' list: some of them had long ago moved to other cities, some to other countries, and some had died.[16] 'The area committees were in a hurry,' says Musa Ozdoyev.

They simply had no time to find voters' names for the enormous number of ballots that were added to the ballot boxes after the polls had closed.... In the already mentioned area No. 67, for example, United Russia won 164 votes, and this is what the precinct committee's records indicate. But in the records of the regional committee, United Russia's total has grown to 1784 votes. The exorbitant difference of 1620 votes was only partly offset by lowering the totals of the other parties; for the most part, this hole was patched up by filling in new ballots for about a thousand citizens.[17]

Nonetheless, in April 2004, Ingushetia's Supreme Court ruled against a claim brought by People's Assembly deputy Musa Ozdoyev against Ingushetia's election commission, and denied his request to invalidate the election commission's final vote count in the December election.

In occupied Chechnya there was a similar pattern. In the Grozny district, United Russia won 97.25% of the vote—a record for Russia, especially remarkable because United Russia was the 'war party' (although the military also voted in Chechnya, in addition to Chechens). Its performance was stellar in certain areas: In area No. 66 (Chechen electoral district No. 32) there were 1005 voters and 886 ballots were handed out: 884 of them were cast for United Russia and two invalidated). In area No. 90 (the same Chechen district): 666 ballots were handed out and all 666 (100%) were cast for United Russia.[18]

According to the head of the CEC himself, Alexander Veshnyakov, in Chechnya and Ingushetia the number of ballots cast

exceeded the number of voters by 11%, which was explained by President Akhmat Kadyrov's press secretary as a result of 'very intense immigration.'[19]
(Other parts of Russia were also the subject of 'intense immigration'. The number of ballots cast was also found to exceed the number of registered voters in the Moscow region by 4.5%, and in the Kaluga region by 5%.[20]) In one of the regions where electoral corrections had always been endemic (Bashkiria, Tatarstan, Kalmykia, and Dagestan), officials were more candid. One Tatar official admitted off the record, 'in the morning we planned to give them 78%, but then we received an order from Moscow not to raise the bar and to stop at 60%.'[21]

The opposition parties to United Russia in the Duma elections fought back as best they could. The pro-West Union of Right Forces (SPS) and Yabloko, as well as the Communists were able to collect a rather large number of copies of area records. Both Yabloko and the Communists used their copies to recount the votes. And they immediately discovered significant discrepancies, even at this level of the elections. According to Yabloko founder Grigory Yavlinsky, 'we reviewed 12,500 records and found that 16% of them did not match the CEC's official data.'[22]

Boris Nemtsov, the SPS leader, said they their results were similar: 'The party's executive committee laboured day and night to review 14,000 copies. A fifth of them turned out to be falsified.'[23]

According to Galina Mikhaleva, head of Yabloko's analytic centre at the time, the most common discrepancies were found in column 10 (number of valid ballots) of the area copies and the composite records of the regional election commissions and the national CEC. For example, the 'records from Smolensk region area No. 389 indicate that the committee counted 964 valid ballots. The CEC lists 1020 valid ballots for the same area.... Udmurtia, area No. 817: the precinct records show 762 valid ballots; the CEC indicates 1108.'[24]

From official records Yabloko found that at least 250,000 unaccounted absentee ballots had been handed out for voting in the 'common federal district'. Citizens voting outside their home area are given absentee ballots by their election commissions. If they are voting not only outside their home area, but outside their home district, they are given ballots for voting in the common federal district, but receive no ballots for voting in single-constituency districts. A total of 572,926 people voted by absentee ballot on December 7, 2003, but 424,926 of them nonetheless voted in their own districts. The difference was the number of voters in the common federal district, or 147,997. However, the official records indicated that the election commissions handed out not 147,997 ballots for voting in the federal district, but 403,809.[25] The mystery votes were for the party 'with the President'.

According to Yabloko's analytic centre, for 'area No. 284 in North Ossetia, the record given to our observer proves that Yabloko got 16 votes. The CEC sharply reduced the number of 'wrong' votes to six. In area No. 233 17 people voted for our party; we were given only seven votes.... Also in area No. 233, the records indicate 218 votes for United Russia, but the CEC's records give United Russia 356 votes.'

According to the Communists, records from area No. 925 (Orenburg region) indicate that 536 people voted for the CPRF; in other official records, these votes shrank to... 136.[26] 'They said we got 12%, but I think our actual outcome was more of the order of 18%,' comments Ivan Melnikov, deputy head of the CPRF Central Committee and professor of mathematics at Moscow State University. 'Two thirds of the election commission record copies that we possess differ from the records that were used to establish the official vote count. And most importantly, they contain internal contradictions. If you add up the votes that were cast for all of the parties, you find that it is greater than the number of people who voted.'[27]

According to Fair Game, a parallel system for vote-counting created by the Communists, the figures on 60,000 records (i.e. two thirds of their total number) differ from the official outcomes announced by the CEC. 'The number of all ballots that were handed out and the sum of all valid, defaced, annulled, etc., ballots do not coincide. This can mean only one thing: extra ballots were physically added to the original total. FairGame's operators find that 3.5 million extra ballots were added in the country as a whole.' The greatest numbers were added in the Kurgan, Rostov, Samara, Orel, Tver, and Stavropol regions, Dagestan, Tatarstan, Bashkiria, and Moscow. According to the Communists, Yabloko and the SPS had actually passed the five-percent threshold, while United Russia was given an extra 3%-4%.[28]

But, as in earlier elections, the CEC declined to accept the area copies of voting records. By law, election commissions are allowed to correct 'mistakes' of lower level commissions. In addition, copies are not admissible in court. Area election commissions are required to hand out copies of their records upon request. But they are not considered reliable as it is thought they are filled out hastily, incompletely, and with obvious mistakes to observers who may not understand election rules. With regards to the Duma election of 2003 the head of the CEC, Alexander Veshnyakov stated that 'only about 20 copies of the records are filled out correctly from a legal point of view. The rest have no legal significance.'[29]

Nonetheless, based on its copies of the records, Yabloko filed about 100 lawsuits in 44 regions to have the election outcomes invalidated. In most instances, the courts simply refused to hear the case. The Novgorod Regional Court, for example, refused to hear Yabloko's suit to invalidate the Duma election outcomes in the region by claiming that such cases must be heard by district courts. On June 23, 2004, the Supreme Court upheld the Novgorod Regional Court's decision.[30] About 15 of Yabloko's claims (out of almost 100) were granted a hearing. By June 2004, all of them had been thrown out of court due to the fact that the record copies had 'no legal weight.'[31] In fact, the courts declined to review the overwhelming majority of claims brought against the outcomes of the election in various districts (by the CPRF, Yabloko, private citizens).

The Kremlin had landed two flies with one blow in the Duma elections. Without irregularities, the pro-Western Yabloko (and perhaps the SPS as well) would have had more than 5% of the vote and representation in the fourth session of the Duma. (As it was, its candidates later joined United Russia.) In addition United Russia—together with its allies from the NPRF—would have been able to get a majority of Duma seats, but enough for a qualified majority. In order to pass many different laws, particularly those requiring a constitutional majority, Putin's regime would have had to take into account either the opinion of the Communists or the opinion of the liberals (the way it happened in the third convocation of the Duma).

The Presidential re-election

In the summer of 1996, over the course of two weeks between the first and the second rounds of voting in the presidential election that Yeltsin won, the number of voters had increased by 100,000. Between the Duma election of December 1999 and the presidential election of March 2000, i.e. over the course of three months, the number of voters grew by 1,300,000. But in 2004, the government chose a different approach. This time, no one doubted that Putin would win in the first round—what was open to doubt was voter turnout. Therefore, the list of eligible voters was now reduced by 842,000 compared to what it had been in the Duma election of December 2003.

Also in contrast with the Duma election, in which the Kremlin restricted the number of candidates and parties, in the presidential election the Kremlin aimed to expand the list of candidates. This was done, first, in order to present voters with abundant choice and thus to render the election legitimate in the eyes of the West. And second, arguably more importantly, it was done in order to prevent an 'obscenely low' voter turnout, which was a real possibility.

An 'obscenely low' voter turnout was secretly decided to be a voter turnout below that of 2000 election (68.74%), and the goal was set at 70%-75% (the voter turnout in the Duma election in December had been only 55.75%, but as the experience of the past 14 years has shown, voter-turnout in elections for heads of state is always considerably higher than in other elections). The likelihood that voter turnout would be below 50% (which would invalidate the election) was equal to zero. The deliberately overwrought discussion in the media of this possibility was itself in reality an instrument for raising voter turnout.

Sergei Mironov, the speaker of the upper house of the Russian parliament (head of the Russian Party of Life), was roped into participating as a candidate, and attempts were made to persuade liberal leaders Yavlinsky (a Yabloko founder) and Zhirinovsky (of the Liberal Democratic Party of Russia, LDPR). Yabloko, resenting the way it had been treated in the Duma elections, refused to play the Kremlin's games and even returned to the opposition. It initiated a pact among the democratic parties not to participate in the presidential election if the democrats were unable to agree on a single candidate (and the democrats were not able to agree on a single candidate, as expected). Vladimir Zhirinovsky carried out the Kremlin's order with fine line in subversive irony. The LDPR did nominate a candidate for president—not Zhirinovsky himself, however, but his boxer-bodyguard Oleg Malyshkin. The Communists also played down the significance of this election as far as they dared, nominating as the CPRF candidate not their leader Zyuganov, but the left-wing agrarian Nikolai Kharitonov. The democrats' pact was soon broken by the Kremlin with the nomination of Irina Khakamada, who ended up representing the liberal voice in the election—despite the wishes of Yabloko and Boris Nemtsov's SPS.

The CEC helpfully ignored electoral violations during registration, mainly the purchase of falsified signatures by the headquarters of practically all of the candidates nominated by non-parliamentary parties (with the exception of Putin—signatures for his nomination were genuine).[32]

Nonetheless, the Kremlin's attitude toward two candidates, the left-leaning populist Sergei Glazyev and Ivan Rybkin, the candidate supported by Boris Berezovsky, was ambivalent. On the one hand, they increased voter turnout. On the other, they were capable of raising unpleasant topics in their election campaigns (the liberal voice Khakamada turned out to be capable of doing this as well, but she quickly stopped doing so after being called to order). In addition, if Glazyev won the second highest number of votes, his candidacy would gain dangerous momentum for the next presidential election in 2008 (the Communist Zyuganov was invariably defeated and so no one worried if his candidate Kharitonov won). In other words, Glazyev's participation gave the president's campaign team a headache: the runner-up to Putin had to be Kharitonov, not Glazyev.

The bureaucrats in Putin's election team were in favour of barring Glazyev from the election, but Putin's political strategists insisted on—and obtained—'democratic' methods of eliminating this candidate through Bashkirian technology. Indeed, the political strategists took up the project of 'destroying Glazyev' with creative delight—they also periodically used Glazyev to frighten their own bureaucratic management and to obtain budget increases for their department.

The political strategists' attitude toward Rybkin's participation in the election was similarly laissez faire: 'let him be!' But the 'Rybkin problem' had certain special aspects in Putin's eyes that ultimately resulted in its being solved completely separately.

Apart from ample choice of candidates high voter turnout was also boosted via administrative means. The administrative head of St Petersburg's Frunzensky district, Vyacheslav Khmyrov, for example, sent the following letter to the district's housing cooperatives:

Please have your housing cooperative's management office submit a work plan to the district administration before 02.01.04 to ensure that residents vote on 03.14.04 in the Russian presidential election. Your work must guarantee a turnout of at least 79% of the eligible voters among your residents. The results of your work will be evaluated after the outcomes of the election are calculated.[33]

Called to account by St Petersburg's Yabloko office Khmyrov explained that it 'was my own idea, exclusively my own initiative. I did not do it on anyone's instructions.' But subsequently he offered what was probably the real course of events, 'Our district has two district election commissions. As district head, I am obliged to assist them. I am in constant communication with them. The committees have not criticized this letter in any way.'[34]

Rybkin's vanishing act

Ivan Rybkin's disappearance, reappearance, and the awkward and contradictory interviews that he gave after returning to Moscow, were the only major fly in the ointment during the 2004 presidential election.

As an official candidate, Rybkin had to be given the opportunity to state facts and hypotheses on television. Given Rybkin's connections with well-informed people, he was expected to produce certain sensational revelations which were extremely unpleasant for the president himself in general, and for certain members of his chekist-commercial inner circle in particular.

As it turned out, however, Rybkin had nothing to say that was not known already (or no chance to say it). In his interviews, the candidate merely hinted at the fact that he possessed information about the 'stash' kept by Putin and his collaborators Gennady Timchenko and Yuri Kovalchuk, and also about the role of the Rossiya Bank controlled by St Petersburg chekists. There was little new in what he said: practically all of it had already been published in the print media and/or on the internet, and usually in a more reliable form (for example, while Rybkin talked about the Kovalchuk 'brothers,' it would have been more accurate to say 'father and son,' since the third Kovalchuk has no direct relation to the brother's and nephew's business). Nonetheless, what the administrative oligarchy (still) had to tolerate on the internet and in low-circulation magazines, it found unacceptable and dangerous on mass media such as television.

The government had ample opportunity to decline Rybkin registration as a candidate. The signatures gathered in support of his nomination were quite dubious (this was also true of all the other candidates from non-parliamentary parties). But denying registration to the most oppositional of all candidates would have looked manipulative to the West and, diluting the spectrum of opposition candidates to Putin, might have lowered voter turnout.

In order to silence Rybkin and to prevent him from repeating and elaborating on television the theme of the web of corruption surrounding the president, the secret service conducted a vintage special operation—possibly, the only operation conducted by the secret service in recent years that has been wholly successful and effective. In one week, the dignified and moderately respected politician was transformed into a comic figure who no one would believe anyway and could henceforth be allowed to produce any revelations he felt like.

In February 2004, he disappeared under mysterious circumstances, a day after he accused the Putin administration of complicity in the 1999 bomb attacks in Moscow apartments. Five days later, Rybkin appeared in Kiev. He stated he had been lured to Ukraine under the pretense of meeting the former Chechen leader Aslan Maskhadov. Upon arrival he was offered refreshments in the apartment, at which point he became 'very drowsy,' waking on February 10th. Upon waking he was shown a videotape in which he was performing 'revolting acts' conducted by 'horrible perverts'. He was told that the tape would be made public if he continued with his presidential campaign. He initially continued the campaign from overseas, but, on March 5, 2004, he withdrew from the race, saying he did not want to be part of 'this farce.'

Presidential election irregularities

In the final analysis, the re-election proved to be quite a struggle for the Kremlin. The excessively high expectations at the Kremlin of Putin's popularity had taken a heavy toll on the election commissions throughout the Russian Federation. Official observers from Yabloko and the SPS were not able to monitor the election as they had not entered candidates. But the Communist CPRF had stationed around 200,000 observers.

In April 2004, campaign headquarters of the Communist candidate Kharitonov had analyzed and published the materials which they had collected. It consisted of copies of records from 18 area commissions in Moscow and composite tables provided by the regional committees of the Ramenki, Troparevo-Nikulino, and Vnukovo districts. A typical example was area No. 2572 [in Ramenki, where], on March 14,1430 ballots were handed out according to the area election commission's records, and 2214 ballots were handed out according to the regional election commission's records. The area election commission reported that 1377 ballots had been taken out of stationary ballots boxes, while the regional election commission corrected this number: 2214 ballots had been taken out.[35]

Tables published in *Nezavisimaya Gazeta* showed the totals for the four presidential candidates in three Moscow precincts. The first column gave the number of votes won by each candidate according to the precinct committee records, the second column indicated the same figure according to the territorial committee records, and the third column showed the difference between the two numbers.

In area No. 2565 (Ramenki), there were 100 less for the liberal Khakamada, 50 less for the populist Glazyev, and 50 less for the Communist Kharitonov, and 46 less for 'none of the above'; Putin's total was 650 higher. In area No. 2572 (Ramenki), there were 170 less for Khakamada, 50 for Glazyev, 50 for Kharitonov, and 150 less for 'none of the above'; Putin's total was 1257 higher. In area No. 2620 (Troparevo-Nikitino), there were 70 votes less for Khakamada, 20 for Glazyev, 10 for Kharitonov, and 60 for 'none of the above'; Putin's total was 170 higher.[36]

After analyzing the information from their Moscow observers, the Communist party's lawyers identified five patterns:

1. The regional committees reported a higher voter turnout than was indicated in the records of the precinct election commissions.

2. All of the additional votes that appeared in the regional election commissions' records were given to one candidate, V. V. Putin. In 18 electoral areas, this candidate received a total of 5479 additional votes. Only in two areas did several dozen additional votes go to S. M. Mironov and O. A. Malyshkin.
3. The greatest losses from the area committees' 'corrections' were sustained by [liberal] candidate I.M. Khakamada. In one precinct, she was given only 35 out of a total of 135 votes that had initially been cast for her; in another, 41 out of 181; and in 18 precincts overall, this candidate lost a total of 870 votes or 35.4%.
4. Almost everywhere, votes were taken away from 'none of the above.' Evidently, this ... this 'candidate' would definitely not complain.
5. The difference between the area and the regional committees' figures is usually divisible by 10: 30, 50, 70, 110. Kharitonov's lawyers explain that this makes counting easier: round numbers are easier to add and subtract than not round ones. It is true that this also makes it easier for investigators to spot falsifications—provided, of course, that they are interested in doing so.[37]

Even CEC head Alexander Veshnyakov agreed with these compelling findings:

A review of the complaint has determined that falsifications have taken place in the Ramenki and Troperevo-Nikulino territorial election commissions,' Veshnyakov stated. 'The Moscow municipal election commission, which reviewed these matters under the CEC's supervision, has resolved to file a claim with the prosecutor's office to investigate and hold the guilty parties accountable. Wrong-doing must be punished, and it must be punished firmly.[38]

The Moscow municipal election commission's resolution was passed on March 30, 2004, and on April 6 it was sent to the Moscow prosecutor's office. After which the file... was lost.

Elsewhere in Russia, the top supporting regions for Putin were the usual suspects. According to official CEC figures, Ingushetia turned out to be the frontrunner in terms of voter turnout and votes for Putin. Voter turnout: 96.23%; Putin's total: 98.18%. In terms of voter turnout, Ingushetia was surpassed only by Kabardino-Balkaria (97.72%), which, however, fell somewhat short in terms of Putin's total (96.49%). The other top performers are no less familiar: Dagestan (94.59% for Putin, voter turnout 94.08%); Chechnya (92.35% for Putin, voter turnout 94.19%); Bashkiria (91.79% for Putin, voter turnout 89.09%); Mordovia (91.35% for Putin, voter turnout 94.57%); North Ossetia (91.25% for Putin, voter turnout 89.24%).

Musa Ozdoyev, the Ingushetia People's Assembly deputy who uncovered the falsification of the Duma election outcomes in Ingushetia, conducted his own investigation of the presidential election in the republic, too. According to him, 'not even half of Ingushetia's voters participated in the presidential election. The election was basically subverted.' Ozdoyev collected copies of all lists of voters from all area committees in Nazran and compared the lists used in the Duma election with the lists used in the presidential election. A remarkable thing was discovered:

On December 7, a voter obtained a ballot by presenting one passport, while on March 14, he obtained a ballot by presenting a different passport. And he signed his name differently in both cases as well. Here, for example, are the lists of Nazran's electoral area No. 67... Citizen Magomed Zalikhmanovich Abiyev, born in 1983, voted in December with passport No. 26 01 132102, while in March he presented passport No. 26 01 001477.[39]

Among such 'two-passport' voters, Ozdoyev found his own brother Mikail and a great number of his friends. He concluded not unfairly: 'In reality, these people did not vote. Their passport details were supplied by the election commission. And their signatures, too. The election commissions evidently did not expect anyone to check them, so they simply made up the passport numbers.... as long as they had 10 digits and the same republican series number, 26. Notice that the passport numbers are the same in both lists in about 10% of the cases. This indicates the actual voter turnout in Ingushetia on March 14. The rest was added.[40]

At the end of March 2004, the advisory member at the CEC from the Communist CPRF (Vadim Solovyev) sent a claim to the General Prosecutor's Office, requesting 'criminal proceedings in connection with signs of voter fraud in the presidential election in the Republic of Adygea. Such signs have been identified by observers from

Kharitonov's campaign headquarters in 13 of the republic's electoral areas. The pattern is the same in all cases: candidate Putin has everywhere been given a greater number of votes than is indicated in the precinct election commission records (in large areas, 300-500 votes have been added to his totals), while his opponents have been given a smaller number.... [In Adygea], the greatest number of votes has been taken away from the "red" candidate Kharitonov.'[41]

While the CEC had agreed that the election outcomes had been falsified in Putin's favour in two Moscow districts, it however refused to acknowledge similar evidence of voter fraud in other regions—citing the familiar fact that the record copies had been improperly filled out from the legal point of view. The CEC Alexander Veshnyakov regretted in an interview with *Nezavisimaya Gazeta* that, 'in terms of handing out the record copies, although there are rules for everything, unfortunately the observers' poor understanding of legal procedure leads to completely unfounded objections....' Short attention spans were really to blame:

> The observer must wait for the vote totals to be counted and for the records to be signed. But if he gets tired of waiting, writes down the preliminary totals that he overheard while the votes were being counted, and then takes this document, which has not been signed by anyone, and goes with it to his party's headquarters—should the committee be blamed? ...

Nor was the federation committee to blame, it had gone beyond what could be expected:

> If there are objections that some committee refused to hand out copies of its records, then there are indeed grounds for a claim against it. But I do not accept such objections against our committee. The first thing that we did in the parliamentary election, and then in the presidential one, was to publish a special reminder for observers (although this is in principle not our responsibility).

He further wondered whether the complaining candidates had brought their claims with sufficient vigour:

> When observers collect materials—including materials that have no legal weight—and send them to their party headquarters and two months later start complaining that they weren't given real copies... Well, how can we establish that two months after the fact?[42]

In the final analysis, all the hard work that had gone into the election throughout the Federation had yielded only half the desired result for the Kremlin. 71.31% of the electorate had voted for Putin, which was within the range predicted and therefore pleasing.

However, official voter turnout on March 14, 2004, was purportedly 64.39%, lower than the turn-out for Putin's first election, and therefore the 'obscenely low' result that pre-election guidance had sought to avoid.

CHAPTER EIGHT

The Self-Censor

The 2nd term Duma and Presidential elections had revealed that there were still problems with the election laws and in August 2004, the CEC proposed introducing a new package of amendments to facilitate its 'ministry.' The most radical reform proposed by the agency was to increase the 'proportional-representation component' in the election of Duma deputies so that all deputies were elected on a proportional basis via a party list, rather than returned through constituency elections. The CEC also proposed reducing the allowed percentage of inauthentic and invalid signatures collected in support of a candidate from 25% to 5% in order to weed out dubious candidates more effectively. On September 13, 2004, President Putin also expressed support for the idea of allowing only party-list candidates to run for the state Duma and announced the upcoming repeal of direct elections for the regional governors. The reason he gave was fighting terrorism, It also strengthened the vice-like grip of the Kremlin over the regions, as governors would once again be appointed by the president and then confirmed by local legislative assemblies.

By this time, the criticism both in Russia and abroad had become highly vocal. A group of over one hundred foreign scientists and politicians sent an open letter to the heads of the European Union and NATO, accusing the Russian president of rejecting democratic values and harbouring dictatorial ambitions. In the West, Putin's political trajectory was seen as a threat to Russian democracy and the country's economy. To foreign analysts, Russia appeared to be shifting toward a social-political model characteristic of Latin

American countries. The Kremlin noted the opposition, and moved ahead nonetheless to pass amendments to the election law through the Duma—safe in the knowledge that a constitutional challenge would fail due to the qualified majority it enjoyed.

The Kremlin was also anxious about the continuing high level of criticism that kept swirling around the country. In principle, the feeling was that the media was free to say what it wanted—but if it was allowed to talk 'filth', it was a small wonder that the electorate had been turned off from voting in the Presidential elections. This created uncertainty that did not help anyone.

Regulating the internet

One culprit was doubtless the growing size of the Russian internet community, as Russian cities became ever more prosperous as a result of the surging demand for Russia's mineral deposits. The idea of the government regulating the world wide web has always been close to the hearts of Putin's bureaucrats. Pronouncements in favour of filtering it from 'falsification' became especially common in 2004 when the first signs of voter apathy reared its head. Given Putin's ostensible popularity, the apathy clearly had to come from somewhere.

Just before the elections, in March 2004, information was leaked to the media about proposed legislation to regulate the internet and internet media outlets. One bill, according to the leaked information, proposed that special permission be required to access the web. Another bill would have required all internet media outlets to register with the government (at present, the registration of internet media outlets is voluntary).

On April 13, 2004, the president's old collaborator, former and current Minister of Communications, Leonid Reiman, once again expressed his concern about the rights of information consumers: 'It is necessary to regulate the relations between providers and consumers, and not to allow information that goes over the internet to be subject to distortions.'[1]

Shortly before this, the widow of Sobchak, Lyudmila—the Federation Council deputy from Tuva—also repeatedly expressed her deep concern about 'simple people' who 'suffer' because 'no one carries any responsibility for unreliable information published on the internet.'[2] (It was suggested that high among the 'simple people' who 'suffer' from the internet, a prominent place was occupied by the Sobchak family. Her daughter's romantic adventures were diligently monitored on the web, as were those of Lyudmila.)

On June 16-17, 2004, a special meeting of the Organization for Security and Co-operation in Europe (OSCE), devoted to internet-related issues, took place in Paris. The official position of the Russian government was represented at the meeting by secret service General Viktor Ostroukhov, who proposed increasing international cooperation in controlling the content of the web and holding internet service providers accountable for websites that promote xenophobia, terrorism, extremism, non-traditional religious sects, and anti-globalization movements.

The Russian representative expressed particular concern towards the popular Russian search engine 'Yandex,' which enables 'anyone who wants to do so to become easily acquainted with the teachings of the Aum Shinrikyo sect, the Jehova's Witnesses... to access the websites of the Hare Krishna organization... to learn about various Satan-worshipping cults.'[3]

Since 2004, bills for new media regulations have periodically been passed by the Duma to address these concerns ahead of the next Presidential election. Proposals have included revising the definition of 'media' to include all communication and materials that pass over the internet, as well as permitting internet media outlets to be run only by legal or physical persons who have registered with the government as individual private business owners.

In 2006-2007, the government's pressure on the internet increased, although it did not yet introduce an all-encompassing new law. Inconvenient websites were blocked or forced to find foreign hosting when law enforcement organs threatened Russian internet service providers (the websites of Limonov's party and the internet outlets of the Another Russia coalition at the end of 2006 and beginning of 2007; the Antikompromat internet library of political articles in March 2007); shut down websites accused of making 'extremist' and 'libellous' pronouncements (the court decision to close down the critical site 'Novy Fokus' in Khakassia at the end of 2006 'for not registering as a media outlet'); or, finally, employed hackers' methods to achieve their ends, such as the so-called 'ddos-attack' (the 'hacker' terrorist campaign against oppositional internet resources at the end of May 2007 looked like a trial run for the possibility of a future crisis, a dress rehearsal).

NTV's final demise

Despite its good behaviour, the privately-owned mass media continued to feature on the Kremlin's radar for various infractions. NTV had done so well in becoming a reality and entertainment channel under its latest head. But even he was unable to provide the degree of loyalty that was expected of him in the Kremlin. NTV's news policies continued to overstep the safety norms that the two public channels One and Rossiya observed to the letter. The state-run Rossiya ('button two'), even had a formal list of 'prohibited words.' Thus, the following expressions cannot be uttered on the air: 'substituting money payments for benefits' (reporters must say 'benefit payments'), 'banking crisis,' 'shahid [Muslim martyr],' and even 'Chechnya' (reporters must say 'the Chechen republic').[4]

NTV, however, did not remain silent about the grandiose fire in the nineteenth-century Manezh Exhibition Hall, which cast a shadow over Putin's re-election triumph on the evening of March 14, 2004. Something analogous was seen, too, on May 9, 2004—Victory Day, a national holiday—when the president of Chechnya and the speaker of Chechnya's parliament were blown up in a stadium in Grozny, while the prime minister survived only by a miracle, having left for Moscow the day before. NTV's special editions showing Kadyrov's bloody body at 11:40 a.m. and reporting his death at noon formed a stark contrast with the silence observed by the government channels, which did not wish to 'spoil Victory Day.' Reporting the death of the Chechen leader, the anchor of the program 'Segodnya' Alexei Sukhanov was pulled off the air in the middle of a word. The three-hour silence of the government channels ended at 2 p.m. when the news show 'Vesti' reported that the assassinated Kadyrov had been 'wounded'.[5]

Although the privately-run NTV had already been through the wringer twice, it was the only nationally televised channel where one could see reports about the death following a hunger strike of a worker involved in liquidating the consequences of the Chernobyl disaster; about demonstrations by pro-West Yabloko's youth organization against the cult of Andropov and Putin; about the provocative anti-Putin protests of the National Bolsheviks. When the test-firing of a ballistic missile in the Northern fleet went awry, it was only NTV's 'Strana i Mir' ('The Country and the World') that even alluded to the fact that the missile had failed come out of its silo—the two public channels continued busily to describe the 'large-scale' test-firing.

In addition, two main havens for free-thinking lingered on in the NTV schedule: Leonid Parfenov's 'Namedni' ('The Other Day') and Savik Shuster's 'Svoboda Slova' ('Freedom of Speech'). In fact, due to its audience figures, 'Namedni's' ad time was the most expensive on NTV: one minute cost $141,600. Alexander Gerasimov's news and analysis program 'Lichny Vklad' ('Personal Input') did not broach forbidden subjects—in contrast to Parfenov's show—but it cultivated an objective, disinterested tone that contrasted strongly with the Putin-mania of 'Vesti' on Rossiya and 'Vremya' on Channel One. (Presenter Gerasimov was also the deputy manager of the station.)

Not long after Putin's re-election, NTV's independent course ground to a halt on June 1 when Parfenov was dismissed. Shortly before, NTV's management had cancelled a 'Namedni' segment featuring an interview with the widow of the former president of Chechnya-Ichkeria Yandarbiyev, who had been killed by Russian GRU agents in Qatar. Reporter Yelena Samoilova's segment, 'To Marry Zelimkhan,' was taken off the air in the European part of the country, after being shown in the Far East, Siberia, and the Urals. According to Parfenov, deputy manager Gerasimov had 'cancelled the segment at the request of the security services.'[6] Another account, published in *Kommersant*, was that the order had come from the President's press office.[7]

After being instructed to cancel the segment, Parfenov requested a written confirmation from Gerasimov. He then sent a copy of this order to *Kommersant*, where it was published on May 31, 2004. This NTV argued was an 'unacceptable infringement of corporate ethics' and the cause of Parfenov's dismissal.

The mystery about this was that Parfenov had actually already self-censored the segment and cut out all the parts that might have been unpleasant to Kremlin eyes. For example, he had deleted a fragment about the fact that Yandarbiyev (who was killed in February 2004), acting on his own initiative, had telephoned the Chechen terrorists who had hijacked the 'Nord-Ost' theatre audience and demanded from them that they should commit suicide and not allow the death of a single hostage. This revised version of the interview was the one already been seen by viewers in the Far East—and it had not contained anything particularly revealing. Nor had it contained anything that might have made life worse for the agents who had been caught in Qatar.

It is more likely that the real reason for Parfenov's firing were his ironic remarks about the president and his 'sovereign style,' which in the spring of 2004 had become a constant leitmotif of his programs, and that this had exceeded the patience of Kremlin officials and Putin himself.

The last straw was an advertisement for an upcoming episode of 'Namedni'—the episode that was supposed to feature the interview with the window of the Chechen separatist. 'Who is Mr. Putin?' asked Parfenov's voice in the commercial. 'Nobody and nothing!' replied the voice of Putin (then, after a pause, came Putin's words to the effect that 'nobody and nothing will be able to do anything bad to Russia'). On the Saturday before the final episode of 'Namedni' on Sunday, this mocking advertisement was played every hour on NTV. The station authorities were too embarrassed to censor the commercial. Instead, they instigated a conflict around the Chechen interview that drew attention away from their actual grievance.

After four years of Putin's Kremlin, the self-control exercised by the free media had become exemplary. As Alexander Ryklin of the magazine *Yezhenedelny Zhurnal* wrote:

When the channel's managers state that they fired Parfenov independently, without any pressure from above, I believe them completely. Today, the trust and understanding that exist between Kremlin officials and our media generals have reached such high levels that direct instructions are no longer necessary: everyone already understands perfectly well what kind of television the country must have today. As the Kremlin says: 'Don't teach Dobrodeyev [head of the docile Channel One]—you'll only ruin him.[8]

A former co-owner of NTV believed that 'the cancellation of "Namedni" and the firing of Parfenov demonstrate that a new degree of control has been established. Parfenov walked a certain fine line and played hide-and-seek with his bosses and with the ruling party (not United Russia, of course, but with the party of the security services, let us call it that).... Previously, reporters were controlled by being made to remove certain segments; after that they were allowed to talk about what they liked. But now that is not enough. Today, reporters must be controlled to the point of not being allowed to think....'

But it was the secretary of the Reporters' Union, Igor Yakovenko who hit the nail on its head. 'If before this we all knew that we had censorship and government control over national channels, but at least we got doses of glasnost when the TV maestros were allowed to do something, then now it turns out that even they are not allowed to do anything, and that the TV channel is not even concerned about its ratings.'[9]

At the beginning of July 2004, the next round of purges followed. NTV's head was promoted to head of Gazprom Media's board of directors, and his place was taken by a reporter who had come over from the Rossiya Channel. On July 7, 2004, at a meeting of the channel's new management, the new management declared its intention to terminate all political programming on the network: Shuster's 'Svoboda Slova,' Gerasimov's 'Lichny Vklad,' and the Pilot TV-produced show 'Krasnaya Strela' ('Red Arrow')—a substantially toned down version of the popular TVS show under Yeltsin, 'Shut the Lights!'.

NTV's ending of 'Svoboda Slova' left little to the imagination:

The show was considered a forum for the exchange of opinions. But not all opinions. People with a certain status, people who made decisions, remained in the minority or did not participate at all, and as a result the show stopped being an objective reflection of the arguments going on in society today.... Often, it looked like a club of armchair warriors who were essentially intent on proving one proposition: that Putin doesn't know what he's doing.[10]

It did not matter that NTV's new overseer was not entirely correct. The opinion that 'Putin doesn't know what he's doing' was not expressed by most guests on Shuster's program—on the contrary, most argued the opposite. For all of 2004, 'Svoboda Slova' was dominated by Dmitry Rogozin (Homeland) and Alexei Mitrofanov (Zhirinovsky's LDPR), who on key issues in Russian politics (Chechnya, 'managed democracy,' freedom of speech, the redistribution of large-scale property) are more pro-Putin than Putin himself. However, along with Zhirinovsky-supporters and Putinoids of various stripes, 'Svoboda Slova' did sometimes offer critics of the regime a chance to express their views—from both left-wing (communists, Limonov) and liberal perspectives (Yavlinsky, Nemtsov, Khakamada).

If Parfenov was banished for doing what he did (ridicule Putinmania), then Gerasimov was asked to leave for what he did not do (praise Putin). The level of Kremlin paranoia about NTV could be measured by the fact that the new head of the channel had to report to a newly created supervisor—a certain Tamara Gavrilova. Very little is known about her, except that she was Vladimir Putin's classmate at the university.

Mention should also be made of REN TV, in particular, of Olga Romanova's news and analysis programme '24' on this channel. The channel broadcasts predominantly in Moscow, and even in Moscow is not available in all districts and was under the economic and ideological influence of Anatoly Chubais, the author of Yeltsin's privatization and a man of influence, too, with Putin. Olga Romanova's '24' was allowed to take a considerably critical stance toward the government, both in its choice of news and in its approach to presenting it—until November 2005 when she was fired. (Certain lonely vestiges of freedom can still be seen on REN TV—in Marianna Maksimovskaya's programme 'Nedelya' ['A Week'].

The desired results were quietly obtained through property transactions. At the end of July 2005, 70% of REN TV's shares were sold, another 30% of the shares, which belonged to the family of the channel's founder and head were bought by RTL Group, a German media concern. In October, half of its REN TV shares to Surgutneftegaz. As a result, the a new head was appointed (after the founder was fired) who ordered on that two segments in the '24' show be deleted from the program: one on the closing of the criminal case against the son of Minister of Defence Sergei Ivanov (in May, the minister's son had struck and killed an elderly woman while driving), and another about the building of a new chapel on Manezh Square, designed by Zurab Tserteli and costing $15 million. Romanova threw out the segment about the minister's son, but left in place the one about the chapel.

On the following day, November 24, 2005, employees from the Eurasia private security agency, which had been hired by the channel's management, prevented her from entering the TV studio.

On November 28, 2005, the new management announced that Romanova had broken corporate ethics rules and that she would remain off the air for at least three months, which she was being given 'to prepare a concept for a new show.' On December 5, 2005, Romanova resigned.

The Beslan crisis

The first serious test of Kremlin policies came months after the elections. It was on a scale of the Kursk submarine and the 'Nord-Ost' theatre crises. At the beginning of September 2004, Russia was shaken by the actions of Northern Caucasian terrorists: in the Ossetian city of Beslan, terrorists occupied a school and took 1200 people hostage. During the operation to free to hostages, a large number of children were killed.

During the crisis and immediately following it, it seemed as if the government was worried less about rescuing the children than about accurate information leaking out (about the number of hostages, the terrorists' demands, actions of government and law enforcement officials). Putin himself explained that 'war on Russia has been declared.'

What the President's ellipsis meant was quickly elucidated for the public by Channel One's political commentator Mikhail Leontiev:

> In times of war, one doesn't fight one's own government. That's called a 'fifth column'.... In times of war, the laws of war go into effect and certain public procedures are suspended....The only way to re-establish order quickly (and in times of war, it must be done quickly) is undoubtedly to expand the authoritarian component [of the government].[11]

Thus in order not to allow certain reporters to reach Beslan, authoritarian action was taken against them: Anna Politkovskaya (*Novaya Gazeta*) was poisoned in an airplane and ended up in a hospital in serious condition; Andrei Babitsky (Radio Liberty) was initially not allowed to board an airplane. The reason was suspicions of a bomb having been planted in his luggage, and then accused of disorderly conduct.

Other reporters were made to understand the new situation, too. On September 6, 2004, in Mineralnye Vody, the head of the Al Arabiya News Channel's Russian bureau—a Russian Citizen—was taken off an airplane and detained (an AK-47 bullet was 'found' in his luggage). In Beslan itself, two Georgian TV reporters, Nana Lezhava and Levan Tetvadze, were detained for two days. The apparent reason was that they had no entrance visas—despite the fact that they were legal residents of Georgia's Kazbeg district, which is located on the Russian border and whose residents, according to an agreement between Russia and Georgia, have the right to cross the border without visas and to remain in North Ossetia for up to ten days). In North Ossetia, Anna Gorbatova and Oksana Semyonova (*Novye Izvestiya*), Madina Shavlokhova (*Moskovskiye Novosti*), and Yelena Milashina (*Novaya Gazeta*) were also detained, albeit briefly, to make a point.[12]

Vladimir Pribylovsky, co-author of this book, received assassination threats from an unknown person in an airplane from Rostov to Moscow. This was followed by a six-hour detention at Vnukovo airport during which he was not charged with anything, but threatened to be put in jail for 'resisting police'.

The law, too, was used. On August 25, 2004—before the Beslan hostage crisis—agents from the North Ossetia regional secret service directorate raided the premises of Radio Liberty correspondent Yuri Bagrov. They conducted searches at his home, office, garage, and his mother's apartment. In all, about 40 regional secret service agents participated in the raids, headed by the director of the counterintelligence department, Lieutenant Colonel Sergei Leonidov.

On September 17, 2004, criminal charges were filed against the reporter: he was accused of using a forged court decision to obtain Russian citizenship. In 1992, Bagrov had moved from Georgia to Vladikavkaz, where his mother, wife, grandfather, and grandmother live, all of them Russian citizens. In 2003, when his Soviet passport expired, Bagrov exchanged it for a Russian passport—and in order to do so, he was required to obtain a court decision. But in the spring of 2004, Bagrov had published materials about the secret service's involvement in kidnappings in Ingushetia. After this, he became the object of surveillance, and his place-of-residence registration was removed from the passport office.

Vladikavkaz's Iristonsky Court denied a request from the defendant's lawyers to have experts analyze the handwriting and seal on the court decision to grant Bagrov Russian citizenship. In December 2004, the court found Bagrov guilty of knowingly using a forged document, sentenced him to pay a fine in the amount of 15,000 rubles, and revoked his Russian passport. In January 2005, the Supreme Court of North Ossetia let the lower court's decision stand. Bagrov, who had become a person without a citizenship (and from the point of view of the secret service, this seemed to mean he had become a citizen of the hostile Republic of Georgia), began consistently encountering difficulties in the fulfilment of his professional duties. Thus, in September 2005, he was arrested in Beslan when attempting to attend mourning services at the former school No. 1, because he had no accreditation from the Ministry of Foreign Affairs.

At the beginning of 2007, impossible working conditions and threats from law enforcement organs forced Bagrov to leave his homeland and to seek political asylum in the United States. In June 2007, Bagrov was granted asylum—at the same time as Fatima Tlisova, a reporter from Kabardino-Balkaria.

The printed media

Despite episodic persecution and the provocation of 'economic' conflicts, the press was never subjected to the same kind of systematic control and pressure during Putin's first term as the televised media. This was partly an instance where Homer nodded. Putin watches all news programs on all channels daily but stopped reading newspapers and magazines after becoming president. In the government's daily overviews of the press, he pays special attention only to what is written about him by Western reporters. In another part, Putin's entourage considers rigid control over the press an excessive measure. Mainly the preserve of wonks and intellectuals, the influence of the printed media did not reach far enough to matter in the vast Federation with its many regions, cultures and languages.

It therefore came as a surprise when on September 6, 2004, Raf Shakirov, editor-in-chief of *Izvestiya*, resigned. *Izvestiya,* which at that time was owned by billionaire Vladimir Potanin's Prof-Media concern, was in no respect an anti-government publication. The tone of the newspaper was set by right-liberal and right-conservative (in the Western sense of the word) statists—writers who with a touch of Islamophobia were absolutely hostile to all forms of separatism, and loyal to moderate forms of authoritarianism. However, Putin's Kremlin is supported by *Izvestiya* without being sycophantic. The newspaper will criticize the actions of specific agencies and officials. In addition, it also publishes liberal writers, whose attitude toward 'managed democracy' is not extremely negative, but nonetheless questioning.

Shakirov stated in an interview that Prof-Media, the newspaper's publisher, had objected to the way in which *Izvestiya* had covered the events in Beslan, above all, to the Saturday, September 4 issue, which focused on the Beslan tragedy. Eight columns of the newspaper had been devoted to the battle for the school in Beslan. Large photographs of bloody children appeared on the front and back pages, and there were many large photographs inside the body of the paper as well, some showing dead bodies.

According to Prof-Media their disagreements with Shakirov were not political but stylistic in nature: 'the Saturday issue was excessively naturalistic.'[13] It is also possible that Prof-Media's apprehensions were triggered by a television overview, which was more biting and emotional than usual. Petrovskaya wrote about the way in which state-run TV channels had lied to the people and pandered to government officials during the Beslan crisis.

Reporters and political pundits interpreted the firing of *Izvestiya*'s editor-in-chief as the sign of a new phase in the Kremlin's policies toward the print media—after TV, it trembled, it was next. Appropriately, it was a news anchor from the docile Channel One to explain what had happened:

This was decided in the Kremlin... Muscovites believe newspapers more than TV. That's why you couldn't buy any newspapers in those days. They were giving readers what television was not.[14]

No Kremlin organised assault on the printed media followed, however. A minor tweak had already been put in place earlier, and print journalists were not worth a further look. In the spring of 2004, the Interagency Anti-Terrorist Commission recommended that Moscow's metro and surrounding areas be cleared of retail commercial activity. Although this was a 'recommendation' and not an order, Moscow municipal offices stopped renewing licenses for selling newspapers and magazines in the metro and within 25 meters of metro stations. By the beginning of October 2004, practically all mobile newspaper kiosks inside metro stations and within 25 meters of them had been liquidated. The Kremlin reckoned that the market would sort print mess out from here on.

It was expected that the place of mobile newspaper kiosks in the metro would be taken by special automatic newspaper dispensers (which, however, would not be able to sell more than six different publications at the same time), while outside the stations they would be replaced by pavilions run by large companies that deal in printed matter (whose owners may not always be willing to sell printed matter that is not wholly enthusiastic about the government—whether of a Communist or liberal stripe).

The reform led to a rise in the prices of practically all newspapers and magazines, but above all hit such critical publications as *Novaya Gazeta*, *Nezavisimaya Gazeta*, *Russky Kurier*. The number of places where these newspapers could be bought in Moscow very visibly shrunk. In addition, the metro was completely cleared of 'unaffiliated' distributors of printed matter, who dealt mainly in the marginal and semi-marginal publications of left-wing and right-wing radicals (including, Eduard Limonov's quite popular *Limonka*, Alexander Prokhanov's *Zavtra*, and Yuri Mukhin's *Duel*).

The advance guard for this creative move had been led by the pro-Putin youth organization 'Iduschie Vmeste'. In April, it had sent a request to the Moscow prosecutor's office to look into the activities of *Novaya Gazeta*, *Yezhenedelny Zhurnal*, *Nezavisimaya Gazeta*, and the Kommersant Publishing House, to ascertain whether everything was being done in accordance with Russian media regulations.

To support its concerns, 'Iduschie Vmeste' put forward articles it thought libellous about their own organization, and the publication of texts containing false information which 'Iduschie Vmeste' had itself placed in the newspapers—through middlemen—as paid advertisements. In some cases these newspapers had agreed to conceal the fact that the texts were being published as paid advertisements.

The balloon let up by 'Iduschie Vmeste'—pro-government youth organizations 'Nashi,' 'Molodaya Gvardiya,' 'Rossiya Molodaya,' 'Mestnye,' show the same industry—sounded out public opinion for the 'terrorist measures' that were to be announced later.

The Kremlin was not far off. Overtime recalcitrant papers returned to the fold under market pressure. In March 2005, the former (Berezovsky-owned) *Novye Izvestiya* reporters who had begun publishing their own newspaper, *Russky Kurier*, were fired once again. The paper had been acquired by Moscow publisher Mediapress Corporation. Initially, Mediapress was interested neither in the content of the newspaper, which sharply criticized 'managed democracy' and President Putin personally—nor in the fact that it operated at a loss. However, at the beginning of 2005, Mediapress' owner, Soskin, wanted to become a Duma senator for the Koryak autonomous district, for which he needed the support of the Kremlin.

Soskin simply shut the newspaper down and fired the entire staff. After a while, he started publishing a tabloid weekly under the same name—moderately pro-government in tone and equally unprofitable. Nonetheless, he failed to get the reward that he expected from the Kremlin. A lurid five-year-old scandal dug up by *Kommersant* at the start of Soskin's 'Koryak campaign', ended his career prematurely. In 2000, when the publisher was going through a divorce and dividing his property, Soskin's wife tried to shoot him. Sadly and accidentally (according to the official records), she accidentally shot herself while trying to shoot him.[15]

A shift in ownership also steered the course at *Izvestiya.* At the beginning of June 2005, the semi-state-owned Gazprom Media Holding Company acquired 50.19% of *Izvestiya*'s shares from the Prof-Media publishing house. On November 8, 2005, a new editor-in-chief was appointed. Gazprom Media's general manager (who had overseen NTV's return to normalcy) declared that the replacement of the editor-in-chief had no political subtext and that *Izvestiya*'s editorial policies would remain unchanged.

The former editor-in-chief of *Izvestiya*, Shakirov, was less convinced. 'Did Gazprom buy *Izvestiya* in order to deviate from the party line? They want to radically clean up the press.... They want to turn *Izvestiya* into *Pravda*.'[16] After settling in, the new editor-in-chief laid out his vision of the newspaper's future in a special and rather expansive 'Memorandum' to the newspaper's employees. The 'Memorandum' showed up on the internet (its authenticity has not been contested):

Izvestiya is not an opposition newspaper. Our front door says: 'national public newspaper.' Today, this sign is deceptive. Often, we are very far from the people.... It is odd for us, who belong to a practically state-owned corporation, to pretend that we are radically anti-government. This contradiction is enough to make one lose one's mind.

Those who are not satisfied with such a stance—and that is

precisely how things will be from now one—should look for another job.

We must become a genuinely liberal, influential, vital, respectable, interesting Russian newspaper. No one will prevent us from providing a forum for competing opinions, but it will be good always to stay within the bounds of common sense. The limit (and best example) of liberalism for me is A. Chubais. He stands for liberalism, and he is also building the Bureya hydroelectric dam.

I want to assure you: with the arrival of the new editor-in-chief, and those who have already come and are yet to come with him, the period of *Izvestiya*'s strange journalistic life outside the political and social mainstream of the country is over.[17]

In the spring of 2005, the Kremlin delegated the head of United Russia's information directorate (Ilya Kiselev), to fill the position of *Izvestiya*'s deputy editor-in-chief. He replaced a liberal reporter close to Chubais.

The looming 2007 presidential elections

On March 12, 2007, less than a year away from the elections for his successor as President, Vladimir Putin started preparing for an orderly hand-over of power. He ordered the merging of the Federal Service for the Oversight of Mass Communications and the Protection of the Cultural Heritage into one agency (the Rossvyazokhrankultura). In this way, the functions of media licensing and media oversight were taken away from two separate ministries (the Ministry of Culture and the Ministry of Communications) and combined in a powerful single new service, under the direct control of the office of the prime minister.

On March 27, he appointed Boris Boyarskov, an secret service officer of the active reserve as the new head. His first important act as agency head, in July 2007, was to send an inquiry to the General Prosecutor's Office concerning the publication of the interrogation of the Foreign Minister of the Chechen-separatist movement, Akhmed Zakayev, by the General Prosecutor's Office. Investigators had questioned Zakayev in connection with the Russian investigation into the murder of former secret service officer Alexander Litvinenko, and *Kommersant* had published a transcript.

Boyarskov suspected Kommersant of divulging secret information pertaining to the investigation. In addition to the inquiry to the General Prosecutor's Office, Rossvyazokhrankultura demanded that the website's editor-in-chief Pavel Chernikov desist from 'the publication of materials that might lead to violations of the law.' The agency denied that its inquiry represented an official warning to Kommersant. The letter had been sent merely as a 'preventive measure', because so far Rossvyazokhrankultura had no claims against the Kommersant Publishing House and its publications.[18]

It would seem, Kommersant had rattled the Kremlin's cage. The 'preventative measure' was obviously aimed at its reporting on the war in Chechnya. The war—though it had been declared over years ago by Putin—continued to look like ablaze in the region itself. Like Iraq for the George W. Bush administration in the US, the Chechen peace that had broken out was an aching Achilles heel.

On May 10, 2007, Putin introduced amendments to the law 'On opposing extremist activity', lifting its provisions to felonies. On June 27, 2007, a further series of amendments were passed by the Duma on July 4, 2007 aimed 'to improve' government procedures for opposing extremism. In particular, 'hatred or enmity with respect to any social group' would henceforth be a cause of an aggravated charge.

The nub was the definition of 'social group'. Federal courts had long decided that this included groupings of state officials. In 2005, for example, Stanislav Dmitrievsky, the editor-in-chief of the newspaper *Pravo-Zaschita*, appeared in court in Nizhny Novgorod. One year earlier, in January 2004, *Pravo-Zaschita* had published Akhmed Zakayev's appeal to the Russian people not to vote for Putin in the Presidential elections. The regional prosecutor had brought criminal proceedings under a charge of 'public appeals for a forcible change of the constitutional system of the Russian Federation'. But the investigation had led to nothing and in September 2005 the charge was changed to 'incitement to national and racial enmity'. The prosecutor demanded four years in prison.

On February 3, 2006, Nizhny Novgorod's Sovietsky District Court gave Dmitrievsky a suspended sentence of two years in prison and four years of probation. According to the text of the court's decision, the 'national and racial groups' toward which Dmitrievsky had incited and promoted 'hatred or enmity' were the 'leadership of the Russian Empire' and the 'mindless, bloody Kremlin regime.'

(The court struck from the record Dmitrievsky's question to a witness whether such a thing as the 'leadership of the Russian Empire' was currently in existence.)

Similarly media criticism of such 'social groups' as 'Kremlin officials,' 'the government of Mordovia,' and even 'bad cops,' had been construed by the courts as incitement to social strife. The new codification—'for motives of hatred or enmity with respect to any social group'—made it possible to define the criticism of any government official or government organ as an extremist crime, if necessary.

An article added to the 'Administrative Violations Code' created criminal liability for the 'mass distribution' of extremist materials. Such materials would also be put on a special watchlist. Furthermore, whenever a media organization was found to be 'extremist' by the courts, the mass media are required to mention this fact in their reports.

According to political commentator Andrei Piontkovsky (who had two books investigated in May 2007 to determine whether they were of an extremist nature),

this law—and the latest amendments are merely a continuation of the same logic—has been passed, of course, not in order to fight with people such as Basayev. Because the Criminal Code contains enough instruments for fighting terrorists and murderers. Rather, this is simply a direct replication of article 58 from Stalin's Criminal Code—about counter-revolutionary agitation; and of article 190 from Brezhnev's Criminal Code—knowingly distributing false information about the Soviet social order. This is an instrument for fighting political dissent, any political opposition.[19]

Yet another offence of an 'extremist' nature was created in the new legislation: 'knowingly, falsely, and publicly accusing' a government official 'of committing acts, during his term in office, that are named in the present article and constitute extremist crimes.'

Commenting on the changes in anti-extremist legislation in an interview with the magazine *Vlast*, Putin's representative in the Federation Council, Alexander Kotenkov, explained:

The media cannot make accusations against government officials. A governor by definition cannot engage in extremist activity. He enjoys a presumption of innocence, just like any other citizen. To accuse a government official of extremist activity is not simply to insult him personally, but to undermine people's faith in government. And *that* is extremism.[20]

A year earlier, on July 27, 2006, President Putin had introduced a related law 'On Personal Data'. This law prohibited any government department from divulging 'personal data' about physical persons without their written consent. It both insulated the clans from laundering their enemies' clothing in public as well as offering general relief against intrusions.

The law is drafted in such a way that it can easily be given a broad interpretation: for example, it can be read as denying the right to divulge personal data to the media, sociologists, political analysts, historians, etc. Moreover, according to the letter of the law, 'personal data' can include any information about a person—such as his name, date of birth, address, political views, and so on. In principle, reporters who quote political activists, businessmen, or other newsmakers, must from now on obtain their written consent to mention their names.

Obviously, such a requirement cannot be fulfilled in principle, but like all laws that are impossible to carry out, it creates discretion for the Public Prosecutor's Office. It can be used to prohibit the dissemination of uncomplimentary information about politicians without their written consent (for example, how a deputy voted on the issue of substituting money payments for benefits or the issue of ceding islands in the Khabarovsk region to China). No prosecution under the new law has been brought to date, though this does not mean that—like all the new legislation introduced under Putin's Kremlin—it is serving the purpose for which it was designed.

CHAPTER NINE

Where Are the Bodies?

The secret service's Basic Instinct

How was Putin's Kremlin able to achieve its iron control over the unruly clan-driven internecine strife of the Federation in such a short period of time? It is the elephant in the room of the investigation in our book. It starts with a misconception in the West about the Russian secret service agencies. It is thought that they are similar to, for example, MI5 and MI6, or the FBI and CIA. They are not—neither in mind-set nor in methods. The core function of the Cheka (from which all subsequent agencies are incarnations) to the secret service has always been to gather information about dissent among the population, rather than deal with (more or less) serious threats to the state. Whereas the threats constantly change as international politics change, the nature of dissent is that it is always there. From its first creation, the Cheka has played a long game and assassination has been an essential part of its armour of last resort. Unlike the Western secret agencies, it has always found being bracketed with liquidation helpful in its functioning (countering dissent) rather than detrimental.

The NKVD was the prototype of the KGB, the same organization that is known today as the secret service. When Trotsky was murdered on 20 August 1940 in Mexico by a man who had befriended and killed him with an ice-pick, the NKVD did not go out of the way to cover over the tracks of its involvement. On June 6, 1941, almost a year later, the head of the NKVD Lavrenty Beria put a request to Stalin that the six plotters of Trotsky's assassination be decorated with high state honours. This was granted in secret. But after Ramon Mercador—Trotsky's actual assassin—spent 20 years in a Mexican prison, he first moved to Cuba and then to the USSR. He was given further decorations and an apartment in Moscow, as well as a dacha in Kratovo (a prestigious Moscow suburb), and a pension equivalent to that of a KGB general—400 rubles per month (a very high pension in the USSR at that time).

When the Cold War began after World War II, the chekists stopped the kidnappings on foreign soil it had organised until then, and returned to assassinations. It often left a signature like a serial killer would. On September 15, 1957, shortly after publishing his memoirs, the chekist defector Nikolai Khokhlov fainted in the Palmengarten in Frankfurt at a political conference. One witness who had been present, later recalled that Khokhlov had taken a sip from a cup of coffee that had been brought to him at his request by an attendant. Khokhlov had then heard that an interesting speech was about to begin and ran to hear it without finishing his drink. The doctor at the university hospital to which Khokhlov was taken suspected food poisoning.

Five days later, however, red and brown stripes, dark spots, and black and blue marks appeared on Khokhlov's body and face. A sticky liquid started to leak out of his eyes, blood appeared in his pores, his skin became dry, tight, and inflamed. Big clumps of his hair fell out from the slightest touch. His skin became rigid and cracked when it was stretched. In places where the skin is particularly thin, such as behind the ears and under the eyes, his blood did not have time to dry, and Khokhlov constantly used tissues to wipe it off himself. He could not be bandaged because the bandages rubbed off his scabs and reopened his wounds. His blood was undergoing a rapid process of decomposition that the doctors were unable to understand. Tests conducted on September 22 revealed that his white blood cells were being quickly and irreversibly destroyed, having fallen to a count of 700 from a normal level of 7000. Khokhlov's salivary glands atrophied. Then a bone marrow sample was taken. It turned out that a large part of his blood-forming cells was dead. Necrosis of the mucous membranes of the mouth, throat, and oesophagus set in. It became difficult for him to eat, drink, and even speak.

Khokhlov was transferred from the German hospital to an American military hospital in Frankfurt. Six American doctors began to treat the poisoned patient. They gave Khokhlov continuous injections of cortisone, vitamins, steroids, and other experimental medications, while keeping him alive through intravenous feeding and almost continuous blood transfusions. An anaesthesiologist was always at hand to relieve Khokhlov's suffering. Solutions were prepared for his mouth, which had absolutely no saliva. Various specialists were called in for consultations. New medicines were sent to Frankfurt.

After three weeks, Khokhlov's condition began to improve. Soon, he left the hospital, although for many more months he remained completely bald and covered with scars. Somewhat later, in New York, a famous American toxicologist studied the history of Khokhlov's illness and came to the conclusion that Khokhlov had been poisoned with radioactive thallium.

The attempt on Khokhlov's life was followed on October 9, 1957, in Munich, by a capsule of hydrocyanic acid shot (using a specially designed tube) into the face of one of the leaders of the Ukrainian émigré community, Lev Rebet—inside his apartment building. Rebet died on the spot. The autopsy revealed that he had died of a heart attack. Two years later, on October 15, 1959, in Munich, the operation was repeated with a cyanide-filled capsule shot into the face of the Ukrainian nationalist leader Stepan Bandera. Bandera also died on the spot. (Two years later, it was confirmed by chance that the murderer was KGB agent Bogdan Stashinsky. He had fallen in love with a West German woman, defected, and confessed.)

On November 3, 1961, the émigré journalist and writer Mikhail Baykov was poisoned in Buenos Aires. Soon, attempts were made to poison dissident writers in the USSR as well: Alexander Solzhenitsyn and Vladimir Voinovich. They survived, Solzhenitsyn was banned and expelled from the USSR, while Voinovich was asked to emigrate.

In 1978, the 49-year-old Bulgarian dissident Georgi Markov was killed in London. Markov was poisoned with ricin (manufactured in the USSR). Along with poison, Soviet agents had given their Bulgarian colleagues a specially designed umbrella that fired poison capsules. On September 7, 1978, Markov was returning to work after lunch. Near a bus stop by Waterloo Bridge, he felt a sharp pain in his right leg. Turning around, he saw a man of about 40 years of age who was bending over an umbrella that had fallen down. After picking up the umbrella, the man departed in a taxi that had been waiting for him. Markov started choking, his head started to spin, and on his leg he discovered a bleeding wound. After making his way to the BBC's Bulgarian studio where he worked, Markov told his colleagues about the story with the umbrella. Soon, he became completely ill and was taken home. Four days later, he died. The diagnosis at the time was heart disease, but a microscopic capsule was found.

A couple of weeks before Markov's murder, Bulgarian security agents tried to eliminate another Bulgarian dissident, Vladimir Kostov, who had been granted political asylum in Paris. While going down on the escalator in the metro, Kostov felt a sharp, light pain in his buttock. In the evening, he suddenly developed a high temperature. On the following day, constant fevers began. Kostov saw a doctor, but the doctor could not give him a diagnosis (it was August, all serious doctors in Paris were on vacation, and the doctor who examined Kostov turned out to be an intern). Only when news of Markov's sudden death reached Paris was Kostov examined again. This time doctors discovered and removed from Kostov's soft tissue a microscopic capsule similar to the one that had been found in Markov's leg. The outside of the capsule was made of 90% platinum and 10% iridium, and it contained ricin.

In 1980, Boris Korzhak, a Soviet citizen and a CIA double agent, felt a pinprick resembling a mosquito bite while he was in a store in Virginia, in a suburb of Washington D.C. He developed a temperature. Several days later, he developed internal bleeding and arrhythmia. A doctor extracted a capsule from the 'mosquito bite.' Just as in Paris and London, the capsule had two small holes which had been sealed with wax. Inside the body, the wax melted and the poison penetrated into the organism.

The 1990s were an unsettled for the old Soviet *nomenklatura* and Yeltsin led (briefly) an assault on the KGB's power by carving the organization up rather than abolishing it. But with the spreading widely of secret service active reservists (such as Vladimir Putin) into post-Soviet society, monitoring continued as before, as did the other standard KGB activities.

On August 1, 1995, Ivan Kivildi—the president of Rosbiznesbank, head of the Free Labour Party (PST)—died at Moscow's Central Clinical Hospital. He had had ambitions to become a political force that would, in the words of *Kommersant-Daily*, protect 'entrepreneurs from the tyranny of the government.' At a press conference in

St Petersburg on October 27, 1994, He announced with Anatoly Sobchak that they had decided to unite in a bloc called Russian Democratic Reform Movement. After Sobchak, the third name was Kivildi's. On October 29, he declared at a Russian Business Round Table (RBRT) meeting that he chaired 'All of the apparatchiks are making nefarious attempts to climb on the backs of entrepreneurs'. Now 'they will have to reckon with the entrepreneurs for real.'

In 1995, Kivildi became a State Duma deputy. For his ill-wishers, it seemed, he had become unapproachable and untouchable. However, it was precisely because the Russian business world had turned to politics that 1995 saw an unprecedented wave of assassinated entrepreneurs. On April 10, 1995, Vadim Yafyasov, the 33-year-old vice president of Yugorsky Bank, was killed in Moscow. He became the forty-third banker to be killed. On the night of July 20, the forty-fourth banker—Oleg Kantor, president of Yugorsky Bank and a member of the council of the Russian United Industrial Party (ROPP)—was brutally murdered together with his bodyguard. The murder took place at the Kantor's dacha, on the territory of the Snegiri government sanatorium in the Instrinsky district in the Moscow region. Kantor's body had been stabbed and shot; his eyes had been gouged out. Indeed, of the 30 members of Kivildi's Round Table's board, eight had already been killed.

When several days after the Kantor murder, the heads of the RBRT called a press conference, Kantor's party chairman Vladimir Scherbakov remarked that the Round Table had begun to resemble a funeral parlour: 'We meet on a regular basis to take note of the fact that another entrepreneur has been murdered and to call on the government to put an end to this lawlessness.' Kivildi described what was happening as the 'genocide of the brains of the nation.... Not one murder of a factory director or bank director has been solved.... Private security agencies in banks have their weapons taken away from them.'

The next victim was Kivildi himself. He was the forty-fifth banker to be murdered, the ninth member of the board of the RBRT to be killed and the fifty-second major Russian entrepreneur to be eliminated in 1995. On August 1, Kivildi was brought to Moscow's Central Clinical Hospital in a coma. On August 2, Kivilidi's secretary—who had spent the whole previous days answering phone calls on Kivilidi's mobile phone—had a seizure and was also taken to the First Municipal Hospital. On August, 3, Ismalova died. On

August 4, without coming out of his coma, he died. Their death certificates cited acute heart failure as the cause of the death. However, the hospital pathologist refused to perform an autopsy on the corpse of Kivildi's secretary, and in the history of her illness he wrote: 'There are indications of poisoning with an unknown poison.'[1]

On August 18, 1995, it was reported in the press that that Kivildi and his secretary had been poisoned with a radioactive poison slipped into his mobile phone. The newspaper *Tverskaya Zhizn* reported that the poison was a heavy metal of the cobalt group, while ITAR-TASS claimed that a 'military employee [had] been arrested' and that 'containers with radioactive materials' that had likely been used in the poisoning of Kivildi and Ismalova 'had been confiscated from him.... Law enforcement organs are investigating the incident.' This was the first and last time that the words 'military employee' and 'law enforcement agencies' were mentioned in the same sentence with regards to Kivilidi's murder.

The media obtained new information from the governor of the Saratov region, Dmitry Ayatskov. The poison had been produced at the state chemical defence centre in Shikhany, in the Saratov region. Ayatskov was indignant at the fact that military chemists were not paid their salaries for months at a time, which forced them to take jobs on the side. In 1997, Russia's Ministry of Internal Affairs also reported that analysis had confirmed this information. The chemical agent that was the basis of this poison had been discovered in Sweden in 1957. It penetrates the body through pores in the skin or respiratory pathways. The person dies several hours later. Without extremely sophisticated analysis, the cause of death is impossible to determine. The administrative head of Shikhany, however, gave this helpful clue: 'This is a super-modern poisonous substance whose formula is strictly classified. Neither I nor the local secret service know of a single case of such poisons being sold illegally. If this were the case, there would be an enormous international scandal. Can you imagine: in Shikhany, at the state institute of organic synthesis, anyone who wants to can buy poison, moreover poison that's used by professional spies!'[2]

On April 19, 1997, the *Kommersant-Daily* reported:

> ...he would sharply criticize [secret service-General Korzakhov's] Security Service... Ivan Kivildi supported com-

> petitive auctions and was against backroom decisions and deals between government officials and business fat cats. We have concrete information that one of these people threatened him with physical retribution if Kivildi did not shut his mouth.[3]

On July 22, 1999, the newspaper *Moskovskaya Pravda* suggested another person from the same clan who had an interest in Kivilidi's death: Soskovets. The newspaper also reported that Rosbiznesbank's surveillance cameras, which monitored the bank's surroundings, had been turned off by someone on the day that Kivildi was poisoned.[4]

In December 1999, Moscow criminal investigators announced they had arrested a man (whose name was not made public), who had testified that he had personally sold poison to a man called Ivan Khutsishvili—Kivilidi's business partner and a member of Rosbiznesbank's board of directors. (Khutsishvili had first been arrested on October 31, 1995, but was released 30 days later for lack of evidence.) Khutsishvili was not arrested in 1999 and left the country, nor was an application made for an international arrest warrant. Subsequently, Russia's law enforcement organs officially announced that 'the case had reached a dead end.' The Moscow municipal prosecutor's office, which headed the investigating into the crime, issued a statement that 'Investigators have thus far been unable to obtain any evidence that might indicate who could have been interested in committing this crime.'[5] (On January 17, 2001, Russia's Ministry of Justice announced that it, too, had conducted a forensic analysis of the cause of Kivilidi's death. It confirmed, the substance with which Kivildi had been poisoned had a 'rare formula and a name that is highly classified.')

In 2006, Khutsishvili returned, believing that the ten-year-old case had been closed. But at 8:30 in the morning on June 30, outside No. 7 Yefremov Street, where he was staying with a friend, Khutsishvili was arrested again. On October 9, 2006, Moscow prosecutor Yuri Semin stated in an interview that investigators had fully established the mechanism of Kivilidi's murder. 'He was poisoned with a substance which simply has no analogues. And we know how it is made.' How Khutsishvili could have obtained poison and how he had placed this poison into the receiver of Kivilidi's mobile phone were details that the Russian General Prosecutor's Office was unable to explain.

With interest in the case renewed, here is what Yefim Brodsky, the head of a laboratory at the institute for the evolutionary morphology and ecology of animals, told a *Moskovskiye Novosti* reporter:

> A: Using special equipment, we were able to determine the formula of the toxic substance relatively quickly. It is a nerve agent like zarin.
> Q: Is it known where such toxic substances are produced?
> A: I know several such laboratories.
> Q: Could you name them?
> A: No.
> Q: Who, in your opinion, could have placed the toxic substance inside the receiver?
> A: Only someone who knows how to handle it.
> Q: Let's suppose that the killer who bought the toxic substance had received detailed instructions.
> A: It's impossible to teach an outsider how to conduct such a difficult operation without putting him at risk of poisoning himself.

Ivan Khutsishvili was neither charged nor released.

Polonium and its by-product Thallium

Polonium was discovered by Marie Curie. A Russian by birth, Marie Sklodowska (Curie) was born in 1867 in Poland, then a part of the Russian empire, and became the only woman to win the Nobel Prize twice, for research on radioactivity. She received the first of these prizes with her husband, Pierre Curie, who died in a carriage accident. Marie survived her husband by 28 years and died of exposure to radiation. One of Marie and Pierre Curie's two daughters, Irène, followed in her mother's footsteps and, together with her husband, Frédéric Joliot, also received the Nobel Prize for research on radioactivity. Irène and Frédéric died of the effects of prolonged exposure to radiation. Irène was 59, Frédéric was 58. Marie and Pierre Curie discovered radium and polonium. Polonium was named in honour of Marie Curie's homeland—after the Latin name for Poland.

Thallium is a silver-white metal with a greyish tinge, soft and malleable. It was discovered in 1861 in England by Sir William Crookes. This extremely toxic chemical element is mentioned as a 'murder weapon' both in detective novels and in contemporary history. Thallium has no taste or smell, which makes it useful to criminals—it is a poison that cannot be recognized. Thallium poisoning is all the more dangerous because the symptoms of poisoning that appear in the victim resemble inflammations that doctors have learned to deal with. The poison's effects are diagnosed as a flu or pneumonia. The antibiotics usually prescribed in such cases have no therapeutic effect and allow the illness to develop uninterrupted. Thallium is a slow-acting poison. It kills from within, slowly and irreversibly. Everything depends entirely on the dosage. The only known antidote against thallium is another poison, the so-called 'Prussian blue.'

In order to understand how poison is used as a murder weapon by the secret service, it is important to note that radioactive poisons such as polonium-210 produce thallium as a by-product as they decay. It is thallium that experts often detect when they encounter poisonings today. And it is usually not asked whether the victim has indeed been poisoned with thallium or whether a more sophisticated poison has been used, such as polonium-210. In Russia, such a question could be answered only by the secret service, which controls the secret laboratories that produce these poisons and which has no interest in making information about them public. Outside Russia, suspicions regarding the use of radioactive poisons did not arise until November 2006 when Alexander Litvinenko was poisoned with Polonium 210, nor was there mobile equipment that could detect the presence of such poisons in the victim's body on location.

Yuri Schekochikhin

Yuri Schekochikhin was a State Duma deputy from the pro-West Yabloko party, a member of the Duma anti-corruption commission, a reporter, and the deputy editor-in-chief of *Novaya Gazeta*. It was he who initiated a 2001 Duma investigation of the secret service crimes prompted by those that Yuri Felshtinsky (co-author of this book) and Alexander Litvinenko documented in their book *FSB vzryvaet Rossiu* (*Blowing up Russia*).

Schekochikhin first felt ill on June 16, 2003. On that day, he was in Ryazan for the opening of an anti-corruption commission and took part in a press conference. On June 18, his condition grew worse. On June 19 and 20, his skin started to peel off, as after a severe burn. On June 21, he was taken to Moscow's Central Clinical Hospital in a grave condition, he died after almost two weeks of agony, on July 3, 2003.

According to medical analysis, the immediate cause of Schekochikhin's death was severe general toxicosis—Lyell's syndrome (toxic epidermal necrolysis)—an acute allergic reaction that usually develops in response to medications.

Lyell's syndrome occurs relatively rarely: one case in a million. Signs of a systemic toxico-allergic reaction in Schekochikhin were evident. He entered the hospital in Moscow with a high temperature, loss of mucous membranes and epidermis, impaired kidney function, and increasing respiratory failure, due to which he was later put on an artificial respirator. It was not ruled out that such a 'rare allergic reaction' could have been provoked by an 'unknown agent,' that is a poison.

It was never determined how poison (the 'unknown agent') could have penetrated into the victim's body, since no analysis was conducted and the forensic documents were not made public. On the contrary, the results of Schekochikhin's autopsy and the history of his illness were classified as a 'medical secret.' They were even kept secret from his family and Schekochikhin's relatives never received an autopsy report. When they tried to initiate criminal proceedings, their request was denied—even though on the day of Schekochikhin's death, the chairman of the Duma's Committee on Security (of which Schekochikhin was the vice-chairman), had filed a request with the General Prosecutor's Office to initiate criminal proceedings in connection with his colleague's death.

Schekochikhin died shortly before a planned trip to the United States, where he was intending to tell the American public, congressmen, and senators about the major corruption cases that he was investigating. One of the most important among them was the case of the company Tri Kita, which was under the protection of high-ranking officials in the General Prosecutor's Office and the secret service.

In an interview he gave before he died, he said:

> I'm forced to work on two fronts—as a deputy in the State Duma and deputy head of the Committee on Security, whose aim is to fight terrorism and cross-border crime, and also in the Duma's anti-corruption commission and in *Novaya Gazeta*, which also occupies an important place in the fight against corruption. I don't like the word 'fight,' however. This is more of an analysis of the situation, of what is happening today. Many years ago we... gave summed up the mafia in the following phrase: 'The lion has jumped.' This year, in January, we gave the mafia a new characterization: 'The lion has jumped and is already wearing epaulets.' By comparison with what is going on today in our security services, in our prosecutor's office, all bandits are simply boy scouts. Today, it is precisely the people who are needed to fight crime and corruption that have raised the flag of corruption and crime. This has not bypassed the secret service; what has never happened before happens constantly now—the protection that they provide, the enormous amounts of money that they receive, and the control over ports and banks that they exercise. I'm not even talking about the police.... The whole system and its foundations must be changed. I'm not even talking about the fact that there are too many policemen. For example, there are about 110,000 policemen in Moscow alone. In London, there are about 40,000, although you feel safer in London.

The deputy editor-in-chief of *Novaya Gazeta*, described Schekochikhin's activities during the last weeks and months of his life as follows: 'In recent days, Yuri Schekochikhin was intensively working on the Tri Kita case. In addition, he was actively preparing materials connected with the Chechen problem, with the search for peace, and with this whole topic in general. He travelled to Chechnya as part of a Duma commission. This was immediately before his trip to Ryazan. And naturally, he was working on new materials for another session of the Duma's anti-corruption commission. This was again connected with Tri Kita and facts connected with it that concerned the General Prosecutor's Office.'[6] It was the General Prosecutor's Office that decided not to start an investigation into a possible criminal cause for Schekochikhin's death.

Anna Politkovskaya and Nana Lezhava

The Russian reporter Anna Politkovskaya almost died on several occasions. The first known attempt to poison her occurred aboard a plane to North Ossetia (as described above). Politkovskaya was intending to cover the hostage crisis in Beslan, which began on September 1, 2004. It was believed that Politkovskaya, who enjoyed great respect among the Chechens, could take part in negotiations with the terrorists and obtain the release of the hostages. Politkovskaya was also intending to try to get in touch with Aslan Maskhadov, the president of the self-proclaimed Chechen Republic, and to ask him to risk his life and to come to Beslan to negotiate with the terrorists, which might have induced them to end their takeover of the school.

It was for this reason that it was vitally important for Russia's security services to prevent Politkovskaya from arriving in North Ossetia, since in such an event the credit for putting an end to the crisis and for rescuing the children would go not the Russia's security services, but to Politkovskaya and Maskhadov—a reporter and a president unrecognized by Moscow. Aboard the airplane, Politkovskaya, who had prudently refused to eat any food, asked the flight attendant for a cup of tea. Then she fainted, fell into a coma, and woke up in a hospital. Politkovskaya survived, but she was too late for the negotiations with the terrorists in Beslan since she had spent those tragic days in intensive care.

In contrast with Anna Politkovskaya, Nana Lezhava, a reporter for Georgia's independent TV channel Rustavi-2, managed to arrive in Beslan and to send back several sensational reports about the terrorists' takeover of the school there. On September 3, she was arrested with her cameraman Levan Tetvadze after reporting that the first explosion inside the school had taken place on outside the wall of the gym. From this it followed that it was not the terrorists who had opened fire first, as the Russian authorities claimed, but the Russian security services, who had blown up the wall in order to penetrate into the school building. During her five-day stay at the secret service's detention facility, Lezhava was repeatedly interrogated. At some point, she was offered coffee to drink. She drank it and fainted. Subsequently, a life-threatening toxin was identified in her body. The toxin belonged to the class of strong psychotropic substances that cause diffuse changes in the brain and lead to permanent brain damage.

Chechen Separatists

On March 19, 2002, field commander Amir Khattab—a Saudi Arabian-born international terrorist and one of the leaders of the Chechen insurgency—was poisoned. The poisoning took place in the Nozhay-Yurt district of Chechnya by means of a letter. The secret service managed to intercept a letter from Saudi Arabia that was addressed to Khattab and to treat it with a poisonous substance that caused the heart to stop functioning. On April 11, the secret service announced that the operation had been carried out successfully. According to the secret service's Centre for Public Relations, Khattab was liquidated in a 'meticulously planned special operation whose details will remain classified for at least 10 years.'

According to one account, an agent from the secret service's Dagestan office—officer M.—had used a certain Ibragim Magomedov for the purposes of the operation. Magomedov was a young man, an Avar by nationality, born in the village of Gimry in the Untsukulsky district in Dagestan. Ibragim was a trusted agent of Khattab's and acted as a courier for him. He constantly went out of the country through Azerbaijan and Turkey to receive money and then brought this money back to Chechnya. In this, he was assisted by officer M. Ibragim Magomedov's trust in M. was so great that the latter succeeded in treating an envelope addressed to Khattab with a special solution. Two or three days after reading the letter, Khattab died. Shortly afterward, it was reported that Chechen fighters had executed Dagestani resident Ibragim Alauri (Magomedov), who had unwittingly given Khattab a poisoned letter.

On June 1, 2004, Aslan Maskhadov's Georgian representative Khizri Aldamov, his son, and his nephew, were brought to a hospital in Tbilisi and diagnosed with poisoning. The Georgian Ministry of Internal Affairs determined that the Aldamovs' car had been treated with a toxic substance that contained phosphorus. Aldamov claimed that he had been the victim of an assassination attempt ordered by the secret service.

In the fall of 2004, Chechen fighter Leche Islamov, sentenced to nine years in prison, was poisoned in jail with an unknown substance. After he was sentenced, but before he was sent to prison, Islamov was seen in jail by three secret service agents. They proposed that he collaborate with them and gave him tea and sandwiches. Islamov refused to collaborate with the secret service. Shortly after this conversation, Islamov's health suddenly and sharply deteriorated. His body turned red, his skin began to flake and peel off, he developed a high temperature, his hair started to fall out. Islamov died shortly afterward.

Elena Tregubova

In November 2003, the journalist Elena Tregubova wrote a spicy expose, *Tales of the Kremlin Digger*, of her time as a Kremlin reporter, one of the Russian 'pool' journalists allowed unrivalled access to the corridors of Russian power. It included an unflattering picture of the then Director of the secret service, Vladimir Putin. On February 2, 2004, a bomb exploded in the hallway next to the door of Elena Tregubova's rented apartment on Nikitsky Boulevard. The unknown terrorists had tapped her phone and detonated the bomb right when Tregubova—preparing to catch a taxi that she had ordered—said on the phone that she was about to leave her apartment. The reporter was saved only because she stopped in front of a mirror for a few seconds.

Pavel Basanets

At the beginning of August 2007, Pavel Basanets, the 50-year-old first secretary of the Communist CPRF's Western district committee, a father of four, was poisoned with an unknown poison in Moscow.

Basanets had graduated from the Dzerzhinsky Higher Red Banner School of the KGB. He had served for ten years in foreign intelligence and was a resident in Dresden when Putin was stationed there. Basanets is fluent in Chinese, English, Indonesian, and Malay. For 15 years, he practiced various forms of single combat and had a brown belt in karate. In terms of his political views, he was considered a Stalinist. In 1991, he did not leave the Communist Party but remained involved in party work and public service. In particular, he was the co-chair of the Committee for the Defence of Citizens'

Rights and a member of the Council of the Veterans of Labour, War, and Law Enforcement.

On December 7, 2006, at a meeting of the secret service in the Lubyanka building celebrating the eighty-sixth anniversary of the founding of Soviet foreign intelligence, Basanets spoke out in harsh criticism of Putin, calling him a traitor to Russia, to his own people, and to officers' honour. The response was immediate. Basanets started receiving threats directed at him and his children. The Communists tried to expel him from their ranks. But the expulsion fell through, although it was attempted six times. Certain influential Communists stood up for Basanets, including some members of the State Duma.

But what might have passed had he been a civilian was unacceptable for an secret service agent. Basanets's former colleagues warned him that very serious people were angry at him, that he would not be forgiven his Lubyanka speech, and that there would most likely be an attempt to assassinate him. In July, Basanets was contacted by his former foreign intelligence colleagues from one of the former republics of the USSR and warned that an assassination attempt was being prepared against him. They suggested that Basanets leave Russia and move to one of the Soviet Union's former republics. But Basanets refused, understanding that he would not be able to escape from the secret service in a new location.

At the beginning of August, Basanets suddenly felt ill. A rash appeared on his body; he became extremely weak. The symptoms did not go away, which was unusual for ordinary food poisoning. His condition continued to get worse. Serious medical experts became involved in his treatment. By the end of August, in addition to his general symptoms associated with poisoning, Basanets was diagnosed with unstable angina and stable hypertension (previously, his blood pressure had been completely normal; Basanets was always distinguished by his good health and sound constitution). His doctor's main diagnosis was poisoning with an unknown poison.

Basanets did not go to the hospital, understanding that it would be easier to finish him off there. At the end of August, he commented on his condition as follows: 'I refused to go to the hospital and am now at home with an IV. I think that I'm safer here. What is most interesting is that the doctors who examined me did not find an allergen in my body. My echocardiogram shows a serious blow to the heart. But, to be honest, I now feel a little better than I did three weeks ago. Only the sores on my body won't heal.'

Anna Politkovskaya and Paul Klebnikov

On October 7, 2006, Vladimir Putin's birthday, Anna Politkovskaya was murdered in Moscow. Rejecting the possibility of any involvement by the Russian government in the murder, President Putin said: 'This murder has done more harm to Russia than Politkovskaya's articles.' In January 2007, during a Russian-German meeting in Berlin attended by former German Chancellor Gerhard Schröder, President Putin's advisor Igor Shuvalov had this to say to reporters concerning Politkovskaya's murder:

We see Politkovskaya's murder as a provocation. The president has given orders to solve this crime. It is silly to connect the murder with the leadership of the country. Polonium, Litvinenko, Politkovskaya—all of these are connected. There are powerful groups which have joined together in order constantly to attack the president's program and the president personally. We have nothing to gain from any of these murders. From a political point of view, they only cause harm, while in human terms, of course, one is sorry for the victims.

On August 28, 2007, Russia's General Prosecutor's Office announced the arrest of several individuals who, according to the prosecutor's office, had organized and carried out the murder of Anna Politkovskaya. Among the people arrested was Lieutenant Colonel Pavel Ryaguzov, an employee of the secret service's Moscow office. According to General Prosecutor Yuri Chaika, this same group of hired killers may have been involved in the murder of the Paul Klebnikov, an American journalist and editor-in-chief of the Russian edition of *Forbes*, in July 2004.

Paul Klebnikov may have been killed by the hero of his book *Conversation with a Barbarian*, published in July 2003: Khozh-Ahmed Nukhaev, also known as 'Khozha.' In an organized crime database compiled some time ago by Russian law enforcement, this man was given the following brief description: 'Date of birth, 1954; place of birth, the Kyrgyz SSR; resident of Chechnya. Has prior convictions; is capable of murder. Lives in Moscow without a resident permit in apartments belonging to criminals.' Klebnikov knew that

Nukhaev was dangerous. In September 2001, in New York, Yuri Felshtinsky (co-author of this book) had given him a printout of the organized crime database.

Nukhaev was repeatedly arrested but always released. Whenever criminal charges were brought against him, Russia's Supreme Court would close the case. Nukhaev fought in Chechnya and it was believed that he was on the side of the separatists. He was wounded, received medical treatment in Austria, and returned to Moscow. In Moscow, surprisingly, he lived in one of the city's best hotels and gave interviews at Ostankino TV studios. Although he was on the federal wanted list at this time, for some reason no one pursued or arrested him. His instructions were carried out by secret-service agent Max Lazovsky and Lazovsky's supervisor, SVR staff employee Pyotr Suslov.

On a show on Ekho Moskvy radio, the Russian journalist Yulia Latynina revealed:

Klebnikov was sent to Nukhaev by [secret service General] Korzhakov, the former head of the Presidential Security Service. They had a rather complicated relationship.... This relationship has been best described by Korzhakov himself in his memoirs. Being a fairly simple-minded man, he wrote with transparent resentment' that 'two thirds' of Klebnikov's book on Berezovsky, *The Godfather of the Kremlin*, was based on Korzhakov's own account. 'It was Korzhakov that sent Klebnikov to Nukhaev.' It was the publishing house of Korzhakov and his former subordinate, head of the 'P' Department of the Presidential Security Service Valery Streletsky, that 'published [Klebnikov's] book. It is obvious that Korzhakov understood Chechen psychology and everything that it might entail better than Klebnikov. But what is interesting is that neither Korzhakov nor Streletsky told Klebnikov anything about a possible danger to himself.

Korzhakov and Streletsky didn't tell Klebnikov anything about a possible danger because the whole project had been coordinated at the top levels of the secret service. Except for one aspect: the financial component. Nukhaev agreed to help Klebnikov write a book that would discredit the Chechen people in return for the money that Klebnikov promised to pay Nukhaev out of his royalties. Just how much money Klebnikov had promised to Nukhaev is probably something that we will never know. Nukhaev gave Klebnikov a year to pay the money. And when he did not get it by the appointed time, he killed Klebnikov—exactly one year after the publication of the book—on July 9, 2004.

By stating that Klebnikov's and Politkovskaya's murders were organized by the same people, the General Prosecutor's Office has helped us a great deal. It is highly likely that Politkovskaya's murder was also organized by Nukhaev. But Nukhaev could not have put out the contract on her. Politkovskaya was never involved in investigating his activities, and Nukhaev had no personal motives to kill her. Nukhaev could have been asked to kill Politkovskaya by several possible contractors. Possible contractor number one: the central leadership of the secret service—as a birthday present for Putin. Possible contractor number two: Ramzan Kadyrov, also as a birthday present for Putin, in the hopes of receiving a present in return—the presidency of Chechnya (the hope was realized). Possible contractor number three: Chechnya's current representative in the Federation Council, Umar Dzhabrailov—a well-known Moscow-based Chechen businessman and owner of the Radisson Slavyanskaya Hotel—as a favour to Kadyrov, and again as a birthday present for the president.

It should be added that Dzhabrailov is suspected of organizing at least two other crimes: the murder of the American businessman and the Radisson Slavyanskaya Hotel's former co-owner Paul Tatum, on November 3, 1996; and the assassination attempt against Moscow's deputy mayor Iosif Ordzhonikidze, on June 20, 2002.

Yegor Gaidar

On Friday, November 24, 2006, Yegor Gaidar, the former prime minister of Russia's first democratic government and the director of the Institute for the Economy in Transition, spoke at a conference at the National University of Ireland, Dublin. The conference was on 'Ireland and Russia: History, the Rule of Law, and the Changing International System.' Gaidar started to feel unwell in the morning, after eating breakfast. According to Gaidar's daughter Maria, the breakfast had been simple—a fruit salad and a cup of tea. Ekaterina Genieva, the organizer of the conference, recalled that Gaidar had eaten breakfast in the cafeteria of Maynooth College, where the delegation from Moscow was staying. Of the ten people who had eaten breakfast together with Gaidar, he alone became ill.

During his presentation at the conference, Gaidar felt sick, left the lecture hall, and fainted. He lay unconscious on the floor, with blood was gushing out of his nose and mouth. He remained in this condition for over half-an-hour. Then he was taken to the intensive care unit of the James Connolly Memorial Hospital in Blanchardstown. The former prime minister spent about three hours in intensive care without regaining consciousness. Then he came to, but was unable to move, and for another day his life hung by a thread.

Gaidar was given a full preliminary detoxification—the standard complex treatment for patients showing signs of food poisoning. The symptoms of the poisoning were so ambiguous that doctors hesitated to give a diagnosis. Gaidar checked out of the hospital on Sunday, November 26. His condition was no longer life-threatening, in the doctors' opinion, and he felt somewhat better. After leaving the hospital, Gaidar telephoned the Russian embassy and asked for permission to spend the night there. 'It would be safer,' he said. The request was granted. On Monday, he was still pale, complained of nausea, weakness, and pressure. Nonetheless, he immediately left for Moscow, where he was hospitalized at once. On his way to Moscow, Gaidar tried to make sense of what had happened and remembered: 'That tea didn't taste very good...' The doctors who examined Gaidar reached the unanimous conclusion that he had been poisoned in Ireland, although the nature of the poison was not determined.

Alexander Litvinenko

'Congratulate me. I just became a British citizen. Now they won't dare to touch me. No one would try to kill a British citizen.' These were the words with which Alexander Litvinenko greeted Yuri Felshtinsky on October 13, 2006, in London, at a memorial service for Anna Politkovskaya, who had just been killed. Nineteen days later, on November 1, 2006, Litvinenko was poisoned.

On that day, he met with several people who had come to London from other countries: secret-service agent Andrei Lugovoi, secret-service agent Dmitry Kovtun, secret-service agent Vyacheslav Sokolenko, and apparently with one more—unknown and unidentified—agent of the secret service (or maybe Litvinenko did not meet this fourth agent on this day, although that agent was, apparently, also in London and took part in their meeting without being noticed by Litvinenko). Finally, Litvinenko also met with Mario Scaramella, an Italian citizen. With his former colleagues from the secret service, former secret service Lieutenant Colonel Alexander Litvinenko drank green tea. Litvinenko met with Scaramella in Picadilly at 3 p.m., ate sushi and drank mineral water at a Japanese restaurant. Scaramella did not eat. He just drank.

In the evening, Litvinenko felt ill. He experienced nausea and began to vomit. Litvinenko realized that he had gotten poisoned. He dissolved some potassium permanganate in water—a common Russian treatment, which he learned in the army—and started drinking it and throwing up intermittently. He developed stomach spasms and difficulty breathing, his temperature dropped, his pulse became irregular. This is how Litvinenko spent the first day after his poisoning.

On November 2, Litvinenko got a call from Lugovoi. He was still in London. They had agreed earlier that they would meet on November 2. But Litvinenko told Lugovoi that he was sick and that he would not be able to meet with him. An ambulance was called. The doctor said that it was a seasonal infection. Litvinenko was told to drink water. He continued vomiting, but instead of vomit some kind of foamy liquid came out of his mouth, approximately every twenty minutes. He had stomach cramps and developed severe diarrhoea with blood.

Lugovoi and company were still in London. They flew back to Russia on November 3, when it became clear that their mission had been accomplished. Meanwhile, former secret service Lieutenant Colonel Alexander Litvinenko—who had spent his whole life working in the Russian military and the KGB, who had entered into conflict with the secret service in 1998, who had spent nine months in prison in 1999, who had fled from Russia in October 2000, who had written (as a co-author) the book *Blowing Up Russia*, and who had since then published dozens of articles against the secret service and Putin—had no idea on November 2, 2006 that his three former colleagues from the secret service would be suspected of adding a slow-acting poison to his green tea. Had such an idea occurred to him on November 2, though, Scotland Yard would not have had to request for Lugovoi's extradition from Russia.

On November 3, another doctor was called. He said that

Litvinenko was suffering from an infection, but did not rule out the possibility of poisoning (no one suspected deliberate poisoning). An ambulance was called and Litvinenko was taken to the hospital. He was put on an IV and his blood was taken. The results of the blood analysis were not bad. But the doctors said that he should remain at the hospital. Alexander was promised that he would be able to leave in three or four days. His wife, Marina, said that they would keep him at the hospital for the time being, since they had found some kind of bacteria. All this time, Litvinenko kept his condition secret. Neither his friends nor the police were told anything about it. He did not want people to find out that he had gotten food poisoning from sushi. Who knows—later on he might be poisoned for real but everyone would think that he just has food poisoning again, as on November 1, 2006.

By this time, Alexander could not eat or drink. He had lost 33 pounds. But he believed that he had survived. By the end of the first week of his illness, he had already realized that he had been poisoned, but he thought that he had saved himself by washing out his stomach with potassium permanganate, as he had been taught in the army.

'You know, if I were given a choice: either to go through all this a second time or to spend a year in a Russian prison, I would choose a year in prison, honestly. You can't imagine how bad I feel,' he told Yuri Felshtinsky.

But Alexander no longer had the option of spending a year in prison. He had only 15 days of suffering left. Abscesses appeared in his throat. Doctors thought that this was a reaction to the antibiotics—the flora had been killed and an irritation had appeared. After another couple of days, the patient could no longer open his mouth. All of the mucous membranes were inflamed, the tongue could not fit inside the mouth. His hair started to fall out. At this point, doctors thought that his spinal marrow had been harmed. Litvinenko was transferred to the cancer ward.

Thallium poisoning was mooted and the police became involved in the investigation. Litvinenko was prescribed a thallium antidote ('Prussian blue'). But the antidote was already useless, since it could have worked only during the first 48 hours after the poisoning and a week had passed. In addition, the antidote was effective against thallium. But Alexander had been poisoned with polonium-210, which became known only on November 23, a couple of hours before his death, when Litvinenko's urine was sent for analysis to the Atomic Weapons Establishment at Aldermaston—the only laboratory in the U.K. that could detect radiation poisoning from a poison that emitted alpha radiation.

From a bus ticket for city bus No. 134 that was found in Litvinenko's pocket, British investigators established that Litvinenko had not yet been contaminated with polonium-210 when he had gone to meet with Lugovoi and his colleagues, and that the exact scene of Alexander's poisoning was the Millennium Hotel. The bus ticket had been purchased near Litvinenko's home in North London. From there, Litvinenko had gone to meet with the men from the secret service at the Millennium Hotel. The hotel was the first location that Litvinenko visited after he came out of the bus. Traces of polonium-210 were found on the saucer and cup from which Litvinenko had drunk green tea with the Soviet agents. It followed from all this that it was not Litvinenko who had brought polonium to his meeting with Lugovoi and company, but that the group of secret service operatives from Moscow had brought polonium with them for their meeting with Litvinenko.

CHAPTER TEN

Rewards for Old Friends

From Yeltsin, Vladimir Putin inherited twelve presidential residences and mansions: Novo-Ogarevo (Moscow region), Vatutinki (Moscow region), Rus' (Zavidovo, Tver region), Gorki-9 (Moscow region), Valday (Novgorod region), Bocharov Ruchey (Sochi, Krasnodarsk region), ABTs (Moscow), Shuyskaya Chupa (Karelia), Volzhskiy Utyos (Samara region), Sosny (Krasnoyarsk region), Angarskie Khutora (Irkutsk region), and Tantal (Saratov region).

In March 2001, as a small gift to himself on the first anniversary of his Presidency, the Presidential Property Management Department sent the economic ministries a request to approve a project to rebuild the Vatutniki presidential mansion. The project included plans to install several jacuzzis at a cost of $2.7 million. Also in 2001, the atmostpheric Konstantinovsky Palace in Strelna near St Petersburg was added to the list of presidential residences. The palace had to be rebuilt for this purpose. The cost of the project was estimated at a range $50-$150 million. At the beginning of 2003, Putin issued an order for the building of the Vavilov Horticultural Research Institute, located on St Isaac's Square in St Petersburg, to be transferred to the Presidential Property Management Department with a view to using it as a residence, since Strelna was located too far from the centre of the city.

On April 29, 2003, the Moscow Shipbuilding and Repair Factory launched the newly manufactured yacht 'Pallada,' costing approximately $4 million and intended for the president's use during sea trips. Previously, Putin had used the motor ship 'Rossiya,' listed on the accounts of the Moscow River Fleet (the ship was modernized in

1994 for Yeltsin in Finland), as well as the motor ship 'Kavkaz,' which belonged to Federal Border Security.

It was probably on the banks of Komsomolskoye lake that Putin first developed a passion for constructing residences for himself. While the builders were rebuilding his St Petersburg dacha in 1996 (it had gone up in flames on the day he was ousted from the St Petersburg council offices by his colleague, the newly elected mayor Yakovlev), Vladimir Putin, in order not to lose any time, created a whole dacha cooperative. They offer a fascinating insight into the anatomy of the Putin galaxy.

On November 10, 1996, eight co-founders signed an agreement establishing the Ozero Cooperative on the shore of the Komsomolskoye lake (in the Leningrad region, the St Petersburg equivalent of Moscow's fashionable Zhukovka and Rublyovka districts). The co-founders of the cooperative included Vladimir Putin, who was at that time the deputy head of the Presidential Property Management Department under Yeltsin; the owners of the Strim corporation and Rossiya Bank shareholders Yuri Kovalchuk and active reserve officer Vladimir Yakunin (Yakunin, a former KGB officer under diplomatic cover, later chief vice president of the Russian Railways Company); Andrei and Sergei Fursenko (brothers); Nikolai Shamalov, a Rossiya Bank shareholder and businessman who delivered equipment manufactured by the Siemens Company to St Petersburg's dental clinics, and whose son Yuri was appointed the head of Gazfond, Russia's largest pension fund. Vladimir Smirnov was another one of the co-founders. He was the head of the Ozero Cooperative. The eighth co-founder was Rossiya Bank head Viktor Myachin.

The cooperative was protected by the Rif private security agency, owned by Vladimir Barsukov-Kumarin, the head of the 'Tambov' crime gang (he was arrested on August 24, 2007, for 'murder and the attempt to organize a contract killing'). He was an associate of the well-known Roman Tsepov, a former body-guard of Vladimir Putin during his St Petersburg time under Mayor Anatoly Sobchak.

As Vladimir Putin's career progressed, there was a growing complex to protect at the lake: three-story dachas built right in the middle of the forest, a radio tower, a meteorological station, a landing for helicopters used by President Putin, secret service director Nikolai Patrushev, the President's representative for the

Northwestern District Viktor Cherkesov. Like Stalin, Putin seems to prefer to have his friends at close hand when he rewards them. These rewards over the past 10 years offer a lucid X-ray of the modern, non-Soviet secret service and its corporate structure that is now firmly in place.

Previous associates

At the end of the 1980s, a rather charismatic man appeared in Moscow. His name was Sergei Chemezov. Today, his name is quite widely known in Russia; among other things, he is a friend of President Putin. Chemezov's occupation is selling Russian arms, and he does this quite successfully as head of the Rosoboronexport company. Russia is the second-biggest arms dealer in the world, surpassed only by the United States. The volume of the Russian arms trade exceeds $5 billion per year. When he first settled in Moscow in 1989, Chemezov was unknown. He had grown up in Irkutsk. After graduating from the local polytechnic institute, he worked for a short time at the Irkutsk Scientific Research Institute for Rare and Non-ferrous Metals. He got married, was hired by the KGB, and served in the KGB's second counterintelligence department for the Irkutsk region. Then he was sent to East Germany to work for Soviet foreign intelligence—the KGB's First Main Directorate.

The official (public) side of his job was working for the Luch association in Dresden, which was involved in developing nuclear energy. Chemezov's main task, however, was to obtain Western countries' technical and technological secrets for the 'T' Directorate of the First Main Directorate of the KGB. In an October 2005 interview, responding to a question about his joint work with Putin, Chemezov remarked: 'Why deny what happened? It's true, we worked in East Germany at the same time. From 1983 to 1988, I was the head of the Luch association in Dresden, and Vladimir came there in 1985. We lived in the same house and spent time with each other both as colleagues and as neighbours.'

Back in the USSR Chemezov became a senior operative of the Eleventh Department of the Fifth Directorate of the KGB. This department had been created in 1977 in order to provide for counterintelligence oversight of the channels of international sports exchange. The most pressing concern at the time had been to provide security for the upcoming 1980 Olympics, which took place in Moscow and Tallin.

The appearance of Chemezov in 1988—a new employee, and moreover a new employee who came from the provincial city of Irkutsk—was frowned upon in the department, since Chemezov had been appointed by the generally-disliked General Kubyshkin. The extremely direct and rigid Kubyshkin, who had a liberal taste for women, managed to make powerful enemies among the top rank of the KGB. Moreover, the new employee's arrival was accompanied by a series of 'irregularities,' which violated the usual procedures through which employees of the KGB's peripheral outer reaches were normally transferred. As a rule, an employee who was transferred to the central head quarters would be appointed to a position several notches below the one that he had occupied at his previous (provincial) place of work. Chemezov, however, was appointed to the same position that he had held previously—senior operative—evidently because he had come to Moscow from Dresden.

In addition, as an officer of the active reserve, Chemezov was appointed deputy general manager of Soyuzsportobespechenie and assigned to an agency that oversaw the purchase of foreign sports clothes and inventory for all Soviet athletes. Chemezov was also given an apartment in Moscow, which was a significant bonus in Soviet times (many Moscow KGB employees spent years on a waiting list in order to move to better living quarters). At Soyuzsportobespechenie, Chemezov became close with general manager Viktor Galayev, head of one of the sports directorates of the USSR's State Sports Committee, and secretary of this agency's party committee. Soyuzsportobespechenie's monopoly over the purchase of athletic equipment allowed Galayev and Chemezov to enter into agreements with foreign firms in such a way that a part of the money from the contracts would end up in their own pockets, and, by the standards of the time, the money was not trivial—tens of thousands of dollars.

In the early 1990s, Galayev and Chemezov began selling chicken legs in St Petersburg, a popular business at the time. They invested about $100,000 in their enterprise. The business operated unofficially, through proxies, since as government employees Galayev and Chemezov (as a KGB officer) had no right to engage in private commercial activities. They got cheated out of their proceeds and were thus confronted with the problem of getting their money back.

Luckily, one of Chemezov's chekist colleagues was a young officer, Senior-Lieutenant Yuri Zaitsev. For several years, Zaitsev had worked as a civilian specialist (without military rank) in one of the subdivisions of the KGB; at the same time, he was enrolled at the National Legal Correspondence Institute (VYuZI). After he graduated, Zaitsev was ordered to oversee Soyuzsportobespechenie, where he met and became close with Chemezov. Soon, Zaitsev left to go into business as an officer of the active reserve.

Zaitsev had, with the son of a Soviet marshall, set up a business in selling aviation technology to China. Zaitsev believed that hid partner had not paid him his full share and he organized a 'fighters' brigade,' headed by ex-boxer Pechenochkin and the debts that were owed were settled satisfactorily. Shortly afterward, the head of a company that had been a client—and who owed a large debt to one of the banks—was killed under unclear circumstances.

So when it came Chemezov's turn to collect $100,000 for chicken legs that had never been delivered, he turned for assistance to Zaitsev. It turned out that Chemezov's $100,000 had been stolen by an organization that was protected by the Kazan group—an all-powerful crime clan in St Petersburg. Zaitsev's 'fighters' were unable to get his money back and, after a shootout with the Kazan gangsters, barely escaped from St Petersburg with their lives. At this point, Chemezov had one last hope left: his old acquaintance from Dresden.

Roman Tsepov

Roman Tsepov was born in 1962 in the town of Kolpino near Leningrad. After graduating from high school, Roman was employed as a metal-worker at the Izhorsky factory. Then he was drafted into the army. Roman's mother was chief dental surgeon in the system of Leningrad and Leningrad region correctional facilities. This was what allowed a young man with the Jewish last name 'Belinson' (Tsepov's real name) to enrol in the Ministry of Internal Affairs' Higher Political School after coming out of the army. It was here that he changed his name to 'Tsepov,' when he joined the ranks of the Communist Party. Roman Tsepov served in the internal security troops and resigned (or, according to other sources, was fired) at the very beginning of the 1990s with the rank of captain in the internal troops.

In 1992, Tsepov opened one of the first private security agencies in St Petersburg, the Baltik Eskort company. The idea to create a private security agency had come from Viktor Zolotov, a former officer in the Ninth Directorate of the KGB and subsequently of the Federal Protection Service (FSO). As an officer of the secret service's active reserve, Zolotov formally oversaw the private security agency for the secret service, while at the same time serving as head of security for the mayor of St Petersburg, Anatoly Sobchak, as an official employee of Baltik Eskort. The private security agency's second secret service supervisor was Igor Koreshkov, a colleague of Putin's from the Leningrad KGB directorate.

Thus, Sobchak, who because of his position had a right to federal security protection, was protected by the FSO, while Sobchak's family (his wife Lyudmila Narusova and his daughter Kseniya) and the city's deputy mayor, Vladimir Putin, none of whom had a right to federal security protection, were protected by Tsepov's private security agency, where Zolotov was listed as an employee—although he was simultaneously an officer in the FSO and head of security for Sobchak. It was not easy to unravel these complicated arrangements, but the upshot was that Sobchak, his family, and Putin were all protected by the same people from the Zolotov-Tsepov team.

In a 1999 interview with the newspaper *Versiya*, Tsepov recalled those years: 'I provided security for Sobchak's daughter and sometimes his wife. Not more than that.... In St Petersburg city government, steamship navigation was supervised by Putin. And the government contacted our agency. We made a contract and we worked with Putin. Our work consisted in watching: he went into the house, he came out of the house, he got inside his car, he got out of his car.... At that time, Putin's status didn't entitle him to security protection from the FSO. Today, all of St Petersburg's deputy governors have security protection and all of them employ private security agencies. Naturally, the question comes up: who pays for all this? It costs money, after all. But at that time, in 1996, I took a only a few kopeks from Putin, because he was useful to me—the fact that the agency provided security for the deputy mayor increased its prestige. Putin paid only for the salaries of his two bodyguards, $400-$500 per month. And he could afford it. He was a useful client.'[1]

However, Tsepov did not reveal everything about his relations with Putin. It was precisely Tsepov who collected money from businessmen for the St Petersburg's International Relations Committee headed by Putin. It was to Tsepov that Putin sent his old friend Chemezov, when the latter turned to Putin for help; and by contrast with everyone else, Tsepov was able to return to Chemezov the $100,000 that had been stolen from him. Thanks to Putin, Tsepov was able to take part in major commercial transactions, such as the privatization of the Baltic Sea Steamship Company.

Baltik Eskort became the main private security agency that provided security for St Petersburg's city hall. It was among the first in St Petersburg to receive a license granting its employees the right to carry firearms. Tsepov himself became a staff officer of the Seventh Department of St Petersburg's Regional Directorate for Combating Organized Crime (RUBOP) and had documents from St Petersburg's Directorate of Internal Affairs and the regional secret service directorate (when necessary, Tsepov could present papers from a panoply of state enforcement organization). Many of Baltik Eskort's cars were equipped with sirens and flashing lights, while Tsepov himself had a 'free pass'—a special document that guaranteed that his car would not be stopped or searched.

Baltik Eskort immediately obtained contracts to provide security for prestigious buildings in the centre of the city, cruise ships, and visiting pop stars. By putting many employees of St Petersburg's government and law enforcement agencies on their payroll, including Zolotov himself, Tsepov and Zolotov created a system that allowed businessmen to use Baltik Eskort to resolve conflicts with partners and gangsters. Baltik Eskort could also protect the traffic of off-the-books cash that was used by the city's government and businessmen when they wanted to make deals with one another, by gangsters and businessmen when they wanted to make deals with the mayor's office, and by businessmen when they wanted to make deals with gangsters. Alexander Tkachenko—also known as 'Tkach,' and considered to be the head of the Perm organized crime group—worked for some time at Baltik Eskort. Tsepov had dealings with Alexander Malyshev (head of the Malyshev organized crime group), who was later killed; with the Shevchenko brothers, one of whom was killed and the other of whom was given a suspended seven-year sentence for extortion. It should be noted that the 1990s in St Petersburg, and in Russia as a whole, were the bloodiest years in terms of shootouts and contract killings. But not one person who received protection from

Tsepov's security agency was killed. For the most part, Tsepov was on the attacking side rather than on the defensive one.

Heavy-metal salts

Not everything in Tsepov's business career went smoothly. In 1994, his rivals and opponents managed to initiate criminal proceedings against him for illegally possessing and carrying firearms. He was the head of a private security agency—yet did not have the right to bear firearms. It was a profitable arrest, he later recalled: 'When I was in jail at the pretrial detention facility, the St Petersburg crime boss Malyshev was in the next cell. He told me: 'When you come out, protect my family.' And I protected them, because they paid me for it. And many crime bosses, I won't mention any names, are today also protected by my people.' In this way, business relations were formed between Tsepov's private security agency and St Petersburg's largest crime organizations.

In March 1998, criminal charges were again brought against Tsepov. During the investigation, it came out that Tsepov was simultaneously an agent or employee of several different law enforcement agencies: the secret service, the Ministry of Internal Affairs, and the Foreign Intelligence Service (SVR); and that he had five different documents to cover up his identity. In 1999, without waiting for the outcome of the investigation, Tsepov used his foreign passport and driver's license (both of them issued under a different name) and left for the Czech Republic. He soon returned, however, and continued to run his operations, controlling (rarely formally heading) a number of legal commercial enterprises and extralegal 'businesses,' collecting protection money and distributing and redistributing these resources.

His sphere of activity thereafter gradually expanded. It came to include the security and pharmaceutical businesses, ports, tourism, shipping operations, insurance, and even the mass media. After Putin moved to Moscow and became president, Tsepov maintained close contacts with many of the *siloviki*—from Minister of Internal Affairs Rashid Nurgaliyev to the head of the president's security, Vladimir Zolotov. In addition, Tsepov lobbied for the appointment of various Ministry of Internal Affairs and secret service officers, was on close terms with Igor Sechin, the deputy head of the presidential administration, and even with Vladimir Putin himself.

Tsepov began to feel ill on September 11, 2004. In the morning, he ate breakfast at his dacha. Then he went to the St Petersburg secret service office at Liteiny Prospect, 4. There he drank tea. Then he went to the St Petersburg Directorate of Internal Affairs, where he met with a department head and ate ice cream. At 4 p.m. he started feeling sick. But the doctors could not establish an exact diagnosis. His symptoms resembled severe food poisoning. Tsepov was taken to one of St Petersburg's private clinics in critical condition. Two days before his death, he was transferred to the Centre of Leading Medical Technologies (formerly Sverdlov Hospital). Plans were made to fly Tsepov to Germany for emergency medical treatment. But the disease developed too quickly and before he could be flown to Germany, Tsepov died on September 24.

Tsepov's physician was the head of a department at hospital No. 32, Pyotr Perumov, he was baffled by what was happening to his patient:

> Everything began on a Saturday in September. His wife called me: 'Pyotr Ashotovich, Roman is feeling sick. He has some kind of poisoning.' What are the symptoms? 'Vomit and diarrhoea.' Although I was 300 kilometres away from the city, I called my hospital and sent a team of people to his home. I know from my work in Afghanistan that this combination of symptoms is very dangerous: if it's not stopped, the organism become dehydrated and desalinated, the person quickly loses his strength... The problem is to fill him up. To give him fluids and to detoxify him. The only thing that immediately gave me pause was that there was no temperature. Usually, toxico-infection is accompanied by a sharp rise in body temperature.
>
> All night long, from Saturday to Sunday, he was treated by a team of emergency physicians. He started feeling a little better, but his symptoms did not go away. I arrived on Sunday and persuaded him to check into a hospital. His condition was bad. He wasn't vomiting any more and had less diarrhoea. But most importantly, there were no signs of infection. This was a poisoning without a poisoning.
>
> I invited a major specialist in this field from the Botkin Hospital. We made bacteriological analyses and continued treating him at the same time. The thing that we didn't like

right from the start was that there was no leukocytosis. Usually, the body fights the illness, and the number of leukocytes rises sharply. In his case, his body wasn't reacting.

I should say that Roman had spent almost the entire previous week in Moscow and had only arrived in St Petersburg on Friday. We asked him what he ate on that day. 'Nothing,' he said, only drank. Everything indicated that he had gotten poisoned already in Moscow.

You had to know Roman—he was very careful about his food. In recent days, he had become a vegetarian. I don't know what the reason for this was—health or some other reason—but he did not eat in random places.

I spent the whole first night in his hospital room. We gave him all the necessary medicines intravenously, protected all of his organs, worked very hard. He started feeling better. But we still had no clinical picture of the poisoning. And this very much alarmed me. Moreover, his leukocyte count started going down gradually. At first it was something like 7000. Then it fell to 4000. I already started suspecting that something was going on. And Roman—he became more and more silent and didn't really respond to my questions about what he had eaten and where.

Just in case, I decided to check him more thoroughly. I went through all the labs in St Petersburg, looking for those that could identify heavy metal salts. I found only one. With difficulty, I persuaded them to make an urgent analysis. Three days later, we got the answer: everything is normal, but there's mercury in his urine. This was also within normal limits, but still no one expected to find such a quantity.

Meanwhile, with all the treatment that he was receiving, he gradually started to feel better. I sent him to get a light massage and little by little he started to come back to life. And on the following Friday, Roman decided to check out of the hospital. Moreover, he got behind the wheel himself and said that everything was coming back to normal. But his leukocyte count continued to drop, and on the day that he checked out it was already 2500. I told him: it's very dangerous to go around like this, your organism can't resist anything, it's open to any infection. If this is the lowest it's going to get, good. But if it isn't? But Roman insisted on checking out of the hospital, saying that he would be careful.

On the day before he checked out, we arranged a consultation with St Petersburg's leading doctors... discussed all of the analyses, and I calmed down somewhat—no one made any especially bad prognoses. We thought that it might be... radiation poisoning—the clinical picture was the same as with radiation sickness. But we used a dosimeter and found everything within normal limits.

Nonetheless, on Saturday I sent a nurse to his home to set up an IV and to take his blood. She called me on Sunday and said: 'Pyotr Ashotovich, I don't like his condition.'

I dropped everything and went to see him. He had developed stomatitis. It was as if someone had torn off the skin from his tongue and lips. His symptoms were the same as if he had just gone through chemotherapy. We thought that this was some kind of allergic reaction to medicine. But there's no medicine that will produce such a reaction. Everything looked as if he had been given chemotherapy for leukaemia. Because the point of chemotherapy is to kill the tumour, to kill the fast-growing cells. At first, the person doesn't notice anything; then his leukocyte count starts dropping and he develops stomatitis. After that, his bone marrow cells start feeling the damage and his platelet count drops. And then the third stage begins, which in medicine is called cytopenia. This is when you can't even come close to the patient; he picks up any infection at a distance of five to seven meters. In Roman's case, everything resembled the symptoms people have when they're treated for leukaemia with chemotherapy. By this time, the second stage had just begun—a pronounced reaction that led to the depletion of the spinal marrow. The leukocyte count was down to 1000.

We arranged another consultation and said that he needed to be put in a general hospital where he could receive blood transfusions and be monitored by infectious disease doctors. And Prof. Golofinsky offered to take him to the Medical Academy's hospital. They had everything he needed there, all kinds of specialists. But Roman categorically refused....

Finally, his family made the decision to put him in hospital

No. 31. I immediately called up an acquaintance of mine at that hospital, a very capable person—Prof. Belogorova. I asked her to return from her dacha, because it was the weekend. She called me three hours later. 'You know,' she said, 'everything is very bad here. He's literally disintegrating in front of our eyes. This looks a lot like... there's a kind of hemotoxic poison that's used to treat leukaemia.'

On the next day, I sent the results of all the tests to the hospital. But it was already too late—Roman died shortly afterward.

The examination was very unprofessional. Infinitely less serious cases have been examined far more thoroughly. I wasn't even asked for a history of the illness. And then there was a strange phone call. 'Hello, Pyotr Ashotovich,' they said. 'We are forensic specialists from such-and-such a place. We would very much like to hear your opinion about what happened.' I told them that I could come to see them. 'No,' they said, 'let's have a conference call.' Fine. I described the whole clinical picture to them. I told them my theories about hemotoxic poison. They listened to everything carefully, and then they said to me: 'Pyotr Ashotovich, we've already determined what he died of. Roman Igorevich had prostate cancer and he himself medicated himself to death.' I told them: 'You should be ashamed of yourselves. What did you do? Talk to the nurse? I didn't just give him all kinds of ultrasound tests—we examined him from top to bottom twenty times over, and believe me, we would have found this cancer, we would have found it a hundred times over. And what kind of cancer is going to give you a complete depletion of the spinal marrow?! This is what you're telling me?'

The church service at Tsepov's funeral was attended by the head of the president's security service, the head of the secret service's Departmental Security Directorate, at the time the head of the Main Directorate of Internal Affairs for the Northwestern Federal District and later a deputy minister, the head of the St Petersburg Directorate of Internal Affairs, a 'liquor-and-vodka oligarch' and Federation Council member from the Nenetsk District and secret service general Dmitry Yakubovsky; and Tsepov's long-time business partner and collaborator in many clandestine operations, the mafia leader Barsukov-Kumarin. Only close friends and relatives went to the burial afterwards—Barsukov-Kumarin among them—in St Petersburg's famous Serafimovskoye cemetery. A troop of policemen honoured Tsepov's memory by firing into the air. This was unusual because under military rules, such honours are bestowed only on officers with a colonel's rank or higher—it was not hitherto known that Tsepov had held this rank.

The official cause of death was quickly diagnosed: poisoning with a radioactive poison. Doctors pointed to damage to his spinal marrow accompanied by pronounced symptoms of radiation poisoning. Preliminary forensic analysis revealed that Tsepov's blood contained a large amount of medicine used to treat leukaemia. In contrast to Schekochikhin's death, a criminal investigation was begun in connection with Tsepov's death—presumably because the deceased did not have cancer. According to doctors, a lethal dose of the medicine—in the form of a solution or crushed pills—could have been added to Tsepov's food. Experts had different opinions: radioactive isotopes, an unknown poison, 'heavy-metal salts'. The results of the investigation were not made public, and no arrests were made.

One newspaper, however, *Moskovskiye Novosti*, pointed to an unnamed 'top-ranking official in Moscow', who some of its readers assumed to be Vladimir Putin:

> Tsepov's name is well known in St Petersburg. But few people are aware of this person's real status. Seven years ago, I obtained a document that, by all appearances, had been put together by one of Russia's security services. The document stated that Tsepov collected protection money from a number of St Petersburg's casinos for one of the secret service's top-ranking officials. I tried to get Yuri Vanyushin, the General Prosecutor's Office investigator for cases of special importance, to corroborate this information about Tsepov. The team that Vanyushin supervised was looking into a criminal case connected with deliveries of imports into St Petersburg that avoided customs by passing through a military port. Vanyushin (who has since died) confirmed this information: according to facts possessed by his team of investigators, Tsepov indeed collected money from commercial enterprises

and personally handed it over to a 'top-ranking official in Moscow.' So that rumours about Tsepov's special role, which have circulated both in Moscow and St Petersburg, are not groundless. For example, rumours about the fact that the scale of the commercial projects in which he participated corresponded to the expanding possibilities of the same Moscow official to whom he had once delivered off-the-books cash.

Anatoly Sobchak

In 1995, as part of their (failed) putsch to take over power in Russia, General Korzhakov and his collaborators decided to unseat Yeltsin's supporter Anatoly Sobchak from his post as mayor of St Petersburg. The St Petersburg secret service began 'working on' Sobchak's family and entourage in May 1995. In December, an interagency operational-investigative group was established to look into evidence of corruption in Sobchak's mayor's office. The group was officially created by an unprecedented joint order from the Minister of Internal Affairs A. Kulikov, the head of the Russian Security Service (SBR, the former KGB and the future secret service—the KGB was being constantly renamed and restructured at that time) M. Barsukov, and General Prosecutor Yu. Skuratov. The political motivations behind Sobchak's harassment were obvious. Everyone knew that the order to have Sobchak removed from his post had come from the all-powerful Korzhakov. But the fact that in St Petersburg—'Russia's crime capital'—corruption flourished and government officials took exceedingly large bribes was also known to everyone.

The St Petersburg investigative group was headed by Leonid Proshkin, the deputy head of the investigations directorate of Russia's General Prosecutor's Office and one of Russia's most famous investigative officials, who was in charge of many important government corruption cases. Over the course of a year, the investigative group collected several dozen volumes of documents (criminal case No. 18/238287-95). According to the investigators, the St Petersburg construction company Renaissance had been given ownership of several apartment buildings in the city on the condition that it would renovate them, and it had paid for this major contract by selling renovated apartments to mayor's office employees and their relatives at reduced prices. The investigation discovered documents signed by

Sobchak that had secured most favourable treatment status for Renaissance, while the company's head, Anna Yevglevskaya, confirmed that she had paid $54,000 to relocate the residents of city-owned apartment No. 17 in building No. 31 on Moika Embankment. This apartment shared a wall with apartment No. 8, which was occupied by Anatoly Sobchak, his wife, and their daughter. After the residents of apartment No. 17 were relocated, the apartment became Sobchak's; to cover up this fact, however, it was officially transferred to Sergeyev, the private chauffer of a close friend of Sobchak's wife, Lyudmila. The mayor's niece Marina Kutina (née Sobchak) also obtained better living quarters, as did the head of Sobchak's staff, V. Kruchinin. Evidence of corruption at the St Petersburg prosecutor's office also came to light. Nazir Khapsirokov, the property manager of the St Petersburg prosecutor's office, had signed a contract with a Turkish firm, Ata Insaat Saanyi Ticaret Ltd., to have the prosecutor's office building repaired and renovated for a sum of $5,855,435. The Turkish firm received $3 million less than the agreed amount. The cost of the repairs was inflated by a hundred percent. The city prosecutor's daughter somehow obtained an apartment.

Sobchak tried to defend himself against the attack from the secret service. On May 20, 1996, the St Petersburg branch of the party Our Home Is Russia sent letters to the president, the general prosecutor, and the prime minister, expressing 'strong objections to the harassment and libel [to which Sobchak was being subjected by] the General Prosecutor's Office.' 'On the pretext of "fighting corruption",' the letter read, 'the General Prosecutor's Office is using its work for political purposes and discrediting the government. L. G. Proshkin's investigative group is giving interviews and, against all procedural norms, publishing unsubstantiated materials in the communist press—*Sovietskaya Rossiya*, *Pravda*, *Narodnaya Pravda*—which are being used as promotional flyers in the election campaign. In view of these facts, the St Petersburg organization Our Home Is Russia demands that decisive measures be taken to put an end to the use of law enforcement agencies for political purposes.' All of this was absolutely true—but so was the evidence of corruption collected by the criminal investigation. Among those who signed the letter was the head of the board of the St Petersburg office of Our Home Is Russia, Vladimir Putin.

From a political point of view, Sobchak lost this battle: on June 2,

1996, Sobchak's deputy Vladimir Yakovlev was elected as the new mayor. The 'apartment affair,' however, did not die down after Sobchak's defeat in the election. In December 1996, a new General Prosecutor's Office investigator, Nikolai Mikheyev, became head of the investigative group. In the summer of 1997, the investigation led to the arrests of the head of the planning and economic department (Glavsnab) of the St Petersburg mayor's office, V. Lyubina; Mayor Sobchak's former assistant on housing issues, L. Kharchenko; and the head of the mayor's staff, V. Kruchinin. By the fall, relying on the testimony of the arrested individuals and other collected materials, the investigative group was already prepared to bring charges against Sobchak himself and members of his inner circle. Plans were in the works for the arrest of a large group of people, including the former mayor of the city himself.

At this time, Putin was already in Moscow at a height that the St Petersburg investigators could not reach; but he covered up for Sobchak, knowing that he was thus indirectly protecting himself as well, since the investigation was also looking into his own financial activities. The investigation's note 'On certain aspects of the work of the operational-investigative group of the St Petersburg Ministry of Internal Affairs' stated:

> We have obtained evidence of crimes—the use of an official position for private purposes—committed by Putin, one of the high-ranking officials in the president's administration, a member of the Chubais team. The official position which Putin currently occupies considerably hinders the work of the operational-investigative group and allows A. Sobchak to feel relatively safe.

Putin, who at that time was deputy chief of staff and head of the Main Control Directorate (GKU), did as much as he could to thwart the 'apartment affair.' The St Petersburg prosecutor's office brought a number of charges against St Petersburg police officers who had been involved in the investigation of the Sobchak case. Some of them, including the supervising officers, were arrested. Sobchak's wife, Lyudmila, began paying regular visits to Putin in Moscow. They always met alone, so the details of their conversations are not known. It was precisely Narusova who informed Putin that, after long debate, Russia's General Prosecutor's Office had made the decision to arrest Sobchak. And Sobchak's arrest would imperil his whole entourage—first and foremost, Putin himself.

On October 3, 1997, the now ex-mayor Sobchak was called in for questioning by the prosecutor's office. It was expected that he would be presented with charges and then arrested. Neither the democrats nor Putin could allow this to happen: the democrats, because Sobchak was their symbol; and Putin, because after Sobchak's arrest the threads of the investigation would lead to him. On Putin's instructions, an emergency response team from the Regional Directorate for Combating Organized Crime (RUBOP) removed Sobchak from the prosecutor's office and took him to a hospital, where the director of the Military Medical Academy Yuri Shevchenko—a person close to Sobchak's family and a close acquaintance of Putin's—at once gave Sobchak a highly dubious diagnosis: heart attack.

Realizing that Sobchak was being freed from arrest, investigator Mikheyev met with the heads of Russia's Ministry of Health and arranged for an independent examination of Sobchak's health by Moscow doctors. However, this examination—which the General Prosecutor's Office had no right to conceal from officials in the Kremlin, who did not want Sobchak to be arrested—never took place. On November 7, 1997, three days before the group of Moscow cardiologists were scheduled to arrive in St Petersburg, RUBOP officers Shakhanov and Milin, led by the first deputy head of the secret service's St Petersburg directorate, Alexander Grigoriev, removed Sobchak from the hospital and took him to France on a private plane. The plane had been chartered from the Finnish airline Jetflite by the famous cellist and conductor Mstislav Rostropovich. The operation to remove Sobchak was organized by Vladimir Putin. An ambulance drove out directly onto the runway at Pulkovo airport: Anatoly Sobchak and Lyudmila emerged from it, boarded the plane, and flew away.

When he became president, Putin did not forget the people who had helped him carry out this operation. Yuri Shevchenko became Russia's minister of health. Alexander Grigoriev became head of the Federal Agency for State Reserves. Rostropovich became a close friend of Putin's. s minister of health, Shevchenko acquired the nickname 'Dr. Death,' since during his tenure mortality among

Russians rose sharply, and during the freeing of the 'Nord-Ost' hostages in Moscow on October 23, 2002, 129 people lost their lives due to inadequate medical treatment after gas poisoning. After five years of failure, Shevchenko was dismissed from his post.

Anatoly Sobchak's Viagra

On February 17, 2000, Anatoly Sobchak, acting as representative of presidential candidate Vladimir Putin, arrived in the Kaliningrad region for a meeting with the region's governor, Leonid Gorbenko. By this time, all criminal charges against Sobchak had been dropped, all of the prosecutors and investigators who had initiated proceedings against him had been dismissed from their posts. A reception had been organized for Sobchak in Kaliningrad, during which Sobchak consumed only a small amount of alcohol. Then he returned to his hotel room in Svetlogorsk and died. This happened on the night of February 19, 2000. Sobchak's heart disease, which had been exacerbated by his past troubles, was well-known, and the cause of death was quickly determined to be heart failure.

However, at the time there were also rumours, from unknown sources, that two other people had been present in Sobchak's hotel room at the time of his death. He had died because a 'drug' which he was taking was incompatible with the alcohol that he had consumed. Between the lines, the message was that Sobchak had been taking Viagra and he had died in his hotel room in the company of two call girls.

Wrily, one newspaper described the tragedy as follows:

> Sobchak arrived in Kaliningrad not as an out-of-favour and persecuted criminal and one of the godfathers of the Russian mafia, but as the mentor, teacher, and representative of the country's acting president. Sobchak entered Kaliningrad as a winner on a 'white horse,' as a man whose political career was once again on the rise. By this time, all the criminal charges against Sobchak had been dropped, not without Putin's help, and his 'persecutors' themselves had been dismissed from their posts—all of them, to a man, from the general prosecutor of Russia down to the run-of-the-mill criminal investigator. Thanks to his favourite student and president, Sobchak had

> won all of his suits against the media, which had at various times 'dared' to publish unflattering information about him. During the whole time of his visit to the Kaliningrad region, Sobchak radiated wellbeing and a smile never left his face. Under such circumstances, one can get a heart attack only from too much happiness.'

Vladimir Putin (Acting-President, and in the midst of his election campaign) himself did a great deal to cement Russian public opinion in the belief that Sobchak had indeed been poisoned. Thus, at the beginning of 2000, shortly before Sobchak's death, Putin said in an interview that the persecution of Sobchak had been initiated by secret service General Alexander Korzhakov and Oleg Soskovets, and that a 'very dirty game was played' against the former mayor. On the day when he arrived in St Petersburg for Sobchak's funeral, Putin remarked in a Baltika radio interview that his former boss and St Petersburg mayor 'Sobchak's departure is not simply a death, but a *travlya* and the result of an attack against him.' In Russian, the word *travlya* has two meanings—persecution or poisoning.

Sobchak's autopsy in Kaliningrad was accompanied by unprecedented security measures on direct orders from Putin. A special police unit blocked all access to the forensic analysis department of the traumatological hospital where, under conditions of extreme secrecy, the autopsy took place. Policemen, traffic police officers, and Kaliningradavia security agency personnel were likewise stationed at Khrabrovo airport, from where a special 'funeral' flight left for St Petersburg on the same day. Sobchak's body was transported to St Petersburg and he was hastily buried on February 24, 2000, without a second examination of the body by the country's leading specialists. Against this background, an announcement by the head of the press service of the Federal Protection Service (FSO), Sergei Devyaty, that an assassination attempt against President Putin had been averted during Sobchak's funeral in St Petersburg, went unheard and unnoticed.

Yuri Shutov

When Putin started working for Sobchak in 1990, Sobchak had people working for him who, according to Putin, 'have since then become notorious and who did Sobchak a bad service.'[2] Putin was referring first and foremost to Yuri Shutov, a shady businessmen and politician who was the unofficial advisor to Lensovet chairman Sobchak during the spring and fall of 1990 (officially, Shutov served as Sobchak's advisor only for several days, from November 5 to November 12, 1990).

In Soviet times, petty bureaucrat Shutov had been charged with attempting to set fire to Leningrad's city hall (Smolny) with the aim of destroying evidence of his financial misdeeds. He was put in prison. During Gorbachev's perestroika, Shutov was pardoned and then exonerated. Obviously, he had had no intentions of setting fire to Smolny. After Sobchak first took him under his wing and then banished him in shame (apparently, not without Putin's advice), Shutov began gathering incriminating evidence against Sobchak and his entourage. The times were difficult ones, everyone broke the laws, and there was plenty of incriminating evidence to be had. Later, part of the materials collected by Shutov went into his book-length pamphlet, 'Sobchak's Heart' (*Sobchachie serdtse*, a pun on the title of Mikhail Bulgakov's famous novella *Sobachie serdtse*, 'The Heart of a Dog') and its sequel, 'Sobchak's Mischieviad, or How Everyone Was Robbed' (*Sobchachya prokhindiada, ili kak vsekh obokrali*). These books were intended to be the first two parts of a trilogy entitled 'Thievery.'

In working on his books, Shutov was helped by Mark Grigoriev, a professional journalist who had once published an article in the magazine *Ogonyok* about the attempt to 'set fire' to Smolny, which had strongly contributed to Shutov's pardon and exoneration. Shutov's office was located in the Leningrad Hotel. Shutov rented a room for his co-author in the same hotel, and the two writers worked on their book in peace—a book that, of course, could bring no great joy to Sobchak.

In February 1991, there was a fire in the hotel, in which Mark Grigoriev died. This did not stop Shutov, and he stubbornly went on with the work that he had begun. Somehow, he had gotten hold of a tape of a casual conversation between Sobchak and the resident of French intelligence in Russia. Sobchak asked Putin to intervene and to prevent the publication of this conversation. And Putin, using the Leningrad Regional Directorate for Combating Organizing Crime (RUBOP), organized a raid on Shutov's apartment and confiscated the tape.

The raid and search were conducted without authority. On the night of October 6, 1991, Shutov entered his own apartment and discovered robbers there. As they fled from the scene of the crime, they broke Shutov's skull with a hammer. When, several months later, in March 1992, Shutov was visited by government officials with an official search warrant and an order for his arrest (for preparing an assassination attempt against Azerbaijan's President Abulfaz Elchibey, which sounded about as believable as the previous charge of trying to set fire to Smolny), Shutov recognized one of them, Dmitry Milin, as one of the robbers who had cracked his skull. The second 'robber' turned out to have been Milin's co-worker Dmitry Shakhanov. Both were top-ranking officials at the Leningrad RUBOP. After spending a year-and-a-half in a pretrial detention facility, Shutov was initially released on the condition that he would not leave the country; and then, in 1996, completely acquitted by a decision of St Petersburg's Vyborgsky District Court.

In his first two anti-Sobchak pamphlets (first published in 1992 and 1993, respectively), the vengeful Shutov did not once mention Putin. But in 1998, Shutov became a deputy in the St Petersburg Legislative Assembly and began to believe that he was now truly protected by parliamentary immunity, which he enjoyed according to his status. Through the *Novy Peterburg* newspaper, which he sponsored and for which he wrote a column entitled 'All the King's Men,' Shutov launched a rumour to the effect that the new director of the secret service, Vladimir Putin, had been recalled from East Germany during his tenure there as a foreign intelligence officer for treasonous offences against Russia: 'During his almost five-year term of service in East Germany, KGB captain Putin achieved no visible results. However, he was observed entering into non-sanctioned contact with a member of the enemy's agent network. After which he was immediately sent to the Soviet Union, where he arrived on a used GAZ-24 Volga automobile, purchased in East Germany, with three German-made rugs.'[3]

In the same article, Shutov proposed his own interpretation of the relations between Putin and Sobchak, when the former was the KGB's overseer of Leningrad State University and the latter a professor at the university's law faculty. According to Shutov, Sobchak had been a freelance agent and Putin's informer. Putin was 'required to collect information for the KGB, to work with agents employed by the university, and to recruit new informers... Professor Sobchak ended up in the net of the KGB's interests [and he] willingly informed the pro-rector's assistant, Putin, about the entire spectrum of issues that interested him. Subsequently, in 1990, a small folder containing this informer's original handwritten reports, which in KGB bureaucratic terminology is called 'the agent's working case,' became a very weighty argument in support of Putin's appointment as advisor to Leningrad city council head Sobchak.'[4]

Novy Peterburg readers never found out whether or not what Shutov had written was true. The response from Putin, who was the director of the secret service, came less than two months after Shutov's controversial article was published. In February 1999, by a decision of the court, Shutov was stripped of his parliamentary immunity and arrested on suspicions of organizing a number of serious crimes, including the murder of a prominent city official, Mikhail Manevich, in St Petersburg in 1997; and the murder of a prominent democratic political activist, Galina Starovoitova, in 1998. In order to attack Shutov, Putin even made use of the famous official TV reporter Mikhail Leontiev, who appeared on Channel One of Russian television demanding punishment for the 'thug and bandit.'

However, in November 1999, St Petersburg's Kuybyshev District Court changed Shutov's pretrial restrictions to a promise not to leave the country and ruled that Shutov be released from jail. Shutov was freed right in the courtroom, but several minutes later, armed masked men burst into the court. A tussle ensued, in the course of which several people were hurt, including a TV cameraman, whose arm was broken, and Shutov himself, who was hit several times on the head with gun butts and fists, and passed out. According to Shutov, the masked men then took him to the building of the municipal prosecutor's office and subjected him to a beating. As a result of this beating, Shutov lost half his hearing and one of his eyes. Independent doctors were not allowed into the prosecutor's office, while the government's medical experts diagnosed the defendant as being in perfect health. However, several days later, a court hearing was called at the request of Shutov's lawyers; and the ambulance paramedics who had been summoned to the hearing submitted a medical report calling for Shutov's immediate hospitalization. But instead of being hospitalized, Shutov was sent to St Petersburg's pretrial detention facility, and after some time, he was transferred to the Vyborg prison.

At first, it was not even clear who had organized Shutov's abduction from the courtroom. Subsequently, the St Petersburg municipal prosecutor's office assumed responsibility for the action. The special forces unit (OMON) that had burst into the courtroom had been sent from Moscow for this operation.

Human rights activists and democrats took a weak and indecisive stance in the 'Shutov affair,' since Shutov's anti-liberal and anti-Western views were undeniable, and since he probably had connections with the criminal world. Despite Shutov's court acquittal and the Russian Supreme Court's subsequent ruling about the illegality of keeping him under arrest,[5] despite Shutov re-election to the city parliament in 2002, Putin's personal enemy spent seven (!) years being shuttled between different pretrial detention facilities without a conviction, and in February 2006 was finally sentenced to life in prison for organizing a number of contract killings of businessmen (the charges of murdering Manevich and Starovoitova were dropped).

It was never discovered who killed Manevich and Starovoitova. Starovoitova was killed in the entrance to her apartment building. Manevich's murder was carried out in a highly professional manner. The killer fired an optical-sight rifle from the roof of a high-rise building at a car that had stopped at a traffic light; the bullets went through the roof of the vehicle. Manevich's wife was with Manevich inside the car at the time of the murder, but she was not hurt. Criminal investigators developed several possible theories regarding this incident. They also discovered how Manevich first met his future wife. A certain secret service agent had asked a young woman courier to take a train to Moscow and to hand a sealed bag to a man who would meet her at the Leningradsky Station. In the train, a young man named Mikhail sat down next to the girl. They spent the whole night talking and exchanged phone numbers. In Moscow, the girl was indeed met by a man when she got off the train. He took the bag, moved some distance away, and believing that he was no longer seen, tossed the bag in a garbage can without opening it. The young man on the train was Mikhail Manevich. The young woman was his future wife. The secret service agent who had asked her to deliver the bag was Vladimir Putin.

Nazir Khapsirokov and Ashot Yeghiazarian

Nazir Khapsirokov, the property manager of the General Prosecutor's Office, was born in 1952, in the Karachay-Cherkessian village of Khabez. His father, Khazir Khapsirokov, was a professor at the Karachay Pedagogical Institute. After graduating from high school, Nazir entered the institute where his father taught. During vacations, along with other students, he made money by working as an instructor at the Dombai downhill ski resort, and here already he displayed an enterprising spirit: he would tell each of the groups that he worked with that it was his birthday, after which money would be collected for a gift, making a decent supplement to his salary.

After graduating from the institute, Nazir became the secretary of his district Komsomol committee, and then an instructor at his district party committee. However, he continued to drink heavily and his habit got so out of hand that the question arose of expelling him from the party committee. He was saved when his father, a respected man in the republic, intervened on his behalf. But his career as a party functionary was over. Nazar left his native city and became the director of a household services factory, organizing underground production of knitted goods at his place of work. In the Soviet Union, such people were called 'shop organizers' (*tsekhoviki*). They produced goods at government expense in government-owned enterprises, but these goods were not mentioned in any documents, just as if they did not exist. And all the money from their sales went to the organizers of these complicated and risky private businesses, which were prohibited by Soviet law. Sooner or later, 'shop owners' were arrested. This is what happened to Nazir. Criminal charges were brought against him and he was put in a pretrial detention facility.

Criminal cases involving 'shop organizers' were handled by the KGB, since large-scale economic ventures were regarded as a form of economic sabotage and a threat to the foundations of the state. The RSFSR's Criminal Code even prescribed the death penalty for illegal operations that involved over one million rubles. At the very least, Khapsirokov was facing a long term in prison. But he was offered freedom and the dropping of criminal charges against him in exchange for collaboration with the KGB.

When in the early 1990s Khapsirokov started building dachas

outside Moscow for federal and Moscow city government officials, criminal charges were once more brought against him for overspending his resources by an amount exceeding half a million dollars. In other words, he was accused of stealing over $500,000. Nazir blamed everything on his deputy, who disappeared. Khapsirokov himself switched to a different job, becoming an executive manager in Russia's General Prosecutor's Office. The general prosecutor at the time was the former head of the president's audit directorate, Alexei Ilyushenko. When Khapsirokov was appointed to his new post, reports appeared in the press that the budget resources allocated to the General Prosecutor's Office for the maintenance of all of the prosecutor's offices in the country were kept on accounts at Moscow National Bank and Unikombank, which were headed by Khapsirokov's friend Ashot Yeghiazarian

Ashot Yeghiazarian was born in Moscow on July 2, 1965. In the late 1970s, he emigrated with his family to Los Angeles. In the 1970s, the USSR opened a general consulate in San Francisco, which provided diplomatic cover for Soviet foreign intelligence activities and handed out visas to Americans wishing to visit the Soviet Union. All copies of forms for obtaining entrance visas were sent to the Consular Directorate of the USSR's Ministry of Foreign Affairs and to the KGB—to the Central Unit of Operational Communications. This made it possible for various subdivisions of state security to take an active part in the process of handing out (or refusing) entrance visas to foreign citizens. The employees of the consular departments of the USSR's—and later Russia's—embassies were usually foreign intelligence officers, working under diplomatic cover. Consequently, the KGB and the secret service were always informed well in advance when any foreign citizen made plans to visit the country.

In Yeghiazarian's biography, everything looked peculiar. In 1991, at the age of 25, Yeghiazarian became the head of the Foundation for the Social-Economic Development of the Moscow Region. In 1993, he created and became the head of Moscow National Bank (whose name—'Moscow National'—does not sound at all Russian). In 1995, the bank became one of the largest in Russia (then it went bankrupt). The bank held the accounts of the Moscow regional government, the Ministry of Defence, Rosvooruzhenie (the state-owned arms export company), the Russian Cosmic Agency, and the General Prosecutor's Office. In 1996, Yeghiazarian left the bank and became deputy chairman of the board of directors at Unikombank. The son of the new general prosecutor, Yuri Skuratov, became one of the managers of this bank; the obliging banker Yeghiazarian repaired and renovated Skuratov's apartment, in return for which he was appointed advisor to Russia's general prosecutor, a post he continued to occupy until 1998. The clue to Yeghiazarian's success lay in the fact that he had been recruited as an agent of Russia's Foreign Intelligence Service (SVR).

It was precisely these two agent-friends—secret-service agent Khapsirokov and SVR agent Yeghiazarian—that were used by Putin to work on the case of Russia's general prosecutor Yuri Skuratov, who was investigating economic crimes committed by members of Yeltsin's entourage. In 1998, Unikombank—where Yeghiazarian was employed—provided the funds to rent the apartment in which certain unknown individuals—subordinates of secret service director Putin—made a videorecording of a 'person resembling the general prosecutor' of Russia, Yuri Skuratov, amusing himself with two call girls. This videorecording ultimately forced Skuratov to resign.

Unikombank soon collapsed. When the bank declared bankruptcy, the Moscow region hard-currency domestic loan bonds that it was holding disappeared, as did $230 million that had been allocated to the MAPO MiG corporation for the production of fighter planes for India. This money was never found. Several lawsuits followed the bank's collapse, but none of them affected Yeghiazarian. And when the amount of incriminating evidence against Khapsirokov and Yeghiazarian attained a critical mass and started to pose the threat of an investigation and an arrest, Khapsirokov took shelter in the president's staff, where he continues to work to this day, while Yeghiazarian found safety in the Russian parliament. He became a Duma deputy from the Liberal Democratic Party of Russia (LDPR), thus obtaining immunity, and is currently deputy head of the Duma budget committee.

Sergei Chemezov

In 1997, Yevgeny Ananiev—former KGB officer, head of MAPO Bank's board of directors, and editor-in-chief of the *Megapolis-Express* newspaper, who had been supported by head of the Presidential Security Service Korzhakov and Deputy Prime Minister Soskovets prior to their resignations—became the head of Rosvooruzhenie.

Shortly thereafter, by order of President Yeltsin, additional organizations were created to facilitate the sale of Russian arms abroad: Promexport and Russian Technologies. The appearance of new arms dealers gave rise to competition among them and a sharp decline in sales. This led to a wholesale review of the activities of Rosvooruzhenie in 1998 by the Main Control Directorate of the Presidential Administration, headed by Putin's appointee Nikolai Patrushev. What the review discovered remained a secret, although in June 2004, the Italian media reported that former head of Rosvooruzhenie Ananiev was being charged by the Italian authorities with laundering $18 million that had been received by him and a group of Russian parties from the government of Peru as a bribe for giving Peru a discount on MiG-29 fighter planes.

After becoming the head of the government, Putin immediately united Russia's arms dealers into a single organization, Rosoboronexport, in order to make it easier to monitor their monetary flows. At the head of the new organization, he installed his old foreign intelligence colleague Andrei Belyaninov, and as Belyaninov's first deputy he appointed Chemezov. The Government Commission for Military-Technological Cooperation with Foreign Countries was headed by Putin personally.

In 2004, Chemezov replaced Belyaninov and became head of Rosoboronexport. In December 2006, President Putin signed a decree 'On certain issues of military-technological cooperation between the Russian Federation and foreign countries' that gave Rosoboronexport monopoly rights over Russian arms sales. Prior to the signing of the decree, 18 other defence enterprises had the right to deliver spare parts and maintenance services for previously sold arms to foreign countries. In addition, a number of major producers of military technology—such as the manufacturers of MiG fighter planes, the KBP Instrument Design Bureau, and the NPO Mashinostroyenia Military-Industrial Corporation—also had independent access to the foreign market. After the president's decree, all Russian arms sales became concentrated in the hands of one of the people closest to Putin, Sergei Chemezov.

In terms of its volume and profitability, the sale of arms is the third largest business in Russia, after oil and gas. Andrei Belyaninov, who headed Rosoboronexport before Chemezov, acknowledged in one of his interviews that the money that remained abroad with agents and middlemen was not subject to monitoring and control. In addition, in the spring of 2007, the Duma Committee for Defence prepared a bill allowing Rosoboronexport, which has 44 offices in foreign countries, to use the accounts of Russian embassies and other delegations in foreign countries, i.e. not to deliver the proceeds from arms sales back to Russia, but to keep them on the diplomatic bank accounts of embassies, consulates, and other representative delegations.

The new law also allowed Rosoboronexport to form barter arrangements for arms sales. In principle, there was nothing new about this. The Soviet Union made extensive use of similar arrangements in selling arms to developing nations that were unable to make scheduled payments in hard currency. Some paid in bananas, others paid in oranges. Such contracts were handled by various subdivisions of the Ministry of Foreign Economic Relations. The same agency also handled the sales of the natural products which it received, disposing of them on the territory of the USSR. The new law entrusted all of these functions to Rosoboronexport. The law was accompanied by an explanatory note:

'The attraction of payments in the form of natural products stems from the fact that developing nations, particularly those of the African region, are not always able to meet payments, as well as from the fact that it is economically expedient for importers of Russian military production to pay for the products they receive with goods that they produce (textiles, palm tree oil, etc.).'

Thus, the note went on to report, $150 million worth of munitions were delivered to Indonesia in 2003-2004; payment was made in palm tree oil and its ingredients. Currently, plans are being made of the sale of $400 million worth of arms to Thailand; payment will come in various food products, which will not be delivered to Russian territory (which means that Rosoboronexport will not have to pay value added tax).

This approach to selling Russian arms and paying for them opened up broad possibilities for manipulating prices, receiving off-the-books commission fees, and appropriating substantial sums of money, since complicated barter arrangements made monitoring and control over sales and payments virtually impossible.

In 2007, Rosoboronexport and all of its daughter enterprises were unified in the newly created Russian Technologies corporation. Chemezov now became the head of the whole corporation. In addition, Rosoboronexport received Oboronprom's packet of shares; the Perm-based Motovilinskiye Zavody munitions plant; two thirds of the shares of Russia's largest titanium corporation, VSMPO-Avisim, which produces 20% of the world's titanium; the Russpetsslal steel company; and the AvtoVAZ automobile factory. The new corporation was exempted from the government's direct control. Its head was appointed by the president personally. In other words, Putin had created a monopolistic military superstructure in Russia for the production and sales of arms, on the model of Gazprom, which deals in natural gas.

Not surprisingly, people who were involved in investigating Russian arms sales to foreign partners, as well as the partners themselves, found themselves in a high-risk area. In March 2007, *Kommersant* correspondent Ivan Safronov 'fell out' of the window of the stairwell of his own apartment building. Safronov, an ex-serviceman, was involved in investigating Russian arms sales to Syria and Iran. In June, Egyptian billionaire Ashraf Marwan, who had made his fortune selling Soviet and Russian arms, fell from the balcony of his apartment in London.

On July 5, 2007, Russian citizen Oleg Orlov was strangled to death in pretrial detention facility No. 13 in Kiev. Ukraine suspected Orlov of involvement in two crimes: illegally selling a P-14F radar station to Eritrea, which was at war with Ethiopia, in the fall of 1999 (false papers stated that the radar station was being sold to Romania); and illegally selling Kh-55SM air-launched cruise missiles to China and Iran. In both cases, the arms had been delivered through the Ukrainsky Spetsexport company. Until 2004, Orlov had lived in Karlovy Vary (Czech Republic). He had asked the Czech government for political asylum, but his request was denied. While attempting to leave for the United Arab Emirates, Orlov was arrested in the Prague airport and then deported to Ukraine, where the Ukrainian Security Service (SBU) had brought criminal charges against him in 2004. The same charges had also been brought against Vladimir Yevdokimov, general manager of the Ukrainsky Aviazakaz company and former SBU employee; Yevdokimov was sentenced by the Kiev Appellate Court to six years in prison. The SBU put one more Russian citizen on the wanted list: Igor Shilenko. His case also involved the former head of Ukrainsky Spetsexport, Valery Malev, and Australian citizen Haider Sarfraz, both of whom died in automobile accidents in 2002 and 2004.

Leonid Tyagachev

There's a Russian saying: an old friend is better than two new ones. Sometimes, however, the opposite is true. Putin's new friend Leonid Tyagachev, head of Russia's National Olympic Committee, is a vivid example. Leonid Vasilievich Tyagachev was born on October 10, 1946, in the Moscow-area town of Dedenevo. For many years, his life was connected with the Turist railroad station, located just outside of Moscow. The landscape around this railroad station is hilly and these hills have long been used by downhill skiers to practice their skills. One of them was the very young Leonid Tyagachev. After becoming involved in sports, Tyagachev graduated from the physical culture faculty of the Krupskaya Moscow Regional State Pedagogical Institute in 1973. The institute was not a prestigious one; it prepared gym teachers for Moscow region secondary schools. Tyagachev's education was insubstantial.

However, he possessed other important qualities. He was friendly, particularly with those who occupied high positions in the Soviet party elite and their children. There were many people who were interested in downhill skiing. But only a very small group was able to try it. The necessary equipment was impossible to find, despite the fact that it was so expensive. By skilfully trading in equipment and making the right connections, Tyagachev was gradually able to reach the very top: he became the coach of the USSR's representative downhill ski team (whose international rating was negligible). Now the necessary people in whom Tyagachev was interested received everything they needed from him, either for a token payment or for free. Coach Tyagachev could afford it.

After working as coach for the USSR's downhill ski team for a short time, Tyagachev was able to acquire influential supporters in the USSR's State Sports Committee, in Moscow's municipal CPSU committee, and in the Central Committee of the CPSU. Tyagachev's house near the Turist railroad station became a kind of elite downhill ski base for his sponsors. He also established good working relations with sports administrators around the USSR at those locations where the downhill ski team's training sessions took place. These local administrators were interested in hosting the Soviet ski team, since the training sessions were all paid for by Moscow. In addition, a small amount of hard-to-acquire equipment would be left over for them. One phone call from Tyagachev to the director of the Elbrus-area council on tourism, former air force pilot Ibragim Timoyev, was enough to find hotel rooms—which were otherwise impossible to obtain—for the necessary person or his children. Through Zalikhmanov, who was in charge of ski lifts on Mt. Cheget, Tyagachev's 'friends' had free access to the ski lift and did not have to wait in line. In short, Tyagachev made skilful use of his 'administrative resource.'

While the young coach Tyagachev was becoming established in his new position (it should be noted that, while Tyagachev was coach, Soviet downhill skiers never achieved any significant successes in international competitions), Lieutenant Vladimir Alekseyevich Livros—a graduate of the KGB's Higher School—started working in the first division of the First Department of the Fifth Directorate of the KGB. He and his older colleague Major Anatoly Sergeyevich Semenov, deputy head of the first division, were ordered to supervise the USSR's State Sports Committee. It was Livros who, in the mid-1970s, recruited into the Fifth Directorate's agent network an agent with the code name 'Elbrus,' who was known in ordinary life as the coach of the Soviet downhill ski team, Leonid Tyagachev.

Lavrov's and Semenov's work at the USSR's State Sports Committee opened up broad opportunities. Through the Directorate for Medical-Biological Provisions for the representative teams of the country, it was possible to obtain expensive and hard-to-acquire foreign medicine for personal use. Through the Sports Committee's Main Athletic Provisions Office and through Soyuzsportobespechenie, it was possible to obtain athletic equipment and supplies. When it came to 'obtaining' all of these products, Semenov and Livros took orders from their boss, the deputy head of the Fifth Directorate's First Department, Lieutenant Colonel Viktor Timofeyevich Gusted.

Before being hired by the KGB, Gusted was the head of the Komsomol Central Committee's administrative-economic department. At this post, he had clearly learned that the essential thing in building a career was good relations with one's superiors, whose good will could be procured in return for various kinds of offerings. All three—Gusted, Semenov, and Livros—did everything they could to provide necessary athletic equipment and supplies (such as bicycles) for the Fifth Directorate's deputy heads, V. I. Nikiski and I. P. Abramov, and the Fifth Directorate's head, Lieutenant General Bobkov. But Semenov, Livros, and Gusted were not liked in the KGB. Semenov was nicknamed 'black.' His younger colleague Livros was nicknamed 'little vermin.' Ultimately, Gusted ended up being demoted and sent into honourable exile to the Dinamo Sports Association, becoming the deputy head of its Central Council.

In February 1979, the USSR's representative downhill ski team, under the supervision of its senior coach, Leonid Tyagachev, was coming back home from another world championship in Austria. When the team's luggage was passing through customs at Moscow's Sheremetyevo-2 airport, instead of finding ski boots customs officers discovered 120 pairs of contraband blue jeans—extremely rare and expensive items of clothing in the USSR. Contraband foreign-made blue jeans, which were almost illegal in the Soviet Union, could create serious difficulties for Tyagachev. In order to determine the circumstances of the case, the State Sports Committee—with the Fifth Directorate's approval—sent its representative Mikhail Volfovich Monastyrsky to Austria. Monastyrsky was the director of a number of international mountain-climbing camps and also a security agent with the code name 'Vladimirov.' During his short trip, Monastyrsky-'Vladimirov' obtained documentary evidence, including invoices signed by Tyagachev, that showed that he had removed 12 pairs of ski boots from their boxes and replaced them with 120 pairs of precious blue jeans.

Tyagachev was facing criminal sanctions. The transport prosecutor's office had brought criminal charges against him for trafficking in contraband on a large scale. Even the KGB was refusing to help. Livros, who had recruited Tyagachev, was apprehensive that he himself would be punished for his agent's actions. He avoided meeting Tyagachev and did not respond to his requests for help.

At this time, the KGB was preparing to make security provisions for the Moscow Olympics in 1980. The Fifth Directorate's Eleventh Department was considered the key agency in this important project, and in particular its third subdivision, which was being urgently expanded to include agents from other departments who had been transferred there for the duration of the Olympics. Among the new employees of the Eleventh Department's third division was a former graduate of the KGB's Higher School, Captain Fyodor Alekseyevich Volkov, who had previously served in the Fifth Directorate's Ninth Department, monitoring Soviet dissidents. And Livros, who had become afraid of possible repercussions arising from the Tyagachev incident, handed the supervision of the State Sports Committee's winter sports directorate over to the newly arrived and unsuspecting Volkov. Volkov had no choice but to deal with the problem that he had inherited from Livros, the problem of agent 'Elbrus.' Volkov arranged for Tyagachev's transfer to a supervisory position in the Russian Sports Committee, and Tyagachev was rescued from being held criminally liable for what he had done. The case was closed.

On April 15, 1980, in connection with the Moscow Olympics, the KGB made a decision to establish new positions for active reserve officers in the USSR's main athletic organizations: the State Sports Committee of the USSR, the State Sports Committee of the RSFSR (Russia), and the Sports Committee of the VTsSPS (the All-Union Central Council of Trade Unions). The decision was ratified by the Secretariat of the CPSU Central Committee and signed by Mikhail Suslov, the leading ideologist of Soviet Union, and by Mikhail Gorbachev, future general secretary of the CPSU Central Committee and president of the USSR. This was how Emerik Merkurievich Shevelev, a long-time employee of the state security organs and a member of the Fifth Directorate, ended up being appointed deputy head of the international department of the RSFSR State Sports Committee.

Tyagachev rather quickly established good informal relations with the new deputy head of his department, and Shevelev and his two sons soon started walking around in clothes made by Western firms—producers of skiing supplies—and developed a passion for downhill skiing, having received all the necessary equipment as a gracious present from Tyagachev.

Shevelev did his part for Tyagachev as well. He reported to his supervisors in state security that Tyagachev was in all respects an exceptionally reliable man, a valuable agent, and that in order to secure greater counterintelligence oversight over international sports exchange channels, it was absolutely imperative to send him on foreign work assignments as a downhill skiing coach. Since the head of the Fifth Directorate's Eleventh Department Colonel N. N. Romanov and the deputy head of the Fifth Directorate Major General V. A. Ponomaryev also turned out to be lovers of expensive skiing equipment, and since they also had sons who appreciated the expensive, foreign-made athletic products, the question of whether or not Tyagachev should be sent on foreign work assignments was decided in the affirmative. Shevelev's recommendations were supported by another person—Tyagachev's boss, the head of the RSFSR's State Sports Committee, Leonid Drachevsky.

Drachevsky, a former coach for the USSR's rowing team, was also an agent of the Fifth Directorate's Eleventh Department. He had been recruited by Valentin Nefedov, an employee of the Fifth Directorate's Seventh Department who had been temporarily transferred to the Eleventh Department. And if Nefedov's career in 'sports' did not work out—he was forced to leave the Fifth Directorate's Eleventh Department after the Moscow Olympics—then the career of his agent Drachevsky ended up being exemplary in all respects. Thanks to the KGB's support, he first became the head of Russian sports, and then was appointed by President Putin as his plenipotentiary representative in the Siberian Federal District. And to replace KGB agent Drachevsky as head of Russian sports, the government installed KGB agent Tyagachev.

In Soviet times, the KGB's Second Main Directorate was the main counterintelligence organ in the country. The directorate included a Thirteenth Department. In the late 1970s, Arkady Guk—a former London resident of Soviet foreign intelligence, whose career had been seriously damaged when one of his London subordinates, Oleg Gordievsky, defected to the United Kingdom—was appointed as the head of the Thirteenth Department. This department oversaw the selection and processing of state security officers for trips to foreign countries in various Soviet delegations (including athletic ones). The processing of agents for foreign travel with athletic delegations was handled by the former goalie of the Moscow soccer team Dinamo, Valery Fyodorovich Balyasnikov. Balyasnikov had climbed up through the ranks of this department to become the head of his subdivision, and shortly before the collapse of the Soviet Union, he was sent to one of the Latin American countries as a state security officer with the Soviet embassy.

State security officers accompanied Soviet athletic delegations only during major international sporting events: world championships, Unversiades, and Olympics. During competitions at lower levels and periods of training abroad, control and monitoring functions were performed by agents permanently embedded within the sports organizations themselves. Active reserve officers who had no relation to sports never travelled abroad with athletic delegations, since this could compromise their cover at their official places of work.

After the creation of the commercial organization Sovintersport in the late 1980s, Chemezov was sent there as an officer of the active reserve. Formally, however, he became Sovintersport's deputy general manager. This firm handled all purchases of foreign-made equipment for Russian teams, which is what led Tyagachev to seek out Chemezov. Shevelev was also helpful in this respect; like Chemezov, he was an active reserve officer and the deputy head of the RSFSR's State Sports Committee's international department. Chemezov and Shevelev worked in the same subdivision—the third subdivision of the Fifth Directorate's Eleventh Department.

Chemezov and Tyagachev quickly came to see eye to eye with respect to purchasing necessary equipment for skiers. They received kickbacks or commission fees either in cash or in kind (ski equipment produced by top foreign firms). Chemezov knew how to please his friend Putin. For a downhill skier such as Putin, good skiing equipment is a matter of pride. Tyagachev did not disappoint. Putin was given the best of everything. This is how Putin and Tyagachev met and how, over the years, they became friends.

The Olympic Games in Sochi (2014)

Putin's, Chemezov's, and Tyagachev's career paths are all correlated with one another. In 1996, Putin and Chemezov joined the Presidential Property Management Department, while Tyagachev became the head of Russia's State Sports Committee. In 1998, Putin was appointed director of the secret service and then prime minister, while Tyagachev became the vice president of Russia's Olympic Committee. In 2000, Putin was elected president. In July 2001, Tyagachev became the head of the Olympic Committee, replacing Russian secret-service agent Vitaly Smirnov, who had occupied this position for over 20 years.

In 2002, the Winter Olympics were held in Salt Lake City, Utah. They were accompanied by a series of scandals involving members of the Russian team. Tyagachev, who spoke no foreign languages and thus had no ability to communicate directly with members of the International Olympic Committee (IOC) and the Olympic committees of other countries, did virtually nothing. After the Olympics ended, Putin's deputy chief of staff Alexei Volin remarked that 'Russian sports officials displayed complete indifference and ineffectiveness at the games in Salt Lake City. We did not see their influence within the IOC, we did not see their presence in the international sports federations, and we did not hear them take an articulate and well-argued position on problems and issue that came up.'

Many believed that the head Russia's National Olympic Committee Tyagachev would resign. However, the controversy remained confined to criticism in the press. Shortly afterward, there occurred a conflict between the two heads of Russian sports—the head of Russia's State Sports Committee Vyacheslav Fetisov and the head of Russia's National Olympic Committee Tyagachev. Exploiting the criticism directed against Tyagachev after the Salt Lake City Olympics, Fetisov tried to remove him from his post and to replace him with his own person, Irina Rodnina, famous in the world of sports as an Olympic medallist and world champion. However, Fetisov and Rodnina lost this particular competition, since Tyagachev had the support of Chemezov and Putin, and their support had a long-standing commitment behind it.

Back in January 1996, Putin joined the council of Klub-2004, an association of St Petersburg industrialists and entrepreneurs established to promote the city as a host for the 2004 Olympics. At the time, St Petersburg did not even make it to the final round of the Olympic selection process. However, Putin did not abandon the idea of holding the Olympics in Russia. When he moved to Moscow, this idea turned into a project to host the Winter Olympics in Sochi, Putin's favourite downhill skiing destination, where he had often spent time with Chemezov and Tyagachev, in a little village called Krasnaya Polyana.

For those who have never been to Russia, we should reveal an important state secret. In the winter, a great part of Russia is covered with snow; its Siberian expanses and numerous mountain peaks form natural sites for holding Winter Olympics. There are hundreds of such locations. There is, probably, only one place that is obviously unfit for this purpose: the southern Russian Black Sea resort city of Sochi. Sochi is as hot as Florida. But this is the most expensive and popular destination for all 'new Russians,' and for all Russians in general, because Sochi in Russia is like Nice in France. It is clear that it is most profitable to invest money in Sochi, and the Winter Olympics are merely a pretext to pump billions of dollars in foreign investment and Russian government resources into the summer resort.

With the same zeal with which Putin in 1996 had supported the idea of holding the 2004 Olympics in St Petersburg, where he was the second in command, he now supported hosting the 2014 Olympics in Sochi, where he was first in command. The project promised large profits, since by the time of the International Olympic Committee's deciding vote on the issue, Sochi had been entirely 'privatized' by Putin-controlled organizations. In other words, all of the most important sites and locations involved in the Sochi-2014 project had been bought up in advance, in accordance with a previously coordinated plan, by private organizations and people controlled by Putin and the secret service.

Thus, when Putin spoke about realizing his dream of holding the Olympic Games on territory under his control, it was not sports that was at stake, but business. In order to realize the project, Putin needed a proven, reliable man, and he selected Tyagachev for the job. Fetisov, despite his fame and connections in the world of sports, lost his struggle with Tyagachev because Tyagachev's team turned out to be stronger: it included both Chemezov and Putin.

The contest in the international arena took place in 2007. The International Olympic Committee (IOC) had to decide where the 2014 Winter Olympics would be held. The contenders for hosting it were Austria, Korea, and Russia. The IOC met to vote on July 9, 2007, in Guatemala City.

The IOC's decision to offer the right to host the Winter Olympics had been preceded by a serious struggle among the contending countries. Victory in any sporting event requires money. As usual, the winner is the one who has invested the greatest amount of money to secure a victory. Russia's rivals, Austria and Korea, had spent $12 million and $21 million, respectively, to promote their cities as hosts for the Winter Olympics. Russia had spared no expense and had spent $50 million to promote Sochi. But this was not all. In order to snatch the victory from Russia's rivals, Putin himself came to Guatemala. On the eve of the IOC's deciding vote, he personally met with the IOC's most influential members and its head, Jacques Rogge. Putin also did not neglect the IOC's honorary president Juan Antonio Samaranch, a respected figure in international sports circles and among the members of the world's most important sports organization, the International Olympic Committee, all of whose members had been elected to what are in effect life-long positions under Samaranch. What Putin and Samaranch talked about, we do not know. What we do know is the IOC voted to hold the Winter Olympics in the Russian summer resort of Sochi. Moreover, since this vote took place, many of Putin's subordinates have repeatedly stated that President Putin intends to inaugurate the Sochi Olympics in person.

In achieving this ambition for Putin, the Kremlin was able to rely, in particular, on the help of an influential person who was very close to the IOC. This member was a diplomat whose position had been supported in the past, not only by the Soviet Union, but also by all the countries of the Eastern Bloc. His selection was preceded by a something of a detective story. As a diplomat the diplomat had developed an interest in Russian history and culture and grew particularly fond of Russian antiques, which he collected with the love of a genuine connoisseur and had shipped home. However, the USSR prohibited taking objects of cultural and historic value out of the country. This prohibition could be easily circumvented by using diplomatic mail, which was not subject to customs inspections. Since in Soviet times all antiques were closely monitored by the KGB, as a perpetual buyer of increasingly valuable rarities, the purchases by the diplomat was taken note of. After some time, an agent from the KGB's Second Main Directorate, which monitored the relevant embassy, met with the diplomat and smoothly explained to him that his actions were subject to prosecution under the RSFSR's criminal code (each republic had its own criminal code; there was no general criminal code for the USSR) and were classified by Soviet law as the smuggling of contraband goods. The diplomat was then offered a choice: he could either be compromised through the publication of articles in the Soviet and foreign press detailing his purchases, which would undoubtedly have put an end to his diplomatic career, or he could collaborate with the KGB.

In order to galvanise support for the recruit, the leadership of the KGB had directed the Fifth Directorate's Eleventh Department to prepare an encrypted telegram for its 'friends'—the heads of the state security organs of the other Eastern Bloc countries. The telegram requested that the foreign agents embedded in the various National Olympic Committees and Olympic sports federations be briefed concerning the necessity of showing world-wide support for the diplomat. The telegram was signed by the KGB's deputy head, V. M. Chebrikov, former head of the whole Fifth Directorate. It did not specify whether or not the diplomat was an agent, but indicated that he was supported by the USSR and asked that it also be supported by its 'friends', agents among the heads of the National Olympic Committees and Olympic sports federations. The KGB officer who had recruited the important diplomat was not forgotten either. By secret decree (without an announcement in the press) of the Presidium of the Supreme Council of the Soviet Union, he was awarded the Order of the Red Banner for Military Valour.

Other secret service agents were also involved in working on IOC members before the vote in Guatemala City. IOC vice president and Russian sports activist Vitaly Smirnov had been recruited by the KGB during the preparations for the Moscow Olympics in 1980. His immediate supervisor was the head of the Fifth Directorate, Lieutenant General Bobkov, and as Bobkov's protégé, Smirnov even called Bobkov's deputy General Abramov by his first name—Ivan—despite the difference in their ages and in front of Abramov's subordinates.

Shamil Tarpischev, who had been head of Russia's State Sports Committee during the Yeltsin presidency, also helped as much as he could. He, too, had been recruited by the KGB during the preparations for the 1980 Olympics. The agent who had recruited him was Major Albina Gavrilovna Demidova, a former track and field athlete who had served for a number of years as an officer in the KGB's Seventh Directorate—which monitored the activities of persons of interest to the KGB—and had then been appointed senior operative in the third subdivision of the Fifth Directorate's Eleventh Department. Finally, the head of the State Sports Committee's soccer and hockey directorate (and subsequently president of the Russian soccer federation), Vyacheslav Ivanovich Koloskov, also exerted his influence on the members of the IOC. He had been recruited in the late 1970s under the code name 'Yantar' by the deputy head of the third subdivision of the Fifth Directorate's Eleventh Department, Lieutenant Colonel Ernest Leonardovich Davnis. In short, Putin had no shortage of assistants. But the most important one among them turned out to be Tyagachev. He was ordered to keep silent during all of the meetings in Guatemala City. Tyagachev executed this task with consummate skill.

Who is Mr. Zubkov?

In February 2007, Anatoly Serdyukov became Russia's defence minister. On February 16, in a Radio Liberty interview, Vladimir Pribylovsky commented on Serdyukov's appointment:

> Of course, the most amusing and most surprising innovation here is the appointment of a former major furniture dealer to the post of defence minister. He is, by the way, a classic oligarch, since oligarchy really means political rule by a rich minority. And Mr. Serdyukov is a classic oligarch of this kind: a millionaire, and now a defence minister to boot. One can only guess what motivated this appointment.... For example, perhaps Serdyukov himself is not being groomed for the post of successor. But Serdyukov is married to the daughter of the head of the Federal Financial Monitoring Service, Zubkov. Zubkov is quite close to Putin. Maybe they want to make Zubkov the successor?[6]

Viktor Zubkov, Russia's ninth prime minister, is a friend of Vladimir Putin's, Viktor Ivanov's, Boris Gryzlov's—and the father-in-law of Anatoly Serdyukov.

Zubkov was born on September 15, 1941, in the village of Arbat in the Kuvshinsky district of the Sverdlovsk region. He is a Russian by nationality. In 1965, he graduated from the economic faculty of the Leningrad Agricultural Institute. Zubkov holds a doctorate in economics. In 2000, he defended his dissertation. Its title: 'Improving the Tax Structure of the Mineral and Raw Materials Complex. On the Example of the Leningrad Region.'

From August 1958 until August 1960, Zubkov worked as a metal worker. After graduating from the institute, he served in the army in 1966-67. Zubkov joined the CPSU in August 1967 and remained a party member until August 1991. From 1967 until 1985, he worked at state farms in the Leningrad region. From 1985 until 1991, Zubkov worked in Soviet and party organs in the Leningrad region, serving as head of the Priozersky municipal executive committee (1985); first secretary of the Priozersky party municipal committee of the Leningrad region, and head of the department of agriculture and food industry and the agrarian department of the party's regional committee (1986-89); and first deputy head of the Leningrad region executive committee (1989-91).

From January 1992 until November 1993, Zubkov worked under Putin at the International Relations Committee (IRC) of the St Petersburg mayor's office as deputy head in charge of agriculture. In other words, he served as Putin's deputy, since Putin was head of the IRC at the time.

On November 3, 1993, Zubkov was appointed head of the State Tax Inspectorate (GNI) for St Petersburg and deputy head of the State Tax Service (GNS). From August 14 until September 6, 1996, the GNS was called the Federal Tax Service of Russia. In May 1995, Zubkov joined Our Home Is Russia (Putin was the head of the organization's St Petersburg office at the time).

On November 30, 1998, Zubkov was relieved of his duties as deputy head of the GNS 'due to a transfer to a different place of work,' according to his resignation papers. Zubkov was then appointed head of the Ministry of Taxes and Receipts for St Petersburg. On July 23, 1999, he was appointed deputy minister of taxes and receipts for the Northwestern District. A few days after being appointed deputy minister, he was also appointed head of the combined Ministry of Taxes and Receipts Directorate for St Petersburg and the Leningrad region. He occupied these positions until November 2001, supervising the activities of 12 regional tax inspectorates.

On August 12, 1999, Zubkov was registered as a candidate for the position of administrative head of the Leningrad region. Zubkov's election campaign was managed by Boris Gryzlov, the future minister of internal affairs. Zubkov came in fourth out of sixteen candidates in the election on September 19, 1999, with 8.64% of the vote

(Valery Serdyukov—not a relative of the future defence minister with the same last name—was elected governor with 30.30% of the vote).

In 2000, Zubkov joined the St Petersburg initiative group (headed by Sergei Mironov and Vladimir Litvinenko) to elect Putin as president. He was 'candidate Putin's election agent.'

From February 2001 until October 2004, Zubkov was part of an interagency task force for the preparation of proposals for improving the Russian Federation's migration regulations (the task force was headed by Viktor Ivanov).

On November 5, 2001, Zubkov was appointed first deputy minister of finance—head of the Committee on Financial Monitoring. Zubkov's committee, which worked on preventing money laundering, became unofficially known as 'financial foreign intelligence.'

On June 11, 2002, Zubkov joined the Central Coordinating Council of the supporters of United Russia. From June 2002 until April 2004, he was a member of the government commission on migration policy. On March 16, 2004, Zubkov was appointed head of the Federal Financial Monitoring Service within the Ministry of Finance (under Minister A. Kudrin). Since July 2004, he has been deputy head of an interagency task force to develop national strategies for preventing the legalization of criminal profits. In June 2006, he joined the government commission on preventing substance abuse and illegal drug sales.

Zubkov received Soviet honours: the Badge of Honour (1975) and the Order of the Red Banner of Labour (1981); and he has received Russian honours as well: the order 'For Service to the Fatherland' in the fourth degree (2000) and 'For Service to the Fatherland' in the third degree (2006).

Zubkov's appointment as prime minister in the middle of September 2007 means that President Putin will have not one successor, but at least two. The name of one of them—the one who will become the next president—remains unknown and is unlikely to become known until December. But the second successor—the one who will occupy the position of prime minister in the next few years—has been revealed to us. His name is Zubkov.

No matter how loyal a friend, student, and colleague of Putin's the next president will be, he will still be faced with the temptation to appoint his own prime minister. A decision by the new president to dismiss Fradkov in May-June 2008 would have looked natural. Putin's supporters (in the Kremlin and in society at large) would have understood such a move. But the new president will find it much more psychologically difficult to remove Zubkov, a brand new prime minister, and, like the new president, an appointee of Putin's. By the spring, both of them—the new prime minister and the new president—will have practically identical 'credit histories' and the same level of legitimacy: one was appointed by Putin in September, the other will have been appointed by Putin a few months later. The real power will be in the hands of those who gave them this divided legitimacy—the secret service corporation.

But why was it specifically Zubkov that was appointed prime minister? What will be required of both successors is, above all, loyalty to the boss. Until 1989, Zubkov was the first secretary of the Priozersky municipal committee. The Priozersky district of the Leningrad region is the equivalent of Moscow's Rublevka: the favourite dacha location for all of Russia's elite. It was in the Priozersky district that dachas were purchased, through Zubkov's assistance, by Putin, and Yakunin, and Kovalchuk, and the Fursenko brothers, who in 1996 united their newly built estates into the Ozero dacha cooperative, which today, along with the secret service, rules Russia.

CONCLUSION

The Corporation

On May 7, 2000, Russia became a new kind of republic—a Corporate republic. A corporation took over the government of the country and put its own president in charge. It was called the Russian secret service (or FSB, the Federal Security Service). President Putin, who until August 1999 had been the president of the FSB *kontora* ('company'), and who on March 26, 2000, was elected the president of the country, began to rule Russia in the corporation's name. For the first time since seventeenth-century European East-India companies ruled entire countries in Asia for their shareholders, a modern company owned the largest land mass in the world—the Russian Federation.

Unlike the foreign owners of the East India companies, however, the shareholders were local and had been handed control over the state by its ruler. In 1999, the Russian tycoons and the state security men who were close to Yeltsin had explained to the president that only a former head of the secret service would be able to guarantee him and his family's immunity after he left office. If the Communists came to power, they would put Yeltsin in jail for using tanks to dissolve the parliament in 1993; if the democrats came to power, they would put him in jail for starting the first and second wars in Chechnya and for the genocide of the Chechen people. And whoever came to power would certainly try to put Yeltsin and his family in jail for his privatization of the Russian economy and the large-scale corruption that followed.

Yeltsin believed them, and with his own hands—the same hands that in August 1991 took the government of the country away from the Communists—gave the government of Russia to a top official from the Russian secret service by appointing him as his own successor before his Presidential ended.

The country's government would henceforth be run and be controlled by people who hated America and Western Europe, who had no experience in building anything, who acted in secrecy while belonging to an organisation of which—as with the Gestapo in Nazi Germany—not a single good word can be said in its defence.

After eight years in power, Vladimir Putin is leaving the Russian Presidency with a golden parachute of enormous proportions. From a position in 1990, when he received no salary, he moved to one in 2008 where he controls 37% of 'Surgutneftegaz', Russia's fourth-largest oil producer. The market value of this 37% is approximately $20 billion. He also controls 4.5% of the shares of 'Gazprom', Russia's natural gas monopoly. His package of shares is equal to approximately $13 billion. Finally, through his representative Gennady Timchenko he controls 50% of the oil company Gunvor. Last year the turnover of this company came to $40 billion dollars, and its profits to $8 billion.

The question that lies ahead is what the retired leader of the Russian Corporation will have to do to maintain his wealth and prevent history from turning on him....

Appendix

CHEKA—WHAT'S IN A NAME?

On December 20, 1917, the Council of People's Commissars of the Russian Republic passed a resolution, signed by Lenin, establishing the All-Russian Extraordinary Commission for Combating Counter-Revolution and Sabotage (VChK). In August 1918, the VChK changed its name to the All-Russian Extraordinary Commission for Combating Counter-Revolution, Speculation, and Corruption. The VChK's first head was Felix Dzerzhinsky.

On February 6, 1922, the All-Russian Central Executive Committee (VTsIK) of the Russian Soviet Federative Socialist Republic (RSFSR) passed a resolution abolishing the VChK and establishing State Political Directorate (GPU) as part of the RSFSR's People's Commissariat of Internal Affairs (NKVD).

On November 2, 1923, after the formation of the Union of Soviet Socialist Republics (USSR) in December 1922, the Presidium of the USSR's Central Executive Committee established the Joint State Political Directorate (OGPU) as part of the USSR's Council of People's Commissars.

On July 10, 1934, the Central Executive Committee passed a resolution making the OGPU part of the NKVD.

On February 3, 1941, the NKVD was split up into two independent organs: the NKVD and the People's Commissariat of State Security (NKGB). But already in July of the same year, the NKGB and the NKVD merged once again into a single People's Commissariat, the NKVD. In April 1943, the NKGB was created anew.

On March 15, 1946, the NGKB was transformed into the Ministry of State Security (MGB) of the USSR. Also at that time, all People's Commissariats started being referred to as ministries.

On March 7, 1953, two days after Stalin's death, the Ministry of Internal Affairs (MVD) of the USSR and the MGB were merged into a single MVD of the USSR.

On March 13, 1954, the Committee for State Security (KGB) was established as part of the Council of Ministers of the USSR. In 1978, the reference to the Council of Ministers was eliminated from the name of the agency. From then on, it was known simply as the KGB of the USSR.

On May 6, 1991, the head of the Supreme Council of the RSFSR, Boris Yeltsin, and the head of the KGB of the USSR, Vladimir Kryuchkov, approved the formation of a Committee for State Security of the RSFSR (the KGB of the RSFSR), with the status of a national republican state committee.

On November 26, 1991, the president of the USSR, Mikhail Gorbachev, signed a decree 'On the establishment of temporary provisions for the Interrepublican Security Service (MSB) of the USSR.'

On December 3, 1991, the president of the USSR, Mikhail Gorbachev, signed a law 'On the reorganization of the organs of state security.' This law abolished the KGB of the USSR and replaced it with two new agencies: the Interrepublican Security Service (MSB) and the Central Foreign Intelligence Service of the USSR (SVR).

On December 19, 1991, the president of the RSFSR, Boris Yeltsin, signed a decree 'On the establishment of a Ministry of Security and Internal Affairs of the RSFSR' (MBVD). With the creation of this agency, the MSB was effectively abolished. However, on January 14, 1992, the Constitutional Court of the Russian Federation ruled that Yeltsin's decree went against the constitution of the RSFSR and repealed it.

During the period 1992-1993, the Russian Federation's state security organs were part of the Ministry of Security (MB, Barsukov) of the Russian Federation. On December 21, 1993, Yeltsin signed a decree abolishing the MB and establishing the Federal Counterintelligence Service (FSK) of the Russian Federation.

On April 3, 1995, Yeltsin signed a law 'On the organs of the Federal Security Service in the Russian Federation,' on the basis of which the FSB became the successor to the FSK.

All these years, the VChK-FSB was located in the same building-at the very heart of Moscow, on Lubyanka Street. That is how the building was called: Lubyanka.

ST PETERSBURG CRIME RING

At the end of 1991, St Petersburg's law enforcement agencies, steered by Putin's IRC, entered into partnerships with the city's organized crime groups. This period saw the first divisions of property between two groups of people who controlled St Petersburg: the chekists and the criminals. The formal agreement between the 'city' (the KGB) and the 'businessmen' (the gangsters) concerning the joint organization of and control over the gambling business became a classic example of this kind of partnership. The gambling business was supervised by Putin personally under the following provision.

APPENDIX

MAYOR OF ST. PETERSBURG

Order No. 753-r of December 24, 1991

ON THE REGULATION OF THE ACTIVITIES OF ENTERPRISES THAT DERIVE AN INCOME FROM THE GAMBLING BUSINESS IN THE ST. PETERSBURG FREE ENTERPRISE ZONE

In order to regulate the activities of all forms of enterprises that derive an income from the gambling business:

1. A permanent supervisory council will be established at the mayor's office for monitoring casinos and the gambling business. The supervisory council will include:

V. V. Putin, head of the International Relations Committee
G. S. Khizha, head of the Economic Development Committee
S. F. Medvedev, head of the Main Financial Directorate
D. N. Filippov, head of the Tax Inspections Office
N. M. Gorbachevsky, deputy head of the St Petersburg Internal Affairs Directorate
A. I. Karmatsky, deputy head of the Federal Security Agency (AFB)

V. V. Putin will serve as the head of the supervisory council. [Emphasis Added]

2. By January 15, 1992, in accordance with city council resolution no. 38, passed on October 15, 1991, the supervisory council will develop rules for operating gambling machines, proposals for fees, and procedures for levying municipal taxes on enterprises that have the right to operate gambling machines, card tables, roulette tables, and other gambling operations, on the territory of the city and the districts within the administrative jurisdiction of the St Petersburg city council. The proposal packet will be submitted for review to the city council in January 1992.

3. A task force will be created in order to develop standard documentation for the regulation of activities associated with the gambling business. The task force will include: ... By January 20, 1992, the task force will prepare a resolution on licensing the activities of businesses that derive an income from gambling operations.
4. By January 30, 1992, the heads of the district offices, the St Petersburg Internal Affairs Directorate, the Main Financial Directorate, and the Tax Inspections Office will review the rights of all forms of enterprises involved in the gambling business to engage in the said form of business.
5. By January 30, 1992, the task force will prepare plans for a competition to find the best approach to organizing casinos in St Petersburg. The task force will organize an open competition in accordance with this project once the project is approved.
6. By April 1, 1992, the city property committee, in coordination with the supervisory council, will allocate the necessary facilities for housing casinos.
7. The taxes collected on the casinos' profits will be used to finance top-priority social programs.
8. Oversight over the execution of this order is assigned to the head of the International Relations Committee, *V. V. PUTIN* [Emphasis Added].

Mayor of St Petersburg, A.A. Sobchak

APPENDIX

THE KUCHMA TAPES

In 2000, the Ukrainian government, headed by Leonid Kuchma, suddenly became involved in the intrigues surrounding the SPAG affair. By this time, Russia's security services had spent a large amount of money in Germany to buy up documents that could compromise President Putin. However, one set of files concerning Putin turned out to be in the possession of Ukrainian intelligence (having been transferred to the head of the Ukrainian Security Service, Leonid Derkach). None of this might have ever come to light. But in 2000, a group of Kuchma's security officers directed by General Yevgeny Marchuk, the former head of the Ukrainian KGB, started illegally eavesdropping on and recording conversations in Kuchma's office. Among the hundreds of hours of recorded covernsation, there were some that concerned the German intelligence file on Putin.

First Conversation (June, 2000)

Derkach: Leonid Danilovich, we have acquired interesting information from the Germans here. All right. This person has been arrested. He has not yet been transferred. Here.

Kuchma (reading): Ritter, Rudolf Ritter.

Derkach: Yes. In the case against these. For drug trafficking.... Here they are, the documents. Here, they have taken out the documents. And here is Vova Putin.

Kuchma: This is about Putin?

Derkach: So the Russians have bought up all of this. All of these documents here. We have the only ones left. And I think that Patrushev will be [in Kiev] on the fifteenth-sixteenth-seventeenth [of June]. This is for him to work on....

Kuchma: Hmm.

Derkach: But we'll keep them ourselves. They want to shut down everything here.

Second Conversation (June, 2000)

Kuchma: Give them out to Patrushev only if he signs from them! Are these truly valuable materials or not?

Derkach: About...

Kuchma: About Putin.

Derkach: Yes. There is a lot that's very valuable. This is really a company that...

Kuchma: No, you tell me, should we give this to Putin or tell him that we have these materials?...

Derkach: Well, we can. But he will still know where we got these materials....

Kuchma: I'll say that our security service has interesting materials. I won't even send them to him.

Derkach: And say that we got them from Germany, and that everything they had is in our possession.... No one has anything else.... Now, I've prepared all the documents about Putin and I've given them to you.

Kuchma: All right, if it comes down to that. I'm not saying that I'll hand them over personally. Maybe you should give them to Patrsuhev?

Derkach: No, I just... No matter how we decide, we'll have to hand them over in any case. Because they have bought up all these documents from all over Europe. Because ours are the only ones left. This security service in Germany.... Therefore, he is very interested.

Kuchma: What if I say that we have documents, authentic documents in Germany. Without going into details.
Derkach: Aha.
Kuchma: I'll say: 'Give your people an order. Let them get in touch with our security service.' And when they get in touch with you, you'll tell them: 'I gave them to the president. Shit, I can't take them back from him.'
Derkach: Good.
Kuchma: We have to play a little too.

Third Conversation (June, 2000)

Derkach: And another question, about Putin....
Kuchma: I said, 'Our security service got some materials from the Germans. They might be of interest to your country. So if you don't object, we will hand them over to Patrushev. The head of my security service will hand them over to Patrushev.' I said: 'I don't know whether the documents are valuable or not.' So I was very proper about everything.
Derkach: That's what you said, yes?
Kuchma: Yes, yes. Did you meet with Patrushev?
Derkach: I met with him, but I can't go ahead without you.

Fourth Conversation (June, 2000)

Kuchma: ... from here on, our security services will continue working with the Russian security services. We have normal cooperation, and the process is in motion.... They have also begun looking into Putin.... I've been shown materials from Germany, absolutely reliable ones, about the creation of a company in St Petersburg, in which Putin was involved.... The materials are authentic.... We have one stolen set, so to speak. The Russians have bought up everything else, down to the smallest details.

Transcript of a conversation between President Leonid Kuchma with the head of Ukraine's tax administration, Mykola Azarov.

First Conversation (April 17, 2000)

Azarov: So you will now meet with Putin tomorrow, yes?
Kuchma: Yes.
Azarov: All right. Maybe you can give him the materials? For us, who we're dealing with is very important. If we're dealing with offshore companies, then not only does our money vanish, nor only does Russia's money vanish into offshore accounts, as is happening now, but there is real documentation of actual contracts. If an agreement for the delivery of oil products, gas, has been made with an offshore company, then we have no idea about anything and no control over anything. We don't know where everything is going. Therefore, I think that Putin must become interested in the question of where his money is going. Why shouldn't we work without intermediaries? Here, we can give him a report. The transactions go through eight or nine offshore companies. If we made agreements directly between our countries-our organizations and their organization, the Russian organization, directly, what objections could there be? We don't receive a kopek for any of this.... Practically everything is delivered through the offshore

companies. I prepared this file for you. In general, of course, it would be good to work something out, so that we might be given information about all of these issues. But for now, Russia is a dark forest for us. It is sometimes easier for us to obtain information somewhere in Latvia than in Russia. I understand why, of course. Because all of them are implicated.

Kuchma: Implicated. You said it.

Azarov: All of them are implicated, involved.... Now about Ukrainian Aluminum. In general, are you aware of how all of that was privatized?

Kuchma: Well, basically, Russian Aluminum was behind it.

Azarov: Sibaluminum.

Kuchma: Sibaluminum

Azarov: But in principle, it was privatized-you can laugh if you want to-by the Cyprus offshore company, White Orient World Invest Ltd. Cyprus, Limassol.

Kuchma: This is where the money will come from?

Azarov: Yes. Where the money will come from.

Kuchma: This is Russian money.... Now, they are effectively under Putin's protection.... But these are enormous sums.

Azarov: Yes. But Cyprus, Limassol.

Kuchma: They don't pay anything from Cyprus.

Azarov: Well, now let's think about where this money will go. After all, we're also looking at this whole business in a strange way. We're building a budget. Our budget and Russia's budget. If all of this was done not through Cyprus, but directly, the way it was supposed to be done, then the Russian budget would have gotten its 20%, and we would have gotten ours.

Kuchma: Yes.

Azarov: But now we are going through all of these clients, and so on and so forth.... I'm just telling you so you know.

Kuchma: Well, I know that already. The most important thing is that it was sold for $100 million.

Second Conversation (July 15, 2000)

Kuchma: Where did all the money go? Figure it out. Before the election in Russia, at Putin's request, we paid, I don't know, something like $50 or $60 million. In cash. An export-import bank gave one loan and someone else also gave.

Azarov: Ukraina. Ukraina Bank.

Kuchma: Yes? Ukraina Bank?

Azarov: Yes.

Kuchma: The export-import bank settled its accounts with Ukraina Bank. It made an additional two million.... They told me that it gave about twenty million dollars out of thirty. So, go and make sure. This first thing I can go and make sure myself, if they won't give you the information. You must know how much Russia wrote off. I'm certain, and when they asked me, they told me, so to speak, that they wrote off not 53.7 million, but that they wrote off five times that amount.

Azarov: The opposite.

Kuchma: The opposite! In other words, they wrote off much more than that.

Azarov: Much more.

Kuchma: So then, did he show this 'more much' or not? And this difference-

Azarov (interrupting): In our mutual accounts.

Kuchma: In our mutual accounts. And this difference, where did it go? It went through Itera, so as not to go through Gazprom. It would have been too noticeable there, so to speak. It was taken out directly through the offshore zones. Right? So just go and make sure.

HUMAN RIGHTS IN RUSSIA

Since the spring of 2001, Russia has regularly figured in the reports of various human rights organizations as a country with serious problems in the area of press freedom.

On May 3, 2001, on World Press Freedom Day, the international Committee to Protect Journalists (CPJ) named its Ten Worst Enemies of the Press for 2001. President Putin of Russia came in fifth-after Iranian Ayatollah Ali Khamenei, President of Liberia Charles Taylor, President of China Jiang Zemin, and President of Zimbabwe Robert Mugabe. According to the CPJ, 'Vladimir Putin has presided over an alarming assault on press freedom in Russia. The Kremlin imposed censorship in Chechnya, orchestrated legal harassment against private media outlets, and granted sweeping powers of surveillance to the security services.... the Kremlin-controlled Gazprom corporation took over NTV, the country's only independent national television network. Within days, the Gazprom coup had shut down a prominent Moscow daily and ousted the journalists in charge of the country's most prestigious newsweekly. Despite Gazprom's insistence that the changes were strictly business, the main beneficiary was Putin himself, whose primary critics have now been silenced.'

Also in May 2001, the international organization Reporters Without Borders (RSF), which likewise compiles an annual list of 'Enemies of Press Freedom,' named its thirty enemies of press freedom for 2000, giving Putin twenty-second place (the four top spots were occupied by Fidel Castro, Saddam Hussein, Kim Chen Ir, and Alexander Lukashenko).

On May 3, 2003, Reporters Without Borders published its press freedom index for 2002. The index included 156 countries and a list of the 42 greatest enemies of press freedom, which once again included President Putin.

At the end of February 2004, Reporters Without Borders again included Putin on its list of 'Enemies of Press Freedom' (along with the presidents of Belarus, Kazakhstan, Turkmenistan, and Uzbekistan).[1]

At the end of April 2004, the international human rights organization Freedom House published an index of press freedom in various countries. Out of 193 countries on the list, Russia came in at number 148.

On October 27, 2004, Reporters Without Borders published an international index of press freedom, in which Russia was number 140 out of 167 (in 2002, it had been number 121; in 2003, number 148). For comparison: the three top spots were occupied by Denmark, Finland, and Iceland; the United States was number 22; and the two last spots (166 and 167) were occupied by Cuba and North Korea.

In December 2004, Freedom House published its yearly 'Freedom in the World' survey (192 countries), which ranks countries as 'free,' 'partly free,' and 'not free.' In the 2004 survey, for the first time since 1991, Russia was classified as 'not free.'

On December 20, 2005, when the next Freedom House survey came out, Russia was still among the 45 'not free' countries (out of 192), but had moved several places down the list, which ends with Turkmenistan and Uzbekistan.[2]

On May 3, 2006, Reporters Without Borders published its list of 37 'Enemies of Press Freedom' for 2005, which once again included the president of Russia. A report published on the RSF website states: 'Putin is using the techniques he learned as a KGB officer to bring all media outlets in Russia under his control. The government controls the press, radio, and television through the powerful energy conglomerate Gazprom, and Putin appears on television more and more often, usually lecturing his ministers.'[3]

Along with Vladimir Putin, other enemies of press freedom in RSF's survey include President of Belarus Alexander Lukashenko, President of Turkmenistan Turkmenbashi Saparmurat Niyazov, President of Uzbekistan Islam Karimov, President of Kazakhstan Nursultan Nazarbayev, as well as Fidel Castro, Kim Chen Ir, and King Gyanendra of Nepal.[4]

In Freedom House's index of May 3, 2006, Russia is listed as one of 67 'not free' countries. In terms of its press freedom, it is ranked 158th out of 194 countries, on the same level as Bahrain and Venezuela.

According to the press freedom index published by Freedom House at the beginning of May 2007, in 2006 Russia moved six more places down the list: it shares the 164 spot with Azerbaijan, coming in below Brunei, Kazakhstan, Tajikistan, and Swaziland. (The first place in the index is occupied by Finland and Iceland, the last place-number 195-by North Korea, unchanged from last year. The last ten spots also include three CIS countries-Turkmenistan, Uzbekistan, and Belarus.) The report also notes that Russia continues to oppress the independent media and has plans to regulate the use of the internet.[5]

In June 2007, President Putin was awarded the international Closed Oyster prize. This prize was awarded to him in Hamburg, at an annual international conference of media representatives specializing in press-related issues. Putin was cited for 'destroying the free press.'

The German reporters' association Netzwerk Recherche awarded Putin a prize for his 'bad attitude toward reporters,' for 'obstructing the development of the free media,' and for the absence of results in the investigation of Anna Politkovskaya's murder.[6] Putin is the first head of state to receive the Closed Oyster award.

Notes

Chapter 2

[1] Derived from '*silovye ministerstva*' (literally, power ministries)—Internal Affairs, Defence, Justice, the secret service and the Attorney General. The top members of these ministries are called *siloviki*. According to the Moscow Centre for the Study of Post-Industrial Society, 15% of men working in Russia are employed by *siloviki* in various state enforcement agencies. In the top tiers of the government, 43% come from the security services, the police, the prosecutor's office, or the army. Other researchers believe that the FSB's share of the political and economic elite is even greater—between 70 to 80%.

[2] *Gevorkyan, N., Kolesnikov, A., Timakova, N.,* Ot pervogo litsa. Razgovory s Putinym. I., *Vagrius*, p.43.

[3] *Kommersant*, March 10, 2000; Ot pervogo litsa, p. 47.

[4] *Versiya*, No. 3 (77), January 25-31, 2000.

[5] Moskovsky komsomolets, August 18, 1999.

[6] *Moskovskie novosti*, No. 2 (1021), January 25-31, 2000.

[7] *Usol'tsev, V.* Sosluzhivets. Moscow, EKSMO, 2004, p. 287. V. Usoltsev (real name: Vladimir Gortanov) served with Putin in Dresden during the years 1985-1988 and retired, like Putin, with the rank of lieutenant colonel. A year before the publication of these memoirs, an interview with the author and excerpts from his book were published in *Izvestiya* on March 4 and 5, 2003, under the pseudonym Vladimir Artomonov.

[8] Ot pervogo litsa, p.76.

[9] *Blotsky, O.*, Vladimir Putin. Doroga k vlasti, I., INIIN-PRESS, 2002, p. 271.

[10] Ibid, pp. 271-273. Blotsky refers to this colleague as Gleb Novoselov—and adds that 'his name has been changed.' Presumably, this is Boris Miroshnikov—since 2001, the head of the Ministry of Internal Affairs' Main Directorate for Special Operational Arrangements.

[11] Ibid, pp. 307-308.

[12] *Moskovskie novosti*, No. 2 (1021), January 25-31, 2000.

[13] *Blotsky, O.*, Vladimir Putin, p. 283. According to Putin himself, his position at the university was called not 'assistant to the rector on international *issues*,' but 'assistant to the rector on international *relations*' (Ot pervogo litsa, p. 77).

[14] *Brichkina, L.* Vladimir Putin. Poslednyi patron, *Profil*, No. 32 (154), August 30, 1999.

[15] Ot pervogo litsa, pp. 78-79.

[16] Ibid, p. 79.

[17] *Vishnevsky, B.*, Smertel'naya oshibka Lensoveta, *Politichesky zhurnal*, May 23, 2005.

[18] Bobrova, I., Markina, M., Bychkob, C., Rostovsky, M., Khinshtein, A., Deev, E., Sem' mgnoveny iz zhizni preemnika, Moskovsky komsomolets, August 18, 1999.

[19] *Usoltsev, V.* Sosluzhivtsy, pp.7-8.

[20] *Blotsky, O.*, Vladimir Putin, p. 154.
[21] Ot pervogo litsa, p. 41.
[22] *Blotsky, O.*, Vladimir Putin, p. 309.
[23] Ot pervogo litsa, pp. 104-105.
[24] *Blotsky, O.*, Vladimir Putin, p. 331.
[25] *Novye Izvestiya*, December 26, 2002.
[26] Ot pervogo litsa, pp. 81-82.
[27] Companies that received 'Putin's' registrations can usually be easily recognized in the mayor's office database by the prefix 'AOL' in their license numbers (for example, AOL-165, AOL-244, etc.).
[28] *Blotsky, O.*, Vladimir Putin, p. 327.
[29] Ot pervogo litsa, pp. 89-90.
[30] *Bonimi, K., D'Avantso, D.*, Gody Putina mezhdu mafiei I KGB, *La Repubblica*, July 13, 2001.
[31] *Salye, M.*, Putin—'prezident' korrumpirovannoi oligarhii. However, the original copies of the documents have disappeared. By all appearances, they vanished sometime between 1997 and 1999, when Putin was the head of the president's Main Control Directorate and director of the secret service, while the St Petersburg Legislative Assembly (which acquired the Petrosovet's archives in 1994) was headed by people close to Putin—Yuri Kravtsov, Viktor Novoselov, Sergei Mironov. But copies of the materials of the Salye-Gladkov commission have survived, in part. In March 2000, Marina Salye published an article entitled 'V. Putin—the 'President' of a Corrupt Oligarchy!' (Putin—'prezident' korrumpirovannoi oligarhii!) on the website of Sergei Grigoryants's Glasnost Foundation. See also: *Ivanidze, V.*, Nerazborchivye svyazi severnoi stolitsy, *Sovershenno sekretno*, August 2000; *Lur'e, O.*, Kolbasa dlya Pitera, *Novaya gazeta*, No. 10 (581), March 13-19, 2000.
[32] Ot pervogo litsa, p. 91.
[33] *Salye, M.*, Putin—'prezident' korrumpirovannoi oligarhii!; *Bonimi, K., D'Avantso, D.*, Gody Putina mezhdu mafiei I KGB, *La Repubblica*, July 13, 2001.
[34] *Pitch, I.*, Pikantnaya druzhba. Ì., *Zakharov*, p. 171.
[35] *Salye, M.*, Putin—'prezident' korrumpirovannoi oligarhii!
[36] Ibid. Here is one such agreement: 'Agreement No. 11/92. On organizing barter operations in order to provide St Petersburg with food. January 13, 1992. St Petersburg. / The International Relations Committee at the St Petersburg mayor's office, represented by the deputy head of the committee, A. G. Anikin, referred to below as 'the Committee,' and the Dzhikop Corporation, represented by deputy general manager S. V. Ivanov, referred to below as 'the Provider,' have entered into the present agreement about the following: / *The Object of the Agreement.* The Committee will issue to the Provider licenses to export rare-earth materials, 8 positions, in accordance with the appended list and certificates. The total amount available in stock is 13,997 kilograms. The Provider will carry out barter transactions by exchanging the indicated materials for food products.' / The agreement's Supplement No. 1 listed these '8 positions': anodized niobium, niobium pentoxide, tantalic pentoxide, terbium, cerium dioxide, yttrium, scandium, zirconium—indicating the amounts, in kilograms, and the prices per kilogram in German marks (niobium pentoxide: 3000 kg at 711 DM; scandium: 7 kg at 72.6 DM; and so on). (Lur'e, O., Kolbasa dlya Pitera, *Novaya gazeta,* No. 10 (581), March 13-19, 2000). / The joint enterprise Dzhikop had two other co-owners, Dzhangir Ragimov and Sergei Viktorovich Ivanov—apparently, the same Ivanov who, as deputy general manager of the Dzhikop Corporation signed a contract with the IRC, 'represented by the deputy head of the Committee, Anikin.' Beginning in September 1992, Anikin became the general manager of the Lenfintorg Foreign Trade Financing Association, which in December 1994 became a co-founder of the Kontrast-Tur Company. Dzh. Ragimov became the head of Kontrast-Tur. In another one of Ragimov's companies—the Russian Trade Chamber—Sergei Mironov made his start as a builder of capitalism in Russia when he served as the company's executive director in 1991-1993. Somewhat later, Mironov became a manager for the Molchanovs, father and son; then, under Putin's patronage, a deputy in the St Petersburg Legislative Assembly; and then the speaker of the

upper house of the Russian parliament. Dzhangir's brother was Ilgam Ragimov—Putin's university classmate, the head of his student cohort, and one of Putin's four closest friends from his student days. The three others were Vladimir Cheremushkin, who died while during judo practice, Nikolai Yegorov, and Viktor Khmarin.

37 *Salye, M.*, Putin—'prezident' korrumpirovannoi oligarhii!

38 *Ezhkov, D.*, Problema 2000-2008, *Novaya gazeta*, March 16, 2007.

39 *Lur'e, O.*, Kolbasa dlya Pitera, *Novaya gazeta*, No. 10 (581), 13-19 iadoa 2000.

40 Ot pervogo litsa, p. 90.

41 *Salye, M.*, Putin—'prezident' korrumpirovannoi oligarhii!

42 *Bonimi, K., D'Avantso, D.*, Gody Putina mezhdu mafiei I KGB, *La Repubblica*, July 13, 2001.

43 *Ezhkov, D.*, Problema 2000-2008, *Novaya gazeta* ('colour' issue *Svobodnoe prostranstvo*, No. 9 (19), March 16, 2007).

44 *La Repubblica*, July 13, 2001; Kakie dokumenty est' za razoblacheniyami I. Rybkina i M. Salye, *Novaya gazeta*, No. 9, February 9-11, 2004.

45 From Cheka, the first Russian secret service.

46 Ot pervogo litsa, pp. 93 94

47 *Kommersant-Daily*, No. 169, September 4, 1993

48 Ibid.

49 A significant detail. D. Rozhdestvensky was the head of the Russian Grand Priory of the 'Maltese Order,' based in Cannes—one of the numerous, self-proclaimed, illegitimate 'Maltese Orders.' But even here, in the 'Maltese Order,' in Cannes, Rozhdestvensky's deputy at the Russian Grand Priory was the former head of the Leningrad KGB's 'T' service ('terrorism'), Colonel Vladimir Grunin.

50 *Tsyganov, A.*, U Putina takih firm shtuk 800 ili 1800, *Kommersant*, No. 60 (2899), April 5, 2004.

51 Excerpts are included in the appendix.

52 *Izvestiya*, August12, 1999.

53 *Obschaya gazeta*, No. 2, 2000; Ot pervogo litsa, pp.114-117.

54 Ibid.

55 Prezident tebe tovarisch. Ekho-TV's reporters have once again tried to answer the question: 'Who is Mr. Putin?' But Russians won't see their answer on the air, Moskovskie novosti, No. 25, July 9, 2004.

Chapter 3

1 *Solzhenitsyn, A.*, K nyneshnemu sostoyaniu Rossii. *Obschaya gazeta*, No. 47 (175), November 28-December 4, 1996.

Chapter 4

1 *Kommersant*, September 15, 1999.

2 *Express-khronika*, No. 46 (601), December, 1999.

3 *Literaturnaya gazeta*, No. 51/52, December, 1999.

4 Moskovsky komsomolets, February 1, 2000.

5 *Larionova, O.*, Skolko materei u Putina? *Sobesednik*, March 2, 2000.

6 Ibid.

7 Vakha Ibragimov has researched the Georgian period of Putin's life. In 2000, Vagrius Press published in Russian a small number of copies of Ibragimov's book, *The Secret Biography of the President of Russia* (226 pages). He has also recorded numerous video interviews with V. V. Putin and the residents of the village of Metekhi, which he has kindly placed at our disposal.

8 *Ibragimov, V.*, Tainaya biografiya presidenta Rossii, p. 69.

9 *Vignansky, M.*, U i.o. presidenta Rossii v Tbilisi est i.o. sestry, *Segodnya*, March 1, 2000.

10 *Borisova, Y.*, And the Winner Is? *Moscow Times*, September 9, 2000.

11 *Saliy, A.*, Dagestanskaya tekhnologiya falsifikatsii, *Sovetskaya Rosssiya*, April 27, 2000.

12 Ibid, April 6, 2000.

13 *Kasyanenko, Zh.*, Saratovskaya nepreryvka, *Sovetskaya Rosssiya*, Marh18, 2000.

[14] *Borisova, Y.*, And the Winner Is? *Moscow Times*, September 9, 2000.
[15] *Duel*, No. 4 (184), October 10, 2000.
[16] *Germanovich, A.*, Korrektirovka? Klub edinodushnogo golosovaniya, *Vedomosti*, March 28, 2000.

Chapter 6

[1] Panfilov, I., 'Svyashchennye korovy' rossiiskoi verticali, *Nezavisimaya gazeta*, September 22, 2003.
[2] *Segodnya*, February 5, 2000.
[3] *Izvestiya*, February 5, 2000.
[4] *Nezavisimaya gazeta*, February 8, 2000.
[5] *Shenderovich, V.*, 'Zdes bylo NTV' i drugie istorii. I., Zakharov, 2004, p. 14.
[6] *Bossart, À.*, Zashchita Buratino, *Novaya gazeta*, No. 26 (669), April 12-15, 2001.
[7] *Shenderovich, V.*, 'Zdes bylo NTV' i drugie istorii, p. 16.
[8] Ibid, p. 26.
[9] *Stringer*, No. 7, May 2003.
[10] *Ryklin A.*, Beseda s Borisom Berezovskim, *Yezhenedelny zhurnal*, No. 48 (99), December 8-14, 2003.
[11] Ibid.
[12] *Shenderovich, V.*, 'Zdes bylo NTV' i drugie istorii, p. 51.
[13] *Albats, Y.*, Komu prodali NTV. Chekisty podminaut pod sebya SMI, *Novaya gazeta*, No. 72 (810), September 30-October 2, 2002.
[14] *Tsurganov, Y.* Neudavshiysya revansh. Belaya emigratsiya vo Vtoroi mirovoi voine. Ì., *Intrada*, 2001, pp. 116-118.
[15] *Kommersant*, July 4, 2001.
[16] *Vremya novostey*, June 21, 2004.
[17] *Agafonov, S.*, Kremlyevsky napyerstok, *Novye izvestiya*, October 27, 2002.
[18] *Pasko, G.*, Yury Shmidt: Stukachei nado berech. I dannye o nih hranit v taine, *Novaya gazeta*, 29 naioyaoy—1 ieoyady 2003.
[19] *Simonov, A.*, Brakonerskiy udar kartech'u, *Nezavisimaya gazeta*, June 26, 2002.
[20] *Strana.ru*, July 15, 2003.
[21] *Latynina, Y.*, Ya sam budu vashim tsenzorom. Televidenie—edinstvennaya otrasl economiki, kotoruiu kontroliruet lichno president Rossii, *Novaya gazeta*, No. 4 (837), January 20-22, 2003.
[22] *Kommersant*, February 21, 2003. (The author of this article in *Novye izvestiya* is Vladimir Pribylovsky.
[23] *gazeta.ru*, February 20, 2003.
[24] *Komarov, Y.*, Ushcherb radi 'svobody slova', *Novye izvestiya*, No. 95 (1101), June 7, 2002.

Chapter 7

[1] Nezavisimaya Gazeta, April 2, 2003
[2] *lenta.ru*, October 2, 2002.
[3] Moskovskie novosti, July 9, 2004.
[4] *Latynina, Y.*, Kluchevye vybory, *Yezhenedelny Zhurnal*, No 35 (86), August 25-31, 2003.
[5] Ibid.
[6] *Kommersant*, March 12, 2002.
[7] Zayavlenie o narushenii federalnogo zakona 'Ob osnovnyh garantiyah izbiratelnyh prav i prava na uchastie v referendume grazhdan Rossyiskoi Federatsii,' June 12, 2002, No 67; FZ prezidentom RF Putinym V. V., *Yezhenedelny Zhurnal*, No 35 (86), September 8-14, 2003.
[8] *Izvestiya*, January 31, 2004.
[9] *Tropkina, O., Skrobot, A.*, Mertvye dushi rossyiskogo elektorata, *Nezavisimaya Gazeta*, December 3, 2003.
[10] Ibid.
[11] *Kornya A.*, Uchetnyi material bolshoi mobilnosti, *Nezavisimaya Gazeta*, February 11, 2004.

12 *Nezavisimaya Gazeta*, December 2, 2003.

13 *Stadnik, I.*, Obratnyi podschet, *Yezhenedelny Zhurnal*, No 49 (100), December 15-21, 2003.

14 Soobshchenie IA 'VolgaInform,' *Agentstvo politicheskih novostei (ÀPN)*, December 9, 2003; www.apn.ru/elections/2003/12/9/41296.html

15 *Vorobyeva, N.*, Bessmyslennoe vorovstvo, *Politichesky Zhurnal*, No 1 (4), January 19, 2004.

16 *Kostukov, A.*, Po dva pasporta v odni ruki, *Nezavisimaya Gazeta*, April 27, 2004.

17 Ibid.

18 *Oreshkin, D.*, Iz getto v Kreml, *Novaya Gazeta*, No 5, February 13-19, 2004.

19 http://www.polit.ru/event/2003/12/26/veshnyakov.html

20 Ibid.

21 *Dyemin, A.*, Koney podkuut do perepravy, *Yezhenedelny Zhurnal*, No 35 (86), August 25-31, 2003.

22 *Gromova, N.*, Grigory Yavlinsky: 'Strana uhodit, i nichego nelzya podelat', *Moskovsky Komsomolets*, January 30, 2004.

23 Ibid.

24 *Kitova, O.*, Raznye arifmetiki 'Yabloka' i Tsenrizbirkoma, *Russky Kur'er*, December 19, 2003.

25 *Kornya A.*, 'Yabloko' i KPRF ob'edinilis, *Nezavisimaya Gazeta*, June 24, 2004.

26 *Kitova, O.*, Raznye arifmetiki 'Yabloka' i Tsenrizbirkoma, *Russky Kur'er*, December 19, 2003.

27 *Mitrofanov, A.*, Razdvoenie linii, *Russky Kur'er*, April 13, 2004.

28 *Orkhan Dzh.*, Vybory 2003: Mertvye dushi proshli 5-protsentnyi bar'er, *Novaya Gazeta*, No 6 (936), January 29-February 1, 2004.

29 *Galimova N.*, Listogonnoe sredstvo [Interview with chairman CEC A. Veshnyakov], *Moskovsky Komsomolets*, February 7, 2004.

30 *Kornya A.*, 'Yabloko' i KPRF ob'edinilis, *Nezavisimaya Gazeta*, June 24, 2004.

31 Ibid.

32 At the beginning of January 2004, Saratov's colleges received an order: to submit signatures in support of the nomination of Putin for president of Russia. Students who did not give their signatures would not be allowed to take their exams. *Soborov, V.*, Putin v zachetke, *Moskovsky Komsomolets*, January 10, 2004.

33 *Vishnevsky, B., Donskov, N.*, Sankt-Petersburg: kolybel rezolutsii, *Novaya Gazeta*, No 12 (942), February 19-25, 2004.

34 Ibid.

35 *Kostukov, A.*, Rezultaty ne shodyatsya s itogami, *Nezavisimaya Gazeta*, March 29, 2004.

36 Ibid.

37 Ibid.

38 *Egorov, A.*, Tsennoe pismo Mosgorizbirkoma popalo v rozysk, *Nezavisimaya Gazeta*, April 19, 2004.

39 *Kostukov, A.*, Po dva pasporta v odni ruki, *Nezavisimaya Gazeta*, April 27, 2004.

40 Ibid.

41 *Kostukov, A.*, Po dva pasporta v odni ruki, *Nezavisimaya Gazeta*, April 2, 2004.

42 *Kornya, A.*, Urodov nado lechit, *Nezavisimaya Gazeta*, April 28, 2004.

Chapter 8

1 Sred bela dnya. Zloklucheniya redaktsii. Ograblenie kak biznes-proekt. Anatomiya banditskogo kapitalizma, *Novoye vremya*, No. 24, June 13, 2004.

2 *Korolyev, I.*, Zakon zhizni. Popytki otregulirovat Internet ne prekrashchautsya, *Vremya novostei*, April 14, 2004.

3 Ibid.

4 *Afanasyeva, E.*, 'Ekho Moskvy' v 'Izvestiyah', *Izvestiya*, No. 99 (26656), June 5, 2004.

5 *Plakhova, V.*, Novosti uhodyat v podpol'ye. Duma reshila izbavit telezritelei ot stressa, *Novaya gazeta*, No. 69, September 20-22, 2004.

6 *Izvestiya*, June 5, 2004, p. 9.

[7] *Borodina, A.*, Parfenonsens, *Kommersant*, June 3, 2004.
[8] Ibid.
[9] *Malashenko, I.*, Konets puti, *Yezhenedelny zhurnal*, No. 22 (123), June 7-13, 2004, p. 8.
[10] *Rebel, A.*, Namedni ne stalo 'Namedni,', *Russky kur'er*, June 3, 2004.
[11] *Vedomosti*, September 7, 2004; *Leontyev, M.*, Po zakonam voennogo vremeni, *Nezavisimaya gazeta*, September 9, 2004.
[12] *Plakhova, V.*, Gosteleradio zakazalo Hruna i Stepana, *Novaya gazeta*, No. 51 (981), July 19-21, 2004.
[13] *Serova, Y.* Spetsoperatsiya v Beslane proshla uspeshno. Protiv zhurnalistov, *Novaya gazeta*, No. 69, September 20-22, 2004.
[14] *Voronina, A.*, Dobralis do bumagi, *Vedomosti*, September 7, 2004.
[15] *Borodina, A.*, Na NTV proveli profilakticheskuiu rabotu, *Kommersant*, December 9, 2005.
[16] *Kommersant*, January 28, 2005.
[17] *Rostova, N.*, V 'Izvestiyah' ne pomenyaetsya nichego, krome glavnogo. Interview with Raf Shakirov, Vladimir Borodin, Nikolai Senkevich, *Novaya gazeta*, No. 84 (1109), November 10-13, 2005.
[18] Rossiya: vlast protiv pressy, *Ezhenedelny bulleten tsentra exstremalnoi zhurnalistiki*, vol. 30 (185), July 25-31, 2006.
[19] www.lenta.ru/articles/2007/07
[20] *Sannikova, A., Khronika suda. Prava cheloveka v Rossii* www.hro.org/ngo/about/2006/02/02.

Chapter 9

[1] *Svetlova, Y.*, Kogda vrachi bessil'ny, *Sovershenno sekretno*, October 30, 2001.
[2] *Berres, L.*, Saratovskie himiki zarabotali na smerti izvestnogo bankira, *Kommersant-Daily*, April 19, 1997.
[3] Ibid.
[4] *Kotlyar, E.*, Echshe o gromkih ubiystvah, *Moskovskaya pravda*, July 22, 1999.
[5] V dele Kivildi—nikakih podvizhek, *Argumenty i fakty*, June 9, 1999.
[6] *Sokolov, S.*, Vrachebnaya taina. Obstoyatel'stva, kotorye ne mogut ne vyzvat' voprosov, *Novaya gazeta*, July 1-4, 2004.

Chapter 10

[1] 'Gospodin Okhrannik.' Interview with R. Tsepov, *Versiya*, November 2, 1999.
[2] 'Ot pervogo litsa. Rasgovory s Vladimirom Putinym, Ì.', *Vagrius*, 2000, p. 79.
[3] 'Neuzheli eto Pravda?' *Novyi Peterburg*, December 24, 1998.
[4] Ibid.
[5] *ITAR-TASS*, September 30, 2002.
[6] Pribylovsky told the magazine *Russky Zhurnal* (February 16, 2007): 'The appointment of Serdyukov as defence minister is the strangest part of the whole operation. It is unlikely that the president wanted deliberately to spit in the face of his generals (this happened by itself, as a side effect). There are two possible explanations. First, that he wanted to surprise everyone and make everyone think that 'our president is anything but simple.' Second, perhaps the hoped-for successor and heir to the throne is Mr. Serdyukov's son-in-law, Putin's old friend Viktor Zubkov?'

Appendix

[1] Politichesky Barometr, No. 102, July 2-8, 2007; www.demos-center.ru/reviews/19030.
[2] *Yezhenedelny Zhurnal*, No. 18 (119), May 10-16, 2004.
[3] Strokan, S., 'Rossiya poluchila nezachet po demokratii. Freedom House vkluchil eye v spisok 'nesvobodnyh stran', *Kommersant*, December 21, 2004.
[4] *Kommersant*, May 4, 2006.
[5] 10 stran s samoi zhestokoi tsenzuroi, Komitet po zashchite zhurnalistov, May 2, 2006 (cpj.org/censored/censored_ru.pdf)
[6] grani.ru, May 2, 2007, see Freedom House www.freedomhouseuse.org/template.cfm

Abbreviations

AFB	Federal Security Agency
APR	Agrarian Party of Russia
ASSR	Autonomous Soviet Socialist Republic
BKA	German Federal Criminal Police Office (*Bundeskriminalamt*)
BND	German Federal Intelligence Service (*Bundesnachrichtendienst*)
CEC	Central Election Commission
CEER	Committee for External Economic Relations
CIS	Commonwealth of Independent States
CPRF	Communist Party of the Russian Federation
CPSU	Communist Party of the Soviet Union
DVR	Democratic Rebirth of Russia (party)
ESA	European Space Agency
FAPSI	Federal Agency for Government Communication and Information
FESCO	Far Eastern Shipping Company
FOM	Public Opinion Foundation
FSB	Federal Security Service
FSFO	Federal Service for Financial Health and Bankruptcy
FSK	Federal Counterintelligence Service
FSO	Federal Protection Service
FSU	Former Soviet Union
GIU	Main Engineering Directorate
GKU	Main Control Directorate
GNI	State Tax Inspectorate
GNS	State Tax Service (GNS)
GPU	State Political Directorate
GRU	Main Intelligence Directorate
GUVD	Municipal Directorate of Internal Affairs
IOC	International Olympic Committee
IRC	International Relations Committee
KGB	Committee of State Security
KSTU	Krasnoyarsk State Technical University
LDPR	Liberal Democratic Party of Russia
LSI	Leningrad Shipbuilding Institute
LSU	Leningrad State University

MB	Ministry of Security
MBVD	Ministry of Security and Internal Affairs
MGB	Ministry of State Security
MGSU	Moscow City Social University
MNVK	Moscow Independent Broadcasting Corporation
MSB	Interrepublican Security Service
MSGU	Moscow State Social University
MSTU	Bauman Moscow State Technical University
MVD	Ministry of Internal Affairs
NBP	National Bolshevik Party
NDR	Our Home Is Russia (party)
NKGB	People's Commissariat of State Security
NKVD	People's Commissariat of Internal Affairs
NPRF	People's Party of the Russian Federation
NPSR	Popular-Patriotic Union of Russia
NTS	National Alliance of Russian Solidarists
NTV	Independent Television
OGPU	Joint State Political Directorate
OMON	Special Forces Police Squad
ORChD	Society of Russian-Chechen Friendship
ORT	Public Russian Television
OSCE	Organization for Security and Cooperation in Europe
OVR	Fatherland-All Russia bloc (party)
PACE	Parliamentary Assembly of the Council of Europe
PGU	First Main Directorate
PST	Free Labor Party
PTK	St. Petersburg Fuel Company
RBRT	Russian Business Round Table
ROIPP	Russian Public Institute of Electoral Law
ROPP	Russian United Industrial Party
RSF	Reporters Without Borders
RSFSR	Russian Soviet Federative Socialist Republic
RUBOP	Regional Directorate for Combating Organized Crime
SBP	Presidential Security Service
SBR	Security Service of Russia
SED	Socialist Unity Party of Germany
SPS	Union of Right Forces
SSR	Soviet Socialist Republic
SVR	Foreign Intelligence Service
TOTs	Tatar Public Center
TsEZh	Center for Journalism in Extreme Situations
TsOS	Center for Public Relations (KGB)
TsSN	Center for Special Operations
UBEP	Directorate for Fighting Economic Crime
UPS	Directorate for Government Communications
USB	Directorate of Departmental Security
VChK	All-Russian Extraordinary Commission
VTsIK	All-Russian Central Executive Committee
VTsSPS	All-Union Central Council of Trade Unions
ZGV	Western Group of the Soviet Army

Index

INDEX

INDEX